Praise for *Jacques Plante:*
The Man Who Changed the Face of Hockey

"Jacques Plante was an innovator, a difference maker and a different person, and this book has captured the essence of one of the greatest goaltenders ever." – Scott Morrison, hockey journalist, appears regularly on the "Satellite Hot Stove" feature on *Hockey Night in Canada*

"A well researched and thorough examination of the life of an extraordinarily talented hockey player and complex man." – Al Strachan, regular panelist on *Hockey Night in Canada* and co-author of *Don Cherry's Hockey Stories and Stuff*

"The Hockey Hall of Fame should have a room preserved for those very few who actually change the way the game is played. Bobby Orr would represent the defence, Wayne Gretzky the forwards – and none other than Jacques Plante the goaltenders. This is a long overdue examination of one of hockey's pivotal players and most colourful characters – but Todd Denault has made the wait worthwhile." – Roy MacGregor, *Globe and Mail* columnist and bestselling co-author of *Home Game* (written with Ken Dryden)

"Ontario journalist Todd Denault chronicles that fateful night in *Jacques Plante, The Man Who Changed the Face of Hockey*, an entertaining biography that reminds readers that Plante's enduring legacy is not his six Stanley Cups or seven Vezina trophies but the innovations he brought to hockey." – *Winnipeg Free Press*

"… a complete, well-researched portrait of a complex man who truly did 'change the face' of hockey – and not just because he was the first goaltender to wear a facemask. The book is more than that. Plante's story is inextricably linked to the greatest era the Canadiens will know, the five straight Stanley Cups during the late 1950s." – Montreal *Gazette*

"After just a few pages into this book it was obvious Todd Denault had written an instant classic. I can not recommend this book enough. Plante was one of the game's true great players. He is sadly unknown to many of today's generations of fans. He is truly worthy of such a fine commemoration." – hockeybookreviews.com

"While there are many sports books as anyone who delves into the subject will soon find out, *Jacques Plante* is a sports book like few others. Even those not enthusiastic about hockey will find this book hard to put down. It has the drama of a good mystery and the excitement of a thriller. It will be of considerable interest to anyone who watched Plante play. It will bring back memories of the Canadiens and their opponents when the league only had six teams. It will also be popular with younger hockey fans eager to learn how the game used to be played." – *CM* magazine

"This is a remarkable book and what makes it more remarkable is it is the first book by Denault – and won't be the last. Denault not only covers Plante being an innovator with the mask, but an innovator with many other things in hockey that we now take for granted." – www.Post-Journal.com

JACQUES PLANTE

TODD DENAULT

McCLELLAND & STEWART

Cloth edition published 2009
Paperback edition published 2010

Library and Archives Canada Cataloguing in Publication

Denault, Todd
    Jacques Plante : the man who changed the face of hockey / Todd Denault.

ISBN 978-0-7710-2627-0

    1. Plante, Jacques, 1929-1986. 2. Hockey goalkeepers – Canada – Biography.
3. Hockey players – Canada – Biography. I. Title.

GV848.5.P5D45 2010   796.962092   C2010-901544-4

We acknowledge the financial support of the Government of Canada through the Book Publishing Industry Development Program and that of the Government of Ontario through the Ontario Media Development Corporation's Ontario Book Initiative. We further acknowledge the support of the Canada Council for the Arts and the Ontario Arts Council for our publishing program.

Published simultaneously in the United States of America by McClelland & Stewart Ltd., P.O. Box 1030, Plattsburgh, New York 12901

Library of Congress Control Number: 2010927461

Typeset in Electra by M&S, Toronto
Printed and bound in Canada

ANCIENT FOREST
FRIENDLY

This book is printed on paper that is 100% ancient-forest friendly (40% post-consumer waste).

McClelland & Stewart Ltd.
75 Sherbourne Street
Toronto, Ontario
M5A 2P9
www.mcclelland.com

1   2   3   4   5   14 13 12 11 10

To my mother, my brother, and my father – who back in the day was also a "guardian of the goal" who quite often found himself staring down an approaching puck without the benefit of a mask

In his time, Jacques Plante was called a lot of things, not all of them complimentary. Iconoclastic? Yes. Hypochondriacal? At times. Idiosyncratic? Yes. Superstitious? Definitely. But, above all, Frère Jacques was a unique individual, a marvelous teacher, ahead of his time, and the man who quite literally changed the very face of hockey.

NEW YORK TIMES, MARCH 16, 1986

There are a lot of very good goalies; there are even a fair number of great goalies. But there aren't many important goalies. And Jacques Plante was an important goalie.

KEN DRYDEN

Jacques Plante's impact on the game is forever.

JACK FALLA

CONTENTS

FOREWORD
By Jean Béliveau

In the fall of 1948, I began playing in the Quebec Junior A Hockey League as a member of my hometown Victoriaville Tigers. We were an expansion outfit and were primarily made up of the other teams' extra players. Despite all of this we were playing close to .500 hockey through the fall as we got set to face off with the first-place Quebec Citadels on November 25.

I didn't know it at the time but that night would prove to be auspicious for two reasons: It was my first visit to the Quebec Colisée where in the next few seasons I would enjoy some of my greatest successes, initially with the Citadels and later with the Quebec Aces. And it was also the first time I met and shared the ice with Jacques Plante.

By then, Jacques had already garnered a considerable amount of attention for his wandering ways and his habit of charging out of his net to play loose pucks, frustrating the attacking forwards. I was very fortunate that evening to score two goals on Jacques, including one where I beat him to a loose puck and then tucked it into the open net. Years later I would tease Jacques about my open-net goal that night at the Colisée.

In the fall of 1953, I joined the Montreal Canadiens, playing alongside many of those talented players whose exploits I had closely followed while listening to my family's radio only a few short years before:

Maurice Richard, Elmer Lach, and Butch Bouchard. That first year, I tried to learn as much as I could from my new teammates, about what it took to be a professional hockey player and how one should represent the Montreal Canadiens. I wasn't the only new player with the team that season. Players like Dickie Moore, Bernie Geoffrion, and Doug Harvey had established themselves, and Jacques Plante was into his first year as the team's starting goaltender after helping the Canadiens to a Stanley Cup in 1953, and a repeat appearance in the finals the spring before.

Jacques took his position very seriously. He approached his profession with a scientific precision and was always looking to better his game. Jacques was a fast, smooth, and agile skater, and used these skills to revolutionize the game. He was able to do things in the net that other goalies couldn't match. He would stay back in his goal until the last possible moment before striking out to quickly poke-check the puck away from an onrushing forward. He also possessed a quick glove hand and an aptitude for finding the perfect position to face a shooter.

In my third year with the team, Toe Blake became the Canadiens' head coach. One of the more critical adjustments that Toe made to our team was implementing an attacking style that became famously known as "firewagon hockey." We could afford to play such a style because of our talented forwards and quick-thinking defencemen and because we had Jacques Plante in our net.

There were times that we found ourselves caught in the wrong end as the other team rushed towards our goal with the puck. It would be up to Jacques to bail us out, and more often than not he would succeed. On nights that our team got off to a sluggish start, and even when the opposition was out-shooting us, the period would often end in a scoreless tie. Jacques would hold the fort until we got our footing and could come back to win the game. With Jacques Plante in the net we were always in the game.

He was certainly responsible for many of our Stanley Cups. The players on the team that won five consecutive championships all shared a dedication to their responsibilities. Each of us had a specific role to play on that team and Jacques did his as well as anybody. We all shared a passion for winning and a disdain for losing. In hockey, without a really good goalie you're in trouble. As a team we respected Jacques because we knew we had a great goalie backing us up. On the other hand, when a goalie makes a mistake there is nobody to back him up. Jacques accepted that responsibility and thrived on the pressure.

In addition to his play on the ice, Jacques received a lot of attention for what he did off the ice. Like many goaltenders, Jacques tended to be a solitary sort, and he spent his spare moments in a dressing room or on the train knitting. Some of the practical jokers on the team were tempted to bug Jacques about his pastime, but I always tried to dissuade them. I would remind them that Jacques was doing the job in the nets and helping the team win and urged them just to let him be. Luckily for us, they almost always did.

Back in those days we spent a lot of time travelling from city to city by train. Sometimes I would take the seat beside him and the two of us would talk for hours, and not just about hockey, but about family, life, and the future. These are my fondest memories of Jacques.

There has not been a goalie since Jacques Plante with the same talent and determination. He will always be Mr. Goalie to me.

PROLOGUE

IN THE DAYS BEFORE flight became the preferred mode of travel, players spent interminable amounts of time anchored within a little cocoon. In a league made up of only six teams there was no such thing as a short train trip. Often the team would get off the train, head straight to the arena, play the game, and rush back to the station in an effort to get to the next city in time for the next game. A trip from Montreal to Toronto took five hours on average, Montreal to Detroit nine hours, and the worst and the longest of them all: the twenty hours that separated Montreal and Chicago.

There wasn't much for the players to do on those train rides. For the majority, endless games of cards in small groups made time go a little bit faster while helping many feed their competitive instincts. Others attempted to sleep the ride away; some played pranks on unsuspecting victims.

Jacques Plante didn't play cards or sleep much or play pranks. When not immersed in a book or knitting, Plante generally passed the time with his fellow passengers, discussing the one subject that each of them knew most intimately – the game of hockey. When Plante discussed the game it was always in the most serious of tones, well thought out, well reasoned. Almost without exception, what made his point stand out was its pragmatism.

In the early months of 1963, on the way to another city, one discussion transcended the boundaries of that train and erupted into a league-wide scandal that dominated the headlines.

When he spoke, Jacques Plante always gathered a crowd. A veteran of the National Hockey League wars for a decade, Plante was the circuit's most decorated goaltender. Winner of six Stanley Cups and five Vezina trophies as the league's top goaltender (a sixth Vezina would follow in a few months' time), he also was also the sport's greatest innovator, it's most outspoken superstar, and a true eccentric who marched to the beat of his own drum. In other words, he was a reporter's dream. So when the media caught wind of a heated discussion between Plante and Ken Reardon, the Canadiens' vice-president, they immediately scrambled to listen in.

With the 1962–63 season passing the halfway mark, Plante had played every minute of every game so far for the Montreal Canadiens, and that was the crux of his argument with Reardon. A goalie playing the entire schedule was the norm in those days, and one of the biggest knocks on Plante was the fact that he had never played the full season of 70 games. After all, it had just been a few months before that Glenn Hall, one of Plante's main competitors, had finally sat out a game after playing in 502 consecutive games.

In those days each team carried only one goalie. As unbelievable as it sounds today, if the visiting team's goalie was unable to play, the home team would provide a "house goalie" that was at best a backup junior goalie and at worst the opposing team's assistant trainer. Obviously, neither was an appealing option for the visiting coaches, so quite often they would hold the game, sometimes for up to half an hour, while a physician attended to their injured goalie in the bowels of the rink. The injured goalie would then have to come out and finish the game.

In his discussion with Reardon that day on the train, Plante passionately argued that each team should be able to dress two goalies for each game, saying that it was impossible to ask a goalie to play the entire schedule and at a high level.

Reardon asked Plante why the goaltender should be considered "special." After all, weren't the other players on the ice expected to play the entire season? Reardon was unwilling to budge from the widely held belief that for a goalie to maintain his sharpness he had to play constantly. A backup goalie, according to Reardon, would waste away at the end of the bench, his skills declining by the minute.

Plante furthered his argument for a two-goalie system by comparing his sport with baseball and his position with that of a catcher. "You don't see baseball doing it," he said. "When a catcher is injured you don't borrow a catcher from the other team."

Despite Reardon's objections, it would be only a few years before a two-goalie system would become the rule in the NHL. But it was at this moment that Plante, his expansive mind in constant motion, turned the conversation to another issue that had been bothering him for some time.

"Another thing about baseball, all the home plates are the same size."

"What's that got to do with it?" asked Reardon as a small group of curious newsmen closed in, awaiting Plante's response.

"The goals aren't the same size in all the rinks."

"You're nuts. They're all the same everywhere – the official goal nets," insisted Reardon.

Plante nonchalantly shrugged. "The crossbars at the top are two inches lower in New York, Boston, and Chicago. I know because they hit my back lower there than in the Forum, Toronto, or in Detroit – two inches lower."

The reporters' jaws collectively hit the floor. Plante was claiming that there had been a violation in the rules that had resulted in a competitive edge, a violation that had gone undetected by the league.

"Even if you're right," protested an incredulous Reardon, "isn't it the same for all of you goalies playing the circuit?"

"No, it isn't the same for everybody!" responded Plante. "Glenn Hall plays 35 games at home in Chicago with less goal to protect than I have to protect for 35 games at the Forum in Montreal. We're both in a race for the Vezina Trophy and that gives him an edge. Do you call it fair?"[1]

If it had been anybody other than Plante, the reporters may not have given the argument much thought. But after a decade of chronicling the man, they had come to realize that no player took the game or his profession more seriously. So when the train reached the station the reporters rushed their copy to their editors. By this point in his career Plante was no stranger to the newspaper headlines. His status as one of the league's most decorated players was matched by the notoriety he had gained through his revolutionary style of play, his pioneering use of a protective mask, and his candour and outspokenness, which were rare in players of that time.

What had begun as a casual conversation on a train ride was featured prominently the next day in the Montreal newspapers and quickly spread to the highest level of the hockey world.

Days later in his office in New York, General Manager Muzz Patrick was staring at the report on his desk. The results of the Rangers' internal investigation into the size of nets were spread out before him. Patrick quickly placed a call to his brother, Lynn, the general manager of the Boston Bruins.

"What do you know, Lynn," Muzz began. "I had our nets measured after reading the Jacques Plante sound-off about our nets being two inches lower and –"

"You don't mean to say Plante was right?" an incredulous Lynn interrupted.

"Yeah, he was right. You better have yours measured, too."[2]

Much to his chagrin, Lynn was forced to publicly admit that, like the Rangers, the nets used by his Bruins were also two inches lower than the league specified. That left the nets in Chicago.

An enterprising reporter from Montreal placed a phone call to Johnny Gottselig, the director of public relations for the Black Hawks.

"That Plante guy is riding another publicity brain-wave," responded Gottselig, adamantly proclaiming, "We're using the official goal nets here."

As chance would have it, the Black Hawks' very next game was against the visiting Canadiens and Jacques Plante. Skating out for the warm-up, Plante saw that night's referee, Eddie Powers, and linesman Marty Pavelich at his goal measuring the net.

Plante couldn't contain a broad smile. "Having some trouble, chaps?" he called out as he approached the net.

"It baffles me," said Powers. "We got a blast from [NHL] President Campbell, who ordered all nets to be measured. We had simply assumed all these official nets are the same size, but this one is two inches lower and, for the life of me, I can't figure out why."

"Don't bother measuring the other one," replied Plante. "It's two inches lower as well."[3]

So why were the measurements of the nets in New York, Boston, and Chicago different from those in Montreal, Toronto, and Detroit? The league's investigation offered a simple explanation. The two upright posts on the nets are a regulation four feet high, and the crossbar that connects the two posts is supposed to be welded on top of the two uprights. In the three rinks that were in violation of the rule, the crossbar instead had been welded to the inner side of each upright. Since the crossbar is two inches deep, the goalmouth was two inches lower.

"Plante, a lean, temperamental veteran, caused much disbelief and some ridicule when he claimed last week the nets in three of the six National Hockey league rinks were smaller than regulation four foot by six foot size," wrote the *Toronto Star*. "That smile on the lips of Montreal goalie Jacques Plante could be called the last laugh."[4]

Jacques Plante was no stranger to criticism or ridicule. Throughout his entire career he was a thorn in the side of those who opposed change, innovation, and originality. He was a man who stood on his own and blazed a trail through the sport of hockey, charting a new course for the game we know today.

1

THE SEEDS OF THE MAN

LOCATED ON THE Saint-Maurice River, almost halfway between Montreal and Quebec City, at the turn of the century Shawinigan Falls (as it was known then; in 1958, the city dropped the Falls from its name) was a thriving town that was the first in the country to produce aluminum and employed thousands in the pulp and paper, chemical, and textile industries.

In the 1930s, with the onset of the Depression, many of those factory jobs disappeared under the weight of the economic downturn. In an effort to help families hit by the loss of employment, the city council enacted a variety of public works programs that included building a hockey arena.

Bolstered by their new arena, Shawinigan was granted a franchise in the nascent Quebec Senior Hockey League in the fall of 1945. A semi-professional league that operated in the area between the junior league and the National Hockey League, the QSHL, then made up of seven franchises, produced a high quality of hockey that gave many players overlooked by the professionals a chance to continue playing for money while keeping their NHL dreams alive. Overnight, the Cataractes became the toast of the town, a source of civic pride, and gave the youngsters a team of players to idolize.

That same fall, a teenage boy, full of dreams and self-assurance, stood in front of the newly built arena and asked if the Cataractes needed any help.

"I was standing outside the door of the rink in the Shawinigan Arena where the Shawinigan team in the Quebec Senior Hockey League played its home games," remembered Jacques Plante many years later. "I noticed that they had only one practice goalie and asked the trainer whether I could help out. Although I was fifteen years old by this time, he told me to 'go away. You're still wearing a diaper.'"[1]

The name of that condescending trainer has been lost to history. What this trainer had no way of knowing was that in fifty years this young man's name would be emblazoned over the door when the arena was named in his honour.

Jacques, the oldest child of Xavier and Palma Plante, was born in a wooden farmhouse near Mont Carmel in Mauricie, Quebec, on January 17, 1929. Soon afterwards, Xavier moved with his wife and baby to Shawinigan Falls, where he had secured employment with the Aluminum Company of Canada Limited.

"Dad was a machinist who had to work hard – harder than any man I have ever known," Jacques later said. "He even got a temporary job during his holidays while working for the aluminum company – just to raise a bit more money. He had a bicycle to get him to and from work, two miles each way. I can't recall him taking a single day off. Whenever I won an award in the NHL, I thought of my father and the pride he would get in reading about it and having people mention it to him."[2]

Jacques was not an only child for long. Over the next thirteen years, he would be joined by five brothers and five sisters. With a burgeoning family, Palma Plante found her time at a premium, so as they got older each of the children was expected to help with the household chores. Being the oldest in such a large family meant that Jacques was given responsibilities rare for many his age. His chores included scrubbing floors, cooking, and changing diapers. With not much in the way of extra money, most of the children's clothing was handmade, and Jacques became proficient with a needle, some thread, and yarn. These were skills he carried into his adulthood and contributed to his legend.

With such a big brood and only one income, everyone in the Plante house was required to sacrifice some of the things that others better off were able to enjoy. This was most apparent to little Jacques in the hot summer months, when he was allowed to wear shoes only for Sunday Mass or the odd special event. Most times he went barefoot.

"The shoes proved everything is relative," Plante wrote later. "All of us kids in the neighbourhood had to go shoeless for the same reason – all except the landlord's son, because his father had more income."[3]

Years later, when his hockey career had taken him away from his impoverished beginnings, many teammates as well as members of the press were taken aback by Plante's habit of knitting his own undershirts, socks, toques, and scarves. But he would always speak with pride of his ability to knit a pair of socks in a day and a toque in a mere three and a half hours. Throughout his life, Plante used knitting as a form of relaxation, oblivious to the reaction of those around him; this was his way to unwind after being the target of onrushing pucks. However, typical of the man, there was also a practical side to his needlework.

"I can't get what I want in the stores," Plante explained of his choice in undergarments, "so I knit [them]. I use four-ply wool. They must not be too warm. I use larger needles because small ones produce a thicker weaving and the holes are too small."[4]

As an adult, Jacques Plante was misunderstood by many around him. They questioned why he continued to knit, why he was so frugal with his money, and why he kept his distance from those closest to him. The answers to many of these questions lay in his childhood.

"He grew up poor and was very proud of it," explains sportswriter Frank Orr. "He learned a lot of good lessons from it. He was deprived because there was no money around, but it taught Jacques the value of a dollar."[5]

"He was very careful with money," confirms his former teammate Dickie Moore. "He came up poor and he grew up the right way. He didn't spend what he didn't have and he saved what he had. I admired him for that – he was an individual. There's a reason he kept his money. He wanted to end up with something, and that's what he did."[6]

Plante never forgot his impoverished roots. It's what drove him, what motivated him to always reach higher. It instilled in him self-confidence, and a belief that he alone could shape his destiny. And despite the poverty, Plante always retained a certain fondness for his childhood.

In the early 1970s, when Plante was plying his trade with the Toronto Maple Leafs, Frank Orr, a writer with the *Toronto Star*, was commissioned by his editor to write a special Christmas column. Orr was given the assignment of asking each player to share a remembrance of their most cherished Christmas memories.

Plante told Orr how his father would buy two bottles of ginger ale on his way home from work every Christmas Eve. This was the only day when the Plante children would taste a carbonated beverage.

"We'd have soft drinks then and I can still taste them," Plante told Orr. "Would you believe that the champagne I have drank on six occasions out of the Stanley Cup didn't have the same tang? Being poor doesn't necessarily mean no enjoyment from life."[7]

Another source of enjoyment for young Jacques was the outdoors. He and his friends played games at every spare moment, whether during recess at school or on the weekends. Sports provided an escape from hard reality.

Baseball was extremely popular with many, and Plante always felt that this may have been the sport he was best at. But for any child growing up in Quebec at that time, all other sports took a back seat to one overriding passion: hockey.

Jacques Plante couldn't tell you when he began playing hockey. He was told by others that he started playing a form of the game, with a ball and without skates, at the age of three, the same age he learned to skate. "Growing up, Shawinigan was a big hockey town," recalls Marcel Pronovost, a childhood friend of Plante's. "We organized and managed a lot of the games ourselves. In all the schools we had an hour and a half for lunch and every class had a team and we played at noon. Every school had an outdoor ice rink then."[8]

Like most children, Jacques was naturally curious about goaltending, but he quickly discovered that a frozen tennis ball hurt, and that a puck hurt even more. Besides, he found that he had an affinity for skating.

And then at the tender age of five, something happened that would forever alter Jacques' path in life. He was climbing up the ladder of the playground slide when suddenly he lost his balance and fell hard to the ground, breaking his left wrist. However, the real damage took place in the ensuing weeks and months when the wrist didn't heal properly, leaving Jacques unable to turn his left palm outward, which made it especially difficult to catch pucks.

Jacques had quickly fallen in love with the game of hockey. He enjoyed skating, but when he skated hard, he had trouble getting his breath. He was soon diagnosed as being asthmatic. Unlike his wrist, which was surgically healed decades later, asthma was a constant companion throughout his life.

"If it wasn't for my asthma," Jacques said later, "I would certainly have remained on defence and possibly never gotten beyond school hockey."[9]

When it became clear that Jacques had no choice but to play in net – where no fast skating was required – his supportive father presented his five-year-old son with his first goal stick, carved from a big tree root. When he was seven, his father bought him a proper goalie stick for Christmas. That same year, Xavier stuffed potato sacks into wooden panels to give Jacques his first set of goalie pads.

It was during these early days spent outdoors that Jacques developed one of his most enduring trademarks. Standing alone in the net in those bitterly cold winters, bare-faced and bare-headed, Jacques soon found himself frantically knitting toques to cover his frostbitten ears. The toque would become a staple and would be worn indoors and outdoors right up until his professional debut.

During this time Plante also discovered that he didn't always fit in with the other children. "Looking back I know it began when my father gave me my first real goaler stick for Christmas," Plante told reporter Andy O'Brien years later. "Although I was only 7 years old that stick got me invited to play with kids 11 and 12 years old. But after we played they didn't want me around. I was left alone off the ice. I didn't resent it because I didn't know any better."[10]

When it came to goaltending and the game of hockey, Plante demonstrated a seriousness about the game not found in many others his age. "For me to be the best possible goalie, I had to learn as much about the game as I could," Plante later explained. "Nobody ever taught me the way to play goal. I was never coached at the position. The skills I developed were learned from personal experience and from studying the mistakes made by other goalies. Of course, hockey is a physical game, and maintaining the best conditioning is important. But playing goal is really a very scientific thing, and that's the approach I tried to take."[11]

Such was Jacques' talent and confidence that at the age of 12, while attending Ecole St. Maurice, he managed to land the goaltending position on the high-school team, which consisted of boys 17 and 18 years of age.

"I still remember the day as if it were yesterday," reflected Plante. "Cold? It was really cruel and the team was practicing on the outdoor rink. What happened between the coach and the goalie wasn't quite clear but the only thing that interested me was the empty net. The goalie had been bawled out, didn't like it and left. I offered to take his place. There was nobody else available. The coach looked around before agreeing with some reluctance to allow a 12-year-old between the posts. But I skated into the net and stayed there – not only that day but for the rest of the season."[12]

Being the goalie on the school team was the first step towards Jacques' ultimate goal: manning the nets for the Montreal Canadiens. Hockey had always been a passion; now he dreamed of making it his livelihood.

"It was the dream of every boy growing up in Quebec in the thirties and forties to one day put on the uniform of the Montreal Canadiens," Plante's future teammate Jean Béliveau wrote later. "I was no different from anyone else who loved playing hockey during that era. We would practice for hours after school in the rink we had in our backyard. By playing outdoors we learned to stickhandle and develop other skills that might one day allow us to play for the Canadiens."[13]

"We couldn't afford a radio," Plante recalled, "but, luckily the man upstairs used to turn up the hockey broadcasts real loud. By standing on the bureau in the girls' room I could hear the broadcasts through the ceiling. In the spring of 1944, when the Canadiens beat the Black Hawks for the Stanley Cup, I listened to those exciting Canadien names coming down through the ceiling – Rocket Richard – Toe Blake – Elmer Lach – Butch Bouchard. When Bill Durnan made a big save in goal, I would try to 'help' him by sticking out a leg or a hand. Believe me, all of those Canadiens seemed to be 10 feet tall!"[14]

Soon afterwards Jacques Plante was so rudely dismissed by a trainer at the entrance of the Shawinigan Arena. This rejection would have shattered a less self-assured 15-year-old, but Jacques, even at this young age, was bursting with confidence. He disregarded the trainer and went straight to the coach of the Cataractes and boldly asked if the team required a practice goalie. Expecting Jacques to fall flat on his face, the coach inserted the boy into a practice of semi-professional players, but was stunned when Jacques not only held his own but shone. Jacques, who had never skated in the Shawinigan Arena before, now found himself the centre of attention. The manager of the arena, in awe of Plante's play, told him that from this point forward he was always welcome at the arena.

Suddenly, at the age of 15, Jacques Plante was in demand. In addition to being the practice goalie for the Senior League Cataractes, he was playing goal in three other age levels simultaneously: midget, juvenile, and junior. "We played together in midget category for Quebec schools," Marcel Pronovost remembers. Plante "was in the nets when we won the Quebec provincial championship."[15]

Unlike many of his classmates, who dropped out of school to chase their hockey dreams, Jacques stayed in school to get the high-school diploma that his parents desperately wanted him to receive. Not that the offers weren't tempting.

The word on Jacques Plante started to spread beyond the local rink and the boundaries of Shawinigan. The wooden benches at the Shawinigan Arena were now filling up with people eager to see the local prodigy, who almost always seemed to be patrolling the goal no matter who was playing. He received an offer to play in England with the pay starting at $80 a week. He was offered a tryout with the Providence Reds of the American Hockey League. His parents stood firm and refused the offers; Jacques Plante had to finish high school first. However, there was one offer he did accept. The local factory team, which played once a week, asked the 15-year-old to join them.

Soon after Jacques started with the factory team, his father pointed out to him that he was in a unique position. All the other players worked at the factory and were paid accordingly. Having watched a few games, Xavier Plante knew that his son was the factor in the team's newfound success, and since he didn't work at the factory, he also was aware that his son was playing for free. Perhaps there was some way that Jacques could be financially compensated? It didn't take long for Jacques to approach the coach, who quickly accepted the weakness of his own bargaining position and capitulated.

"It wasn't my best contract," Plante laughed years later, "but it looked big at the time. I would receive fifty cents a game on the condition that I didn't tell the other players. Fifty cents a week is important money when you're part of a family where soft drinks were only served at Christmas."[16]

Plante may have missed out on his best offer, however. "I grew up in Shawinigan with Marcel Pronovost. We were close friends and played a lot of hockey together. I almost ended up going to Detroit with him. What happened was, a Detroit scout from Quebec City came to Shawinigan to look at four players: Marcel, the Wilson brothers, Johnny and Larry, and me. I wasn't there that night so he signed up the other three and went back home. It was lucky for me that I didn't sign with them. Their regular goalie was Harry Lumley and they had young guys like Terry Sawchuk and Glenn Hall in their system at the time and I might not have gotten a chance to play. I would have disappeared somewhere, especially in Ontario where they had their farm clubs and I didn't speak a word of English. I would have been lost."[17]

And so Jacques Plante stayed behind, and while his friends followed their dream, he continued on with his studies, and graduated from high school at age 18 in the spring of 1947.

He immediately took a job as a factory clerk alongside his father to help the family. But it was apparent to everyone in town that his future lay elsewhere. He had been given a brief taste of semi-professional hockey that year when he played in one game for the Cataractes. Now when he wasn't working at the factory, he was working on what he considered his true profession – goaltending. Spending up to four hours each day in the nets, he kept himself sharp for the opportunity that he was sure would present itself.

2

THE ARCHITECT

ON AUGUST 1, 1946, a diminutive middle-aged man walked through the front door of the Montreal Forum, the home of the Stanley Cup champion Montreal Canadiens. Frank Selke radiated a quiet dignity as he stood in the lobby. Though he was barely taller than five foot and weighed around 150 pounds, his presence was felt. Almost immediately, he noticed the foul odour emanating from the hallways. In spite of knowing only the rudiments of the French language, he quickly issued his very first order, in both languages. "Clean the toilets! Nettoyez les toilettes!"

From this most humble of beginnings, the most successful hockey franchise of all-time was born.

"I'll never forget that first afternoon at the Montreal Forum," Selke said almost 40 years after the fact. "The place was filthy and the stench of poorly managed urinals knocked you down when you opened the front door. I had come from the working class and I would not stand for sloppiness at any level. The local fan deserved to sit in comfort and enjoy a high quality of entertainment, so my first task was to invest more than $100,000 in a new plumbing system and undertake major renovations in the building."[1] Selke, at the age of 53, after 40 years in the sport, had just made the first independent decision of his professional hockey career.

For as long as he could remember, Selke had been involved in the world of hockey. Born in the hockey hotbed of Berlin, Ontario (now Kitchener), the son of Polish immigrants, he left school behind at the age of 13 to pursue his hockey dream. For most kids this dream meant playing the game, but Selke, realizing the limitations of his size, instead began organizing teams made up of his friends and acquaintances.

Selke's acumen for organizing successful hockey teams saw him slowly rise in status within the amateur hockey world. In 1912, he assembled his first junior team, the Berlin Union Jacks, in the Ontario Hockey Association, and three years later coached the team to the league finals, where they lost to a Toronto team captained by a 20-year-old Conn Smythe.

With the onset of the First World War, Selke, like most men his age, joined the Army, but war didn't prevent him from continuing to make use of his organizational talents. Selke quickly cobbled together a soldier's squad that competed in the Ontario Hockey Association's intermediate league.

After the war, Selke turned his focus towards raising his family, while working as an electrician at the University of Toronto. But he still found time to coach and manage youth hockey for the churches he attended, in addition to coaching the University of Toronto's hockey team to the first Memorial Cup, in 1919.

In 1924 his St. Mary's junior OHA team won its third straight SPA championship. Two years later, the team changed its name to the Toronto Marlboros and again won the SPA championship. After a one-year interruption, Selke once again coached the Marlboros, and once again captured the Memorial Cup.

In the fall of 1929, four members of that championship Marlboros team, defencemen Red Horner and Alex Levinsky and wingers Busher Jackson and Charlie Conacher, made the jump to the Toronto Maple Leafs of the National Hockey League. Frank Selke followed his players and became the team's assistant manager, working under his old opponent Conn Smythe.

Once adversaries, Smythe and Selke had gradually grown closer during the previous decade, with the University of Toronto's hockey team becoming their common passion. The two of them shared not only dedication to a strenuous work ethic but a commitment to the sport. Already possessing an engineering degree from the university, after the war Smythe added a degree in applied science, all the while keeping a close eye on the school's hockey team, run by Selke.

Officially, Selke was in charge of scouting amateur talent, public relations, and producing and creating the Maple Leafs program that was handed out at the team's home games. Behind the scenes, he did far more. Without Selke, Maple Leaf Gardens would eventually have been finished, but it certainly wouldn't have opened in the fall of 1931.

In the face of the Great Depression, with construction under way, many of Smythe's original financial backers did not want to finance the arena's construction and pushed for delaying the work for a couple of years. Selke, using his status as the honorary manager of the local branch of the International Brotherhood of Electrical Workers, took it upon himself to go to the Allied Building Trades Council of Toronto with an inspired and clever solution. In large part because of Selke's persuasiveness, the council decided to allow its membership, many of whom were out of work, to take 20 per cent of their wages in Gardens stock.

Smythe immediately took Selke's proposal to his key backers, who in light of the workers' financial sacrifice allowed an exception for Smythe's project and forwarded him the necessary funds. Thanks to Smythe's determination and Selke's ingenuity, at the height of the Great Depression, Maple Leaf Gardens opened on November 12, 1931, when the Black Hawks defeated the Leafs by a score of 2–1. The next spring, led by the "Kid Line" of Busher Jackson, Joe Primeau, and Charlie Conacher – all brought to the team by Selke – the Leafs won the Stanley Cup, defeating the New York Rangers three games to none.

Despite the role played by Selke in building both the championship team and Maple Leaf Gardens, it was Smythe who put himself out front and took full credit for these achievements. A master of self-promotion, Smythe could take justifiable pride in resurrecting the Toronto Maple Leafs, but it was Selke who had brought in the players that delivered the Stanley Cup.

"Smythe was a single-minded, tough-talking, straight-shooting ego-centric that flirted with megalomania. Smythe was the very antithesis to Selke," wrote Chrys Goyens and Allan Turowetz in their book, *Lions in Winter*.[2]

Also standing in the shadow of Smythe's immense ego was the Leafs' head coach, Dick Irvin, who had guided the team to the Stanley Cup. Hired away from the Black Hawks by a scheming Smythe, Irvin rewarded Smythe's faith by bringing him a much longed-for championship.

Selke quickly developed a close relationship with the team's new coach. Each man had much in common. A year apart in age, they both frowned upon many of life's vices, like smoking, drinking, and gambling, while sharing a passion for raising chickens and displaying exotic breeds. Drawing on the same principle that he used on the farm when raising his beloved chickens, Selke assembled the most players, and then each year "harvested a crop."[3]

Selke seemed content to work in Smythe's sizable shadow as the Maple Leafs became the National Hockey League's model franchise, appearing in six Stanley Cup finals over the next eight years. Selke continued to unearth the talent that kept the Leafs on top of the league. As the decade progressed, however, Smythe gradually grew disenchanted with Irvin as his coach as each of the team's six finals appearances ended in loss. At the conclusion of the 1940 season, Smythe decided it was time to make a change and he let Irvin go. Smythe selected Hap Day, the man who had captained the 1932 championship team, to replace him. (Irvin wasn't out of work long, and quickly resurfaced as the Montreal Canadiens' coach at the beginning of the new season.)

At the age of 45, Smythe signed up for the Canadian Army and headed over to Europe to serve in the Second World War. He appointed a committee of three – including Selke – to run the team in his absence. However, Smythe wanted to retain a degree of control over personnel decisions at the professional level, and required that the committee consult him on such matters. Given the keys to the kingdom in Smythe's absence, Selke thrived, building Stanley Cup winners in 1942 and 1945. Ironically, it was Selke's finest strategic move as the Leafs' stand-in manager that sowed the seeds of his eventual departure from Toronto. The 1943 trade of Frankie Eddolls to the Montreal Canadiens in exchange for a youngster by the name of Ted Kennedy, who became immortalized as a Leaf legend, has to be one of the shrewdest moves of Selke's entire hockey career.

That the trade was an absolute steal in the Leafs' favour did nothing to assuage Smythe, who was outraged that the trade hadn't been presented for his approval. Upon hearing of the deal in France, Smythe publicly attacked Selke for the deal; in private, he tried to get the deal rescinded.

After the Leafs' Stanley Cup championship in the spring of 1945, many on the Leafs' board of directors agitated to put him in charge of the entire operation, whether Conn Smythe was on the scene or not.

"That rankled," Selke remembered later. "It really bothered Conn to have to overhear other NHL governors and managers dropping the little lines like: 'yeah, but he's got that Selke doing all that for him.' It drove him crazy. I remember some incredible messages he would send me from his overseas office. How in God's name can you run a team from France? Besides, winning the Stanley Cup in his absence did not mean a thing: he still had me down as the publicity man and Conn took all of the credit."[4]

In the fall of 1945, Conn Smythe made his triumphant return. His first order of business in the Toronto front office was to appoint a president to oversee the team. Smythe asked Selke to support him in his bid for the Leaf presidency. When Selke demurred, the clock on his days in Toronto started to tick.

While Smythe demanded full credit for the 1942 and 1945 Stanley Cup championships, the titles had been in fact won under Selke's leadership. The 1945–46 season would see the acrimonious end of their partnership. Not only did the Leafs fail to make the playoffs, but Ted Kennedy, the initial focus of their rancour and the Leafs' scoring leader the year before, was in a remarkable slump. That sag saw him register only five points that entire season. Smythe wasted no time laying the blame for the team's rapid descent and Kennedy's disastrous season entirely at Selke's feet. Selke later called it "the unhappiest year of my long connection with the game."[5]

There was now a heightened level of animosity between the two men. In the spring of 1946, Smythe sent a memo to Selke that read in part, "Anytime I am in the building you are not to leave for lunch or any other purpose without my permission in case I need you."

"Lincoln freed the slaves eighty years ago," a resigned Selke replied. "I'm done. Goodbye."[6]

"I think he respected my worth as a hockey manager," Selke said years after the fact, "but he never could admit that my ability for identifying hockey talent and molding a team were far ahead of his own."[7]

Smythe could now savour the glory. And while the Leafs would win four of the next five Stanley Cups with the team largely built by Selke, Smythe had no way of knowing that he had let the genie out of the bottle. Heading to Montreal was a man who would in time build his own hockey empire.

Hired as the Montreal Canadiens' newest general manager, Selke seemed to be walking into the ideal situation. After all, he was now reunited with his close friend and former Leafs bench boss Dick Irvin, who had coached the Canadiens to two Stanley Cup championships in the past three seasons. However, Selke quickly ascertained that beyond the core players (forwards Maurice Richard, Elmer Lach, Toe

Blake; defencemen Butch Bouchard and Ken Reardon; and goaltender Bill Durnan), the team had significant deficiencies. With his core group of players advancing in age, Selke was horrified to find that the Canadiens possessed few prospects in the amateur ranks.

Luckily for Selke, he found his ideal owner in Senator Donat Raymond. Raymond shared his desire to have his own hockey empire. As they discussed their ideas, Selke was pleased to discover that Raymond would be willing to pay for it, while staying in the background and giving Selke total control over all aspects of the team.

"We had to do two things," Selke remembered later, "build an organization which on one hand could recruit the best talent available right across Canada, and at the same time develop the pool of players in our backyard, Quebec."[8] "I'd like to inaugurate a farm system," Selke told the press when he arrived in Montreal, "with a team in every province to build up young reserves, as in Toronto."[9]

Selke soon went to work building a network of Canadiens-sponsored teams that would become unmatched in the sport. He quickly set up affiliates throughout Canada, in such places as Halifax, Quebec City, Trois-Rivières, Victoriaville, Montreal, Peterborough, Fort William, Winnipeg, Regina, and Edmonton.

"We helped teams everywhere in hockey," Selke said. "We had ten teams in the Winnipeg area and we paid for the whole amateur system in Regina. And at one point, we were paying $300,000 a year in amateur development in Edmonton."[10]

Selke had a vision of how he wanted the organization to be perceived, based on the Leafs archetype, which meant that players and team employees had to live up to a certain standard. Selke set out to build the ideal hockey franchise. The first step was to overhaul – and clean – the existing facilities at the Montreal Forum.

In time the Forum evolved into a temple, a shrine to hockey. But when Frank Selke took over the reins in the fall of 1946, sanitation issues were just one of the many building deficiencies facing him in his new role as manager. Three years later, under Selke's direction, the team added a second storey to the Forum, boosting the rink's capacity from 9,300 seats to 13,551, and bringing it in line with the league's other arenas.

Frank Selke's initial season in Montreal was at best bittersweet. Dick Irvin coached the Canadiens to a first-place finish at the conclusion of the regular season, six points ahead of the Toronto Maple Leafs. But in the Stanley Cup finals, Selke's worst fears from the previous fall came true. With Elmer Lach, his top centre, out with an injury, the Canadiens were defeated by the Leafs in six games – a Leafs team that had been built and organized by Frank Selke. As soon as he finished renovating the Forum, Selke turned his prodigious energy and intellect into building his empire.

One of his first moves was hiring a 21-year-old native Montrealer named Sam Pollock as an executive. In essence, Selke had hired a younger version of himself who would have many of the same responsibilities that Selke had first had in the Leafs organization. As well, Pollock would be Selke's conduit to the junior system that was being built. Despite his youth, Pollock had already made a name for himself on the local sporting scene as a master organizer of both hockey and baseball teams. Working together, Selke and Pollock cultivated an unmatched network of contacts throughout Quebec and beyond that would alert them to early talent.

In gathering players, Selke and the Canadiens held two distinct advantages over the competition. In Quebec, the mere thought of one day playing for the Canadiens was enough to get most prospects to sign the form binding them to Montreal. And in the rest of Canada, the Canadiens, able to spend much more than their fellow teams were able to accumulate, could sign many more players.

In 1945, the NHL introduced a new way for professional teams to gather the best young talent. The C-form allowed teams to sign a player and then assign him to one of their sponsored teams. As soon as the player signed the C-form he was effectively the property of that particular NHL team and had no say in the course of his destiny.

Selke and Pollock grasped the significance of this new rule before anyone else. Signing an unprecedented number of players to C-forms, Selke quickly built up a network of teams stocked with the best young talent. In a couple of years, the other teams in the NHL began following a similar path, but by then Selke had a tremendous head start on his competition.

"Each young player progressed through levels of expertise," wrote Goyens and Turowetz in *Lions in Winter*. "They underwent a socialization process during which the cultural values of winning were stressed more and more. As a result the Canadiens juniors tended to be a little more serious, a little more mature."[11]

Selke was looking for players who would put the team first. He sought players who in equal measure were dedicated to winning and who detested losing, players who were self-confident, self-directed, and self-motivated and who would work within the team concept. Each player was expected to transform his personal expectations, attitudes, and motives into team expectations, team attitudes, and team motives.

Selke's theory was that the best players would rise to the top of the organization, and that the Canadiens would have a constant stream of young, hungry, talented players challenging for a place with the big team each fall. With their extensive system in place, Selke and Pollock set out on a quest to sign the best junior talent in Canada. And with their extensive network of contacts, it didn't take long for them to hear about a young goaltender filling the rink in Shawinigan.

NECESSITY IS THE
MOTHER OF INVENTION

IN THE FALL OF 1947, Jacques Plante was invited to the training camp of the Montreal Junior Canadiens of the Quebec Junior Hockey League. Theo Racette, the manager of the Shawinigan Cataractes, had been watching Plante play as the practice goalie for his team in the Quebec Senior League for the past three years, as well as play a game for the Cataractes the spring before, and he was well aware of the young goalie's skill. He recommended Plante to Frank Selke and Sam Pollock. Plante's discovery was a perfect example of how the Canadiens were able to stock up their farm system with the best of Quebec's young hockey talent.

Jacques took two weeks' vacation from the factory in Shawinigan, and Racette drove him to Montreal. He was put up at the Queen's Hotel by the Canadiens and received the standard $40 a week in spending money that was due the team's amateurs.

The Canadiens were eager to get Plante on the Junior Canadiens roster, having placed him on the protected list for the team months earlier.[1] After only a week it became apparent that Plante was going to be the starting goaltender for the Junior Canadiens, and he was offered a contract with the team.

Jacques, however, hesitated to sign the deal. According to a letter Selke wrote a few months later to NHL president Clarence Campbell,

"Plante came to my office and asked whether he could go home to arrange with his father about taking up permanent residence in Montreal where he wished to attend Mont St. Louis School at our expense. He was to receive $30.00 a week in addition toward his living allowance while in Montreal. While at Shawinigan, he extended his visit from one day to almost a week and had Theo Racette call me and advise that he had had a better offer elsewhere, but that he would come to Montreal if we raised his stipend to $35.00 a week. This I agreed to do, and notified the Canadien Juniors accordingly."[2]

In truth, Jacques was concerned about the stipend he was being offered by Selke, which was understandable, given that he was making more at the factory.

The Canadiens were not in the business of paying their prospects high salaries. Instead they offered the prestige of being a member of the organization. It was this prestige that compelled most youngsters to sign on the dotted line rather than taking the time to explore their financial options. After all, they were inexperienced teenagers whose dream was to play in the National Hockey League wearing the uniform of the Montreal Canadiens. If they said no, there were many other youngsters who would say yes in their place.

While Jacques Plante had that same dream, he also wanted to be paid what he thought he was worth. Nor was he bluffing: the Canadiens were not the only team offering to pay him to play for them.

Taking note of the Canadiens' interest were the Quebec Citadels, a newly formed team in the Quebec Junior League that would operate in direct competition with the Montreal Junior Canadiens. The Citadels were offering $85 a week for Jacques to star in Quebec City, $50 more than the Canadiens. Plante took the Citadels up on their offer.

It wasn't unusual for many prospects in Quebec to play for a team not directly sponsored by the Canadiens. However, a majority of them had signed a C-form binding their professional futures to the Canadiens. "As I recall when I was playing," Plante's future teammate Bernie "Boom Boom" Geoffrion wrote in his memoirs, "I think every player in the Quebec Junior League had signed a C-form with the Canadiens. This meant in theory every kid playing in Quebec juniors was the property of Montreal – if they wanted them, that is."[3]

There was one player in the Quebec Junior League that the Canadiens wanted desperately, and he hadn't signed a C-form. Frank Selke was a man accustomed to getting what he wanted, and since Jacques Plante's name was on the negotiation list for the Montreal Junior Canadiens, he demanded that the Citadels immediately release Plante from their team. The Citadels responded by threatening to take the issue to the provincial legislature, where the disagreement would become public knowledge. Then Selke's old adversary Conn Smythe placed Plante on the Toronto Maple Leafs' negotiation list. Smythe thought this move gave the Leafs priority in getting Plante's signature on a C-form. After all, he didn't see Plante's name on Montreal's negotiation list.

Plante had misgivings when he heard of the Leafs' interest. In the fall of 1947, the Leafs were firmly installed as the league's pre-eminent team, having just begun a reign that would see them capture four Stanley Cups over the next five years. With Turk Broda considered one of the game's elite goalies and Gilles Mayer of Ottawa entrenched as his heir apparent, the Leafs appeared to have their goaltending situation well in hand for the foreseeable future. But if Jacques signed with the Leafs, he would almost certainly be sent to one of the various towns that made up their farm system, primarily consisting of English-speaking teams. The same reasoning behind his hesitation about joining the Red Wings a few years before now applied to the Leafs. Possessing very little grasp of the English language, Jacques was understandably nervous about living and playing in Ontario.

At the same time that the Leafs were publicly making a play for Jacques Plante's talents, another NHL team, the New York Rangers, was making a private play with the same thought in mind. Roland Mercier was the business manager for the Quebec Citadels, but on the side he was a scout for the Rangers. Knowing the intimate details of the Citadels' tug-of-war with the Canadiens, Mercier befriended Plante in an effort to get him into the Rangers' orbit.

"If you went with the Canadiens," Mercier informed him, "you'd be third in line behind Bill Durnan and Gerry McNeil. If you went with the Rangers you would have only Chuck Rayner to beat out. Either way you would have to wait, but it could mean a shorter wait with the Rangers."[4]

On November 6, 1948, Jacques Plante made his home debut in front of the Quebec City fans against the Montreal Royals, who were led by a 16-year-old prospect from the Park Extension neighbourhood in Montreal named Dickie Moore. Plante's "inspiring defensive play," in the words of the Montreal Gazette, went a long way to securing the Citadels' 5–3 win.[5]

Selke may have been angry about the Plante situation, but he was a practical man.

The same month the NHL head office informed Smythe and the Leafs that Plante was unavailable, since his name now appeared on the Canadiens' negotiation list, Smythe responded by requesting a league investigation. It was understood that if the Leafs pressed their case, Plante would have remained on their negotiation list, but, given the sheer number of talented goalies in the Leafs system, it wasn't worth their effort. On December 12, Smythe sent a letter to the head offices of the NHL releasing the Leafs claim on the future of Jacques Plante.[6]

Selke and the Canadiens quickly moved to bring Plante into the Canadiens fold. The Citadels agreed to loan Plante to the Junior Canadiens for two games, and on December 13, Plante finally signed a B-form with the Montreal Canadiens.

Whereas a C-form would have bound Plante to the Canadiens in perpetuity, the B-form gave them only his professional rights. In other words, if Plante were ever going to turn professional, it would have to be with the Montreal Canadiens. Relieved the negotiations were settled, Plante played his two games with the Junior Canadiens and then returned to Quebec City to play with the Citadels. In truth, his heart had always been with the Canadiens, and now his attention could be devoted to the Citadels.

Unbeknownst to Plante was a letter Selke sent to NHL president Clarence Campbell on December 15. Selke acknowledged the signing of Plante to a B-form a couple of days earlier and then wrote, "I have had my fill of Jacques Plante."[7]

Jacques began his first season in the Quebec Junior Hockey League, and the opposition quickly took notice.

"I first met Jacques when he was playing with the Quebec Citadels," says Dickie Moore, then starring with the Montreal Junior Royals. "He was one of the best goalies in the league, and we had to figure out a system to beat him. He was very quick, very agile in the net, and he caught the puck as if he was a first baseman. We devised a system to beat him and we started passing the puck from behind the net to make him look the other way. We also tried to take him off his game by giving him the odd bump. It worked for a little while, until he adjusted."[8]

Jacques Plante was nothing less than an immediate sensation in Quebec, a city that had enjoyed major hockey for 40 years. Andy O'Brien noted, "The hockey-mature Quebec City fandom found that very special 'something different' in the Citadels goaler."[9]

The Citadels drew more than 100,000 fans to 22 home games, and Plante was easily the major attraction, quickly establishing himself as one of the top goaltending prospects in amateur hockey. In addition to his performance, Plante drew attention to two other distinctive features of his play.

Upon seeing Plante skate towards the net at the start of the game, spectators couldn't help but notice his toque. At a time when all players were bare-headed, Plante stood out as the only man to sport headware during the game. And he made no bones about telling people that he had personally hand-knitted his toque.

In the annals of hockey, only one man previously had stood out for sporting a toque on the ice. The legendary Georges Vézina, the first goaltender of the Montreal Canadiens, had famously worn one a quarter of a century before. For many observers, wearing a toque signalled that Plante felt he was the natural successor to the Vézina legend. Still, others criticized him, simply because nobody else wore one.

He answered his critics, even back then, by using the media and with a hint of humour. "If they want to get hot because I want to keep my head warm, everybody's cozy, oui?"[10]

However, for all the controversy that the toque created, it paled next to Jacques' endless habit of leaving the confines of his goal and roving after the puck. Traditionally, goalies let the puck come to them; Plante was the first goaltender to go after the puck. He was labelled "wandering" by many in the media, and his coming out and playing the puck provoked tremendous debate in hockey circles.

Throughout his life, Plante always maintained that his roving in search of the puck was not a sign of genius or innovation but instead was born of necessity, a requirement of playing behind a porous group of defenders. "Our four defensemen all had flaws," Plante later explained, "one couldn't skate backwards, one couldn't turn to his left, one couldn't turn to his right and the fourth couldn't pass the puck accurately to our blueline. Somebody had to clear the loose pucks, so I started doing it myself. Because it worked and I felt it helped the team, I continued to do it right up to the NHL."[11]

Quite often, Plante would casually go behind his net, stop the puck, and leave it behind his goal for his defenceman to pick up, making the race for the puck not only shorter but one in which the defenceman could gather the puck up with only the slightest delay.

"The shoot-and-chase approach had become big in hockey," Plante reflected later to sportswriter Frank Orr. "Teams would come up to the blueline and shoot the puck around our boards deep in our zone, then swarm in after it forechecking, trying to regain possession. If I skated out of the crease behind the net, blocked the shoot-in and left the puck there, the other team did not have as good a chance to get it again as when it slid into the corner."[12]

By coming out of the net and taking the puck, Plante eliminated all of those options for the attacking team. However, the thinking at the time was that if the goalie left the net, it was unprotected, and it was therefore much easier for the opposition to score. Plante was one of the first to realize what his critics failed to recognize – he had control of the puck when he handled it, and if he had control of the puck, the other team didn't.

"I took a lot of guff about it before they [the coaches and managers] saw that I was not costing us any goals by my little skates and, in fact, I was saving us some goals by keeping the other teams from getting possession as often in our zone."[13]

It didn't take long for many to see that Plante was right, and slowly other goalies began adopting his tactic.

Still only a teenager, Jacques Plante had already redefined the parameters of the goaltending position.

In 1948, a team from Victoriaville, Quebec, made up mostly of local boys, came to Quebec City to face Jacques Plante and the Citadels. Immediately, the Citadels and the crowd noticed the big, tall teenager playing centre for the Tigers. This unknown player dominated the game, and because of his obvious skill, it wouldn't be long before Jean Béliveau's fame stretched far beyond the arena.

"I ended the game with two goals and an assist," Béliveau wrote in his autobiography, "having scored one of those goals and the assist in overtime, helping to upset Jacques Plante and the Citadels 4–2. My goal midway through the third sent the game into overtime. Back then the rules called for a full, ten-minute overtime period, not a sudden-death finale. About three minutes in, I fed a pass to Gérard Théberge, who one-timed it into the Quebec goal. Several minutes later, the puck was cleared out of our zone and toward the Quebec goal. I took after it, with no one in close pursuit. The Citadels' netminder, who I'd heard was infamous for his wandering ways, decided to come out after the puck. Just as he reached to poke it away, I managed to get my stick on it. The goalie sprawled at the Citadels' blue line while I swung around him and tucked the puck into the open net."[14] In a few short years the wandering goalie and the towering centreman from Victoriaville would be teammates, and Jean Béliveau would never tire of kidding Jacques Plante about their very first meeting.

In the late 1940s, Béliveau wasn't the only future teammate of Plante's plying his trade in the Quebec Junior League. Selke, with the help of Pollock and his scouts throughout Quebec, had wisely stocked the Canadiens with a bountiful harvest of homegrown junior talent, a strategy that soon would begin paying large dividends. There were the gritty Dickie Moore and steady defenceman Dollard St. Laurent, who both starred for the Montreal Junior Royals, and Boom Boom Geoffrion of the Montreal Nationales, who was already terrorizing the league's goaltending fraternity with his slapshot and its alarming tendency to find the back of the net.

The Quebec Junior League, however, wasn't merely limited to helping to supply Montreal's farm system. For example, the Verdun Cyclones were stocked with prospects belonging to the New York Rangers. Guarding their nets was a man who would become Jacques Plante's most frequent adversary in a personal and professional rivalry that would last for the next quarter of a century.

Born just five months apart, Lorne "Gump" Worsley and Plante didn't share much besides a birth year, a profession, and a competitive dislike for each other. Plante was tall and thin; Gump, short and pudgy. Plante took a scientific approach to playing goal, whereas Gump swore by his instincts. Off the ice, Gump was gregarious, while Plante preferred his own counsel. As their careers progressed, the two seemed forever to be facing off against each other; playing for different teams, in different leagues, in other sports, in addition to verbally sparring with each other through the media. They fought their first battles in the Quebec Junior League in the late forties, when their two teams were vying for the top spot, a personal rivalry that endured well into each man's later years.

"Quebec's goaltender at the time was Jacques Plante," Worsley later wrote in his autobiography, *They Call Me Gump*. "And we once locked horns in a classic scoreless tie. I still have the newspaper clipping which reads: 'Goalie Lorne Worsley turned in a terrific game . . . Even though he shared the shutout with Jacques Plante, Worsley took the play away from his rival with his acrobatic performance as he handled 59 shots.'"[15]

Worsley was one of a precious few goalies in the league to get the better of Plante during his two-year stint in Quebec. Nevertheless, at the end of the season, Jacques was named to the league's first all-star team as the circuit's top goalie.

With the onset of spring came the playoffs, and in one of those great twists that sports can sometimes provide, the Citadels' opposition was the team that Plante had shunned the fall before: the Montreal Junior Canadiens. In a best-of-five series that went the limit, Plante was seen as the primary factor in the Citadels' upset over the mighty Junior Canadiens, who were directed behind the bench by Sam Pollock, Frank Selke's right-hand man. Taking in what must have been a disappointing defeat, Pollock told newsman Andy O'Brien, "Plante didn't wander enough for us; he was there to make the stops in the third period when we outshot the Citadels 11 to 7. I have no alibi to offer, Plante beat us."[16]

And while Pollock was no doubt saddened by the outcome of the series, he held closer to his vest a secret delight. It was shared by his boss, Frank Selke, who observed the games from high up in the press box. Selke may have told Clarence Campbell a few months earlier that he had had his fill of Jacques Plante. He now envisioned a future that included the brash youngster who had been such a pain the previous fall. Jacques Plante almost by himself had just spectacularly defeated the Junior Canadiens.

After a summer spent at home in Shawinigan, where he would be named the Player of the Year in the Shawinigan Industrial Baseball League, Plante returned to Quebec City in the fall of 1948 and was even more impressive in his last year in the Quebec Junior League.

Named to the circuit's first all-star team for the second consecutive year, and pocketing an almost 50 per cent pay raise, from $85 a week to $125, Jacques made statistical fact what had been the majority opinion the year before: there was no goaltender his equal in the Quebec Junior League. Playing in 47 games with the Citadels, Plante led the league with 35 wins, eight shutouts, and over the course of the season lost only eight games. Even more impressively, in a league in which the goals-against average was 4.49 goals per game, Jacques gave up only 1.99 goals per game, an astounding difference of two and a half goals per game when he patrolled the net.

The following season, 1949–50, saw the fans come out in droves to see the "Class of '31" rule the scoring race the same way that Jacques had defensively dominated the year before. Boom Boom Geoffrion captured the league scoring title with 86 points, including an astonishing 52 goals. Six points behind was runner-up Jean Béliveau. Rounding out the top 10 scorers was Dickie Moore, who captured his second consecutive Memorial Cup, awarded to the junior amateur champions. The team Moore won the Memorial Cup with was the Montreal Junior Canadiens, coached by Sam Pollock and managed by Frank Selke.

All born in 1931, the Class of '31 dominated hockey discussion throughout the province as the fans pondered the delicious thought of Béliveau at centre with Moore on his left and Geoffrion on his right, and of the day all three would graduate and join the Montreal Canadiens.

Jacques Plante missed out on the offensive barrage of the Class of '31 by one season. Instead, he found himself the target of a shooting barrage every morning in practice at the Montreal Forum. Only now the shooters weren't junior-age players, and they weren't amateurs. They were the Montreal Canadiens, led by the inimitable Maurice "The Rocket" Richard.

Slowly but surely, the elements of a future Montreal dynasty were falling into place.

PATIENCE IS A VIRTUE

ON AUGUST 17, 1949, at a press gathering at the Montreal Forum, Frank Selke announced that Jacques Plante, the top goaltender in the Quebec Junior Hockey League, had just signed a contract with the Montreal Royals of the Quebec Senior Hockey League. Jacques would be paid $4,500 for the season. In addition, he would be paid a $500 stipend to be the practice goalie for the Canadiens for the upcoming season.

In a league consisting of only six teams – and only six goalies – employment as a hockey player was an exceptional achievement. In any given year roughly a hundred professionals plied their trade in the NHL, and understandably they were not too eager to have their jobs usurped, resulting in a professional league that was extremely difficult for rookies to break into.

In the days of the original six, each NHL team played a schedule of 70 games. The goalie on each team was expected to play the complete schedule, and because of that, each team carried only one goaltender on its roster. At a time when safety equipment was virtually unheard of, and goalies played bare-faced and bare-headed, it was not unusual for goalies to experience broken cheekbones, broken noses, severe facial cuts, or worse. Games could be interrupted by lengthy delays while injured goalies were patched up before being sent back out to finish the game, often skating in their own blood.

Despite the hazards of the profession, each of the league's six goalies tenaciously clung to his position. Climbing the ladder could therefore be a long and arduous process for any aspiring goaltender. In time, Jacques Plante would learn this, but on that warm summer day in Montreal, playing in goal for the Montreal Canadiens seemed to be right around the corner for the confident 20-year-old.

"The acceptance of my new goaling technique had built my self-confidence," Plante recalled. "I was convinced that my chance would come any time and all I had to do was play every game and yes, every practice – as if it were a playoff. It was right thinking for a rookie."[1]

The raise in pay would come in handy for Plante, who was no longer playing just for himself in Quebec or for his family in Shawinigan. The previous October, while playing for the Citadels, Jacques had been introduced to Jacqueline Gagné, a native of Quebec City. "She wasn't really fond of hockey when she met my father," Jacques' son Michel recalled in a television interview. "Her sister said to her it's Jacques Plante, he's playing for Quebec. My mother responded 'Who's he?'"[2]

They soon began dating, and two months into their courtship, in December of 1948, they got engaged. They married five months later, when the hockey season had ended.

"Things moved fast in the romance department for me and I was grateful for the newspapers," Jacques said at the time, a sure sign that his growing fame did have some unexpected consequences, including a loss of privacy.[3]

Plante spent the summer in Quebec City, where he led the junior lacrosse team to the provincial championship. It was also during this time that Plante began excelling at numerous other sports besides hockey, baseball, and lacrosse; he also became proficient in tennis and badminton. Like most everything Jacques Plante did, this was by design. From childhood Jacques had been a gifted athlete, but now he used these other sports to help perfect his hockey game. By working hard at a range of sports, he maintained a high standard of cardiovascular conditioning, in addition to sharpening his hand-eye coordination. At this early age, he had recognized the benefits of off-season physical and mental training.

"I felt for certain that my career was in pro hockey and that I was going to go right to the top. Not only was Montreal the place where the action was, but Jacqueline and I felt it a great place to live and raise a family. Also I knew that playing for the Royals and practicing with the Canadiens would keep me constantly under the collective eyes of the organization's headquarters staff at the Forum."[4]

Jacques was now recognized as the number three man in the Canadiens pecking order of goalies, behind Bill Durnan and Gerry McNeil. In the fall of 1949 he had the opportunity not only to practise with the big club at the Forum but also to line up in practice against his hero, the legendary Durnan, who faced him on the other side of the rink.

At the time, he felt close to achieving his goal of playing for the Canadiens. As the years passed, however, he would find out what his predecessor for the Montreal Royals and the man who had been the Canadiens practice goalie in the years prior had learned: that in waiting for your turn in the Canadiens net, the foremost requirement was a strong dose of patience. After all, the man he was replacing in the Royals goal had just finished his sixth season waiting for a call from the Canadiens.

Gerry McNeil attended his first training camp with the Canadiens in the fall of 1943, at the age of 17. In training camp he found himself battling for the starting goaltender's position with a player 10 years his elder named Bill Durnan. Neither had ever played in a National Hockey League game.

McNeil may have lost the starting job with the Canadiens to Durnan in '43, but he was rewarded with the goaltending job with the Montreal Royals. In addition to being the practice goalie for the Canadiens, McNeil was now established as the number two netminder in the Montreal system.

McNeil would spend the next six years starring for the Royals, leading them to the 1947 Allan Cup, awarded to the best team in senior hockey; topping the league in goals-against average in 1946 and 1947; and being named to the first all-star team in 1947, 1948, and 1949. During those seasons, 1947–49, McNeil was not only the best goalie in the Quebec Senior League but also its best player, taking home the most valuable player award in each of those three years.

From the 1943 season through the spring of 1949, McNeil dutifully fulfilled his role as the Canadiens practice goalie – and found action in only eight games in the NHL. Clearly, McNeil was an NHL-calibre goaltender, but two things stood in his way. One was systemic, the other was the legendary Bill Durnan.

Today, players have free agency and some choice with regard to their professional future, but back in McNeil's time, options were few. Having signed an open-ended contract with the Canadiens, McNeil was at the mercy of the team's management. If he wanted to play hockey, it would be wherever the team's brass decided. If he disagreed with management, he faced the prospect of not playing at all.

Unfortunately, no matter what level of success McNeil achieved with the Royals, it paled in comparison to what Bill Durnan accomplished with the Canadiens. In the six years that McNeil waited patiently with the Royals, Durnan won an unprecedented five Vezina trophies as the NHL's top goalie, was named to the first all-star team five times, and led the Canadiens to a pair of Stanley Cup championships.

With the ascendance of Plante and with McNeil's continuing great play, by the fall of 1949 the Canadiens' goaltending situation was a logjam. McNeil, having accomplished everything possible with the Royals, was moved to the Cincinnati Mohawks of the American Hockey League in order to make room for Plante.

The wait for the Canadiens goaltending job had all the appearance of being a long one for Plante. Durnan, at the age of 33, was anchored to the number one position in the organization, while McNeil, only three years older than Plante, and the heir apparent to Durnan, seemed to have a long career ahead of him. If Plante harboured any misgivings heading into his maiden season in the Quebec Senior League, he didn't share them with anybody.

The senior league was essentially a semi-professional league, in which the players were paid a salary, some on par with their NHL counterparts. Many of the league's players were graduates of the Quebec Junior League who were unable to immediately crack an NHL roster. With the NHL consisting of only six teams, senior hockey filled the void with a high-quality, entertaining game that had a large fan base and garnered a good share of media interest.

In a league dotted with past and future NHLers, Plante showed that he belonged, posting the league's second-best goals-against average. During his initial season with the Royals, Plante made full use of all the perks available to the Canadiens practice goalie. For someone as naturally curious as Plante, the chance to study his fellow goalies was a precious opportunity. Always eager to learn different approaches to goaltending and quickly modify them to his own style, he was a true student of the game. And so each day in practice he studied Bill Durnan, his idol.

Durnan finished the 1949–50 season as he had most others, by winning the Vezina Trophy and being named to the first all-star team. But below the surface, the strain and tension that were a goaltender's constant companions were beginning to overwhelm the man. The threat of injury dampened Durnan's desire to play. "It got so bad that I couldn't sleep on the night before a game," he admitted. "I couldn't even keep my meals down. I felt that nothing was worth that kind of agony."[5]

Durnan quietly decided to leave the game behind, but Frank Selke and Canadiens head coach Dick Irvin persuaded him to play one more season. All of this was kept from the public.

In the first round of the 1950 playoffs, the Canadiens, who had finished second in the league standings, were paired off against the fourth-place New York Rangers. In what was considered a major upset, the Rangers quickly jumped out to a commanding three-games-to-none lead over Montreal. With game four on the horizon and elimination staring the team in the face, Bill Durnan abruptly walked away from the game – for good. "I was afraid I was blowing things," he reflected later. "I felt I wasn't playing as well as I did in the past. The nerves and all the accompanying crap were built up. It was the culmination of a lot of thinking and I realized, 'What the hell, I'm quitting and this is as good a time as any.'"[6]

Little could be done in those days to help a goalie – or anyone else – who was suffering a nervous breakdown. With no medications available and few doctors who understood this form of psychosis, many goaltenders chose to retire, leaving the game emotionally shattered and psychologically scarred.

"I couldn't blame him," says Elmer Lach. "I couldn't have done what he did, putting my face in front of the puck like that."[7] Lach was understandably empathetic: he had suffered a host of serious injuries, including a broken wrist, a fractured cheekbone, a fractured jaw on two occasions, and worst of all, a skull fracture. It is easy to imagine the mental and physical strain endured by goalies at that time.

Durnan's decision left the fate of the Canadiens in the hands of Gerry McNeil. Long accustomed to playing under Durnan, a man he worshipped, McNeil was now thrust into the spotlight for the most important game of the season. He backstopped the Canadiens to a win that night but only delayed the inevitable as the Rangers wrapped up the series in the next game.

With just one year with the Royals under his belt, Jacques Plante suddenly found himself second in line to being the starting goalie for the Montreal Canadiens.

At the same time that Jacques was climbing the ladder in the Canadiens organization, his own family was starting to expand. His son Michel was born in 1951 and a second son, Richard, would be born four years later.

Jacques viewed hockey as his vocation, and he studied it to the point of compulsion. He was constantly searching for ways to improve himself. Many of his contemporaries left the game behind when they stepped off the ice. Not Plante. When he wasn't playing, he was thinking about the game, talking about the game, and writing about the game.

Plante didn't limit his study to the legendary Durnan; he spent his off-days hanging around the Forum, taking a seat in the stands behind the net, watching opposing teams practise. Often the players on the visiting team would wonder who was that kid sitting in the stands surrounded by thousands of empty seats. Many assumed that he was a Forum employee just slacking off work to watch practice. They didn't realize that it was a player studying them, and particularly their goalie, in order to gain some valuable insight that would improve his own game.

In studying and analyzing the pros, Plante found one goalie who stood out the most, a goalie whom he sought to emulate more than the others: Terry Sawchuk of the Detroit Red Wings.

Almost a year younger than Plante, Sawchuk had been called up to the NHL in the 1949–50 season, during Plante's first year with the Royals, but really began to make his mark the following season. Rare has been the player in the history of the game who has made such an immediate impact. Sawchuk had captured the Calder Trophy as the league's rookie of the year and was named to the first all-star team in 1951. He repeated the first all-star selection each of the following two seasons, as well as copping a pair of Vezina trophies as the leader in goals-against average. But for most people, it was his performance in the 1952 playoffs that forever cemented his reputation as the best goaltender of his day. In eight games, Sawchuk went undefeated, helping the Red Wings win the Stanley Cup with two consecutive sweeps over the Toronto Maple Leafs in the semifinals and then the Canadiens in the finals. Sporting four shutouts, he surrendered only five goals in the other four games, setting a still standing post-season record goals-against average of .63.

Plante watched Sawchuk intently. If Plante aspired to be the best goaltender, then it only made sense for him to study the best. Two aspects of Sawchuk's game struck Plante. The first was how he would assiduously play the angles when confronting the shooters, a characteristic born of one of Sawchuk's greatest strengths: his fearlessness between the pipes. The second was Sawchuk's stance. Standing just an inch short of six feet, Sawchuk managed to crouch incredibly low into his net. By squatting down as much as possible, he was able to keep his sightlines open when looking for oncoming pucks.

"I couldn't figure out how he was able to block so many screened shots," Plante told the *Hockey News* a couple of years later. "Then . . . I suddenly found out. Sawchuk puts the back edge of his stick flat on the ice, handle and all, blade up. He crouches, watching for the shot to come out of a scramble or from the point. You'd be surprised how many shots are stopped by that stick. You don't have only the blade, which might be turned in and a goal scored on a hard shot, but the full length of the stick. Besides, the goalie is in position to grab a higher shot faster."[8]

In the fall of 1950, Plante began his second season with the Royals. Playing behind a team that focused on its offence, much to the detriment of its defence, Jacques saw his goals-against average rise, although it was still the third best in the league. But the statistics tell only part of the story.

"Without Plante, we probably wouldn't even be in the race this season," admitted Frank Carlin, the Royals head coach. "It wasn't unusual for the Royals to be outshot yet still win the game. It has been happening all season."[9]

Plante stood tall in the face of adversity that entire season. He did it without complaint and at times without concern for his own well-being.

"When I first saw Plante he was wearing a toque while tending goal for the Montreal Royals Senior team in 1951," Dick Irvin Jr., son of the Canadiens coach, recalled years later. "You couldn't help but notice him. In fact, there were games when you hardly noticed anyone else."[10]

That year, in a game facing the Ottawa Senators, during the very first minute Plante found himself on the bottom of a goalmouth pileup, after one of his own defencemen sent an Ottawa player sprawling on top of him. Plante pulled himself up, and in obvious agony limped through the rest of the period against a team unbeaten in their previous nine games. During the intermission, Plante had his throbbing ankle taped, and he went back out for the second period. In the third period, with the Royals clinging to a 2–1 win, his ankle finally gave way, and he had to be helped off the ice.

As the call went out for a replacement goalie, Plante asked to be given a shot of novocaine. That would freeze the injured area, but it wouldn't help the ankle heal. After a substantial delay, Plante gingerly emerged from the dressing room and proceeded to shut out the Senators the rest of the way, preserving the Royals' 2–1 victory.

Toughness was a requirement for a goaltender. A lack of toughness could spell the end of any hope of a professional career in goaltending. If a goalie was going to play the full schedule, he was going to have to possess a tolerance for pain and the ability to overcome it.

That night, under the watchful eye of the Canadiens hierarchy, Jacques Plante passed the toughness test. The Chicago Black Hawks also took notice, and frantic for goaltending help, offered the Canadiens cash and centre Gordie Knutson for Plante's rights. Montreal flatly rejected the offer.

After completing the 1951–52 season, his third with the Royals, Plante was forced to make a decision that he felt would allow him to take the next step towards a professional career. Sitting in the stands, watching the professional goalies compete, he realized that his wrist, never fully healed since his fall when he was five years old, stood as the greatest impediment to his goaltending future.

In an exclusive interview he gave to the *Hockey News* a year and a half later, Plante revealed the depth of the personal crisis he faced and said he had seriously considered giving up hockey. "I knew I couldn't hope to be a top goalie, I couldn't catch the puck with my left hand or block it or knock it down. I used my right thigh to try to block it, but that meant a rebound. Too often the puck would go into the net between my hand and my body."[11]

That summer, Jacques wrote a letter to the Canadiens management revealing to them for the first time his greatest secret and asking them to pay for an operation to fix his wrist. A bold Plante promised them that, if they would cover the cost of the operation, he was sure he would be "as good as any goalie in the NHL, not even barring Terry Sawchuk."[12]

Plante's assuredness was not shared by a doctor he consulted, who told him that surgery might not make any difference to his wrist. However, a bone surgeon he then visited differed on that opinion, giving Jacques a sliver of hope. Frank Selke left the decision up to Plante, but warned him that if the surgery was unsuccessful, he would be responsible for the consequences, not the Canadiens. For the time being, the surgery, and the reason for it, were hidden from both the media and the public.

The medical procedure was considered a huge gamble in light of Plante's age and his potential future in hockey. For a man like Plante, however, who strived for perfection in his profession, there was no decision to be made. He was not content to be anything less than the best goalie in the sport.

The surgeon recommended that Plante be given a general anaesthetic. An always curious Plante refused, instead asking for a local anaesthetic of the wrist and the arm so he could watch what was going on. After becoming nauseous in the middle of the surgery, in which part of a bone in the wrist was removed, Plante finally acquiesced and was given the general anaesthetic. A couple of weeks after the surgery, Plante had the cast removed, and much to his delight, he was able for the first time since his early childhood to move his wrist properly.

As he had predicted, there was marked improvement in his play at the beginning of his fourth season with the Royals. After 29 games, Plante had not only lowered his goals-against by more than a goal but had led the team to first place in the standings. As the season neared the halfway point, he had already matched his shutout total from the previous two years, was leading the league in wins, had the fewest losses, and had the lowest goals-against of 2.08, over a full goal less than the league average of 3.16. Jacques Plante had gambled his career and his future and won.

"He was on the doorstep of the NHL," journalist Andy O'Brien wrote. "He went into the 1952–53 season with determination written all over his every move. From the press box we could sense it."[13]

A GRAND ENTRANCE

A SINGLE INDIVIDUAL dominated the news in Toronto on October 29, 1952. You might have thought this attention would be lavished on a returning hometown hero, a visiting dignitary, or maybe a worldwide celebrity. But all this commotion was over a hockey player, and not even a hometown star but a man who was the idol of the country's French-speaking populace: Maurice "Rocket" Richard.

Toronto was caught up in the pandemonium surrounding his chase of hockey's most prestigious record: Nels Stewart's 324 career goals.

Even the Toronto Maple Leafs, that night's opposition and host for the Rocket and the visiting Montreal Canadiens, took advantage of the public and media frenzy by purchasing two-column advertisements in all the local newspapers:

CAN THE "ROCKET" DO IT TONIGHT?
NELS STEWART 324
MAURICE RICHARD 322
DON'T MISS THIS ADDED THRILL!
CANADIENS VERSUS LEAFS TONIGHT

The object of this attention found himself cornered in a lobby alcove at the Royal York Hotel, where he was forced to engage the suffocating press. Richard, already showing his game face, glared, disgust dripping from his words: "Have you guys gone crazy? I've never had a big scoring night in your damn Gardens. And I have scored only three goals in all eight games so far this season. Who do you think I am?"[1]

As the Rocket shouldered his way to the dining room, his head coach, Dick Irvin, held up a hand in an effort to quell the commotion as well as accommodate the media's demand. "I am stunned at the publicity that the Rocket is getting here in Toronto," he said, "where for years fans along the rail have been yelling nasty things and grabbing his sweater; where the management has been accusing him of every crime except piracy on the high seas – and you fellows have been publicizing the guff. My only fear is that the Rocket himself is stunned."[2]

Lost amid all the hoopla that night at Maple Leaf Gardens was the game itself. The crowd of 14,069, delirious with anticipation, instead focused their collective attention on Montreal's famed number 9, cheering wildly every time the Rocket came anywhere near the puck.

At 11:01 of the opening period, Elmer Lach fired a pass that the Rocket, skating at full speed, received an inch outside the blue line. Suddenly, the Rocket rushed past a startled defence and quickly put the puck into the upper left corner of the net behind Leafs goalie Harry Lumley.

Now only one goal short of the record, the Rocket, a little over six minutes later, again broke in, resulting in a wild skirmish in front of the goal. With throngs of people anxiously caught halfway between sitting and standing, disappointment and exultation, the red light over the Leafs goal lit up and the crowd exploded.

The Leafs fans temporarily forgot that the Canadiens were their most hated rival and that the Rocket had been their most despised adversary. As his teammates streamed off the Montreal bench to congratulate him, the Gardens crowd rose in a standing ovation, the likes of which had never been seen before for an opposing player.

That evening's referee, Red Storey, fished the now historic puck out of the back of the net and gave it to the Rocket, whose ever-present scowl had been replaced by a calm smile of relief. Richard, caught up in the emotion of the moment, showed a rare sign of gratitude by waving his arm to acknowledge the cheering fans. In the utmost sign of respect, Toronto fans never booed the Rocket again.

Buried in Monday's newspapers was a report of an injury suffered in that same first period by the Canadiens goalie, Gerry McNeil. "The accident occurred in the first period when Ted Kennedy of the Leafs fired a low shot from a scramble of players a few feet outside the goal crease," the Montreal *Gazette* reported. "McNeil dived to the ice to block the shot and caught the puck full on the cheekbone."[3]

The Canadiens coach, Dick Irvin, had to choose between allowing the hurt McNeil to finish the game or having the Leafs provide him with a replacement goalie. "The backup goalie in the building was the sub-goalie for the St. Michael's Junior B team," remembers Dick Irvin Jr., the coach's son. "The proposed substitute wasn't even the top goalie on the St. Mike's team, and that's the guy the Leafs were paying $10 an hour to sit in the stands for such an occasion. My dad refused to use him, and McNeil, who had his cheekbone broken and one of his eyes shut, gave up seven goals. The coaches of the time just couldn't face using the replacement goalie provided by the opposing team."[4]

Back in Montreal the day after the game, McNeil was taken to the hospital to be X-rayed. The results confirmed the team's worst fears: McNeil had a broken cheekbone coupled with a displacement. He would be sidelined for at least a month.

While all of this was going on, Jacques Plante was travelling with the Montreal Royals, who had played the night before in his hometown of Shawinigan Falls. He had just completed a brief visit with his parents when he received the phone call he had been waiting his whole life for. Plante was notified that the Canadiens had pressed him into emergency duty in McNeil's absence, on the "lend-lease" rule. Jacques had a signed contract with the Royals, not the Canadiens, but the lend-lease rule permitted NHL teams to take a three-game look at young players before making any professional contract offer. If the team wanted to use the player for a fourth game, he had to be signed to a professional contract. Jacques was still playing based on his amateur contract.

As soon as the announcement was made, Jacques was contacted by the press. Playing for the Royals had brought Plante a certain amount of recognition, but that was merely a prelude to the attention he would endure in the days to follow.

"I am more surprised than anybody," Plante told the press. "I had heard Gerry was injured, but wasn't aware it was that serious. I am naturally glad to aid Canadiens in any way I can during Gerry's absence, but it will be difficult to replace a goalkeeper of his caliber."[5]

On November 1, 1952, Jacques Plante would make his debut as the goalie for the Canadiens before a sellout crowd, the team's largest of the season, all clamouring for Rocket Richard to score that one elusive goal. However, over the two days before the game, the Rocket's chase for the record would be overshadowed by a toque.

With Plante's promotion freshly announced, newsmen asked Dick Irvin about his new goalie's habit of wearing a toque in goal. The Canadiens coach responded that the toque that Plante had worn in every game so far would have to be discarded on Saturday night. "In the first place that stuff is 'bush,'" declared Irvin, "and thinking about keeping it on tends to distract. Plante will be better without it; he will avoid a lot of stupid and unnecessary lampooning without it."[6]

Before embarking on a distinguished coaching career, Dick Irvin had been one of the greatest hockey players in the years before the founding of the National Hockey League in 1917. A veteran of the First World War, he was a tough, no-nonsense coach who shaped his teams in his own image. He believed the toque was a distraction, one that neither Plante nor the team needed. But Irvin found little support in the media for his old-school ways.

"This is the point at which your agent and the Canadiens coach Dick Irvin come to a parting of the ways," wrote Elmer Ferguson, the sports editor of the Montreal *Herald*, in his column the morning of the game. "We find our views do not coincide . . . Your agent, in rebuttal, takes the stand that Plante by conveying his toque into the big time would add a dash of colour, individuality and personality, qualities that are steadily declining in production line hockey now being purveyed in the major league in which personalities are so vibrant that they can force their way into attention."

Ferguson went on to voice a fear that many in the media shared. "We believe that the anti-toque ruling holds a hidden danger. Plante, accustomed to his toque, may become disturbed, lose his poise. It's a dangerous practice to suddenly route an athlete into a strange pathway, or break a standing habit. It gets on his high-strung nerves. If tonight Plante, with his head bared, should succumb to the Rangers, we shall certainly attribute this in part to his toque-less condition."[7]

French journalist Jean Séguin commented that "Plante without his tuque is like a hot-dog without mustard."[8] The press even went so far as to denounce Irvin for taking a slap at the yarn industry.

The media outcry was so intense that Irvin felt the need to expound on his original statement. "I don't want the kid to go out there wearing anything that would distinguish him from every other player on the ice. This would make him a target for a lot of ribbing. Perhaps some of his own teammates would rib him a little, and the boy would get some sort of a complex. They tell me that in a scramble around the nets, if his toque came off, Plante was inclined to grab for the toque first instead of the puck. In this league such an automatic reflex would be fatal. . . . The kid might be laughed right out of the nets. It will be tough enough for him out there without adding mental disruptions that are totally unnecessary."[9]

Ironically, Plante had been anticipating a battle with Irvin and the team's executives not over his toque but over his wanderings from the net. Before he played his first game with the Canadiens, he made the decision to tame his wanderings and stay closer to the net in an effort to avoid a confrontation.

At six o'clock on Saturday night, November 1, 1952, Jacques Plante entered the dressing room of the team he had always dreamed of playing for. Undoubtedly, he had played this moment out in his mind countless times before. He was no stranger to the players in the room; he had been their practice goalie for the past three years. But this was no practice, and he quietly sat down to inspect his goaltending gear. It didn't take him long to notice the absence of all three of his toques from his equipment. The time to be concerned about the toque had passed, however, as Plante sought to prove that his talent in goal far outshone his notorious headgear.

Sitting there with his head down, staring at the floor, Plante was racked with nervousness. He always had experienced butterflies before a game, but this was different. The extent of his jitters was so bad that he began having doubts even about his ability to lace up his skates.

The dressing room was heavy with anticipation as the team mentally prepared for the 60 minutes that awaited them out on the ice. The only sound in the silence was the constant thud of one of the player's skates as he paced across the floor, then stopped directly in front of the nervous Plante.

"I looked up and there was the Rocket," Plante vividly recalled later. "He held out his hands, saying: 'Look at them!' The Rocket's hands were shaking too. He told me it was always that way with him before a game, but the shakes left after the game started."[10]

If there was one person in that room who was facing more pressure than Plante, it was the Rocket, who was searching for the goal that would eclipse Nels Stewart's goals record. Outside the dressing room were 14,787 impatient fans waiting for the game to start, in addition to thousands at home watching the game on television through the magic of *Hockey Night in Canada*, then in its first season. Everyone fully expected the Rocket to break the record that night.

"I calmed down as I looked at my longtime idol," Plante admitted, "and told him that if he scored that night I'd give him my toque. We both laughed and I got back at lacing my skates – without jitters – nervous, yes, but no shakes."[11]

Out on the ice and looking down to the opposite end, Plante saw a familiar face guarding the Rangers net. Gump Worsley, who had opposed Plante in the Quebec Junior League and then in the Quebec Senior League, would once again provide the opposition on this historic night.

In the game's very first minute, Wally Hergesheimer of the Rangers provided Plante with his first shot. He would block 19 more that night, allowing only one, from the stick of Jim Conacher, to pass the goal line in a 4–1 Canadiens victory that left the home patrons with mixed feelings. While Plante had passed his first professional test convincingly, the Rocket was able to muster only an assist on the scorecard, leaving him and Nels Stewart still tied atop the record book.

"Jacques Plante appeared without his famed toque," wrote Dink Carroll in the Montreal *Gazette*. "It didn't seem to make any difference in his work and he didn't look nervous but he received good protection from the defense in front of him."[12]

In the dressing room after the game, the press swarmed the rookie goaltender. "They sure shoot a lot harder in this league," Plante told them. "It was the power of the shots I noticed most, just as soon as I stopped one. How do these guys get to shoot as hard after they leave the minor leagues?" From behind the media scrum a lone voice chirped in, "That's why they left the minor leagues."

Jacques joined in the laughter, and much to the newsmen's delight continued. "This may surprise you but I found it easier guarding the Canadiens nets than those of the Royals. I have never known how comforting it was to have such an experienced array of defensemen ahead of me as Émile 'Butch' Bouchard, Doug Harvey, Dollard St. Laurent, Tom Johnson and Jim MacPherson. I never even thought of wandering from the nets, one of them always seemed to be on top of any loose pucks or rebounds."[13]

The next night, November 2, Plante made his debut at the historic Madison Square Garden, stopping 27 Rangers shots and battling Worsley to a 2–2 standoff.

"Plante had been tested in the fire of big league competition and hasn't been found wanting," wrote Baz O'Meara, the sports editor for the *Montreal Star*. "He has steadied down in the fast company and is no longer the nomad of the nets who wanders far afield, as he so often did with the Royals."[14]

Four days after the tie with the Rangers, Plante played the third and final game of his lend-lease deal when the Canadiens played host to the Leafs. Much to the home fans' dismay, the Rocket once again was unable to score that elusive goal. It was the goalie sensation Jacques Plante who stole the spotlight yet again, and despite the Leafs out-shooting the Canadiens 28–24, it was Montreal that claimed a 3–1 victory.

In his three games with the big club, Plante had allowed only four goals and went undefeated, proving to all that he was ready to join the professional ranks. The only question that remained was when.

The Rocket finally scored his record-breaking goal against the Black Hawks in the Canadiens' next game in Chicago.

By then, Jacques Plante was back in the same spot he'd held for the previous three years: starting goaltender for the Montreal Royals and the practice goaltender for the Canadiens. He must have wondered if his three-game stint with the Canadiens had been only a dream.

However, one thing had changed. In Plante's first home game back in the senior league, the Royals drew a senior-league record crowd of 14,500 spectators to the Montreal Forum. Undoubtedly, many of them came to see hockey's latest sensation roam the Royals net.

JAKE THE SNAKE

CLOSE TO TWO MONTHS after playing his initial three games with the Canadiens, Jacques Plante stood in the office of Frank Selke, upstairs at the Forum. Resting on Selke's desk was a document, only a couple pages long, that would make Jacques Plante a professional hockey player. It was a contract with the Montreal Canadiens, dated December 29, 1952.

Ultimately, the Canadiens' decision to sign Plante was a forced one. Months earlier Jacques had begun his fourth season in the semi-professional Quebec Senior Hockey League. Then the Canadiens bought the league and made it professional, all in pursuit of the talented Jean Béliveau.

Béliveau, who in the past few years had emerged as the pre-eminent amateur hockey player of the day, had become a most elusive target for Frank Selke and the Canadiens. Like Jacques, Béliveau was one of those rare players who didn't sign a C-form with the Canadiens. Instead, he signed the same document that Plante had, the B-form, which gave Montreal only his professional rights.

After Béliveau was named to the league's first all-star team in both seasons as a junior in Quebec, the Canadiens were more than eager to sign him in the fall of 1951. The previous season, Béliveau, under the lend-lease rule, suited up with Montreal for two games. On January 24,

1952, he made his professional debut alongside Boom Boom Geoffrion, also starring in his first game. The Boomer potted his first career goal that night, and Béliveau matched him three nights later, before returning to the minors.

After leading the Quebec Citadels to the junior hockey Memorial Cup finals, and setting league records for goals and points, it was assumed that Béliveau would join the Canadiens that fall alongside Geoffrion and the Canadiens' other junior superstar, Dickie Moore. But much to the surprise of many, especially Selke, Béliveau declined to sign with the Canadiens and instead returned to Quebec City to play with the Aces of the Quebec Senior Hockey League, where he was paid the princely sum of $10,000 for the season, an amount that was comparable to the salary of the top players in the National Hockey League.

And while Geoffrion and Moore were getting their feet wet with the Canadiens, Béliveau proceeded to lead the senior league in both goals and assists, some of them at the expense of the star goalie for the Montreal Royals, Jacques Plante.

In the fall of 1952, Béliveau once again attended the training camp of the Canadiens, and just like the year before he spurned Montreal and returned to the Quebec Aces, this time for $20,000 a season – a sum that made him the highest-paid hockey player in the world.

That winter, a few weeks after Jacques Plante's spectacular three-game audition, Béliveau came up to the Canadiens for his own three-game trial. Put on a line with Bert Olmstead and Rocket Richard by Dick Irvin, Béliveau put to rest any whispers about his place among the game's best by scoring three goals (all assisted by the Rocket) in his first game. His performance during his three-game stint only increased the fans' eagerness to see him in a Canadiens jersey full time. In his three games, Béliveau totalled five goals and was named the NHL's player of the week. He then promptly returned to Quebec City.

Sitting in his office, Selke shared the feelings of his fans, and finally decided that he had to have Béliveau on the Canadiens team. Knowing that Montreal owned Béliveau's professional rights, Selke hit on an ingenious if not costly idea to get him into a Montreal jersey. He decided that the Canadiens would buy the Quebec Senior Hockey League and turn it professional. And so they did. And since Montreal owned Béliveau's professional rights, he now had no choice but to play for the Canadiens, which he began doing the next season.

As for Jacques Plante, playing without a professional contract, the rules stipulated that if he played 30 games that season with the Montreal

Royals, he would become available to the other five NHL teams. Selke, unwilling to let this happen, summoned Plante to his office after the Royals' twenty-ninth game. That was when Plante signed his first professional contract, with the yearly salary of $9,100.

Signing that contract ended Plante's days with the Royals, and with Gerry McNeil firmly entrenched with the Canadiens, the obvious question was, where was Plante going to play? Selke's plans had him taking a one-way trip to Buffalo.

The Buffalo Bisons operated in the American Hockey League, which was in the process of establishing itself as the predominant development circuit for the National Hockey League. For a young man like Plante, the prospect of playing in Buffalo must have been a daunting one, and not only in a hockey sense. Jacques, whose skill with the English language was still evolving, would be leaving behind the comfort of all that he had known. Not only that, but he would be crossing the border into the United States, a country that he was hardly familiar with, to play with a team of strangers in a town he barely knew about and had never even been to.

With his wife, Jacqueline, and year-old son, Michel, in tow, Jacques boarded a train for Buffalo a few days into 1953. Ken Reardon, a former Canadiens star and now the team's vice-president, accompanied Plante and his family to make sure the trip went smoothly.

This was all routine work for Reardon, until the train reached the border. It was then that he and the customs officials, opening Plante's luggage, found out that their prized passenger was not your ordinary hockey player. "Out came some paintings," a bemused Reardon remembered later, "and then two balls of wool with knitting needles, a toque – a knitted toque. I could see the customs guys looking at me thinking what kind of hockey player is this?"[1] Nevertheless, the perplexed customs officials let Plante into the United States.

At the time of Jacques' arrival, the Buffalo Bisons were at the bottom of the American Hockey League standings. The Bisons were only two years removed from a first-place finish; now the team was the league's doormat. Of greater concern to the team's ownership was the indifference of the public, which began to show at the box office: the average attendance was a bleak 1,000 at their games. Buffalo's management, newly associated as the Canadiens' primary farm team, spent day after day burning up the phone lines to Montreal, begging them to send one of their better prospects in the hope that they could generate some sorely needed excitement.

As fate would have it, Jacques' debut with the Bisons saw him taking the nets in Cleveland against the league-leading Barons, anchored by the extraordinary Johnny Bower in goal, the finest goalie in the league. It had been two long years since the Bisons had managed to win a game in Cleveland.

That night, before an unsuspecting group of Cleveland fans and players, Buffalo skated off with a surprising 2–1 win. Plante then back-stopped the resurgent Bisons to back-to-back wins over Pittsburgh and Syracuse, shutting both teams out. With Plante onboard, the Bisons embarked on a six-game unbeaten streak, a streak that was widely seen as being entirely the result of his stellar play. All of a sudden, fan apathy transformed into a furious demand for tickets. Attendance jumped to over 9,000 per game.

One of the local newsmen christened the city's newest sensation "Jake the Snake" after observing him strike in and out of the net when the play was in his own end.[2] Almost overnight, there was a sudden demand in Buffalo for all things Jacques Plante. He appeared on TV, on radio, and all over the papers. While not yet proficient in English, Plante was able to cleverly articulate his thoughts about the game, his play, and his position. Journalists descended on him, asking him for his secrets in stopping the AHL's best, many of whom he had never played against before, much less seen in action.

In a game made up of players who tended to answer questions by rote, Plante turned out to be a wonderful exception. He never tired of answering questions or explaining his craft, and his answers were always honest and never less than candid. It didn't take long for the legend of Jake the Snake to spread beyond the borders of Buffalo.

In the days before television channels that were dedicated to sports 24 hours a day, people received their information mainly from newspapers and magazines that detailed the exploits of their favourite performers. In the world of hockey, there was no greater authority than the *Hockey News*. Founded in 1947 and published weekly, the *Hockey News* devoted itself to covering the sport at all levels, and was considered essential reading for those inside and outside the sport. To be mentioned in the *Hockey News* conveyed that you had achieved a certain status within the game. To be the subject of a headline and full-page article meant that you were up there with hockey's most important figures.

The February 7, 1953, issue announced the arrival of Jacques Plante. Under the headline "'Jake the Snake' Plante Big Boon to Buffalo

Bisons," the *Hockey News* ran a full-page spread on the young phenom. "Not since George Ratterman of football fame stepped off the University of Notre Dame campus into the lineup of the defunct Buffalo Bills in 1947 has any athlete captured the imagination of Buffalo sports fans as Jacques (The Snake) Plante, the fast reflexed goaltender of the American League Bisons," wrote Jack Horrigan. "Superlatives often are misused in describing the play of athletes. Yet, Plante has been just that – superlative – in his first games in Buffalo livery."

Many in the press were soon comparing Jacques with Johnny Bower – until then the man who represented the standard for goaltending excellence in the AHL – thanks to Plante's two victories over him in their head-to-head confrontations. "This Johnny Bower is a great goaltender," a humbled Plante conceded in the *Hockey News* feature. "I cannot understand why he is not in the National League. He certainly is good enough."

The article also expressed the unsaid dread of the Buffalo fans that Plante was too good to be with the Bisons and would return to the Canadiens before long. "I got my biggest thrill in hockey in playing those three games with the Canadiens this year," Plante admitted. "I have looked forward to being a National League goaltender for a long time. That was it. Some day I hope the stay will be longer."[3]

As much as Jacques thrived in the public eye, his wife, Jacqueline, struggled in private. Lacking Jacques' increasing fluency in English, she struggled to do the most basic of tasks, like shopping for groceries. She missed her friends back home, and when Jacques left on a road trip the isolation was almost unbearable.

Despite Jacques' noteworthy play, the Bisons failed to make the playoffs. Come spring, Jacqueline was relieved when the family returned to Montreal at the conclusion of the season.

Jacques rejoined the Canadiens, who were preparing for the playoffs after finishing in second place. As he had the previous two springs, Jacques joined the team as one of the "Black Aces," a group of players kept on the sidelines as insurance in case of injury to one of the team's starters. There was nothing to indicate that this spring would be any different.

According to the rules of the day, each team was required to carry a backup goalie for the playoffs, whereas in the regular season the opposite was true. Traditionally, the backup goalie would practise and travel with the team, but he wouldn't dress for the game, and instead of being in the dressing room, he would sit in the press box.

In the 1951 and 1952 playoffs Jacques sat and watched as Gerry McNeil backstopped the Canadiens in the post-season. As Montreal began their semifinal series against the Chicago Black Hawks in the spring of 1953, it appeared that Jacques was going to have to tolerate another post-season on the sidelines.

"The Canadiens won the first two games of the best-of-seven series against the Black Hawks, and everything seemed to be moving easily along to a Montreal victory," Jacques remembered later. "But the Black Hawks won the third and fourth games, both at Chicago Stadium, and also won the fifth game in Montreal. A big upset was in the making as the Canadiens faced the sixth game in front of the Black Hawk fans in Chicago, trailing three victories to two."[4]

Facing a must-win situation, Canadiens head coach Dick Irvin took the highly unusual step of having his team participate in a shooting session on the morning of the game. Answering a ravenous press, Irvin told them that the oddly timed and awkwardly themed practice was an attempt to revitalize Montreal's dormant offence, which had scored only four goals in the last three losses. Irvin then went out of his way to publicly credit McNeil for the Canadiens' second-place finish that season, all the while disapproving of the team's sputtering offence.

It was a clever smokescreen. Irvin was in fact holding close to his vest a troubling secret: in the day between game five and that night's game six, a nervous McNeil had twice approached Irvin and told him to put the young Plante in the nets. Irvin initially refused the request. The thought of putting the untested Plante in the Montreal net, in front of a hostile crowd, for the biggest game of the year did not appeal to him. Ultimately, his choice boiled down to a goalie who asked to be replaced or a goalie who had played the grand total of three professional games. Thus, the shooting session was designed not to wake up the Canadiens offence but instead to allow a troubled Irvin to make up his mind about that evening's goaltender.

"In the practice McNeil was fanning while Plante was hot as a firecracker," wrote newsman Andy O'Brien, who admitted that all the reporters, still in the dark over McNeil's request, "took little notice, as McNeil was obviously taking it easy for that night's game."[5]

But away from the prying eyes of the reporters, as the team made its way towards the visitors dressing room in the bowels of the Chicago Stadium, McNeil once again approached his coach and again asked to be replaced. "I was trying out there," McNeil told Irvin, "but my nerves are taking over."[6]

Much like the reporters and his teammates, Plante was oblivious to what was going on around him. "I had a sound snooze that afternoon in my room at the Lasalle Hotel," he later wrote, "and why not? What was there for a confirmed standby goaler to get uptight about? Seats were going at scalpers' premium prices and I have one of the best in the house. . . . Then, as I came down into the lobby enroute to the rink, I ran into Irvin. He said to me in matter-of-fact tones: 'You're in goal tonight, Jacques, and you are going to get us a shutout.'"[7]

Jacques Plante, a man never at a loss for words, stood in the lobby speechless. Two members of the Canadiens, Dollard St. Laurent and Johnny McCormack, came over and asked him what was wrong. A stunned Plante told them as they made their way to the waiting taxi that would take them to the stadium. Both men, equally taken aback by what they heard, took some time to digest the news.

"Both Dollard and 'Goose' kept repeating it was only another game and not to get worked up," Plante reflected, "but that only made it worse. I knew it was a boyhood dream and a nightmare all at once."[8]

It had been only three years since the legendary Bill Durnan had broken down and asked Gerry McNeil to replace him in the Canadiens nets as the team was facing elimination. Now, amazingly, the same scene was repeating itself. Irvin admitted months later that Plante "was very raw for this spot, yet I had a hunch he'd make it, and one thing I have learned in twenty-four years behind the NHL benches is to never let a hunch go cold."[9]

Jacques, trying to maintain an outward expression of calm, entered the dressing room and made a beeline towards his equipment. As soon as he sat down he was greeted by Gerry McNeil, who wished him luck. "All I could think of," Plante recalled later, "was how often I had kidded Gerry by warning him not to get sick or I'd have his job."[10] Even Frank Selke made an appearance in the dressing room to reassure the nervous Plante.

Outside the sanctuary of the Canadiens dressing room the atmosphere was tense. Having endured a seven-year absence from the playoffs, the fans in Chicago could feel the upset and were ready to vent their frustration on the Canadiens. They would be loud and they would be boisterous, all in an effort to disrupt the opposing Canadiens and spur their Black Hawks to their first Stanley Cup final in a decade.

"Playoff madness hit Chicago with the force of an A-bomb as the resurgent Black Hawks qualified for their first NHL cup series in seven years," wrote Bud Booth in the *Hockey News*. "The hockey fans in the

Windy City have long been known and somewhat notoriously, for their rabid ferocity, but their reaction to the postseason series with the Hawks in the running made previous outbursts look serene by comparison."[11]

It was a solemn but determined Dick Irvin who entered the Montreal dressing room and stunned his team even more by announcing that in addition to Plante replacing McNeil there would be three other changes. Bud MacPherson, Paul Masnick, and Dick Gamble were relegated to spectator status in favour of Eddie Mazur, a winger from Victoria, and two of Jacques' teammates from Buffalo, Calum MacKay and Lorne Davis.

Earlier, Irvin had made his intentions known to Selke, who was more than a little apprehensive and gently counselled, "You realize, Dick, just how far you are sticking your neck out with such a gamble?"

"Sure I do," answered Irvin, "but is there any sound reason why I should stand pat after losing three in a row? If I take a chance and lose I'm going to be second-guessed to death, but what of it? It's now or never – a loss tonight and our long summer begins."[12]

Selke accepted his coach's decision. But beneath his confident exterior, Irvin was anxious. He placed an afternoon phone call back to Montreal to talk to his son. "I'm putting my job on the line tonight. I'll be fired if we lose."[3]

Irvin went on to deliver his pre-game speech in a fiery tone, reflecting the do-or-die game that awaited the Canadiens. His team hung on his every utterance. Irvin slowly reached inside his pocket and began pulling out some money. Scanning the eyes of his players, he offered to bet anyone in the room a dollar each that Plante would come up with a shutout.

After an awkward pause, Boom Boom yelled out, "Here's a chance for you to make some money, Jacques!" The room erupted into laughter.

"I didn't take up Geoffrion's suggestion," Plante said later, "but it made me feel better – enough better to get dressed myself."[14]

"The Chicago Stadium, never regarded as a becalming spa for jittery goaltenders, was in full-throated form," reported Andy O'Brien. "Plante found himself between the goal posts under a shower of eggs and tomatoes. One overripe egg splattered on his arm. A cleaner sweeping in front of him was hit squarely on the head by a tomato."[15] Plante was far from the only target of the fans' wrath. A few games earlier, Montreal defenceman Tom Johnson tangled in the boards with a couple of Chicago players. Just as the scrum was breaking up, a fan had casually tossed a lit cigarette down the neck of the unsuspecting Johnson.

Perched behind Jacques in the top corner of the arena was a lone man sitting in a cramped booth clutching a microphone inside his clenched fist. Then in the first year of what would become a 32-year career as the English voice of the Canadiens, Danny Gallivan vividly recalled the scene over 40 years later. "I couldn't see past centre ice because of the smoke," he said. As the sellout crowd lit their cigars and cigarettes, the smoke became even denser. "The only reason I would know there was a goal was the red light coming through the smoke."[16]

Jacques Plante was going to have to endure his pressure-filled playoff baptism in the most hostile of environments, through an overpowering shade of smoke, under the menace of not only constant verbal abuse but also under a steady stream of materials being hurled at him.

Finally, the puck dropped and the game began.

The players swarmed the Chicago end of the rink as Black Hawks goaltender Al Rollins faced the Montreal barrage head on. Unable to score, the Canadiens continued to press, and didn't notice as the Black Hawks' leading scorer, Jimmy McFadden, snuck behind their last line of defence and took in a pass on his way to a clear-cut breakaway. Four and a half minutes into this most crucial of games, Jacques Plante was about to endure his first test.

As McFadden skated past their bench with not a defender in sight, the Canadiens bench rose as one in anticipation. There are moments in each game when his teammates become background players, when ultimately the game rests on the lone shoulders of the man guarding the net. This is the loneliness of the goaltender, who in the game's most critical moments carries the weight of the team's expectations.

The onrushing McFadden cradled the puck until only 15 feet separated him and the rookie goaltender. McFadden wound back and forcefully aimed for the right-hand corner of the net.

"I just happened to pick the right corner to cover and was on my way there when the puck left McFadden's stick," Plante recalled. "It was a guess at that distance, but a right guess, and I stopped it. Only after he turned away did I realize I had stopped McFadden."[17]

As soon as it became apparent that Plante had turned back McFadden's challenge, the Canadiens bench began banging their sticks against the boards, saluting their goalie.

Ninety seconds later, two of Plante's former adversaries in the Quebec amateur ranks teamed up when Dickie Moore set up Geoffrion for the game's first tally. The Rocket added a second goal in the middle period, as did Ken Mosdell to conclude the scoring.

At the same time, the Black Hawks were unable to puncture the wall erected by the rookie Plante as their 24 shots were brushed aside. Before a depressed crowd the Canadiens skated off with a 3–0 win.

"Getting a shutout in a pressure game like that, where I hadn't even been told until just before game time that I even was getting the start, had to be a tremendous moment in my life," Plante later recalled. "But over all the years and all the awards and championship teams, I still think back to that April night in 1953 with a bit of a shudder – and a satisfied smile."[18]

"Plante saved the game with the first save," Irvin boasted to any reporter within earshot. Irvin's opposite number, Sid Abel of the Black Hawks, also admitted that Plante had made the difference. "We don't know yet how good that young goalie of the Canadiens is. We had only three good shots on him all night. We'll have another crack at him in Montreal."[19]

Remembered by Danny Gallivan as "the greatest shakeup in the history of the Stanley Cup," Irvin's great gamble had paid off in spades.

After the sixth game, the concluding game in Montreal was decidedly anticlimactic. Yet Plante, his confidence growing by the minute, stirred an already anxious crowd by reverting to his roaming ways. According to the Montreal *Gazette*, Plante "had the crowd in an apoplectic state several times with his tendency to stray out of the nets."[20]

In the eyes of McNeil, a goalie who played the game as tradition dictated, Plante's wandering was a thing to behold, as was the fact that the team's management looked the other way. "He would go after everything. He defied the principles. If I went out of the net, they [Canadiens management] got after me. With him, it was okay."[21]

The tired Black Hawks were able to solve the Plante riddle only once, and behind Jacques' 33 saves, the Canadiens won the last game of the series 4–1.

Jacques Plante could bask only briefly in the glow of his first playoff series win. Two nights later he was the starting goaltender when the Canadiens opened the Stanley Cup finals against the Boston Bruins.

The first game of the finals was a sluggish affair in which the Canadiens' young goalie was rarely tested. In a rather timid and listless game, Plante had to make only 21 saves, in a 4–2 Canadiens win.

Jacques Plante had now played three playoff games. He had won all three and had allowed only three shots to get past him. His sense of belonging was growing with each game. Where there had been doubt in Chicago, now there was belief in Montreal. However, in the next game, the bubble burst.

In front of a surprised Montreal Forum crowd, the Bruins evened the series with a 4–1 win in what was described as a letdown by the Canadiens. Boston was able to withstand 33 shots. Facing only 19 shots, Plante allowed four to cross the goal line, and for the first time looked like he was in over his head.

Many in the media suggested out loud – and some in management whispered privately – that the young goalie appeared to be a little fatigued, and with McNeil shaking off his nerves and pronouncing himself ready to play again, Coach Irvin made the change in the Canadiens nets.

Plante watched from the sidelines as McNeil allowed only three goals over the next three games, backstopping Montreal to the Stanley Cup championship. For the first time, Plante sipped from hockey's holy grail. But as he drank from the championship mug, the taste was bittersweet.

Without Plante the Canadiens would never have won the Stanley Cup, and even though he posed for the team picture the day after, he still felt somewhat detached from the team. However, his disappointment didn't dampen his confidence in himself or in his future. "I was totally and immodestly convinced," he wrote later, "that I was the best damn goalkeeper in the whole, wide world of hockey."[22]

7

A SENSATION

JACQUES PLANTE ATTENDED his fifth Montreal Canadiens training camp in 1953 with minimal expectations. He knew that the job as the team's starting goalie was securely in the hands of Gerry McNeil. After all, during those days of the original six, teams were loath to replace their goaltender, especially when he had won the Stanley Cup the previous spring.

Any talk of a goaltending controversy was buried beneath the biggest story emanating from the Montreal training camp that fall. Finally, after years of pleading from the Canadiens organization, Jean Béliveau had signed a professional contract and joined the Habs for good, fulfilling a dream for the team's front office as well as its impatient supporters.

However, despite the hopes and expectations of their most fervent fans, the Canadiens suffered an outbreak of injuries in the 1953–54 season. Béliveau's rookie season was shortened by 26 games thanks to a broken bone in his ankle, immediately followed by a broken cheekbone. Dickie Moore, another of the team's brightest prospects, played only 13 games that year because of a knee injury. Even Elmer Lach, in the final season of a Hall of Fame career, was forced to sit out 22 games with a broken ankle.

As the Canadiens battled on despite injuries, Plante made his triumphant return to Buffalo, where he was treated like a conquering hero.

His achievements in the Stanley Cup finals had brought him more notoriety and fame in the city. The year before, Bisons player and coach Frank Eddolls had referred to Plante as "the greatest goalie outside the National Hockey League." Now he admitted that after his performance in the playoffs, the word "outside" should have been omitted.[1]

Hailed by an awestruck media as "King Cobra" and "the greatest thing since penicillin," Jacques joined a Bisons team completely made over from the previous season. In addition to Plante and defenceman Pierre Pilote, referred to by Eddolls as "our blue chip kids," the team was made up of an entirely new roster of players. If the year before Selke had answered the Bisons' wishes by sending them Plante, he repeated the gift in the fall of 1953 by loaning the team a young forward prospect named Donnie Marshall. Marshall would go on to be named the circuit's rookie of the year, finishing sixth in goals, third in assists, and third in league points with 96.

Proving that the previous spring was no fluke, Plante continued to set the pace in the American Hockey League through the winter, and crowds filled the Memorial Auditorium to see him. And as always, Plante spoke his mind to an always eager press.

Nowhere was this more evident than in the controversy about the starting goaltender's position in the league's annual all-star game. Emile "The Cat" Francis, the new goaltender for the Cleveland Barons, was chosen by Pat Egan, the player-coach of the Providence Reds, for the starter's role. The night of the announcement, Egan's Reds found themselves facing off against Plante's Bisons. Before the game, Plante proclaimed to the media, "I intend to show that fellow [Egan] who is the best goalie."[2]

Three hours later, after a decisive 35-save performance where only a screened shot separated him from a shutout in the 3–1 Bisons win, a cocky Plante took the time to take another dig at Egan. "That fellow must have flunked in figures at school. How can he ignore the fact that I lead the American Hockey League with a 2.69 goals-against average while The Cat is third with 2.98?"[3]

Months later, on a Sunday afternoon in February, Jacques and the "Bisons Express" again matched up with Cleveland and their all-star goalie, Emile "The Cat" Francis, in front of the largest crowd to watch hockey in Buffalo in three years.

"Not since the days when Howie Morenz and, later, Maurice (The Rocket) Richard first skated out on the ice of the old Montreal Forum has any hockey player immediately gripped the imagination of the customers like this lean young French-Canadian goalie, Jacques Plante," proclaimed Buffalo's *Courier Express*.[4]

In front of 9,332 supporters, the first-place Bisons, led by their wandering goalie, stretched his scoreless play to 198 minutes, 34 seconds. Plante finally allowed a goal before emerging with a hard-fought 2–1 victory that was Buffalo's fifth consecutive victory.

Jacques Plante was the league's leading goaltender, playing on the first-place team. He had just played his fifty-fifth game of the season – and his last as a Buffalo Bison.

In a game against the Chicago Black Hawks on February 11, 1954, Gerry McNeil was crushed into the goalpost by a tumbling Pete Conacher. McNeil, enduring the intense pain of a badly sprained ankle, amazingly finished the game. He travelled with the Canadiens to their next game, in Toronto, and even though X-rays revealed that his ankle was not fractured, his rapidly ballooning foot simply could not fit into a skate. An emergency phone call was placed to Palm Beach, Florida, where Frank Selke was attending an NHL governors meeting.

Selke didn't hesitate: "Bring up Plante."

Clustered with his teammates at the Buffalo train station on the morning of February 13, Plante was as surprised as anybody when he saw the headline in that morning's newspaper: "Bisons Surprised by Plante Recall for Two Games."

As his teammates boarded the train to Cleveland, Plante wished them luck and made arrangements to meet up with the Canadiens in Toronto.

Most people assumed it would be a temporary replacement, but there was no turning back for Jacques Plante. The extent of McNeil's ankle injury was underestimated, and two missed games quickly became three, then four, and by that point there was no need to rush a limping McNeil back into the net for the Canadiens' final 17 games of the season, or for the playoffs for that matter.

"Sensational is the word for Jacques Plante," proclaimed the *Hockey News*. "It's been a long time since a netminder has made headlines so convincingly and there are some hockey observers who believe sincerely that had Plante been with the Habs all season they would have finished ahead of Detroit and he would have won the Vezina trophy."[5]

"The fact is," Dick Irvin told Montreal newsman Elmer Ferguson, "Plante has revolutionized the art of goaling. He just slips around behind the net, blocks off a puck destined to make a complete circuit of the end, thus nipping a play in the bud. That play is the only new thing that has been introduced to goaltending in years."[6]

And while the hockey world buzzed and the fans in Montreal marvelled, down in Buffalo, a city that had once thought a championship was within their grasp, they now realized that without the sparkling Plante, the Calder Cup had once again become a pipe dream. In Plante's absence, the Bisons persevered and managed to claim first place, but their season was ended abruptly by their hated rivals from Cleveland in the opening round of the playoffs.

Amid all the success with the Canadiens, Plante felt a tinge of regret. "I like Buffalo and the players, and I wanted to be on the championship club after last year's poor team . . . but I always wanted to play in the National League with Montreal, and now I am."[7]

With McNeil watching from the sidelines, Plante allowed only 27 goals over the Canadiens' final 17 games.

As good as Plante had been in those final games of the season, the Canadiens were planning on returning him to Buffalo at the onset of the playoffs. But then, in a St. Patrick's Day practice, a puck struck McNeil on the forehead. He retired to the dressing room, where he was stitched up before returning to the ice.

Finally, a conflicted Dick Irvin was forced to choose between his two goaltenders. Because of his stellar play in the season's later games, he chose Plante.

The Canadiens drew Boston as their opponent in the semifinals. The year before, it was the Bruins who had knocked a nervous Plante out of the nets, after game two of the finals. This time, however, a confident, experienced Plante wouldn't need to be replaced by Gerry McNeil, as Montreal easily dispatched the overmatched Bruins in the minimum four games. Plante had been the talk of the one-sided series, shutting out Boston twice and allowing only four goals.

Having now extended his playoff résumé to eight games, Plante could proudly boast of pitching three shutouts, in addition to the five he had in Montreal's last 17 regular-season games. By way of comparison, Gerry McNeil had played in 32 playoff games and had secured four shutouts, only one more than the man the press now dubbed "the Canadiens Mister Zero."

"There is no doubt that the slim, acrobatic Plante is a pressure goaltender," declared an impressed *Hockey News*, "a man who rises to his greatest heights when the going is toughest and the outcome of a game might hinge on the handling of just one accurately fired shot."[8]

"Pressure," observed an increasingly secure Plante, "I'm getting used to it. You know I didn't really expect to be recalled by the Canadiens from Buffalo. The Bisons were in first place, we were sailing along and there wasn't much pressure on me. Canadiens were battling with the Leafs for second place. Every game was a big one. We clinched our spot only on the last day of the season and then we plunged right into the playoffs with the Bruins. Now we're in the finals. More pressure. I'll be glad when the playoffs are over."[9]

"Plante has two qualities that are the hallmarks of greatness," wrote journalist Vince Lunny. "He always keeps his eyes on the puck, never wavering. And he has lightning reflexes. If a man follows the puck at all times and can move fast enough to block the shots, he's going to be hard to elude."[10]

If Plante was the defensive story of the playoffs, three of his former adversaries in the Quebec junior ranks had fulfilled the long-held hopes of Canadiens supporters and offensively crushed the overmatched Bruins. Jean Béliveau, Bernie Geoffrion, and Dickie Moore, the "Class of '31," formed a devastating triumvirate and scored a collective 26 points in the four-game sweep of the Bruins.

"I often said when the three of them were juniors that some day they'd make a great line," beamed Frank Selke. "You know I used the idea of this line as bait to lure Béliveau from Quebec two years ago. But it didn't work."[11]

That year's Canadiens appeared to be superior to last season's champions. After years of planning and preparation, Selke's farm system was starting to reveal its bounty. All that stood in their way was the Detroit Red Wings, hockey's most successful team and the Canadiens' nemesis.

"The Canadiens were our biggest rival," remembers defenceman Marcel Pronovost, once Jacques' childhood friend and teammate and now one of the Red Wings' stars. "The intensity was unbelievable. You'd walk into the Forum or the Olympia those nights and there was electricity in the air."[12]

In those days, in an effort to cut down on costs both teams would travel on the same train between a home and home series of games. In a competition that was as heated as the Red Wings and Canadiens' one, this caused some awkward confrontations. "Detroit was our big rival, there's no doubt about that," recalled Rocket Richard years later. "I remember I used to meet their players in the aisleway of the train. We'd pass by each other and I wouldn't say hello to anybody."[13]

"God, you could hardly look at one another," said Gerry McNeil. "I've seen the police at the station. And on the train, the conductor would tell you what time you could go to the club car so both teams wouldn't be there together."[14]

"I guess any of us who played then remember the train trips when both teams would travel from Montreal to Detroit," said Red Wings legend Ted Lindsay. "Even on the train the rivalry was there. No fights, but there were times it wasn't too far away from that. . . . I say there was never hockey like that before, and there hasn't been since. There'll never be hockey like that again."[15]

In 1954 the Red Wings seemed to be just a little better than the Canadiens. Detroit had finished the season at the top of the standings for the sixth consecutive year – a record in professional sports – with Montreal in second. Gordie Howe, their best player, captured the scoring title for the fourth year in a row, beating out perennial runner-up Rocket Richard. Leonard "Red" Kelly, their star defenceman, edged out Montreal's Doug Harvey for the inaugural Norris Trophy. And they had the imposing Terry Sawchuk manning their goal. They had easily dispatched the third-place Leafs in five games in their semifinal series.

It had been only a few years earlier that a young, eager Plante sat in an empty Montreal Forum studying every move that the great Sawchuk made. Now, having absorbed those lessons, Plante prepared to square off against one of his mentors.

Going into the Stanley Cup finals, Plante had reason to be confident. Since his call up from Buffalo, he had faced off with Sawchuk five times, winning three, losing one, and tying one. In addition, he had surrendered only eight goals to the Red Wings in those five games.

However, as any player can tell you, the playoffs are a different season altogether, and that spring, Sawchuk, still smarting after last season's playoff upset loss to the Bruins that he was widely blamed for, was a determined man.

And then on the eve of the final, it became doubtful whether Jacques Plante would play at all. The next morning the headline in the Montreal *Gazette* screamed, "Plante Uncertain Starter in Cup Series Opener at Detroit." Apparently Plante, "the Canadiens spark-plug goalie," had missed the last practice because of indigestion or stomach flu.[16] There was much speculation as to who would be in net, but when the puck dropped that night, a tired though steady Plante was guarding the Canadiens goal.

In the opening game of the Stanley Cup final, the offensively rampaging Canadiens were stopped cold in their tracks by a textbook display of defensive hockey by the home team. It took the Canadiens almost 10 minutes just to get a shot on Sawchuk. Despite their weak offensive, Montreal entered the third period tied, but two quick goals by the Red Wings sealed the opening game.

As the second game began in Detroit, the biggest concern for the Canadiens was the Rocket's scoring drought, which had continued over from the semifinals. At first, this game provided no relief, with the exception of a 56-second span in the first period. With the game scoreless and having just passed the 14-minute mark, referee Red Storey thumbed Gordie Howe for a high-sticking penalty. A few minutes later Tony Leswick joined Howe in the box, having received a two-minute penalty for slashing. With a two-man advantage, the Canadiens put the game away.

Dickie Moore had a shot bank off Bernie Geoffrion into the back of the net at 15:03 to make the score 1–0. Unlike the rules today, back then when a player received a penalty he had to serve the entire two minutes regardless whether the other team scored. So with Howe still in the sin bin, the Rocket now sprung into action, taking a pass from Moore and ripping a slapper past a stunned Sawchuk to put Montreal ahead 2–0. Under constant pressure, Sawchuk robbed Richard of a second goal as Howe leaped out of the box and back into the play. Howe's mad rush was for naught, as the freshly unburdened Rocket took another pass from Moore and backhanded the puck into the top corner of the net.

Three goals by the Canadiens in 56 seconds and a final score of 3–1 in favour of Montreal, who now returned home with the series tied at one apiece. The fact that in the first two games both teams had yet to score an even-strength goal proved the importance of the power play.

The home team had the benefit of momentum as the third game began in Montreal, but they were at a disadvantage with Béliveau and legendary defenceman Doug Harvey sidelined with knee injuries. And just as Detroit appeared ready to wilt, their goaltender took control of the series.

In the first period, the Canadiens bombarded Sawchuk, who stood tall. At the other end of the rink, Plante seemed to fight the puck all evening. Even though Montreal had the better of the play in the first period, they saw themselves down on the scoreboard 2–0. By the time the Canadiens broke through against Sawchuk in the third, the game was 3–1. But Detroit quickly snuffed out any hope the Montreal fans had with two quick goals and eventually prevailed 5–2. "In the other net Jacques Plante was mediocre, possibly because of Harvey's absence," reported the *Gazette*.[17]

Béliveau and Harvey returned for the pivotal fourth game, and Plante performed much better, but he was second best to the perfect Sawchuk. The scoreless game was broken in the second period at the 2:09 mark when Johnny Wilson put one past Plante, who, according to the *Gazette*, looked weak on the goal. Unfortunately, the Canadiens were unable to beat Sawchuk, and Red Kelly iced the game with an empty-net goal with seven seconds left on the clock.

Wilson's goal had been Plante's only miscue of the night. But now, in the finals, against the great Sawchuk, it was one mistake too many. This is the dilemma of being in goal at the highest level. Even though the Canadiens had failed to score, a good portion of the blame for the loss was being placed at the foot of their goaltender.

The Red Wings left Montreal with a commanding 3–1 series lead, and the praise for Sawchuk was unanimous. "Terry the Pirate more than earned his shutout," reported the Montreal *Gazette*. "Sawchuk was credited with only 28 saves but some of the stops he handled were incredible."[18]

Despite controlling the play, the Canadiens found themselves in the unenviable position of having to win three consecutive games to retain the Stanley Cup. Plante had been excellent in the fourth game, but against Sawchuk it hadn't been enough. Irvin, desperate and facing elimination, decided to gamble – much as he successfully had the season before – and reinserted Gerry McNeil in the Montreal nets.

In the fifth game, held at a raucous Detroit Olympia, before a crowd waiting to celebrate a Stanley Cup championship, Sawchuk was once again perfect as the Canadiens' scoreless streak extended past the 130-minute mark. Much to everyone's surprise, McNeil, playing his first game in two months, matched him save for save throughout the entire game.

As the game entered overtime, the Canadiens found themselves a goal away from elimination. Then, close to the six-minute mark, the previously impregnable Sawchuk finally broke on what had appeared to be an innocent backhand from the stick of Kenny Mosdell. The Canadiens had survived to play another day.

Two nights later in Montreal it appeared that another standoff had begun between Sawchuk and McNeil after a scoreless opening period.

At the 12-minute mark of the middle period, however, Boom Boom Geoffrion unleashed a 25-foot slapshot that not only beat Sawchuk but appeared to unnerve him as well. A mere minute later, Floyd Curry doubled the Canadiens' lead, and a little over a minute after that he made the score 3–0. This three-goal outburst helped Montreal take the sixth game 4–1, setting up the winner-take-all seventh game in Detroit on April 16.

Having won both games five and six, McNeil seemed like the obvious starter in the concluding game of the series. "However," wrote the *Toronto Star* on the eve of the seventh game, "Irvin is toying with the idea of restoring Plante to the lineup for the tell-tale game. The Montreal coach can give several reasons. One is that Plante has had six days of rest. Also, McNeil hasn't been tested to any great degree. His defensemen have allowed few shots to reach his net."[19]

It is not clear whether Irvin was indeed serious about starting Plante or if he planted the story to confuse the Red Wings. Regardless, when the seventh game began, Gerry McNeil patrolled the Montreal nets and Jacques Plante watched the game as a spectator.

Once again, McNeil and Sawchuk faced off in one of the most memorable games in Stanley Cup history. The suddenly hot Curry led off the scoring in the first period, on a 40-foot shot that screened Sawchuk, before the Red Wings tied the game in the second period on a Red Kelly power-play tally. The third period went goalless, leaving the two teams to settle the Stanley Cup in overtime. It was the second and last time that the Stanley Cup would be decided in an overtime period in a game seven.

The end came abruptly at 4:29 of the overtime. Doug Harvey, still hounded by a bothersome knee, grabbed the puck behind the Montreal net and slapped it around the boards towards the Canadiens blue line. But the puck bounced onto the stick of Detroit's Tony Leswick, who was making his way to the Red Wings bench. Coming to the end of his shift and from about 30 feet away, he flipped the puck towards the Montreal net.

Harvey casually reached for the floating puck in an attempt to knock it out of the air, but instead the puck deflected off his thumb and over McNeil's shoulder before coming to a rest in the back of the net.

The crowd sat in stunned silence for a couple of seconds, trying to comprehend what they had just seen. Then the rink exploded and the ice was littered first with debris and next with delirious fans.

The Canadiens had just lost the Stanley Cup.

"Boy, it was a long skate back to the other end of the rink because our dressing room was there," recalled Gerry McNeil years later. "There's no way you can express how you feel at a time like that when you're a goalie. It's like the end of the world. I'll always remember that long skate to the other end."[20]

In the aftermath, the newsmen burst into the defeated Canadiens' dressing room. At the sight of the players staring listlessly, undoubtedly still in shock, or crying openly, the writers held off their questions and let a moment of silence permeate the entire room. Writing for *La Presse*, Pierre Proulx described it as "a silence like one has never witnessed in the Canadiens dressing room, even after the most bitter defeats."[21]

Years later, Irvin's son Dick recalled a story Canadiens announcer Danny Gallivan liked to tell about the train trip back home to Montreal after that loss. "Danny and some newspapermen gravitated to the coach's compartment as the train left Detroit. The mood was gloomy and nobody was saying very much. The coach [Dick Irvin Sr.] pulled a calendar out of his pocket, studied it for a few minutes, did some figuring on a piece of paper, then said, 'Gentlemen, I want you all to note that training camp starts in one hundred and fifty days.'"[22]

THE ROCKET

EVERY YEAR, JACQUES PLANTE attended training camp with the Montreal Canadiens knowing that the position of Canadiens goalie was securely in the hands of Gerry McNeil. No matter how well Plante performed in the camp, he knew he was never going to dislodge the incumbent. But when he arrived at his sixth training camp, in the fall of 1954, that was no longer the case. Plante had been establishing himself over a long period as a more than capable NHL goalie, and since the spring there had been numerous discussions within Montreal management about the Canadiens' goaltending situation. As training camp rolled on, the decision remained unresolved, resulting in an open competition.

The two goalies possessed radically different personalities and approaches to the position. "Gerry McNeil was a heck of a competitor, a great guy who was more with the players than Jacques was," Dickie Moore says today. "He was a part of a team. Jacques was more of an individual."[1]

"McNeil was brooding and self-critical," wrote Douglas Hunter in his study of goaltenders, *A Breed Apart*, "and would take the game home with him. Plante could be self-confident to the point of arrogance."[2]

"He was a guy who was always right," McNeil recalled of Plante. "A goal was never his fault – it was the defenseman's fault. It was a great way to go to sleep. I was the opposite. I would figure if I did it this way or that way, I could have stopped it."[3]

The decision proved too difficult for Dick Irvin, who announced in anticipation of a Saturday night exhibition game against Plante's old team, the Buffalo Bisons, that he would play both McNeil and Plante – and alternate them every five minutes. It never came to that, though. Two days before the game, after the morning practice at the Verdun Auditorium, McNeil decided to walk away for good. "Gerry came to see me," said Canadiens general manager Frank Selke at the time. "He told me that he couldn't sleep nights and that he thought he should give up hockey. I advised him to take a few days off from training and to think things over after a few days rest."[4] Five days later, McNeil stepped into Selke's office and confirmed his earlier decision.

After an exhibition game held the day after McNeil's exit, Selke summoned an unaware Plante to his office. Closing the door behind him, Plante sat down, and Selke uttered the words he had longed to hear: "Jacques, the job is yours." Coincidentally, Plante had achieved his life's goal the same way McNeil had inherited the position four and a half years previously, with the abdication of his predecessor because of mental distress.

"I just figured that I had enough and decided to stay home with the family," McNeil told the Montreal *Gazette* on September 27, 1954. "Hockey had to come to an end for me sometime and I thought that I might as well get out while I had my health. You know sometimes it's a lot tougher than people think it is."[5] He told the *Hockey News*, "I have a nervous temperament, and I want to do something that involves less worry."[6]

"Gerry had trouble with his weight from the start," Plante wrote later. "That, plus his record in the practice games – he gave up 72 goals to my 35 – prompted his decision. He failed to report one day for practice. He was still missing the next day and a rumour spread that he had quit but nobody was certain."[7]

A few days later McNeil entered the Canadiens dressing room one last time. He was much loved by his teammates, and his sudden retirement was traumatic for many of them. McNeil slowly made his way over to a nervous and uneasy Plante. Sensing the awkwardness of the situation, McNeil grasped Jacques' hand and told him, "I knew it had to come, Jacques. You've earned the job." Intent on beginning a new life away from hockey, McNeil had already accepted an offer to operate a service station in Montreal. He never regretted his decision to leave the Canadiens that fall.

The road had been long, but Jacques, at the age of 25, had finally reached his dreamed-of destination: he was now the number one goaltender for the Montreal Canadiens. "I stopped being a rookie right then," Plante wrote later. "Suddenly I felt mature, even a bit old, at realizing that some day it would happen to me, too."[8]

His teammates all accepted Plante's elevation as the Canadiens' undisputed starting goaltender. "Plante had all the best of it during two weeks of inter-squad games," reported the *Toronto Star*. "He had three shutouts and after a string of three games in which Plante had blanked him, Maurice 'Rocket' Richard sadly remarked: 'That guy can't be that good. He must have horseshoes in his gloves.'"[9]

Beyond the Canadiens dressing room, however, there were doubts about Plante's ability and worries that his promotion to the top spot would further the Canadiens' hopes of dethroning the champion Red Wings.

The spotlight that now enveloped Jacques Plante would have unsettled most goaltenders. Instead, Plante led the Canadiens to the top of the standings and gave up the fewest goals in the league along the way.

On November 1, 1954, the Canadian Press reported, "Montrealers are in front of the six-team league race today and Plante is high up in the individual netminding computation. The 25-year-old successor to Gerry McNeil has allowed only 19 goals in 11 games so far in the 1954–55 campaign. That's a sign of Plante's talent and the protection given by the Montreal defence corps. The Montreal snipers on the other hand have scored 36 on the opposition."[10]

And then suddenly, during what seemed like an ordinary shooting drill, Plante endured a painful reminder of the precariousness of his position. Practising on the morning of November 11 in preparation for a game that night against the Black Hawks, he was struck directly under the eye by a puck fired off the stick of teammate Bert Olmstead. Plante was rushed to the hospital with a shattered left cheekbone and was replaced that night by André Binette, a Shawinigan Cataractes goaltender who would help the Habs win 7–4. It would be Binette's only NHL game.

Plante spent the next six days anchored to a hospital bed, while Claude Evans starred in his only four games with the Canadiens, winning two and losing two. Plante's injury was so severe that he spent the rest of November and early December convalescing at home. With his injury turning out to be more serious than originally thought, Charlie Hodge, now regarded as the number two goalie in the organization, guided the Canadiens.

Plante was back after just over a month, on December 16, in a home game against the New York Rangers. Returning to the ice with his face exposed to oncoming pucks must have taken incredible mental fortitude. But the papers made scant mention of this, instead focusing on the scores, the league standings, and so on. Nowhere was there any mention of the courage it must have taken to overcome what must have been a frightening experience and ordeal, and to come back and stare down the opposition once again without the aid of protection. But this omission simply reflected the thinking of the time. Injuries were part of the game, whether it was a broken cheekbone or a broken leg. Once the injury healed you were expected to resume playing. The pressure to return was immense. Those who didn't were branded cowards or worse and were quickly replaced. Others soldiered on, putting their own safety – their careers, in fact – at risk every time they skated onto the ice.

The spotlight that had shone so brightly on Jacques Plante at the beginning of the year slowly began to shift to another familiar target.

It was Maurice "Rocket" Richard who now found himself the main attraction. But he had been down this road before. In a little over a decade he had been the most written-about player in hockey, its greatest star, its biggest drawing card, and a legend in his own time. And as the 1954–55 season continued, he became the focus for both the press and the fans like never before. He became the lead player in a drama that would not only captivate the country but spark social and political unrest in his home province, and as a result catapult him to a godlike figure among his own people.

Richard was 33 years old in 1955. A little over a decade before, he became the first player to score 50 goals in 50 games, a mark that stood for almost 40 years. In the ensuing 11 years he had been named to either the first or second all-star team at the end of each season; four times he had led the league in goals and three times he had helped the Canadiens capture the Stanley Cup.

"In his playing days, Rocket was not the greatest skater or the most efficient playmaker, but he had the biggest heart in the league," Plante later reflected. "They can tell all the stories they want about Gordie

Howe but the Rocket played with fire in his eyes. He would do anything to win the game. . . . The closer he came to the net, the faster he moved. Then all you could see were those big black eyes staring you down. It was like being mesmerized by a cobra; he had a hypnotic ability about him."[11]

For those who followed his every move, the Rocket was much more than a hockey player, especially among his fellow Québécois. Richard stood out as that rare francophone who excelled in a world dominated by anglophones. When the Rocket scored, they all scored; when the Canadiens won, they all won. Although the subject of literary, cultural, and social examination and appreciation, the Rocket considered himself apolitical and a mere hockey player. His followers loudly disagreed.

"When I first arrived in Montreal," remembered Jean Béliveau, "the Canadiens may have been managed by Frank Selke, but they were really Joseph Henri Maurice Richard's team. The Rocket was the heart and soul of the Canadiens, an inspiration to us all, especially to younger French Canadians who were rising through the ranks. He was man and myth, larger than life in some ways, yet most ordinarily human in others."[12]

For the generation of Canadiens players who had grown up idolizing Richard and now were his teammates, he was a mentor, a shining star, an example of what was required to excel at the highest level. But with all that he had accomplished in his career, one achievement had so far eluded the Rocket's grasp. Four times in his career, Richard had finished as the runner-up in the points derby.

The 1954–55 season was one of tumult and turmoil league-wide. On December 2, at the Detroit Olympia, the Canadiens stunned the Red Wings 4–1 in a game that saw the Rocket score his 398th career goal and receive a misconduct for arguing with the referee. With only minutes left in the game, Canadiens captain Butch Bouchard found himself trading punches with Detroit's head coach, Jimmy Skinner. Both teams had to be sent to their dressing rooms. Unbelievably, no fines or suspensions were forthcoming.

On December 29, at Maple Leaf Gardens, the Canadiens and Leafs played to a 1–1 draw. With five minutes left in the game, Leafs defenceman Bob Bailey laid a heavy hit on the Rocket near the boards, sending him to the ice. Richard charged Bailey, and they both threw their gloves to the ice and began to fight. Bailey then attempted to gouge the eyes of an enraged Rocket.

As the referees attempted to separate the pair, Richard hit linesman George Hayes with an empty glove. The referees desperately tried to control Richard, but he kept breaking free and hitting Bailey with one stick after another, supplied by Dick Irvin. Both Richard and Bailey received a major penalty and two misconducts. Ten days later, Richard was fined $250 for his attack on Hayes.

Maurice Richard had always been a target for the worst kind of treatment from the opposition. He had long endured verbal assaults, but it was the physical assaults that brought him to the breaking point. He was not the type to pull back; instead, he would lash out at his tormentors. The result was a total of $2,500 in fines incurred by Richard, all dictated by the president of the NHL, Clarence Campbell.

The opposing teams strived to unbalance the Rocket and get him out of the game by provoking him. At the same time, Dick Irvin encouraged the Rocket to raise his intensity level to the edge, firmly believing that the angrier Richard became, the better he played. The Rocket's rage and Irvin's encouragement of it would have disastrous consequences for both and for the Canadiens.

Heading into Boston for a game on the night of March 13, 1955, the Rocket led the point race with 74 points. Geoffrion was second with 72 points, and Jean Béliveau was in third position with 71 points. The Canadiens also held a two-point lead over the Red Wings for the league championship, and with only four games left on the schedule (including two against the Red Wings), it looked like the chase would go down to the wire.

With six minutes left in the game at the Boston Garden, the Canadiens, riding an 11-game unbeaten streak, found themselves on the wrong side of the score. With Montreal holding the man advantage, Irvin waved for Plante to come to the bench in favour of an extra attacker. An exhausted Plante had just fallen through the open gate when all hell broke loose.

Accounts of how the melee started vary, but it quickly got out of hand as the Rocket repeatedly hit Bruins defenceman Hal Laycoe over the head with a stick. Linesman Cliff Thompson attempted to hold a furious Richard back. The Rocket responded by punching him twice in the face.

"There were 13,900 people in the Boston Garden. You couldn't hear a sound," Bruin Fleming Mackell recalled. "You could have heard a pin drop, everything was so quiet. In fact, when the incident was completely finished, a lot of people, over half the crowd probably, got up and left the building. It was very frightening. The fans were scared when Rocket went after Laycoe with the stick."[13]

Clarence Campbell desperately wanted to project a big-league image to the world. The game was struggling then, as it does today, to identify the role that violence has in hockey. Campbell announced his fateful decision on the morning of March 17. Richard was suspended for the season's final three games and the entirety of the playoffs. Fans and players immediately expressed their outrage. Many in Montreal thought the punishment unreasonably severe. To this day, accusations persist that the league's owners (with the exception of Montreal) had arrived at the verdict in concert with Campbell.

"All these gentlemen demanded that something be done to curb Maurice Richard," claimed a resigned Frank Selke, "whose greatest fault was defeating their teams and filling their arenas to capacity."[14] Former teammate Elmer Lach declared, "They always tried to get the Rocket and now they have."[15]

For many Quebecers, the Rocket's suspension was a turning point. They saw it as the most grievous example yet of the anglo minority in Quebec subjugating the French majority. Campbell had suddenly become the figurehead of the oppressive English. "You could feel the tension building on March 17th throughout the city, particularly around the Forum," recalled Red Fisher, a young reporter for the *Montreal Star*. "I got a seat about ten rows behind the Detroit bench and you could feel the tension building even higher."[16]

Amid all the anger and confusion, the fact that the game between the Canadiens and the Red Wings was for first place was soon forgotten.

"It is hard to describe our feelings," recalled Plante. "We knew it was a big game for us yet the game seemed secondary. All of the players as well as the officials were casting worried glances at the sullen crowd. It was as if we were going through the motions while waiting for the big act to start. At the 10-minute mark in the first period I heard the uproar start. Nobody was watching us. All eyes were turned towards the south end where President Campbell and his fiancée had entered to take their seats."[17]

Before a restless crowd, the Red Wings jumped out to a quick 4–1 lead over the listless Canadiens, further enraging a crowd on edge.

As the period came to a close, Campbell – who had ignored advice not to attend the game – reached out to shake a fan's hand and was punched in the face. Then a tear-gas bomb went off a few rows below him.

The players scurried for cover as the crowd spilled into the streets outside the Forum. A shaken Campbell immediately declared the Red Wings the winners of the game by forfeit, vaulting them into first place, as the police ordered the building cleared.

"We put some towels in the bottom of the dressing room door to keep the smoke from coming in during the first intermission," recalls Red Wings defenceman Marcel Pronovost. "Once we got word that the game had been forfeited we were hustled out the back to our waiting bus and rushed immediately to Westmount station where the train was waiting for us."[18]

The riot that ensued outside the Forum and down St. Catherine Street lasted well into the morning hours. In the end, the damages to the neighbourhood and the Forum itself – all its windows were smashed – totalled $500,000. Along the way hundreds of stores were looted, police cars were overturned, and dozens of rioters were arrested.

The "Richard Riot," as it quickly became known, was headline news throughout Canada. Many sat transfixed in front of their televisions, unable to comprehend the carnage on the screen. In an effort to calm the rioters, the Rocket spoke to the masses from the shattered Forum: "Because I always try so hard to win and had my troubles in Boston, I was suspended. At playoff time it hurts not be in the game with the boys. However, I want to do what is good for the people of Montreal and the team. So that no further harm will be done, I would like to ask everyone to get behind the team and to help the boys win from the New York Rangers and Detroit. I will take my punishment and come back next year to help the club and the younger players to win the Cup."[19] And with those simple but heartfelt words, the man whose actions on the ice had ignited the seeds of an uprising now ended the riot.

The Richard Riot crystallized the relationship between Maurice Richard and his adoring public and emphasized just how much of a cultural institution the Montreal Canadiens had become in the province of Quebec. Red Storey, that evening's referee, perhaps summed it up best when he claimed that "hockey is a religion in Quebec, and the Rocket was bigger than the Pope."[20]

As the years passed, the Richard Riot, once seen as a mere sports riot, took on greater historical significance. Many have come to believe that the sight of rioters in the streets supporting a Quebec cultural icon was one of the precursors to the Quiet Revolution that transformed the province over the next decade.

But at the time, none of what happened would change the ruling handed down by Clarence Campbell. Maurice Richard had played his last game of the season. There would be no happy ending for the Montreal Canadiens that spring. "Without Richard, the team had lost its soul," commented Selke.[21]

Two nights later at the Forum, in the penultimate game of the season, Rocket Richard was given a hero's ovation and Boom Boom Geoffrion was loudly booed by the fans for having the audacity to pass the Rocket and win the scoring title.

Geoffrion had considered deliberately not scoring in the remaining games, his idolatry of the Rocket stronger than ever, but his teammates had quickly dissuaded him from that notion, reminding him that the team was in a battle for first place. For Geoffrion, the pain that the booing caused would take a long time to recede, and it never left him completely.

The Detroit Red Wings won their seventh straight league championship by thrashing Montreal 6–0 in the season finale, their margin of victory in the standings being the two points awarded in forfeit the night of the riot.

The Canadiens, with Rocket watching from the sidelines, once again defeated the Boston Bruins for the right to play in the finals. Aside from Irvin's system of rotating Plante and Charlie Hodge as goalies in the series' first few games – the coach's vain attempt to focus attention elsewhere in the aftermath of the riot – the series was nondescript, and the Canadiens defeated the Bruins in five games.

In the Stanley Cup finals, the Canadiens once again faced their hated rival the Red Wings, this time with the Rocket as a spectator. Having endured a tumultuous season, the Canadiens could be forgiven for being an exhausted team. Yet they gallantly fought the Red Wings to a deciding seventh game before bowing out 3–1.

"It had been pretty close," wrote newsman Andy O'Brien. "There wasn't a shadow of a doubt that the Rocket's blow-up had cost all of the Canadiens the extra bonus money that winning the championship would have meant. Yet I didn't hear a single critical voice raised against Maurice during all those travel days to and from Detroit. He could do no wrong with them."[22]

"I've often wondered what would have happened had the Rocket not knocked over Thompson and whacked Laycoe," wrote Bernie Geoffrion in his memoirs. "For one thing Maurice would have won the Art Ross that he wanted so much. For another we would have finished first and finally we would have beaten Detroit for the Stanley Cup."[23]

Marcel Pronovost takes the opposite view. "We always felt that the Canadiens elevated their game in the Rocket's absence, and used it as motivation for some of the younger players to assert themselves."[24]

It was anybody's guess whether the Canadiens would have won the Stanley Cup that year if the Rocket had been on the ice. What *was* known was that there would be repercussions to what had happened. The first change would come behind the bench.

Throughout the 1954–55 season, a distinct chill had developed between Selke and Irvin. Selke frowned upon some of the coach's methods, particularly when it came to the Rocket, and held Irvin responsible for the uproar that followed. "I could not help but think that Dick's penchant for goading Richard had altogether too much to do with getting the great star in the mood that touched off all the trouble," Selke wrote in his memoirs. "And when Dick launched into another tirade at President Campbell, after we lost our final game that season, I had made up my mind."[25] After 15 years as the Canadiens' head coach, the time had come for Dick Irvin to take his leave.

Irvin went back to the city where it had all begun for him. However, he would never be able to revive the fortunes of the sagging Chicago Black Hawks, a team that just three years earlier had been poised to make a run at a Stanley Cup championship – until they were stopped cold by an unknown goaltender who liked to knit his own toques and roam freely from his net.

What was never widely known was that Dick Irvin, the greatest coach the game had seen, was slowly dying of bone cancer. He passed away on May 15, 1957, a little over two years after he left the bench of the Montreal Canadiens.

THE DAWNING
OF A NEW ERA

IN THE EARLY SUMMER months of 1955, Toe Blake was named head coach of the Canadiens. A former Canadiens player and captain, Blake brought his experience as well as an intense dedication to his new position. When he took over behind the bench, Blake found only two of his former teammates still with the Canadiens. One was Butch Bouchard, the other was the Rocket.

After the previous year's debacle, general manager Frank Selke was eager to find a coach who could rein in the Rocket's notorious temper while getting the most out of him on the ice. He had to find a person Richard would respect as much as he did Irvin. In his former linemate on the famed "Punch Line," and a man Richard had idolized as a youngster, Selke found him. During their days together on the ice, Blake was renowned for being able to help his fiery teammate focus his emotions towards scoring goals. Now, years later, he was entrusted with that same task.

That summer, Blake and Selke scheduled a meeting with a Rocket still reeling from the spring before. "You don't have anything to prove either to the players, the fans or us," Selke lectured Richard. "You carried the club during the lean years and now it's time for the younger players to help out, especially when it gets rough out there. Forget about the past. It's the future – and you – we're concerned about. Your heart is as young as ever, but you're now thirty-four years old. Remember that. We don't want you fighting a world of twenty-four-year-old huskies."[1]

Butch, the team's captain, his mind leaning towards retirement, was the next to meet with the Canadiens' new head coach, who persuaded him to play one more year. Blake convinced a skeptical Bouchard that his presence could help ease the coaching transition. The Canadiens were bringing some rookies into the fold that fall, and Blake felt that Butch could be a steadying hand in their development as well as provide some insurance in case of injury. Butch would be a liaison between the rookie coach and the players, and was like a second coach on the team, a role he relished.

In the Canadiens training camp held in the fall of 1955, the professionals were mixed with the amateur hopefuls and split into four squads, scrimmaging every morning under the watchful eyes of Sam Pollock and Ken Reardon, the two men entrusted with running the Canadiens' amateur system. At noon, they would lunch with Selke and report on the morning's activities.

Both of them enthusiastically talked about a 19-year-old who was carrying the play. In the words of Reardon, "He was spoiling the practices. He's got the puck all the time. The pros can't get it away from him."[2] Selke deemed the kid worth a look.

After seeing him with his own eyes, Selke, despite reservations about the player's small stature, offered him a professional contract. The shy, timid teenager slowly walked into the general manager's office and silently signed the deal, while his much older brother assured a skeptical Selke that the youngster was ready to play for the Canadiens. The young man was Henri Richard – the Rocket's younger brother. The final piece in the Canadiens' championship puzzle had quietly fallen into place.

The arrival of Toe Blake also signalled a new beginning for some members of the team who had struggled under the regime of Dick Irvin. Dickie Moore's frequent inability to stay healthy played a large part in his lack of success, but his poor relationship with the former coach also didn't help. For him the succession of Blake to the Habs' coaching spot was not only career saving, it was career changing. "With Dick Irvin it was four years of hell. He didn't like me," admits Moore today. "Toe Blake's arrival was a great blessing for me – he let me go, he let me be me. I owe all my success to Toe. Toe told me when he first came on as coach, 'I'm going to play you, now don't worry about it.'"[3]

Similarly, Jacques Plante welcomed the coaching change. "During the year and a half I played for Dick Irvin I never received a word of praise. He had come up through the hard school of hockey where your best was always expected, your best he regarded as only normal. I produce best with a little praise now and again."[4]

"When Toe Blake came in '55, I'll always remember his first meeting with us," Jean Béliveau told the *Hockey News* in 1999. "He looked around the room and said, 'Boys, I've got great hockey players here. But if you want a championship, we have to form a unit. We have to help each other.' When you look back afterwards, he was so right."[5]

Jacques Plante also never forgot Blake's initial address to the team. "Some of you fellows know more hockey than I ever did and some of you are better than I ever was," stated a humble Blake. "My job is to keep harmony and help us all to win. Let's all work together with that in mind."[6] Thus began the reign of the man Plante regarded as "the greatest coach I've ever had."

Plante always appreciated the single pat on the back that would be waiting for him at the bench after a well-played period. Although Blake's praise was subtle, it was more than what Plante had ever got when Irvin was behind the bench.

This team was a coach's dream: anchored by Jacques Plante in goal, defended by Doug Harvey, Tom Johnson, and Butch Bouchard, and possessing two forward lines of stars, Henri and Maurice Richard alongside Dickie Moore on the first line, and Jean Béliveau centring Bert Olmstead and Boom Boom Geoffrion on the second. Throw in a supporting cast of players who would be stars on the league's other teams, and one would think that Blake could coach from a rocking chair. "The Canadiens were good and they knew it," newsman Andy O'Brien wrote later. "Blake agreed that with a team like that they shouldn't lose a game, but they had to guard against letdowns against lowly clubs."[7]

The Canadiens opened the 1955–56 season with four wins and a tie, highlighted by Plante's back-to-back shutouts. However, they lost their first game to the Bruins, on October 21. As the players changed in the dressing room afterwards, Blake ruminated to the assembled media about the loss. If there had been any doubts about the level of his disgust at losing, they were soon erased.

"You can't win them all," suggested one of the reporters.

"Why not?" snarled Blake.[8]

Blake also subtly changed the way the Canadiens attacked the opposition by stressing constant motion. By going on the attack, Blake made the most of his offensive strength up front. Under Irvin, the Canadiens' defence was instructed to circle around the red line, while the forwards were in the opponent's end of the rink. Now, Blake wanted his defence-men to move up towards the blue line.

At first Plante was skeptical about having so much space between himself and his defencemen. However, he soon found that the extra area was a tacit approval by his new coach of his wandering style, because it allowed him more room to rove in his own end. It also revealed the level of confidence that Blake had in his goalie.

"We were urged to always pinch, to always take offensive chances," remembers Dickie Moore today. "Sometimes those chances left Jacques all alone. He was the last man on the ice. If I went by him it was over. There was a lot of pressure on him – he was the one who had to bail us out."9

The beginning of the relationship between Blake and Plante was based on mutual respect. Blake had confided to Plante that he couldn't help him much with goaltending because he'd never played goal himself. On the ice, Jacques was free to experiment, and he found his foremost defender in Toe Blake. Plante wasn't alone. Each of the players was allowed to engage his individual skills as long as it was for the good of the team.

Toe Blake treated his players with respect, a respect he as a player had always wanted from his coaches. That's not to say that he wasn't demanding, because he was, or that he didn't berate his players, because he did, though always in private, always man to man.

If Blake was unhappy during a game, he would purposely stare at the scoreboard and let his vitriol out by barking at the clock overhead. If he looked away from the ice and didn't name names, the public would never know which player was being singled out. But the subject of Blake's anger always knew.

Blake's responsibilities were not limited to coaching the team. He handled their travel itinerary and had total control over their train schedules, hotel arrangements, and social gatherings. He always made sure that his team travelled first class and had them dress and act as pro-fessionals, stressing that they represented the Montreal Canadiens both on and off the ice.

"That first year, Toe had help," recalls Dickie Moore. "Butch Bouchard was an important leader on that team. I remember Butch calling a team meeting and telling us 'We have a good guy now, let's not spoil it.' Butch kept us in line. We all looked up to him, all of us."10

Thirty games into the season, the Canadiens were already well ahead in the race for first place. Plante was off to a superb start, giving up on average a goal and a half a game, while sporting a league-leading six shutouts, including at least one against each of the league's teams. With success came emulation, and what was once ridiculed was slowly becoming accepted.

"Doesn't Toe Blake ever blast you for leaving your net?" Andy O'Brien of the *Montreal Star* asked Plante.

"No," answered Jacques. "When Dick Irvin was coach he agreed it was O.K. 'as long as you don't do it too often.' Then this season when Toe took over as coach, I asked him what he wanted me to do about leaving the net and he told me to keep on playing my game – he said he'd tell me when he thought I was overdoing it." O'Brien continued, "Plante believes the other goalers will start doing it now because it works. No wonder this Canadien club keeps packin' 'em in year after year. They're always coming up with something new, and the men on top – like Frank Selke and Toe Blake – are shrewd enough not to glue their minds to old ideas. Like goalers 'must stay in their nets,' for example."[11]

And then, in an incident eerily similar to one the year before, Plante was again felled by a teammate's shot.

In practice on the morning of December 16, Plante was celebrating a shutout victory over the Rangers the night before that had given the Canadiens a 12-point lead in the race for first place when he was struck by a Donnie Marshall shot that had been inadvertently tipped into Plante's face by Butch Bouchard.

He was rushed to the Herbert Reddy Hospital, where X-rays revealed a broken nose and a fracture of his left cheekbone. (The year before, it had been the right cheekbone.) Resting idly in his hospital bed, Plante came to the realization that both injuries could have been prevented had he been wearing a mask.

Toe Blake agreed with him, and upon Plante's return to the ice he began wearing a protective shield in practice. But he found the mask uncomfortable, and he never even considered wearing it in a game.

Plante found himself back in the Canadiens goal a mere twelve days after the accident, having missed only six games. His replacement, Bob Perreault, had performed admirably, and returned to his regular goaltending duties in Shawinigan. It was no wonder that the Canadiens rarely faltered, such was their abundance of available talent.

The Canadiens had a ten-game undefeated streak in November and followed it up with an eight-game winning streak in December. They suffered only one slight hiccup in January, losing four out of five, but rebounded to clinch first place on February 25, with three weeks still remaining on the schedule. Thus ended Detroit's seven-year reign at the top.

"I don't recall any problems at all that year," Jean-Guy Talbot, then a rookie, told the *Hockey News* in 1999. "The only thing I know was, if we lost two in a row, it was like losing the Stanley Cup. But that didn't happen too much."[12]

As the season continued along, Butch Bouchard was eased out of the lineup, as Talbot, the rookie whom Bouchard personally mentored that season, began to assert himself on the ice. Realizing the end was near, Butch asked Blake to allow him to retire immediately. Blake wouldn't hear of it.

The Canadiens' dominance on the ice was so striking that a year-old magazine south of the border started taking notice. "Hockey is Canada's national sport, and the Montreal Canadiens, with the season's top team, are the apple of the Dominion's eye," wrote *Sports Illustrated* in its January 23, 1956, issue, which for the first time featured a hockey player on the cover.[13]

No player inspired more words that year or had more flashbulbs pop around him in the seasons to follow than Jean Béliveau.

The year before, Béliveau had finished third in scoring, but under the tutelage of Blake, he blossomed into the game's premier player, capturing the Art Ross Trophy as the league's leading scorer, winning the Hart Trophy as the league's most valuable player, and being named to the first all-star team, where his 47 goals set a record for centremen that would last for the next decade and a half.

"Béliveau is the key man on our club, there's no getting away from that," Plante told *Hockey Pictorial* in 1956, when speaking about his rival from junior days gone by. "He seems to spur us on. And when he's not playing well you can tell it affects him. He's a worrier . . . doesn't say much but I know it's hurting him inside."[14]

Part of this offensive superiority was due to the overwhelming Montreal power play, so lethal that the league had to step in and change the rules to dull its efficiency. Anchored by Béliveau at centre, alongside Moore and the Rocket on the wings, with Harvey and Geoffrion at the points, the Canadiens boasted the greatest power play that the game had ever seen. With penalized players required to serve the full two minutes, it was not unusual for the Montreal power play to score two or even three goals during the player's time in the box. With Plante giving up on average less than two goals a game, for many opponents, a single Canadiens power play effectively ended any hope of winning the game.

No player in 1956 statistically dominated his position more than Jacques Plante, who won his first Vezina Trophy as the league's best goaltender. That year, he led the league in wins (42), had the fewest losses (12), and had the lowest goals-against average (1.86). It was only in shutouts where Plante trailed one of his contemporaries, falling behind Glenn Hall, winner of the Calder Trophy as the league's rookie of the year.

Plante's unusual style and success brought continued attention from the media. The February 1956 issue of *Hockey Pictorial* featured not only the secrets behind Jacques' goaltending style told by the man himself but also his evaluation of the Canadiens' most hated rival, the two-time defending champion Detroit Red Wings. Plante dissected the Red Wings player by player. In an age when many players expressed themselves on the ice, such articulation was rare. Plante went on to assure the magazine's readers that his roaming ways were always the product of much deliberation and not irrational, rash behaviour. "I'm not a worrier nor am I ever nervous in a game," Plante also wrote. "If I could learn to worry a little I'd have to keep sharper all the time. I never seem to get flustered and consequently I'm not on my toes all the time."

Plante finished the article with a guarantee and a challenge to Jack Adams, the Red Wings general manager: "The Canadiens will win the championship and the Cup. Don't you believe that, Jack Adams," he said confidently. "We won't fold this time."[15]

After such an impressive regular season, the only question that remained for the Canadiens was whether they could maintain their high level of play come playoff time. However, that question was quickly answered as Montreal hammered the visiting New York Rangers 7–1 in the opening game of the semifinal playoff series.

Game two, however, served as a reality check for the confident Canadiens, who were felled by the Rangers and their relief goalie, Gord Bell, in a 4–2 loss, a shock for a team that had rarely faced any challenge throughout the season. The Montreal papers whispered about the carelessness of Plante's performance and later openly brooded over the Canadiens' poor record in New York, site of the next two games.

Suddenly what had once been considered a cakewalk now looked like an unexpected test of Montreal's resilience and grit.

There needn't have been too much concern, however, as the Canadiens swept both weekend games to take a commanding three-games-to-one lead.

"The back-to-back victories showed Canadiens at their dazzling best," wrote Baz O'Meara of the *Montreal Star*, "you could hardly find a weak link in their chain. The Canadiens played what you would term a resolute game, which was shot through with more than the occasional patches of brilliance."[16]

Back in Montreal the bell tolled for the overmatched Rangers. "Class plus consistency told the inevitable tale last night," O'Meara wrote, "as Canadiens eliminated the unsteady Rangers in the fifth game of their Stanley Cup series at the Forum by the conclusive score of 7–0."[17]

The Rocket assisted on five of the seven Montreal goals – equalling Toe Blake's playoff record. In the five-game series, the powerful Canadiens scored 24 goals, and Plante allowed only nine to get past him.

There was little celebration in the Canadiens dressing room, however. The team was no stranger to victory in the first round; it was the next series that crowned a champion. This triumph over the Rangers marked the team's sixth straight trip to the finals, and anything less than a championship wouldn't satisfy Selke, Blake, the players, or the fans. And for the third year in a row they would face the Detroit Red Wings in the finals.

With their first-place finish in the regular season, the Canadiens appeared to have finally gained the upper hand in their ongoing rivalry with the Wings. Part of the credit for this, according to Dickie Moore, goes to a roaming Jacques Plante.

"The Red Wings used to generate all of their offense by dumping the puck into our corners. From there they would send their big guys like Vic Stasiuk or Marcel Pronovost into the corner, bang around, and get the puck towards the front of the net where guys like Gordie Howe were waiting. What Plante did was go and play the puck in the corner, and pass it up to our defensemen. By doing that he completely took away any advantage Detroit may have had. Our defensemen didn't take as much of a pounding, and the Red Wings had to come up with new ways to enter our zone."[18]

That year's Red Wings featured one major difference from the team that had defeated the Canadiens the previous two springs. After Detroit's Cup win the previous spring, the Red Wings unexpectedly traded all-world goalie Terry Sawchuk to the Boston Bruins. Replacing him in the Detroit nets was Glenn Hall, who would go on to be the league's top rookie.

"We let Sawchuk go because we found ourselves with two top goalies," Jack Adams explained. "Hall is more advanced now than Sawchuk was when he joined us and all the players insist Glenn has been NHL material for the past year. . . . It was a case of trading one of them and Sawchuk is the established player. Consequently, he brought a better offer."[19]

Plante was not nearly as well acquainted with the rookie Hall. Over the years, though, Hall would become arguably Plante's greatest rival, and this was only the first of what would be many scintillating duels between the two.

Detroit came in to the finals seeking to match a league record with a third consecutive Cup triumph. Most experts seemed to think that this would be the year of the Canadiens instead. But after the first two periods of the first game, the Canadiens found themselves trailing the Red Wings 4–2. Then, as the third period began, the win slipped away from Detroit's clutches and the Canadiens, just as they'd been doing all year, overwhelmed their opposition. In the space of four and a half minutes they exploded for a burst of four goals past a stunned Hall.

Unfortunately for Detroit, the hole only got deeper after the second game. "The Canadiens won't have an easier win in the series than the one they racked up last night at the Forum by a 5–1 score, which gives them a two game lead, and almost assures them final victory," wrote Baz O'Meara in the next day's *Montreal Star*. "Plante played one of his better games, handling twenty shots, some of them real scorchers, in effective style. 'You couldn't criticize his work tonight,'" added Toe Blake. "'He was very good and he made some real key saves.'"[20]

However, days later and back on home ice, the Red Wings, in front of their loyal and loud fans, showed why they were two-time defending champions as the beaten but unbowed team drew within a game of the Canadiens' series lead.

The Montreal Canadiens now faced their greatest challenge of the season. Before a rabid crowd at the Detroit Olympia, and against a two-time Stanley Cup champion that suddenly felt rejuvenated, they had to find a way to reassert their control over the series.

A fifteen-year-old Jacques Plante strikes a goaltending pose.

During his teenage years Plante was the best goalie in Shawinigan, at one point playing for five different teams at one time.

Plante joined the Quebec Citadels in the fall of 1947. Over the next two years he would establish himself as the top goaltending prospect in the province.

When he played for the Montreal Royals in the early 1950s, Plante's performance and unique style of play brought him great notoriety in Quebec, as illustrated by the front cover of a popular magazine of the day.

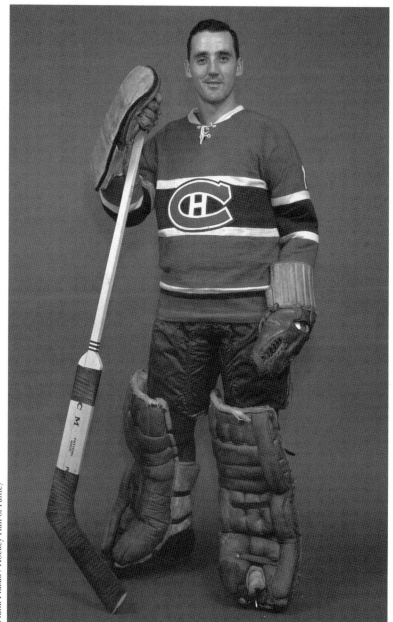

After sharing the Canadiens' goaltending duties for the previous two seasons, Plante finally became Montreal's full-time goaltender in the fall of 1954.

(Imperial Oil-Turofsky / Hockey Hall of Fame)

Plante broke the cardinal rule of goaltending by leaving his net to play the puck. He also wasn't above interfering with opposing forwards as Tod Sloan of the Leafs finds out.

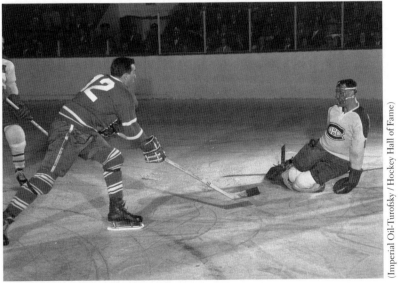

(Imperial Oil-Turofsky / Hockey Hall of Fame)

Plante was obsessive about playing the angles. Here he comes out to challenge the Leafs' Ron Stewart.

(Imperial Oil-Turofsky / Hockey Hall of Fame)

Toe Blake became the Canadiens' head coach in the fall of 1955.
While each man respected the other professionally, their personal
relationship slowly disintegrated over time.

(Hockey Hall of Fame)

Plante waves to the crowd during a parade celebrating the Canadiens'
1956 Stanley Cup win.

In the late 1950s Plante experimented with a variety of masks in practice. With his forehead exposed and because of its tendency to fog up, he never wore this mask designed by Delbert Louch in a game.

215 B 9

SEC.   ROW   SEAT

MEZZANINE $2.50

MADISON SQUARE GARDEN

HOCKEY GAME NO. HVI

SUN. EVE., 7:00 P. M.
NOV. 1, 1959

Aicus-Simplex-Brown, Inc., N.Y. 6

After taking a shot to the face from Andy Bathgate on November 1, 1959, Plante came back wearing a mask, forever changing the game of hockey.

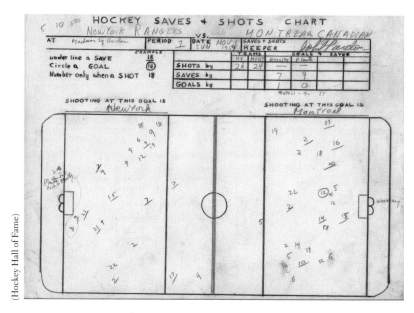

Watching from the stands, John Pardon kept his own homemade shot chart on the night Plante debuted the mask. Above the left goal he has written "Plante out; puck in mouth."

Plante (pictured here with Doug Harvey, centre) continued to wear the mask and was undefeated in the Canadiens' next 11 games, allowing only 13 goals.

With the series on the line, the newsmen in Detroit found their whipping boy in Jacques Plante. On the day of the game the hometown newspapers were full of stories that questioned Plante's manhood. After all, what kind of goalie wore a mask, even if it was in practice? They called him effete, a man who had lost his character, a man marked by weakness, a goaltender who had gone soft.

Plante answered all of his critics in the most convincing fashion he knew: the Red Wings never put a puck past him all night.

"Plante's performance was what you would expect from a great star and he gave us that kind of goaltending. He looked like a million bucks out there tonight," beamed Frank Selke in the wake of the Canadiens' 3–0 win.[21] Toe Blake told the gathered media that the difference in the game was the goaltending of Plante.

The Canadiens now stood one game away from capturing the Stanley Cup. Plante had been tested both before game four (mentally) and during the game (on the ice) and had passed with flying colours.

Plante was not the only Canadien proving that his regular-season excellence was no fluke. Jean Béliveau was busy confirming that he too was no regular-season wonder. His two goals in game four had given him a total of six for the series, as he had scored a goal in each of the games in the finals. "There is acclaim for Béliveau in all quarters," wrote Baz O'Meara in the *Montreal Star*, on the day of the fifth game. "Conn Smythe marveled at his puck control, his ice generalship, his anticipation and above all his quick shot. Doug Vaughn of the *Windsor Star* said on the air the other night that he could spend a whole evening just watching him play. He averred he was the best he had ever seen and his radio mates agreed with him."[22] In another article in the same issue, O'Meara wrote, "The Canadiens stand on the threshold of greatness today while the Red Wings teeter on the brink of disaster."[23]

The fifth game of the 1956 finals felt more like a coronation than a hockey game. Over half the game had been played to a scoreless draw before Béliveau broke the ice, with his twelfth goal of the playoffs, tying the record set 12 years earlier by his teammate Maurice "Rocket" Richard. Not to be outdone, the Rocket himself added another Canadiens goal less than a minute later as Plante continued to stymie and frustrate the Red Wings shooters. Thirteen seconds into the third period, the Boomer put the third Canadiens goal behind Glenn Hall and the celebration began. The Red Wings' Alex Delvecchio scored shortly after, but the outcome of the game and the Stanley Cup were firmly in hand.

As the clock clicked towards the game's end, Butch Bouchard, who hadn't played in months, felt a sudden sensation on his neck as Toe Blake, his coach and former teammate, whipped the towel off and patted him on the back, signalling that it was his turn. To a thunderous ovation, he skated out onto the Forum ice one last time.

"Blake, who has a fine flair for the dramatic, did a kindly thing near the end of the game," reported O'Meara the next day. "He sent Butch Bouchard into action so the latter would have his name written into the records as well as the annals of Stanley Cup play for his last appearance as a competitor. It was a generous gesture to an old teammate, as fine a competitor as hockey has ever seen. No wonder the players idolize their coach who in his greatest moment didn't forget the friend with whom he campaigned and bivouacked for so many seasons."[24]

As the Canadiens almost smothered their goalie in celebration, Dickie Moore and Boom Boom Geoffrion emerged from the crowd, grabbed their coach, and lifted him to their shoulders. Blake, clutching his fedora in his right hand, had his left hand grabbed by his goalie, who had materialized from the group and was thrusting both his arms up towards the rafters.

As the Montreal Forum erupted, the Stanley Cup was brought out to centre ice, where the league trustee, Cooper Smeaton, called on the Canadiens' captain to accept the trophy. Butch Bouchard, in his last act as team captain, made a speech in both English and French, took the Cup, and clutched it close to his heart as he paraded around the rink and skated off into retirement.

Baz O'Meara, writing in the *Montreal Star* the following day, made no secret of who he thought was the team's most valuable player. "When it was all over and the Stanley Cup was trundled out on a table, Plante embraced it in full view of the crowd, who were convinced to the last skeptic that he is a real clutch performer."[25]

When Jacques Plante came tramping into the Canadiens dressing room, he jumped high in the air. He was the happiest Hab of them all, perhaps even more than Toe Blake. For Jacques had been vindicated. "They said and so did we," O'Meara wrote, "that he had been too inconsistent even though he had won the Vezina trophy. . . . Plante showed he had high quality, he silenced critics, he gave two wonderful displays, and now none can say he hasn't arrived at full stature as a twine tender."[26]

After the events of the year before, the city of Montreal was in a mood to celebrate. Mayor Jean Drapeau organized a Stanley Cup parade, the city's first since the Wanderers won the Cup in 1907. Held four days after the final game, the parade covered 36 miles and took six and a half hours. The players, most clad in toques, waved from 35 convertibles to a crowd of at least 250,000, a quarter of the city's population.

As the years went by there would be other parades with other players, celebrating yet other Stanley Cups, but this particular group would prove to have a lasting effect on those who saw them perform. Forty-four years later, as the twentieth century was drawing to a close, the *Hockey News* asked a panel of experts to name the greatest hockey team of the century. They decided it was the 1955–56 Montreal Canadiens.

Among the many members of the team interviewed for the subsequent article, defenceman Tom Johnson described Jacques Plante as "the best goalie I have ever seen. In key games, you couldn't get an aspirin by that guy. He was that good."[27]

And to think that the reign of the Montreal Canadiens and their star goalie, Jacques Plante, had just begun.

DOUG

THE MONTREAL CANADIENS were on top of the world. Rulers of the hockey kingdom, they had it all. Their newest captain, Maurice "Rocket" Richard, was the most recognized athlete in Canada and a legend in his own time. The heir to his throne as the face of the Canadiens, Jean Béliveau, had just completed a season perched atop the league's scoring leaders. Boom Boom Geoffrion was terrorizing young goalies all over the league with his slapshot. Dickie Moore, freed from the shackles of the previous regime, was starting to unleash his considerable talent. And Jacques Plante, the league's best goaltender, was revolutionizing not only his position but the game at large.

Yet none of these men, for all their greatness, was the most valuable player on that wonderful team, or in the league for that matter. That honour belonged to Doug Harvey. Even today, 50 years after his prime playing years, the name still evokes awe.

Harvey's immense talent was equalled by his versatility. He was the quarterback of the most feared power play the game has ever known. He was also the key ingredient in the Canadiens' vaunted transition game, with his crisp and precise passes acting as the springboard for the rush into the opponent's zone. "He controlled the game like an orchestra conductor," recalled his teammate Bernie Geoffrion. "When others were running around like chickens with their heads cut off

Harvey was nonchalantly looking for someone for a pass or easily reliev-
ing the opposition of the puck."[1] At the same time, nobody was a more
tenacious defender. He blocked shots, using his size to his advantage,
all the while making the difficult seem far too routine.

Harvey was named to an amazing 11 consecutive all-star teams and
was a six-time recipient of the Norris Trophy as the league's best defenceman. There were no discernible weaknesses to his game; he excelled in
all aspects and seemed able to bend the game and its outcome to his
will. Once the puck was on his stick, it left only on his terms.

His was a methodical game; nothing was ever too rushed. At times
Harvey would survey the ice before making the perfect pass. Yet he was
also capable of rushing up the ice and, without notice and while in full
stride, dish a perfect pass to a teammate.

Away from the rink, Doug Harvey lived life to the fullest. He enjoyed
a beer and found comfort in many bars throughout the league.

"He loved a challenge – on and off the ice," remembers Red Fisher.
"It didn't matter where it came from – the opposition or constituted
authority. All that mattered was that it was a challenge, something
which had to be addressed and overcome. He was stubborn, aggravat-
ing, unselfish, hard-drinking, fun loving and the best defenseman, by
far, in Canadiens history."[2]

Off the ice, Plante and Harvey went their separate ways. On the rare
occasions that Plante went out to a bar, he would leave soon after the
first beer. For Harvey the first beer was the prelude to a long evening.
Whereas Plante was responsible with his money, Harvey thought
nothing of giving his away. Many found Plante to be distant and aloof,
while Harvey could be kind and generous to a fault.

Once the game started, however, Harvey had much in common with
his goaltender. Both men were stubborn when dealing with authority,
and went about playing their game their own way. Harvey encouraged
Plante in his innovations, immediately noticing that many of them
would also help ease his defensive load.

"I figure Plante takes fifteen per cent of the load off the defence,"
Harvey told Montreal newsman Andy O'Brien. "Whereas we'd frequently get reefed into the corners while going after the pucks that they
[the opposing team] dump into our end, Jacques often saves us the
trouble. Being faster than a lot of forwards, he starts the puck going
back while the opponents are still rushing in."[3]

It was Harvey who suggested that Plante start talking with his
defencemen during plays. By communicating with them, Plante was

able to act as a second set of eyes for his defenders, alerting them to their situation or how the play was unfolding. It didn't take long for the fans to notice Plante's voice during the play, always in constant communication.

When Plante ventured out of his net to gather the puck, he would hear Doug, telling him where to pass the puck, left or right or to leave it behind the net or whether just to fall on it. Plante saved precious time by not having to look up and scan the ice before deciding what to do with the puck.

Plante took the communication a step further by not only yelling when the other team iced the puck but also raising his arm to signal his retreating defencemen that it was an icing situation. In this way a defenceman skating back towards his net, with an opposing player in full chase, would realize that all he had to do was finish the race for the puck.

With the exception of some well-timed suggestions, Harvey left Plante alone to play his game. According to Harvey's biographer, William Brown, "Harvey never considered Plante to be a great team player – he was too self-absorbed, and he always disappeared when it was his turn to buy a round of beers – but he appreciated his value to the team."[4]

On the ice, however, the pair helped to form an almost unbeatable combination. These two men of hockey genius were able to marshal their considerable talents towards common goals: the Norris Trophy, the Vezina Trophy, and ultimately the Stanley Cup.

"Harvey knew that Plante didn't need any heroics by his defensemen," writes Brown. "Harvey would block the shots that came at him, but would rarely throw himself at the puck. The last thing he wanted was to put himself out of position or deflect a shot on goal. The main thing was to let Plante make the stops."[5]

Harvey was adept at slowing down the game. Plante took it upon himself to do the same. The difference is that Harvey did it by having the puck; Plante slowed the game down because of his own ingenuity. He was so successful that the league had to pass another rule specifically designed to thwart the Canadiens.

"Jacques would come out of the net and freeze the puck, especially in key situations," remembered future coach Scotty Bowman years later. "If the Canadiens had a lot of pressure on them, and he wanted to get a face-off, Jacques was the first goalie to stop play. In fact, the league had to make a new rule that a goaltender couldn't stop play from behind his own blueline."[6]

The rest of the league was unable to thwart some of Jacques' other ploys to slow the game. Quite often when facing an opposition power play he would claim to have an equipment malfunction. Skating over to the bench to get a "loose" strap fixed, Plante was actually buying time for his penalty killers to catch their breath as well as leaving the opposition to stir, already anxious for the puck to drop. "I usually do it at the request of a penalty killer," Jacques explained. "These guys are out there going full speed and once in a while one of them will come over to me and say 'Jacques, give me a chance for a breather.' I try to accommodate them and skate over to the boards."[7]

The opposition would howl in protest, but the referees' hands were tied. In time, Plante became a master of gaining his team these unofficial "breaks," and of slowing the pace of the game. At the same time, though, the Canadiens team was so strong that many of Plante's breaks were often unnecessary.

Another facet of his game that drove his opponents to distraction was how he would put himself in between an opposing player and the puck. Running interference, he regularly drew the other team into taking unnecessary penalties.

The Montreal Canadiens entered the 1956–57 season as heavy favourites to repeat as Stanley Cup champions. In the space of one year they had gone from champion-in-waiting to established powerhouse.

"I am a lucky fellow," Toe Blake wrote on the season's eve. "I have the greatest collection of hockey stars in many years, maybe of all time, and yet they are unselfish stars. They play and think as a team. So I stand pat. The Canadiens should win the regular season title and the Stanley Cup again. My men are confident, as they should be, but not cocky."[8]

Much to the surprise of many, the Canadiens faltered a little, in large part because of injuries befalling the team's biggest stars.

On the morning of October 23, Plante was once again felled in practice. This time, however, it was not because of a shot by a teammate but instead from a bronchial attack, which laid him up in a hospital bed for a few days. After a battery of tests, the depth of Plante's asthma was discovered. Having not suffered an attack of consequence for almost a decade, Plante had falsely believed that his asthma had subsided. Gerry McNeil was summoned from the Montreal Royals to take Plante's spot. After a year away from hockey, McNeil returned to the game, albeit in a less stressful situation as a minor league goaltender with the Royals.

Just as Plante prepared to resume playing after a few days, he had to return to the hospital because of an allergic reaction. After another set of tests it was discovered that he was allergic to eggs. Forever afterward his breakfast would consist of fried ham.

McNeil's nine-game-stint with the Canadiens didn't reignite a contest between him and Plante. Giving up 31 goals and winning only four of his nine games, McNeil had the slumping Canadiens eagerly looking forward to Plante's return. When Plante was pronounced healthy again, McNeil was returned to the Royals. He would never play another NHL game.

As the season progressed, the Canadiens found themselves trailing the resurgent Red Wings. On March 17, the Red Wings came to the Forum and escaped with a 2–1 victory, clinching their eighth regular-season championship in nine years. A beaming Jack Adams, the Red Wings general manager, boasted that the Canadiens' time as the league's dominant team had been "the shortest ten years of my life."9

As the regular season came to a close, the only excitement left was the chase for the Vezina Trophy. Glenn Hall, the Red Wings super-sophomore, had proven that his superb rookie season had been no fluke. In those days the Vezina Trophy was awarded to the goalie who had given up the least amount of goals over the season.

"I was two goals behind on Saturday night when we played the Black Hawks in Montreal, but this was our last game and Hall had two," Plante wrote later. "The Red Wings were playing at Toronto. We then started our games at 8:30 p.m. while Toronto games started at 8:00. When we skated out I looked up at the scoreboard; Toronto was leading 1 to 0, which left me only one goal behind."10

Every goalie starts each game expecting to earn a shutout. A shutout is predicated on many things, the least of which is a large chunk of luck. But on that particular night against the Black Hawks, Jacques didn't *hope* to record a shutout. He *needed* to record a shutout if there was going to be any hope of his defending his beloved Vezina Trophy. Of course, Plante was not the only one who felt this pressure. His teammates also sensed the tension, and that night's crowd also betrayed a slight anxiety. Every time Plante made a stop, the crowd roared and cheered.

"Halfway through the second period Toronto scored again," Plante recalled. "That made it even for Hall and me. I tried not to think about it and concentrate purely on handling even the easier shots with utmost caution."[11]

With nine minutes remaining, the final score of the Detroit–Toronto game was posted on the scoreboard. The Red Wings had won, but Hall had allowed three goals. Now Plante held a one-goal lead in the race for the Vezina. All he had to do was keep the Black Hawks from scoring for the next nine minutes.

Not one shot made its way past Plante, who won his second straight Vezina Trophy. As the final buzzer sounded he felt released from the pressure. "I left the ice in a hurry, not even waving at the cheering fans. They must have thought me ungrateful, but I was rushing for the washroom where I was sick to my stomach."[12]

Plante finished the regular season seven wins behind the league-leading Glenn Hall, and once again had the fewest losses in the league. His nine shutouts were twice as much as the next leading goaltender's and five more than Hall's. Plante's goals-against average of 2.02 was the league's best.

And yet Glenn Hall, who finished behind Plante in every statistical category except wins, wrestled the first-team all-star honours from him, and Plante had to settle for being the goalie on the second all-star team.

Recognition among the hockey establishment was hardwon for Plante. For many outside of Montreal, his success was explained more by the skill of those he played with rather than by his own skill. For those who chose to overlook Plante and his numbers, the main reason was ironically Doug Harvey. Adoration for the great Harvey was so immense that many subscribed to the theory that Plante's success was a result of playing behind the unparalleled defenceman. Without Harvey, they reasoned, Plante was an ordinary goaltender, albeit one with a streak of eccentricity.

Widely ignored by the media in the other league cities, Plante's most vocal champion was his coach. "First of all, Jacques is not only great at stopping the puck. He's great at helping out his defense and the forwards by playing the puck for them around the net," argued Toe Blake. "He lifts a team with his chatter and you know as long as he's out there, our fellows will know where the opposing players are. He has the faculty of stopping the very difficult shots. When I say he's the best goalkeeper in hockey today, I'm not over-stating his case one bit."[13]

As the playoffs dawned, many anticipated a fourth straight final involving the Canadiens and the Red Wings. After the tightness of the regular season, however, the playoffs were decidedly anticlimactic. The

Red Wings were once again upset in the semifinals, this time by the Boston Bruins. In the other series, the Canadiens repeated their five-game series victory over the Rangers from the season before, setting up a finals clash with the Bruins.

If there was one team responsible for the Canadiens' slide into second place, it was the Bruins. In their 14 meetings that season, Boston had defeated Montreal seven times and tied them on three other occasions. Even the Rocket, long a Bruins tormentor, had scored against them only twice all year.

Over the course of the series the Bruins came to learn that the Canadiens team they faced in the regular season was a mere shadow of the team they now encountered. In game one, they also found out that the 35-year-old Rocket still possessed a little of the old spark.

"On Saturday," wrote Baz O'Meara in the *Montreal Star*, "the fiery goal getter erupted with a four goal explosion, and when the duel had settled Canadiens were home with a 5–1 victory in the first game of their best-of-seven Stanley Cup series with the Boston Bruins. Nobody this year has so dominated a game as the Rocket did. He wasn't only great on offense, he was wonderful on defense. . . . When it was all over nearly fifteen thousand fans gave him an ovation that he will long remember. . . . At thirty-five years of age he had done something that would live long in the annals of the game as a very singular feat."[4]

Goals would be harder to come by in the second game. The first two periods remained scoreless as Plante battled with Bruins goalie Don Simmons. However, a little over two minutes into the third, Jean Béliveau lifted a backhand over a helplessly prone Simmons to break the deadlock. It was all the offence that Jacques Plante would need. Thanks to his sixth career playoff shutout in the Canadiens' 1–0 win, Montreal found itself with a two-game advantage.

The year before, the Canadiens had allowed the Red Wings a sliver of hope in the third game. The Bruins would enjoy no such luxury in a thoroughly dominating 4–2 win that put Montreal on the brink of a repeat championship. "There was no turning point in the game," voiced a grim Milt Schmidt, the Bruins coach. "We were never in it."[5]

Simmons and Plante hooked up in another display of goaltending acumen in game four, and this time Plante was the only one to allow the puck to pass the goal line. Simmons required no more, and thanks to an empty-net goal, the Bruins were able to make the trip back to Montreal for game five.

Just like the year before, a sense of anticipation surrounded the fifth game as the city of Montreal once again readied itself for a big cele-bration. "If Jacques Plante is as hot as he has been so far in holding Bruins to four goals in four games they will prevail," wrote the *Montreal Star* the morning of the game.[16]

That night's game, held before a record Montreal Forum crowd of 15,286, was a chippy affair. Boston, facing elimination, came out in attack mode. As the first period concluded in a Montreal 1–0 lead, tempers boiled over into an on-ice brawl.

Fourteen seconds into the second period, Montreal upped the lead to 2–0, thanks to a Dickie Moore tally. Fifteen minutes later, Boom Boom Geoffrion made the score 3–0, and the celebration began in earnest as the Canadiens cruised to a 5–1 win.

As Canadiens captain Rocket Richard skated towards centre ice to accept the Stanley Cup before delirious supporters, there were acco-lades all around. In Montreal, Jacques Plante, who had permitted only five goals in the five-game final, was hailed as a goaltending great. Over the course of the two Stanley Cup seasons, Jacques had stopped 2,924 shots, or 92.3 per cent of all shots directed his way.

Beyond Montreal, acclaim for Plante's achievements was decidedly muted, as the *Toronto Star*'s Milt Dunnell pointed out. "Jake has better luck when he's on his own – when he doesn't have to depend on the judgment of others. There's no ballot for the Vezina trophy, the Oscar of the goaltending trade. Jake has that and the grand that goes with it. There's no ballot for the Stanley Cup either. Jake has been good for the Habs and they've been good for him. Beyond the fact that they dis-couraged him from wearing his hand-knit toque, the Habs have per-mitted Plante to play pretty much as he wished – as long as he kept the puck from his net. That's a privilege he wouldn't have enjoyed on many clubs. He'd have been warned, fined, or benched for taking off on solo flights during a game. There's an old belief that a goalie's place is in the net. Jacques may even change that tradition. In years to come, coaches may demand a goalie with legs – one who can help the defense by rounding up stray pucks. . . ."

"It will be called the Plante system of goaling. But first, someone will have to discover Jacques. He's still a secret outside Montreal."[17]

11

THE TRUE TEST
OF A CHAMPION

JACQUES PLANTE WAS A man of routine. It was a routine based
on trial and error, on what Plante had learned through years of exper-
imentation and experience. All with one goal in mind: to be the greatest goaltender the sport of hockey had ever seen.

His preparation was remarkably meticulous and scientific, almost
robotic in its approach. He would always wrap the tape exactly 17 times
around the blade of his stick, ensuring that the balance and the weight
of the stick were the same for every game. He would sharpen his skates
only once each season, exactly at the halfway point. Such was the precision of his routine that he would even schedule certain days to cut
his fingernails and toenails. "There's not a part of goaltending that
Jacques Plante hadn't thought about and analyzed, formed his opinion,
and then blocked out the rest of the world," commented noted hockey
writer Jack Falla.[1]

Plante possessed the game's most analytical mind. As goaltender,
there could be long stretches when he didn't face any shots from the
opposing team. These times of calmness allowed him to contemplate
and then process the many intricacies of the sport.

He was astute enough to recognize any weaknesses in his own game
and then make necessary adjustments. Such had been the case with
his weight, a constant concern in his first few years in the league as it

plummeted to dangerously low levels. He was officially listed as being six feet tall and weighing 175 pounds, but it was not uncommon for him to lose pounds during a game, and by the end of the season his weight could sometimes be as low as 149 pounds. To combat the loss, the Canadiens' medical team prescribed pills designed to help him maintain his weight. He also began eating five meals a day. To maintain his strength, he would take a nap every afternoon and attempt to sleep for at least 10 hours every night.[2] Nevertheless, he always seemed to find himself feeling lethargic right before games, so he began taking a prescribed half tablet of Aspirin two hours before the opening faceoff. According to Plante, the medication sharpened his reflexes and helped relieve his sluggishness.

Unfortunately, Plante's battle with asthma was not as easily solved as his weight problem, as illustrated by his bronchial attack in the 1956–57 season. Plante's difficulties with asthma would continue into the 1957–58 season.

Even worse, Plante's asthma would be only one of many afflictions that would handicap the 1957–58 Montreal Canadiens. Only three players, Dickie Moore, Claude Provost, and Phil Goyette, would participate in all 70 of the team's games that season, though Moore played the last five weeks with his left hand in a plaster cast.

Training camp provided a harbinger of what was to come as the parade to sick bay began before the season was even under way. Boom Boom Geoffrion, who had been unable to play the whole schedule since leading the league in scoring in 1954–55, found himself back in the hospital with a flu that developed into a case of pneumonia that shelved him throughout a large part of training camp and the first five games of the season.

He was soon joined in the hospital by Plante, who underwent a sinus operation that kept him out of the season's first six games. Into the breach stepped Charlie Hodge from the Montreal Royals.

It was three years since Hodge had been called up to replace an incapacitated Plante, and this time he was determined to make an impression. In his six games, the Canadiens won four and tied two. Even more impressive was that the undersized Hodge had allowed only 10 goals during his stint, for a 1.67 goals-against average. Despite his performance, there was no discussion of keeping him with the Canadiens, even as a standby for an increasingly unreliable Plante.

Plante resumed his position in the net on October 26 and backstopped the Canadiens to a 4–3 win over the Boston Bruins.

Four nights later, the Canadiens were in Toronto to play the Maple Leafs. And once again, Plante was felled by an asthma attack and unable to play. Coach Toe Blake was forced to go with the standby goalie provided by the Maple Leafs. Normally the goalie for the Toronto Marlboros (the Leafs' junior team), 19-year-old Len Broderick, was paid $25 per game by the Leafs to sit in the stands and be at the ready. Plante's absence and the presence of an untested youngster didn't help the Leafs, who once again fell victim to the Canadiens' powerful offence in a 6–2 defeat.

After sitting out another two games, Plante made his triumphant return against the Red Wings on November 7 at the Forum, shutting out Detroit in a 6–0 Canadiens whitewash.

The real test for Plante would come six days later, when the Canadiens once again made their way to Toronto, where Plante had suffered his last few asthma attacks. Looking to avoid another attack by changing his environment, Plante, with Blake's approval, checked into the Westbury Hotel, which was farther uptown and closer to Maple Leaf Gardens than the Royal York Hotel where the rest of the team continued to stay. The change appeared to do him good as the Canadiens faced off against the Leafs on November 13, with Plante, asthma free, patrolling the Montreal goal in a 4–2 Canadiens victory. But the real story once again was Rocket Richard – this time, though, for all the wrong reasons.

Despite his advancing age, the Rocket was enjoying the best start of his distinguished career. Heading into that night's game against the Leafs, the 36-year-old Canadiens captain found himself once more in hot pursuit of that long-elusive scoring title. In the first 13 games of the season, the Rocket led all scorers, with 11 goals and 12 assists for 23 points, highlighted a few weeks earlier when he had become the first player to hit the 500-goal mark in career goals.

On this particular night, however, there would be no celebration. On a seemingly innocuous play in front of the Leafs net, the Rocket found himself at the bottom of a pileup when Toronto's Marc Reaume inadvertently stepped on Richard's right foot, almost severing his Achilles tendon. It would be another three months before the Canadiens had the services of their captain, and even then many weren't certain he would come back the same player.

A month later, Jean Béliveau suffered a rib injury that sidelined him for a month. According to the count of Toe Blake, it was the Canadiens' sixth major injury of a season still not halfway completed.

And then, on the morning of January 28, 1958, another accident made all the other injuries pale in comparison. In a spirited practice,

Boom Boom Geoffrion collided with a teammate and fell. Soon, Geoffrion was writhing around on the ice in extreme pain.

He was rushed across the street to the hospital, where doctors immediately diagnosed a ruptured bowel and performed two hours of emergency surgery. His outlook was so dismal that before the surgery, a priest was called in to administer the last rites.

Fortunately, the operation was a success. In the *Montreal Star*, Red Fisher reported on "the delicate, painful sewup job that probably will keep him from active competition for the remainder of the season. The doctors certainly wouldn't want to risk him taking any more body checks this season with that kind of a delicate injury. Geoffrion's injury is a tragic climax to what has been a catastrophic string of injuries to the Stanley Cup champions."[3]

As if that wasn't enough, a week later reports began to surface of a wrist injury suffered by Dickie Moore.

Under Blake's tutelage, Moore had finally blossomed into the league's leading scorer and was hoping to join his two fellow members of the Class of '31 – Béliveau and Geoffrion – in winning an Art Ross Trophy for the most points in the league. X-rays hadn't revealed a break in the wrist, and Moore had played on, but the pain refused to subside, and a week and a half later he was diagnosed as indeed having a fractured left wrist.

Facing the prospect of missing both the remainder of the season and the playoffs, Moore made the daring decision to play the rest of the year. Bill Head, the Canadiens' physiotherapist, who was rapidly becoming the most valuable member of the team in a year dominated by injuries, constructed a cast that left Moore's thumb free and allowed him to slide his plastered hand into a glove. In one of the most courageous displays in the annals of hockey, Moore finished the season, capturing the league's scoring title with 84 points.

If there was one other constant to the Canadiens' season besides the injuries, it was the team's ability to keep winning despite the continued shuffling of players in and out of the lineup. Since his sinus and asthma troubles early in the season, Plante had been at his best, a fact that wasn't going entirely unnoticed as the Canadiens held an insurmountable first-place lead – and as their goalie maintained an overwhelming lead in the race for the Vezina Trophy.

The maladies continued, and even Toe Blake wasn't immune. On February 20, immediately after a game against the Bruins, he entered the hospital to have an unwanted item dislodged from his chest.

Reported the *Montreal Star*, "Blake was probably the happiest ingoing patient in the history of the medical profession after last night's caper in which the remarkable 'Rocket' Richard returned to action after a three months layoff and promptly accounted for two of the Canadiens' four goals in a 4–0 Montreal win."[4]

Despite the plethora of injuries, the team continued to win at an astounding clip, clinching first place on February 27 in Toronto, almost a month before the season's conclusion. It was a true test of the team's mettle, one they were passing with flying colours, but one they would have to take again and again.

In a practice in Toronto on the morning of March 11, Plante took a wicked shot from Henri Richard and slumped to the ground in obvious pain as he gripped his left shoulder. Fortunately for the Canadiens, Plante had suffered no more than a seriously bruised shoulder.

Two nights later, the Canadiens found themselves in Boston, and Plante, despite his sore shoulder, took to the nets. The "game was savage in its conduct, shattering in its bodychecking and brutal in its high-sticking," proclaimed the *Montreal Star*. "It was a game that teetered dangerously out of control on several occasions, and one that finally lost its final vestige of sanity or usefulness at 6:15 of the second period," with the Canadiens leading 1–0.[5]

Vic Stasiuk of the Bruins had parked himself in the Montreal crease with his stick held high. In an effort to remove him, Canadiens defenceman Doug Harvey bumped into him. Stasiuk collapsed into Plante, whose skull struck the crossbar as Stasiuk's stick ravaged his face. Plante would remember nothing of the collision.

"I was watching the puck in the corner of the rink and the next thing I knew I was on the ice and Hector" – Canadiens trainer Hector Dubois – "was pouring water into my mouth. . . . I blacked out for the first time in my life."[6]

"He lay prone on the ice for several moments, and finally was removed from the site where a police ambulance rushed him to Carney Hospital . . .," wrote Red Fisher the following day. "For a time last night when Plante was carried off the Boston Garden ice bleeding profusely and his head rolling from side to side as he fought off the blackness of insensibility there were grave fears that the National Hockey League champions would lose their goalie for a long period."[7] There were in fact fears that he'd suffered a spinal injury.

There still remained 34 minutes to play, and with Plante obviously unavailable, Blake and the Canadiens were forced by the rules of the day to replace him with a goalie provided by the Bruins.

Sitting beside his father was 26-year-old John Aiken, former goalie for Boston University, who had graduated three years before and had played only semi-professional hockey since. He hurried towards the Canadiens dressing room.

Earlier in the season in Toronto, the Canadiens had been able to weather Plante's absence and defeated the Maple Leafs with loaned goaltender Len Broderick. They wouldn't be as fortunate on this evening.

Over the next seven minutes and 19 seconds, four shots eluded an overmatched Aiken. By the end of the second period the Bruins were ahead 6–1 and the game was effectively over. When the final buzzer sounded 20 minutes later, the score read 7–3 in the Bruins' favour.

Plante would spend the night in the hospital with a concussion, his injuries not as serious as initially feared. Not that he emerged completely unscathed: he had two nasty gashes on his face, one two inches in length, the other three inches. Plante would miss the next week's schedule of games, and would once again be replaced by the more than capable Charlie Hodge.

Plante returned for the season's last few games, winning his third consecutive Vezina Trophy, and he was firmly ensconced in the Montreal net as the Canadiens began their playoff quest for a third consecutive Stanley Cup championship.

Injuries had been the recurring theme of the season, with an astounding 32 different players being used. Yet in spite of all the turmoil the Canadiens still finished atop the standings, 19 points clear of their nearest competitor. In many ways the season represented a triumph for Frank Selke. He had built an organization so strong, with such a bounty of talented players, that despite the constant changeover, the inability to ice a consistent lineup, and serious injuries to each of his best players, the team didn't miss a beat.

Boom Boom Geoffrion watched the Canadiens drop the final two games of the season from the sidelines, and over his wife's objections, and those of his parents, he made the fateful decision to return to the ice.

The Canadiens' opposition in the semifinal round that year was the Detroit Red Wings. It was their fourth playoff meeting in the past five years, and while some of the names were familiar – Howe, Sawchuk, Kelly, and Pronovost among them – this Red Wings team was merely a shadow of its former glory, as the Canadiens would conclusively prove in the first two games of the series, held at the Montreal Forum.

In the Canadiens' 8–1 opening-game thrashing, Red Fisher wrote that "for Richard, it was a two-goal, two-assist night, and for Phil Goyette, a wondrous hat-trick, the first he has ever scored in National Hockey League play. And between them, along with goals by 'Boom Boom' Geoffrion, Jean Béliveau and Dickie Moore, they wrote the script for one of the easiest playoff victories in Canadiens history."[8]

Lost amidst the offensive explosion was the play of Jacques Plante, who had allowed only one shot to cross the goal line while keeping the other 39 out of the net. In the second game, two more goals from the Rocket's smouldering stick provided the margin of victory as the Canadiens took a two-game lead with a convincing 5–1 win.

Having been humiliated twice in Montreal, the Red Wings returned home a dispirited bunch. However, game three would be different. It would bring to mind the glorious playoff contests of a few years before. And once again, it would pit Jacques Plante and Terry Sawchuk in a personal battle for goaltending supremacy.

There Plante and Sawchuk stood, once again, on opposite ends at the Detroit Olympia. On one end stared the game's greatest goaltender; while on the other end stared the former owner of the title.

Plante was the first to blink as a long shot from centre ice launched by Forbes Kennedy evaded his grasp. The 1–0 Detroit lead held into late in the second period, when the game was stopped for a long stretch after Plante was victimized by a Bob Bailey charge. A wobbly Plante left the ice, and fearing an extended wait the referees immediately ended the second period and tacked the remaining time into the third period. Suddenly, the direction of the game and the series were uncertain. But Plante returned, and in what was described as the "greatest goaltending display of the season," held the charging Wings at bay until Dickie Moore tied the score minutes later.[9]

Plante and Sawchuk were now taking turns in a performance for the ages. The Red Wings had the better of the play in a scoreless third period but were unable to beat Plante. In the overtime, the Canadiens were turned away by Sawchuk on three breakaways.

It truly was "sudden death." As soon as reserve forward André Pronovost's first shot of the game, 12 minutes into the extra period, made its way past a heroic Sawchuk, the collective groan of a sellout Olympia crowd told the tale.

For the goalie, overtime rewards the one who is able to survive the longest, and celebrates his achievement, and on this night it rewarded Jacques Plante.

"Plante had been tremendous," remarked the *Montreal Star*. "He had been unbeatable in a first period when the clawing Wings, fighting desperately to restore a measure of dignity to their name after 8–1 and 5–1 capitulations in Montreal, threw everything at him. Twelve times they tested this lean, almost unhealthy looking goalie, and 12 times he hardly betrayed a flicker of emotion with miraculous saves. Sawchuk was equally brilliant at the other end of the rink but with only six saves to handle."[10]

Two nights later, Plante, after a scoreless first period, was bombarded by a 15-shot Red Wing attack in the second period that saw three goals go past him. Countering for the Canadiens with their lone goal had been Rocket Richard. The Red Wings entered the third period with what appeared to be a comfortable 3–1 lead over the Canadiens. However, if the Red Wings thought their third-period lead was safe, the Rocket was about to disabuse them of the notion.

The Red Wings made the mistake of taking a penalty two minutes into the period and thus unleashed the game's most lethal power play. Parked at the side of the net, the Rocket made the score 3–2. Four and a half minutes later, the undisciplined Red Wings inexplicably took another penalty, and this time Dickie Moore made them pay, tying the game at three.

The next day's *Montreal Star* told the remaining tale. "The crowd shrieked madly when Henri Richard stole the puck from defenseman Warren Godfrey and was stopped spectacularly by goalie Sawchuk a moment later, but there was still the 'Rocket' to be heard from. He stood about 20 feet in front of Sawchuk, making squishing sounds on the ice with his hockey stick while Moore and the 'Pocket Rocket' battled desperately in front of the net. Then it fell clear and after a split second of hesitation, the shoulders that have powered more shots into National Hockey League goals than any player in the history of the game jerked convulsively, and before Sawchuk could move, the puck had whistled over his left shoulder into the net."[11]

Ten minutes still remained in the game, but now playing with a lead, Plante was unbeatable, and the Canadiens swept the Red Wings out of the playoffs. The final tally from the four-game series saw the incredible Rocket score seven goals, while the entire Red Wings team managed only six.

For the second consecutive season the Canadiens would be facing off in the finals with the Boston Bruins. In the regular season, Montreal finished 27 points ahead of the Bruins in the standings, and the enmity between the two teams had only grown in its intensity. Part of this was because of the Bruins' self-acknowledged ruggedness when playing the Canadiens. Realizing that they couldn't compete with Montreal on a skill level, they tried to shift the focus of the play into the physical sphere.

The opening game featured an astounding 21 penalties. In the end the Canadiens beat the Bruins 2–1; it was surprising that each goal was not scored on a power play. The game also highlighted how important Doug Harvey was to the Montreal cause.

"Harvey, who came out of the game with a slight cut over the eye and two glaring sores on his lips, was the giant of the evening," an impressed Red Fisher relayed to his readers. "He checked and blocked and placed himself unafraid in front of the Boston shots, and he did it without benefit of more than a token rest in each of the periods. He was clocked for 15 minutes and 34 seconds of action in the first period, 15 minutes and 44 seconds in the second, and altogether was on the ice more than 44 minutes during the energy-sapping game. It was a glorious hour for him, but he's had them before."[12]

A certain degree of shock greeted the Bruins' victory in the second game. The shock wasn't that Boston had equalled the series; the surprise was the ease of their 5–2 victory.

Returning for a home game, the Bruins found in the third game that their ability to put pucks behind Jacques Plante had been left back in Montreal, and with the Rocket punching in two goals, the Canadiens had all the offence they needed in a 3–0 whitewash. Plante, however, was not as sturdy in the fourth game, and the Bruins evened the series with a 3–1 win on home ice, setting up a crucial fifth game at the Montreal Forum.

The *Toronto Star*'s Red Burnett described the fifth game as "a hockey classic that rates with anything served up in Stanley Cup play. It was by far the best game of this set, replete with sparkling passing plays and scintillating individual efforts executed at a lightning pace." For the first time in the finals, the Canadiens displayed "the prowess that characterized their march to an easy pennant and new team scoring record during the regular season. But despite this increased tempo, they were life and death to shade this amazing Boston club, chiefly because of the superb goaltending of Don Simmons. The Habs blasted 47 shots at him, compared to 40 leveled at Canadiens goalie Jacques Plante."[13]

In addition to the sellout crowd at the Montreal Forum, millions of television viewers sat watching the game unfold in the comfort of their living rooms or at their local bar. As everyone anxiously waited for the overtime to commence, *Hockey Night in Canada* host Tom Foley asked his intermission guest, Frank Selke, the question on everybody's mind: What did he think was going to happen? "Maurice Richard hasn't done much tonight," Selke confidently replied. "He usually comes through at a time like this. I think he'll score the winning goal."[14]

The astute Selke was correct. In the first three periods the Rocket had been unusually quiet, mustering only one shot on a seemingly unbeatable Simmons. Five and half minutes into the overtime period, however, he posted his second shot on Simmons. Game over.

"Henri won the face-off in our end and passed to Dickie Moore after carrying it out," the Rocket told the assembled media after scoring his fourth game-winning goal of that spring's playoffs. "Dickie gave it to me at the right time and I cut to the left. I was thinking of a pass, but when their whole team folded to the right after I gave a little deke, I just carried on and let go from about 35 feet."[15]

It was a motivated group of Montreal Canadiens that took to the ice in Boston three nights later to try to end this toughest of Stanley Cup finals. And no player was more intent on winning the game and finishing the series that night than Jacques Plante. On the morning of the game he had suffered another asthma attack. In this season, in a year in which the Canadiens had overcome so many obstacles, their goalie would have to overcome his biggest challenge yet.

He had been unable to partake in his usual nap on the day of the game because of a persistent cough and shortness of breath. He walked around aimlessly, feeling as if he wasn't really there.

On the afternoon of the game, Toe Blake took his team to a movie theatre, where they watched the World War II epic *The Bridge on the River Kwai*. It was a savvy move by the canny Blake to have his team watch a movie in which the twin themes of bravery and perseverance in the face of overwhelming circumstances played out.

No doubt inspired by the movie and desperately wanting to end the series, the Canadiens stormed out to a quick 2–0 lead before the game was even two minutes old. Montreal added two more goals in the second period to offset a late first-period goal by the Bruins. With three points, Boom Boom Geoffrion, near death only three months before, was sparking the Canadiens, who in between periods found themselves whistling the theme from *The Bridge on the River Kwai*.

With the temperature at 80 degrees on ice level, Plante's problems became exacerbated. As the air grew stale, his breathing gradually became more shallow. The third period became a matter of survival for him, as the Canadiens clung to their lead, which shrank to a dangerously close score of 4–3 after two goals by the Bruins.

With only seven minutes standing between the Canadiens and a third consecutive Stanley Cup triumph, Plante began to seriously labour. He found himself gasping for air that wasn't there. Standing up was starting to become difficult, and his ability to focus on the opposition was becoming steadily weaker. Somehow, he continued to block the shots of an increasingly desperate Bruins squad anxious to tie the game. He refused to give in. He reached inside himself and found the limits of his fortitude and he pushed past them.

With a little over a minute remaining, the frantic Bruins pulled Don Simmons in favour of an extra skater. Boston quickly attacked, but Doug Harvey stood up at his own blue line, intercepted a pass, and sped towards the vacated Bruins net. His first shot was blocked by a desperate dive from Larry Regan. Harvey then gathered up the rebound and sealed the game and the Stanley Cup.

An exhausted Jacques Plante collapsed into the arms of his teammates. He had gone to a place within himself he had never gone before. Carried off the ice by the team's publicist, Camil DesRoches, and physiotherapist Bill Head, he broke down and sobbed in the dressing room, releasing all the stress and tension that he had been holding in.

"I'm glad it's over," Plante told the *Toronto Star*. "It was a tough series. Tonight it was very tough."[16]

It had been the toughest of years for Jacques Plante and the Canadiens. And on that warm spring night in Boston they sat in a sweltering dressing room with the Stanley Cup, champions once again.

12

SOLITARY MAN

THE MONTREAL CANADIENS of the late 1950s were the true definition of a team both on and off the ice. They were in essence a true band of brothers. Not only did they play with each other, they played for each other. A team made up of great individual talents, they were able to coalesce and form a cohesive unit.

With three consecutive Stanley Cups, they stood at the pinnacle of the hockey world, and there appeared to be no end in sight. They had set a standard for winning. However, it was in many ways a double-edged sword. They had cast a tremendous shadow over all those who came after them. Nothing less than a Stanley Cup was acceptable now, for them or those who followed in their footsteps in Montreal.

Theirs was a team free of division and strife. They played together, partied together, lived near one another, took vacations together. With one notable exception.

"We were a close team," Henri Richard fondly remembers today. "We all got together after the game for a beer. Everyone, that is, except for the goalie."[1]

"Jacques Plante was a loner," says Phil Goyette, who played with him on three teams, including the Canadiens. "He didn't mix with the players that much off the ice. He did his thing and that's it. His manner was similar wherever he played. He was a loner. He didn't share or come to any gatherings or parties with the other players."[2]

Unless it was a meeting called by the team's captain, in which case Plante felt obligated to appear, he would rarely join his teammates in the post-game festivities at the local bar. And if he did, he would always quietly disappear when it came time to pay.

"That's why they sometimes call me a 'loner,'" he told *Hockey Illustrated* in 1962. "I keep to myself a lot during the season. The more a goalie associates with the other players the more chance there is of an argument over something that happened in the game."[3] Many of his teammates attributed Plante's absence more to his legendary cheapness than to anything else.

Instead of spending his evenings out at the bar, Jacques preferred to work on improving his game. If on the road he would retreat to his hotel room and review what had happened that night. In his head he would replay the game, down to the minutest detail. He would jot down notes on what he'd observed during that night's game. These notes were crucial for him. They gave him the opportunity to study the opposing players and discover their weaknesses and patterns.

Of course, these nights spent alone in his hotel room also had the advantage of preserving his finances, and while many of his teammates chided him for his frugality, he was one of the first among them to start investing in opportunities outside the hockey world.

In 1959, much to the amusement of his teammates, Jacques invested as a co-owner of a beauty parlour on St. Hubert Street in Montreal. In time he would expand his investments to include various apartment complexes, all of which brought him a decent income.

He also took time to indulge in some writing. He was not the first hockey player or athlete to write a column for a newspaper or a magazine, but unlike many of his contemporaries, he actually took the time to write his own articles. He used these articles to impart his knowledge of goaltending as well as to discuss the hockey world from his own perspective. Plante described what went into becoming a professional athlete, writing about various diets and different training programs and practice routines.

Writing was also something that could pass the long hours spent on the train. At the time, every NHL team used trains as its main mode of transportation from city to city. Over the years, many on the Canadiens have commented that it was the train travel that brought the team closer. With trips that sometimes took days, the team was clustered together for large stretches of time.

Many of the players passed the time talking about and debating about hockey, playing endless games of cards, or catching up on their sleep. Jacques kept himself apart even on the train. His teammate Jean Béliveau, also not a card player, fondly remembers private conversations between the two, some about hockey, but most about life, family, and a future that looked limitless for both of them.

"Jacques was not a card player so we had many long talks on the train on different subjects, not only sports," Béliveau recalls today. "He was an avid reader. He was knitting at the time as well. But on those long train rides he mostly read. . . . He was an introvert, and he liked it that way. He was very happy like that."[4]

Béliveau was able to gain an insight into Jacques that was rare among his teammates. In Béliveau, the notoriously private Plante found that rare person whom he could open up with – to a certain degree. Their bond was based on a mutual respect, and was one they would maintain for the rest of their lives.

On the ice, Jacques Plante was considered by his teammates to be an individualist. But to a man none ever questioned his commitment to the game, or to the team. They knew that every move he made on the ice was to help ensure a Canadiens victory. If he thought an innovation would improve his own game, he believed the team would also benefit. Though a loner, Plante was unable to separate himself from the team, feeling that what was best for both wasn't mutually exclusive. His teammates didn't always see it that way.

"Like many goalies, Jacques was pretty much a solitary sort, and could be abrasive at times," Béliveau wrote in his memoirs. "That doesn't mean he wasn't a team man. He was, but he had his own way about him."[5]

"He was a very astute hockey man, sometimes too much, sometimes with some of his teammates," remembers Dickie Moore. "It wasn't his fault that the puck went into the net. But that was his determination way of thinking."[6]

In his book *Goaltending*, Plante wrote, "From now on, if you have a tendency to point the finger at the goalie, try to replay each goal and you will notice that the goalie is seldom guilty. Watch what goes on in front of the net and you'll get a better idea of why the goal went in."[7]

Plante always maintained that the goalie had to be a pillar of strength, especially in front of his teammates. He felt that admitting a goal was a sign of weakness. After all, he believed the goalie made up between 50 per cent and 60 per cent of the team.

Not admitting that goals were his fault also served a more personal purpose for Plante. He had seen many of his fellow goalies, including his two predecessors in the Montreal nets, Bill Durnan and Gerry McNeil, succumb to nerves and have their careers end prematurely. He personally witnessed the decline of McNeil, who replayed goals over and over in his head to the point that it consumed him, eventually leading to his early retirement. Plante, however, took an opposite approach. By shirking the blame, he was able to quickly move on, not dwelling on what had come before.

"Jacques Plante was the best goalie as far as I'm concerned," says Henri Richard today. "He was the first at so many things." When asked about the man, he shrugs, then adds, "Goalies are always different, they're lonesome guys, and they're different people."[8]

"A team is made up of different personalities. Some guys have a different way of doing things and you have to respect that, especially if the individual feels that it helps his play," says Phil Goyette. "He was there as a team player all the time."[9]

Perhaps it was Ron Caron, a scout within the Montreal organization, who put it best. "Maybe Plante wasn't a great team player, but players tolerated him because he put money in their pocket. The Canadiens made their money on bonuses for Stanley Cup championships. They respected that about him."[10]

Plante's teammates were grateful that he was on their team, but there were five other teams not as fortunate. So at the NHL annual meetings in the summer of 1958, other teams sought to nullify what they called the "Plante advantage" by trying to pass a rule prohibiting the goalie from leaving his crease to play the puck. The change was voted down by a majority who felt "that a goalie's wanderings outside his crease could not properly be circumscribed by legislation specifying feet, or even inches."[11]

"Jacques Plante, the Montreal goalie, started the wanderlust feature and was beyond the most nomadic puck-stopper in the league," reported the *Toronto Star*. "Several of the netminders on the other NHL teams have copied his roving style, but to a lesser degree."[12]

"Many tried to imitate him," recalls Jean Béliveau. "Jacques was very mobile on his skates. A lot of goalies began roaming out of the net like he did, but had trouble getting back in the net. Jacques was so quick, which was not the case for many of the other goalies who tried."[13]

Thus, Jacques Plante became the rarest of players. The league had already passed one rule aimed at stopping his practice of freezing the puck behind the net. Now they were trying to legislate his roaming out of the game, albeit unsuccessfully. Either way, there could be no question that Plante was having a profound impact on the game.

Jacques Plante was used to spectators hurling insults and sometimes food at him. He had developed a reputation for being immune to the criticisms of others, projecting an air of confidence in the face of doubt and disbelief. But it had never happened before at the Forum, in front of home spectators. The Montreal Forum was his sanctuary, and the goal was his home.

It was the Canadiens' eighth game of the 1958–59 season. In their first seven games, the team had won five games, lost one, and tied one. They had accomplished this despite the absence of the great Doug Harvey. The night of October 25 at the Forum seemed to begin like any other as the Canadiens jumped out to a quick 2–0 lead against the visiting Bruins. The mood began to change after Boston pumped five straight goals past a stunned Plante. The restless crowd slowly began to show their disgust, booing the players but singling out an embattled Plante.

"If the goaler makes a mistake everybody's watching, everybody sees it, you know," claimed a sympathetic Harvey. "If a defenseman makes a mistake it's not as noticeable. And he can say, 'Let's go, now. Let's get that one back.' All Jacques can do is stand there and burn."[14]

The next night was a game against the Red Wings in Detroit, and Plante, with the sound of booing still reverberating in his head, almost single-handedly led Montreal to a 5–3 win. "Canadiens miss Harvey. Plante misses Harvey. But when the Detroit Red Wings threw 45 shots at the Canadiens net last night there was only Plante to stop them," wrote the *Montreal Star*.[15]

After tying Chicago 5–5 on Tuesday night and shutting out the Leafs 5–0 in Toronto, Plante made his return to the Forum the following Saturday night against the Chicago Black Hawks.

Nothing seemed out of the ordinary when Chicago's Earl Balfour shot the puck into the corner of the Canadiens' end, and Jacques darted out of his net to retrieve it. Plante beat a charging Balfour to the loose puck but didn't realize that the Black Hawk was right on top of him.

As soon as Plante did he rushed the clearing attempt, and instead of skimming alongside the backboards the puck plunked the side of the net and bounced back onto Balfour's stick. Circling in front of the empty Montreal net, Balfour scored the easy goal. A chorus of boos echoed through the Forum.

The Canadiens went on to lose to Chicago 4–2 as the press gathered around to mock the roaming Plante. The *Toronto Star* headlined Jacques' misfortune, and the *Hockey News* took it one step further. Under the banner headline "Roaming Jacques Plants One in the Wrong Place," it plastered two photographs over its cover page, one of Plante missing the puck and a second of Plante's reaction as the puck was in the back of the net.

"People have been waiting for years to see Plante caught that way," wrote a sympathetic Red Fisher. "They won't let him forget it for a long time."[16]

As his detractors howled at his misfortune, Plante found himself in crisis.

"Normally, Jacques Plante is one of the first to leave the Canadiens dressing room," Fisher wrote in the aftermath of Plante's public humiliation.

On Saturday night, though, only Dickie Moore was left in the room by the time Plante was ready to leave. Plante was pale and drawn as he shrugged into his coat. He hesitated before opening the door leading from the Canadiens room into the Forum hallway. Then he turned to a visitor who fidgeted at his side.

"Why," he asked, "did it have to happen here? Why here of all places?"

The goalie's hand shook slightly as he pulled on the dressing room door. The hallway empty and cold. People don't wait for autographs from a losing team. Plante thrust his hands deep into his coat pockets as we walked along the hall. He stared at the floor. He recalled that the Forum has been a graveyard for goalkeepers. It's an old story. The people almost drove Bill Durnan from the rink. They did it to Gerry McNeil, too.

Several minutes after the Chicago opening goal, and with the cries of the crowd still curling around Plante's ears, a Black Hawks player threw the puck into the Canadiens zone and Plante raced out almost as far as the blue line to prevent the Chicago player from breaking in on the nets unmolested.

"What made you come out that far after what happened with the first goal?" Fisher asked.

"I had to, that's all," he replied. "After the first period, I felt like staying out of the game. I know how Gerry McNeil felt, but at least the coach is on my side. That's worth more than anything else."

Two youngsters in their early teens looked at Plante, whispered rapidly to each other for a moment, shrugged their shoulders and then approached the goalie. They asked him to sign his name.

"At least," Plante grinned, "I've got somebody on my side."

He walked a little straighter as he disappeared in the traffic.[17]

After a scheduled week off, the Canadiens returned to Saturday night action at the Forum against the visiting New York Rangers. A still shaken Plante permitted six goals in a 6–5 Canadiens loss.

Suddenly the booing was the least of Plante's problems.

"The mighty Montreal Canadiens in town for tonight's game with the Leafs have a host of problems, accentuated by their eviction from first place in the National Hockey League last night," trumpeted the *Toronto Star* under the headline "Jacques' Jitters Woe for Toe." "Biggest of the many worries disturbing coach Toe Blake's customary serenity concerns Jacques Plante, merely the NHL's leading goaltender the past three seasons. Jake's goals-against-average has climbed to nearly three per game, almost one full goal over the mark he's maintained in winning the Vezina trophy for three successive seasons."

"Worse than that is Plante's nervousness," a frustrated Blake told the *Star*. "Our home fans here have been riding him and he's let it get his goat. It's affecting his work. He's been playing much better on the road because of this. He's got to get over it: after all, he's a professional. It isn't anything new. They've been at him a bit for years but it's been worse since he got caught out of his goal and Chicago scored on the empty net. You bet it's serious, any time there's something wrong with your goaltending it's serious. Even the Canadiens can't win a championship with bad goalkeeping."[18]

That night the Canadiens started a three-game road swing with a foray against the Leafs. It proved to be the tonic for Plante's problems, as he allowed only four goals in the three games, and the Canadiens skated off with two wins. Continuing his stellar road play, he was able to regain a modicum of confidence before he returned to the Forum for a home game against the Red Wings on November 20, 1958.

Plante still looked a little tentative as the Canadiens scraped out a 4–4 tie with the visiting Red Wings. But he had turned the corner. The tie against Detroit would kick off a streak of 15 straight games at home where Plante and the Canadiens went undefeated.

As the wins came, doubts about Plante and the Canadiens started to recede. Later in the season the team reeled off a second unbeaten streak – 12 games this time – that left them comfortably in first place. The team once again finished in first place by a staggering 18 points and once again dominated at awards time.

Plante captured his fourth consecutive Vezina Trophy by a whopping 50 goals over second-place Glenn Hall, now with Chicago. Dickie Moore repeated as scoring champion, establishing a new record with 96 points. Ralph Backstrom received the Calder Trophy as the league's top rookie. With an injury-plagued season, Doug Harvey forfeited the Norris Trophy to his own teammate, Tom Johnson.

Plante was joined on the first all-star team by teammates Johnson, Béliveau, and Moore, while Harvey and Henri Richard landed on the second-team all-stars.

On the eve of the playoffs, Toe Blake gathered his team around him. They had won the previous three Stanley Cups and were now gunning for an unprecedented fourth title. As his team sat attentively before him, Blake made them watch the film of last season's championship triumph as Toe, in the words of the *Montreal Star*, "provided the players with a winning spirit he hopes will carry on through the playoffs."[19]

"Toe Blake knew how to prime you for a game," Plante remembered later. "He knew what button to push to get the most out of guys because he always wanted to maintain the edge. Even if it was a so-called nothing game near the end of the season, he would always be saying things like, 'We might see this team in the playoffs so don't let up. If they give you a good run tonight, we'll have them believing that they can beat us and then we're in real trouble.' Toe kept us alert and always prepared."[20]

The Canadiens' opposition was a resurgent Chicago Black Hawks team that was making its first playoff appearance since 1953, the year a young Jacques Plante made his sparkling playoff debut in front of a boisterous Chicago crowd. With Glenn Hall's superior goaltending, and with the leadership of former Detroit star Ted Lindsay, the Black Hawks had started assembling a wealth of talent that would carry them for the next decade: Pierre Pilote, Stan Mikita, and the incomparable Bobby Hull, the game's most exciting player since the Rocket.

The opening contest ended as a 4–2 win for the Canadiens, but the score didn't reveal the true story. The feeble Black Hawks managed to put only 13 shots on a relaxed Plante, while the Canadiens bombarded Glenn Hall with 46 shots of their own. The second game served as a continuation as the Canadiens won again, 5–1.

Now heading to Chicago, Plante and the Canadiens knew they would be dealing with a ravenous home crowd. In the third game, the Black Hawks would exercise a modicum of revenge for past playoff defeats by defeating Montreal 4–2, gaining their first win of the series.

Although Blake was disappointed by the loss, he was more concerned with the health of one of his top stars. Shadowed in the first three games by Chicago's Glen Skov, Jean Béliveau had still managed to produce five points until a check by Skov knocked him out of the playoffs for good with two cracked vertebrae.

"You don't lose a guy like him without feeling it," said a sombre Blake. "He was going so well."[21]

Minus Béliveau in the fourth game, the Canadiens found themselves unable to muster much of an offence against the superb Hall in a 3–1 defeat that evened the series at two games apiece.

This series was going a long way to proving that Plante and Hall were the game's two best netminders. They had split the last four first-team all-star selections, and while Plante had a distinct hardware advantage in the form of Vezina trophies and Stanley Cups, it was Hall who was gradually emerging as his newest rival in the race for goaltending supremacy.

The Canadiens' offence, dormant so long, finally exploded in the crucial fifth game at the Montreal Forum, scoring four goals in the game's first 16 minutes, and then hanging on for a 4–2 victory that left them a win away from a return visit to the Stanley Cup finals.

The sixth game, in Chicago, would prove to be one of the most memorable in hockey history. According to Bernie Geoffrion it was "one of the wildest games I ever had the pleasure, or maybe displeasure would be the more appropriate word, to play in and witness."[22] Refereeing the game would be Red Storey, a man regarded as one of the league's firmest and fairest officials. Described by Red Fisher as "everybody's favourite referee," he had been given the unenviable assignment of maintaining control in a game where the ice was surrounded by 20,000 fanatics who jammed the Chicago Stadium past the point of capacity.

"The tension in the building was something like the night of the Richard Riot at the Forum four years earlier," Storey recalled later.

"I was in that one, too. I didn't let that interfere with the way I handled a game, though."[23]

The game saw the Canadiens emerge for the third period holding a tenuous advantage that soon disappeared in a frenetic period that left the game tied at four apiece with five minutes remaining in regulation.

Then Bobby Hull, the Hawks' swashbuckling superstar in waiting, grabbed hold of the puck and steamed towards the Montreal goal. All that stood between him and the goal was Canadiens defenceman Al Langlois, who lined the unsuspecting Hull up for a perfect hip check. As Hull was laid on the ice, the Black Hawks bench hollered for a tripping penalty. Red Storey's whistle remained in his pocket.

Temporarily losing their focus, the Black Hawks let up, and the Canadiens took advantage as the unheralded Claude Provost slipped the winning goal behind Hall and a stunned crowd with less than 90 seconds remaining.

"The goal didn't officially kill them," recalled Bernie Geoffrion in his memoirs, "but the Black Hawks were mortally wounded and as far as their fans were concerned the murderer was Red Storey."[24]

The crowd sat in shock for a moment and then exploded as one, as garbage and debris filled the air before cluttering the ice. Both the maligned Storey and the Canadiens found themselves dodging and ducking bottles, food, and various other materials. In an effort to get away from the barrage, the stoic Storey skated towards centre ice, where a fan rushed the ice to douse him with beer.

"I grabbed him," Storey recalled later, "and Doug Harvey grabbed him from the other side. Doug realized I was going to hit the guy so he yells at me, 'Red, you can't hit a fan. You can't hit a fan.' And bingo, he drives him. Doug could see I was still mad, so he hits the guy again. We let him go and he staggered off the ice. Doug never left me. He stood right with me at centre ice.

"Another guy had jumped over the screen on the other side. I didn't see him coming across the ice but Doug did and he hollered 'Look out.' The guy jumped on me from behind, so I dipped my shoulder and flipped him up in the air. Doug hit him with his stick and cut him. I think he needed about eighteen stitches. Nobody else came on the ice after that."[25]

The showering of debris continued for the next half an hour as the game was delayed. In attendance that night was NHL president Clarence Campbell, who passively sat in the crowd and remained ominously detached from the chaos. After a prolonged delay the two teams played out the final 90 seconds, with the Canadiens winning the game 5–4 and advancing to the Stanley Cup finals.

Immediately after the game, Campbell gave what he maintained was an "off the record" interview with Ottawa reporter Bill Westwick. Westwick, however, maintained that Campbell never asked for that assurance. According to Westwick, Campbell claimed that Storey "choked" and that he had "frozen" on two calls that should have been penalties against the Canadiens. Campbell went on to insult the beleaguered Storey, using such derogatory terms as "chicken."[26] Upon hearing the remarks, an irate Storey immediately resigned his post as an NHL referee. Campbell, while admitting his mistake, refused to back down or take back his disparaging comments.

After such a tumultuous affair with Chicago, the finals series against the upstart Maple Leafs was anticlimactic.

The thought of setting a record with a fourth consecutive Stanley Cup no doubt rested well in the mind of the Canadiens' general manager, Frank Selke. And to accomplish this, as well as a franchise record-breaking tenth Stanley Cup against the Toronto Maple Leafs, undoubtedly brought the builder of the Montreal dynasty a certain satisfaction. "We want this victory more than any of our preceding three," Selke told the Montreal Star, without confessing his more personal aspirations.[27]

Aside from an overtime loss to the Leafs in game three, the Canadiens proceeded to get the best of the determined Toronto team, taking an imposing three-games-to-one lead into the climactic game five, held at the Montreal Forum on April 18, 1959.

As the third period began, the question of the Canadiens' winning a record fourth consecutive Stanley Cup appeared to be answered, with their commanding 5–1 third-period lead. Then the eyes of the media and the crowd switched to the middle of the Canadiens bench, where, sitting by himself, dry towel hanging around his burly shoulders, was a man unaccustomed to not being on the ice. The crowd started chanting his name, over and over again, louder and louder.

Maurice Richard found himself relegated to the middle of the Montreal bench. Time and the advance of age were starting to take their toll on the proud Rocket. The Canadiens would win their fourth consecutive Stanley Cup without much of a contribution from him. So he sat there stoically on the bench despite the pleading of the crowd.

"I remember only one thing about the game in 1959 that marked the third time I had seen the Stanley Cup won," Dick Irvin Jr. wrote later. "When the final siren sounded at the Forum, the Canadiens had defeated Toronto 5–3. As usual, all the players not on the ice at the time leaped over the boards to start celebrating. All but one. Maurice Richard."[28]

Unlike the great teams that had come before them, Toe Blake's Canadiens were watched across the entire country. They were the first great team of the television era, viewed from coast to coast, and everyone in the country was able to witness their greatness.

The Canadiens were at the height of their reign, and were held up as a model of hockey excellence. And the next season would be their most eventful one yet.

13

CHANGING THE
FACE OF HOCKEY

THE SLAPSHOT CHANGED everything.

It was one of Plante's own teammates, Bernard "Boom Boom" Geoffrion, who became famous as the player who did the most to popularize – indeed originate – the slapshot. Before the slapshot, players had used three types of shots, the wrist shot, the flip shot, and the backhand. However, it was Geoffrion who stumbled upon a mysterious fourth shot, a shot that would have far-reaching consequences not only for his career but for the future of hockey.

"I had skated in on goal," Geoffrion recounted in his autobiography, "and released a wrist shot but missed the net. It always upset me when that happened but this time I blew up and began wildly slapping my stick at the puck as if to give it a spanking. I connected and the puck moved so fast it went through the net. I couldn't believe it! When I saw the puck come out the other side I thought to myself, this is something that goalies are going to be afraid of for a long, long time."[1]

News of Geoffrion's "accident" quickly spread throughout the sport, and soon many of the game's youngest stars were using the slapshot in their repertoire. Members of the goaltending profession weren't as enthusiastic.

Almost overnight, and before many goalies could adjust, the slapshot earned a reputation as the most powerful and, because it was the least accurate, the most dangerous shot in hockey. Because of its speed, the slapshot considerably shortened the goaltender's available reaction time. Coinciding with the increasing popularity of the slapshot was a disturbing rise in devastating injuries to the bare-faced goaltenders who patrolled the nets.

So great was the fear goaltenders had of the slapshot that opposing forwards began using the goalie's fear against him. "High shots to the head drove goaltenders crazy," recalled Geoffrion. "They were a shooter's way of intimidating the puck stopper. . . . Early in every game I would let one high shot go that was not far from the goalie's head. That made him think that all the rest of them were going to be high and it made it easier for me to score."[2] Unfortunately for the goaltending brethren, not all the shots missed.

Long stoppages in play were suddenly commonplace as trainers and doctors rushed to stitch up goalies wounded by pucks travelling at speeds upwards of 100 miles an hour. Also on the rise were concussions, broken jaws, broken cheekbones, and, most frighteningly, eye injuries. The potential for injury led many goalies to abandon their position, and in many cases the sport altogether, because of what became known in hockey circles as "rubber shock."[3]

"You can't be a goaltender and be afraid to get hit in the face," said Jacques Plante. "But you can't be a human being and not think about it."[4]

And yet, despite the threat of injury and disfigurement, even blindness, the goalies of the NHL continued to patrol their nets bare-faced. In their stubbornness, many refused to see that the game they knew was undergoing a significant upheaval.

Yet, in a league of only six teams, and with an abundance of players eagerly waiting in the minors, it was understandable that players were reluctant to challenge the unspoken code of the game. For most seasoned hockey men, the worst thing that could happen to a hockey player was the accusation that he was slowly becoming scared. In his own way, each player had concerns about his protection.

Overshadowing their fears, however, was the ever-present anxiety that seized each player, born of the certainty that this was not only what they did best but also the only profession that they were qualified for. Stuck in an untenable position, the players of the day continued to press on despite mounting concerns about their own safety. A player who refused to play hurt or abide by the owner's wishes faced the knowledge that his career in professional hockey would be a short one. The players were wholly dependent on the league's owners. The loyalty, allegiance, and reliability that the players demonstrated to the owners were not reciprocated in the slightest. As soon as he became a liability, a player was replaced, discarded by the team.

As the injuries to goalies mounted in number and severity, talk of goalies wearing masks increased. Someone was going to have to be the first to wear one. It was only a question of who.

In 1930, Clint Benedict had been the first goaltender in the NHL to sport a mask after having his nose broken by Montreal's Howie Morenz. He wore it only for the last five games of his career, and so it never had a chance to catch on. Since then, no goaltender in the NHL had worn protective facial gear in a league game. If that were to ever change, it would require a player who didn't fear reprisals from management, a player who could withstand the taunts of his peers and the condemnation of the hockey establishment, and, most important, a player who would enjoy success while wearing a mask, therefore dispelling the myth that a goalie's abilities were hampered by a mask.

At seven o'clock on the first Sunday in November 1959, a sellout crowd of 15,925 congregated at the venerable Madison Square Garden to watch the four-time defending Stanley Cup champion Montreal Canadiens, in first place in the NHL standings a month into the 1959–60 season, take on the hometown New York Rangers.

The game appeared to be a terrible mismatch. Opposing the champion Canadiens was a Rangers squad desperately clinging to fifth place in the six-team league. Hovering near the bottom of the standings was not unusual for the New Yorkers. Much to their fans' dismay, it had been a lengthy and torturous decade since the team had experienced any post-season success.

No one player epitomized this decade of dreariness for the Rangers more than their goaltender, Lorne "Gump" Worsley. He had become the recipient of an endless barrage of rubber as he entered his sixth year with the team.

Gaining his unique nickname from childhood friends for his resemblance to the comic-strip character Andy Gump, Worsley was defined by his flaccid, barely controlled goaltending style, and his honest and self-deprecating manner. (Early on in his tenure with the Rangers, Gump was asked by one of the city's beat reporters which team in the league gave him the most trouble. Without hesitation, and in all seriousness,

Gump slyly replied, "The New York Rangers.") This combination of qualities endeared him to a generation of New York sporting fans.

Gump Worsley was the most colourful player on the Rangers' roster but not the most talented. That honour belonged to Andy Bathgate. Proclaimed months before in *Sports Illustrated* as "the finest player to put on the red, white and blue uniform of the New York Rangers since the heyday of the great prewar wing, Bad Bill Cook," Bathgate was seen as one of the game's brightest and most promising stars.[5] He was part of the newest wave of young players who were storming the pro ranks, including Chicago's Bobby Hull. All carried with them hard, heavy, and accurate shots that put fear in the minds of the opposing goaltenders.

"As usual, Bathgate has the satisfaction as well as the responsibility of knowing that he is the heart of the Rangers," wrote *Sports Illustrated*, with Bathgate staring out from the cover. "Bathgate shot magnificently, skated with the puck so well that he stirred old-timers to memories of the great stickhandlers of bygone days and passed the puck with uncanny timing and aim."[6]

Validation of Bathgate's talents had come the previous spring, when he was awarded the Hart Trophy as the NHL's most valuable player. Making his accomplishment more impressive was the fact that the Rangers missed the playoffs, resulting in one of the rare times that a player on a non-playoff team was judged to be the league's best.

Even with Worsley manning the nets and Bathgate up front, the night's task remained daunting for the Rangers. What the Rangers, the Canadiens, and the sellout crowd couldn't have known when the puck was dropped on that cool Sunday evening was that after that night, the game of hockey would never be the same.

As the puck entered the Montreal zone, Bathgate gave chase. "I saw the puck coming around the corner and I thought I could beat Plante to the puck, or I could get there in time to check him," remembers Bathgate almost fifty years later. "Normally, he would come out on the right-hand side of the net and circle and go behind and come out the other side. I was looking at the puck and he let it go and he came back out the short side – the same one he had gone in – and he gave me a poke check and I went head first into the boards, cutting my ear and cheek."

As the play made its way out of the Montreal end and towards the Rangers' goal, Plante began to relax in his net, watching the Canadiens pass the puck from stick to stick. Worsley darted around his net trying to keep up against the game's pre-eminent offensive attack.

Meanwhile, an infuriated Bathgate gathered himself up from the end boards and skated towards the Rangers bench, filled with thoughts of revenge against Plante. "I thought to myself, okay, I can't fight him because the whole team would jump in on me," he recalls, "so I went into the dressing room and quickly got stitched up."

As Bathgate stewed in the dressing room, the Rangers made an offensive push into the Canadiens' zone. Gaining the blue line, Plante readied himself as Worsley, now free of action, rested his arm on the crossbar at the other end. Using his pad, Plante was able to stop the first shot that came from the Ranger point, and then thwart the rebound attempt as the Rangers desperately tried to stuff the puck into the Canadiens net.

The scene in front of Plante's net grew frantic as the Montreal defence failed to clear the puck. The Rangers threw a flip shot towards the goal, a shot that met its end like so many had before it – in the webbed glove of the game's greatest goaltender. The referee whistled the play over.

With that whistle, both teams changed their skaters, the Rangers now led by a stitched-up and fuming Andy Bathgate making his way to the faceoff circle. "I came back out, and I said to myself if Plante wants to play games, I can play games too."

As the linesman readied to drop the puck, Plante lowered himself into his traditional crouch, with one knee brushing the ice and the other knee hovering over the ice a little higher.

Finally the puck was dropped. Each team fought for control, and the puck bounded out towards centre ice. Plante's focus shifted to the contested puck. Out of this chaos emerged Andy Bathgate, carrying the puck forward, possessed with a singular purpose.

Entering the zone first, Bathgate slowed, giving his teammates time to rush towards the Montreal net, where they were immediately met by a mass of humanity erected by the Canadiens around their goaltender. Plante found his vision severely compromised as he struggled to keep his eye on the puck through a tangle of limbs and torsos.

Bathgate saw that Plante was ill prepared for a shot. However, he also saw that the path of the puck to the net was blocked by the players in front. He made his decision. "I got the puck and I went down the left wing, and being a right-hand shot, Plante used to sort of sit with his rear end in the net so he could get across quickly, and his head was sticking out there just like a chicken, just so he could see what was going on."

Plante moved around in the net desperately trying to find an unobstructed view, but it was too late by the time he realized the puck had left Bathgate's stick and was speeding towards the net.

What happened next has been the stuff of hockey legend for the last half a century. But as in most legendary tales, the details have grown fuzzy over time, with different variations emerging of what took place. But for Bathgate, the memory is still incredibly vivid today.

"It was actually a wrist shot. It wasn't a hard shot but I tried to give to him the same as me and I guess I caught him. It was a shot with feeling in it, it wasn't a blast, and I wasn't trying to score because the angle was really bad, but his head was sticking out and I decided if he wanted to play those games . . ."[7]

Plante never did see the oncoming shot, but he felt the puck rip into his unprotected face before careening into the corner of the rink.

Sitting in the press box directly above the ice was Red Fisher, the Canadiens beat writer for the *Montreal Star*. Almost fifty years later, the dean of all hockey writers remembers that historic night in all its gory detail. "Plante promptly sprawled on his stomach, his head cushioned in an ugly pool of blood. Bathgate raced to the fallen goalie and lifted his head. Blood poured from the wound onto the New York player's fingers. It was obvious that this was serious stuff and the Canadiens trainer, Hector Dubois, skidded out to the crease."[8] The puck had struck Plante directly in the face, opening a cut from the corner of his mouth up through a nostril.

A shocked silence descended upon the Garden crowd as Plante was escorted off the ice by his teammates. The game was indefinitely delayed as Plante struggled to stop the flow of blood, helped only by a single white towel.

Fifty years after the event, many have questioned whether Bathgate's actions that evening were the result of an accident or something more ominous in nature. Andy Bathgate, however, doesn't hesitate when asked what his intentions were.

"It was deliberate on my part," he confirms, "because of what he did to me. He could have ended my career. I knew that I was just giving him a little love tap."[9]

At that moment these concerns weren't weighing heavily on the mind of the Canadiens' head coach, Toe Blake. He was faced with a sudden, difficult decision. Just as had happened the season before in Toronto and Boston, Blake had the option of using the "house goalie" if Plante was unable to continue the game.

While Plante was being helped towards the Rangers medical clinic, Blake rushed over to Rangers general manager Muzz Patrick, who informed him of the depth of his predicament. On this particular night, Blake's options for the house goalie were a 33-year-old usher named Arnie Knox, who used to play in the New York City League and occasionally practised with the Rangers, and a junior-aged player named Joe Shaeffer, who hadn't been on skates all year.

Memories of the spring before, when Plante was knocked out, and the ensuing debacle in Boston when Blake was forced to go with the Bruins' house goalie, must have occurred to him. Toe Blake hated to lose, and he knew that placing either of the Rangers' house goalies in the Montreal net would have ensured a Rangers win.

Meanwhile, Red Fisher bolted from the press box and made a beeline downstairs, where an enormous decision was about to take place, a decision with vast implications, not all of which were foreseen that evening. In the Rangers medical clinic, Fisher found Plante "staring into the mirror and using his fingers to separate the ghastly cut."

"Pretty ugly," Plante remarked.

"Yeah, well, you had a good start, Jacques," replied Fisher as he tried to hide the abhorrence he felt as he looked at Plante.[10]

Fisher stepped aside as Rangers physician Dr. Kazuo Yawagisawa began to repair Plante's wound. "The doctor scraped away bits of loose flesh from the wound before inserting the stitches. Plante lay there, soundless, his fingers locked, as the needle knifed through the raw flesh."[11]

Once he was stitched up, Plante made his way back out to the ice and immediately skated towards the Canadiens dressing room for a fateful meeting with his coach. With his uniform caked in dried blood, and his nose held together by stitches and covered by a large white bandage, Plante was serenaded by Rangers fans who sang "For He's a Jolly Good Fellow" in his honour.

Plante had already made up his mind about his next move as he entered the dressing room. He was well aware that he now held the upper hand with his unsuspecting coach, and after months of dispute, he was not going miss this opportunity.

It was not a coincidence that Plante had his goaltending mask with him that Sunday night in Madison Square Garden. He had been carrying a mask with him for the past few years.

In 1954, while practising with the Canadiens, Plante had suffered a fracture of the right cheekbone when a shot from his teammate Bert Olmstead struck him. Plante had missed five weeks of action. Only a year later, and again in practice, Plante had his left cheekbone fractured on a shot from Donnie Marshall. It was after this second injury that Plante received an anonymous gift that would forever change his life and the face of goaltending.

The small plastic mask extended from just above his chin to halfway on his forehead. Despite the primitive design, Plante was eager to use the mask in practices. "I wore it for a while but it obscured my vision," he later wrote. "I was just thinking of taking it off when a puck hit the mask right in front of the eyeholes. I kept it on religiously in practices from then on, wondering all the while about what kind of mask would be practical for wearing in games."[12]

After using his initial mask in practice throughout 1955, Plante spent the next few years experimenting with different masks, all the while searching for the one he would feel the most comfortable wearing in an NHL game. He cut a crude, broad hole through a plastic shield designed by Delbert Louch of St. Mary's, Ontario. However, despite being advertised as "the shatterproof face protector for all sports," the Louch design was not without fault; it left the forehead exposed and had a tendency to fog up.

During a game in the 1958 Stanley Cup finals against the Boston Bruins, Plante was struck with a puck directly in the forehead and was knocked out. After a 20-minute delay, Plante returned to the Montreal net, valiantly continuing for the rest of the game. Sitting in the crowd at the Montreal Forum that night was a 35-year-old marketing rep from Fiberglass Canada named Bill Burchmore.

The next day at work, Burchmore couldn't escape thoughts of what he had witnessed at the game. Sitting alone at his desk, he found himself gazing straight ahead at the fibreglass head of one of his mannequins. Burchmore began to ponder the possibilities of a fibreglass mask.

A fibreglass mask would be lightweight, yet strong enough to protect the face from injury, and if it could be moulded to fit a player's face, it would provide the goaltender with a full range of vision that previous masks couldn't.

A few months later, Burchmore wrote to Plante about the mask he had in mind. Plante, however, was initially lukewarm to both Burchmore and his concept. Since posing in the paper wearing his practice mask a few years before, Plante had grown weary of being sent various ideas and schemes, most of them utterly impractical.

It would take the better part of a year, with the continuous urging of the Canadiens' club physician, Dr. Ian Milne, and the team's physiotherapist, Bill Head, before Plante finally agreed to proceed with Burchmore's mask.

Plante took the first step when he spent a summer's day in 1959 at the Montreal General Hospital, where, under the supervision of Dr. Milne, a plaster cast of his face was made. With Plante's facial plaster cast in hand, Burchmore began constructing the mask. What finally emerged was a mask the likes of which had never before been seen. Soaked in polyester resin, and only one-eighth of an inch thick, the mask was lightweight and impregnable at the same time. The inside of the mask featured thin strips of padding around the forehead, cheekbones, and chin to help cushion the impact of a puck. In testing the mask's durability, Burchmore swung a steel ball from a pendulum and struck the mask with the simulated force of a Bernie Geoffrion slapshot. Despite repeated attempts to damage the mask, Burchmore was unsuccessful.

However, the true test of the mask came when Plante entered the nets. Once in goal, facing his teammates in training camp, all of Plante's previous fears were assuaged. Clearly this mask was the most protective shield he had yet encountered. Most important for Plante, for the first time his vision wasn't compromised by Burchmore's mask.

Armed with his new mask and confident that it would serve its purpose, Plante visited the offices of NHL president Clarence Campbell in September 1959. Campbell was a lawyer and a war veteran, and a noted traditionalist. After careful deliberation and study, Campbell surprisingly gave Plante his blessing to wear the mask in league play. "We're anxious for goalies to wear anything that will cut down injuries," Campbell proclaimed in his authorization to use the mask. "After all, the goalie is the most important man in our game."[13]

Campbell praised Plante as an original thinker. "His whole approach of goaltending has been very professional," said Campbell. "He has studied every aspect and developed some gimmicks of his own that are pretty wonderful. He didn't actually invent the nomadic goaltending idea but he exploited it and made it pay off."[14]

Getting Campbell's permission to wear the mask was one thing. Getting the approval of Toe Blake would be far more difficult. Clarence

Campbell may have run the NHL, but Toe Blake ran the Montreal Canadiens, and anything and everything to do with the team was his responsibility. "He can practice with one, if he wants," Blake told reporters, "but no goaltender of mine is gonna wear one in a game. We're here to win."[15]

In the team's training camp in the fall of 1959, Plante began making serious noises about wearing the mask in the upcoming year. And while Blake allowed Plante to wear his mask in practice and in exhibition games, he drew the line at letting him wear it in a game that mattered.

Plante "had the mask on for the exhibition outings and reported that he was highly pleased with the results," wrote the *Hockey News* in October. "But club officials had other ideas about Plante actually wearing it in league games. They reasoned that Jacques had been very successful these past four years without it and they were content to leave well enough alone. It's doubtful that Jacques will wear the mask this season, other than in practice sessions."[16]

For most hockey players of the day, this would have been the end of it, such was the authority wielded by management. But Jacques Plante wasn't most players.

"Jacques Plante was different," remembers Red Fisher. "He wasn't intimidated easily. He had firm ideas about what was good for his game and for him. The puck stopped with him, and nobody else. He would do what he felt was right for him – on and off the ice. What was good for him, he insisted, was right for the Canadiens. If Canadiens management didn't think so, well, there were other teams."[17]

Jacques Plante and Toe Blake were both very stubborn men, described by Jean Béliveau as "strong personalities unafraid to speak their minds." And while Plante knew that Blake's word was law with the Canadiens, that didn't stop him from proclaiming his displeasure to anybody who would listen, including the media – a rarity at a time when players most often disagreed in silence.

In the October 1959 issue of *Hockey Pictorial*, in an article entitled "Plante Plumps for Face Masks for All Goalies," Plante stated that masks should be mandatory for all goalies, blaming the lack of young goalies on the absence of facial protection. He went on to extol the advantages of his new mask, claiming to have been "saved [from potential injury] between 20 and 25 times in workouts by having the mask," and as for the future, Plante claimed that "the day is coming when goalies will wear them – they'll have to."[18] In the next month's issue, Plante went even further, claiming that no one was better qualified than a goal-tender himself to determine what's good for him.

In an effort to quell the emerging controversy, Blake attempted to coddle Plante through the media. In that same issue of *Hockey Pictorial*, Blake countered that Plante "was jumping the gun" by switching to the mask. "Plante tells me the mask will keep him in the league after his reflexes and eyesight aren't as sharp as they used to be. But it seems to me that neither his sight nor his reflexes have been impaired. So why the mask?"[19]

In the fall of 1959, the Canadiens broke training camp and began playing their traditional series of exhibition games in preparation for the regular season. Plante decided that this was the time to try the mask in game action, but Blake remained unconvinced, claiming that "the mask is causing Plante to lose sight of the puck when it's at his feet."[20]

Privately, Blake urged Plante to discard the mask: "If you wear it when the season starts and have a bad game the fans will blame the mask and get on you," he warned.[21] Blake simply couldn't understand why Plante felt the need to wear a mask. After all, none of the other goalies in the league wore one. What Blake didn't tell Plante but expressed to others was his fear that the fans and players on the opposing team would openly ridicule Plante for his decision and use the mask as evidence of Plante's becoming puck shy.

Blake was supported by the Canadiens' general manager, Frank Selke, who strongly felt that the Montreal fans wouldn't accept the mask, claiming that they liked to see their Canadiens, and that "a man has to be able to look at the puck face to face."[22]

For Toe Blake, Plante and his mask represented an unwanted and unneeded distraction for himself and for the Canadiens. The one thing Blake wanted to avoid was change, because in his eyes there was no need for it. The Canadiens were the most dominant team in NHL history, and Blake was determined to keep it that way.

Standing in the Canadiens dressing room on November 1, 1959, waiting for Plante to arrive, Blake had a lot of things to ponder. Yet, despite the security of a comfortable first-place lead, he wasn't about to sacrifice a game, any game, even to the lowly Rangers.

As Plante skated towards the dressing room where Blake was waiting, Canadiens reporter Red Fisher raced through the bowels of the Garden, hoping to glimpse the imminent confrontation between the two. In his long career, Fisher has become the principal chronicler of the Canadiens' great tradition for thousands of his readers. But at that moment, Fisher was more than just a chronicler of history; he was a part of it.

Staring at his injured goalie, Blake came to the unsettling realization that Plante had to wear the mask if he was to go back in goal for Montreal. Faced with having either a masked Plante or house goalies in net, Blake abruptly found himself with no choice at all.

"How bad is it?" he asked.

"It's sore," Plante wearily replied.

"Why don't you wear your mask for the rest of the game?" Blake suggested.

"I don't think I can go back in without it," said a relieved Plante.[23]

Plante had finally found the right time and place to attempt his experiment. With the unwitting assistance of Andy Bathgate, he had put Blake in a position where there could be no objection. And while Blake was strenuously opposed to Plante's wearing the mask, he realized that without Plante in the net his team's chances of success were severely weakened for that night and perhaps beyond. Blake's desire to win was what drove him, and on this night it won out over his objections to the mask, in part because Blake thought of the mask as only a temporary solution.

Plante reached down into the bag beside him and grabbed for his mask. He gently placed it over his battered, swollen face, and slowly began walking up the flight of six stairs that led to the ice and towards his place in history.

14

SELLING THE MASK

WHEN JACQUES PLANTE stepped back out onto the ice with his mask covering his injured face and skated towards his crease, the crowd let out a gasp that combined both shock and amazement.

They weren't the only ones startled by what had happened. Many of the players on both teams were also surprised. To this day the fact that Plante came back into the game at all, even with a protective mask, amazes Jean Béliveau. "I don't know how he did it," said Béliveau, "his nose was over here, but Jacques went back into the game. I don't know if I would have."[1]

"We were used to seeing Plante wear the mask in practice," recalled teammate Bernie Geoffrion, "but the Rangers and the 15,000 people filling the Garden were shocked, Jacques looked like something right out of a horror movie."[2]

Plante, however, was oblivious to the murmurs from the crowd or from the players as he took his place in front of the Montreal net. Talking after the game to *Time* magazine, Plante, ever the iconoclast, professed to not care about how the mask appeared to others. "I may look like Frankenstein but I'm not out there to stop pucks with my face."[3]

"I already had four broken noses, a broken jaw, two broken cheekbones, and almost 200 stitches in my head. I didn't care how the mask looked. The way things were going, I was afraid I would look just like the mask."[4]

Stan Fischler, a 27-year-old reporter covering the game for the *Hockey News*, recalled the scene from high above the ice in the press box: "He's wearing a mask," screamed a reporter as they all looked down with a mixture of astonishment and admiration. A heckler in the crowd shouted towards the Canadiens end, "Hey, Plante, take that thing off. Halloween's over!"[5]

If Plante was experiencing any after-effects of his injury or any limitations of his mask, it didn't show that night. Despite the continued pain and the fact that he had never worn the mask in a game, Plante never betrayed any weakness. In a 3–1 Canadiens win, Plante stopped all but one of the 30 shots the Rangers fired at him.

"If Jacques was nervous he didn't show it," said Geoffrion. "Actually, he was overjoyed because the very fact that he was wearing the mask was a triumph over Blake and the other critics. Plante's confidence was evident as the Rangers fired shot after shot at him. Jacques was near perfect. He took the three-goal lead into the third period and gave nothing to the Rangers until Camille Henry finally beat him with just over nine minutes remaining."[6]

After the game, Rangers coach Phil Watson held court with the media. "Plante was steady and not jittery as he usually is in Madison Square Garden because of the mask," claimed an impressed Watson. "I think Plante played a marvelous game. The mask was the best thing that ever happened to him. It was his best game in New York." He added that "it may be the start of a new trend."[7]

Across the aisle, Montreal coach Toe Blake admitted that "he thought the Canadiens played their finest game of the season after Plante donned the mask," before confessing that "a better mask could be made."[8]

Everyone in the Canadiens dressing room after the game was in a celebratory mood, and the centre of attention was Plante. Plante entertained the gathered media. "After the puck hit me, I didn't think any bones were broken. But what bothered me most of all was that I swallowed some blood. I didn't feel too good and my teeth felt numb."[9]

"Plante was the happiest guy in the rink that he got cut," Canadiens defenceman Bob Turner later told Dick Irvin Jr. "Don't ever feel sorry for him because he was looking for the opportunity [to put on the mask]."[10]

While Plante told the press about the benefits of his facial protection, Blake sat quietly in the background, happy about the victory, but in denial about the long-term effectiveness of the mask. "After the Ranger game Toe still wasn't completely sold on the mask," Plante recalled years later, "but he suggested that I keep wearing it until the wound healed and as long as I kept on going good."[11]

Blake was certain the mask would be discarded when Plante's injuries healed. He firmly believed that Plante was a weak goaltender when wearing the mask.

Blake was not alone in his thinking. In the Rangers dressing room after the game, their general manager, Muzz Patrick, expressed his opposition to Plante or any other goalie wearing a mask on the novel grounds that "female fans wanted to see the faces of the players."[12]

"I'm against helmets and masks," continued Patrick. "We start out with goalies wearing masks. Every club has a defenseman or two who goes down to smother shots. Soon they will want masks. All the forwards will wear helmets. The teams will become faceless, headless robots, all of whom look alike to the spectators. We can't afford to take that fan appeal away from hockey."[13]

Maurice Richard harboured some doubts, thinking that the mask caused "blind spots, especially at the goalie's feet."[14]

Before the Canadiens' next game four nights later in Montreal against the same Rangers team, Blake privately assured Fisher, "Plante wasn't going to wear the mask." The ace reporter immediately found Plante to gauge his reaction to Blake's proclamation. Plante, never short of self-confidence, responded in a forceful tone, "If I don't wear the mask, I'm not playing."[15]

Toe Blake was seen by many as the embodiment of an old-school hockey man, but he was also a realist. He didn't approve of the mask, but he also wanted to avoid a full-blown feud with his goaltender. So he and Plante developed an unspoken policy of not mentioning the mask to one another. The loser in any type of Blake vs. Plante blowup was the team itself, and for Blake the team was paramount.

And while Plante openly vowed never to go bare-faced again, Blake bit his tongue and bided his time. Supported by general manager Frank Selke, Plante was submitted, at the Canadiens' expense, to a battery of vision tests with the mask and without. These tests supported Plante, all noting that the mask didn't impair his sightlines or vision.

These tests didn't budge Blake. That could only happen on the ice, not in a doctor's office. Nobody was more of a hockey traditionalist than Toe Blake, and to him a goalie who wore a mask was betraying a fear of the puck and was showing signs of cowardice.

The fear did not lie within Plante; instead, it consumed Blake. The two goalies who had preceded Plante in the Montreal net had both retired prematurely in large part because of their inability to overcome the anxiety and nervousness of being the last line of defence. Blake was haunted by the possibility of this happening to Plante. He knew that he couldn't afford to lose Plante for any period of time.

The schism between Plante and Blake was shared among members of the media, who were divided in their opinion about the merits of the mask. "Plante had good reason to violate the code of his craft, which allows goalies mattresses of protection around their body and legs, but nothing over their faces to protect them from a hard-rubber puck driven at speeds up to 100 miles per hour," wrote *Time*.[16]

Surprisingly, some of Plante's harsher critics were fellow members of the goaltending fraternity. "How the hell can a mask protect you when it's hit flush against the face?" questioned Plante's opponent that historic night, Rangers goalie Gump Worsley. "My objection to the mask is that it is not necessary. Why, all of a sudden, after hockey has been played for seventy years, do they decide we should wear masks?" In response to a reporter's claim that the mask was an evolution in goaltending, Worsley angrily responded, "Aww, don't tell me that, and don't tell me that the game has changed. Do boxers wear masks? Plante may make a pot full o' money on that mask idea. He can have it, I don't want the thing."[17]

"Plante is a good goalie . . . and not because of the mask," proclaimed Terry Sawchuk of the Detroit Red Wings. "I've been a pro goalie for more than a dozen years and I've never worn a mask in a game. I don't see any reason to start now."[18]

"I thought he was a wimp," recalls Glenn Hall of the Chicago Black Hawks.[19]

Worsley, Sawchuk, and Hall would all resort to putting on a protective mask before they retired from the game.

Right from the start, what garnered the most attention was the look of the mask. Both the press and the public were drawn to the spectacle. "Crouched in the cage with the sun-white glare of hockey rink floodlights carving his artificial 'face' into deeply shadowed eye sockets and a gaping hole of a 'mouth', Plante looks like something out of a horror film," proclaimed *Modern Man* magazine.[20] Even Plante's teammates on the Canadiens admitted that looking at the mask took some getting used to. The mask gave Plante a psychological advantage over his opponents. It was so striking, so unusual, that it took the attention of the opposition off the task at hand.

"When I first put on my mask, the boys all told me I would scare the women," Plante joked later.[21]

Many in the media focused on the look of the mask but at the same time applauded Plante's decision. Writing in the *Toronto Star*, Milt Dunnell remarked that the mask made Plante "look like a man who died, from the neck to the top of his head . . . while the rest of the body decided to carry on. He knows that he stalks elderly ladies when he leers at them from the screens of their TV sets but all this he feels bound to accept as the price of survival. The selfish fellow simply decided he was too young to die."[22]

"Don't knock his talent or throw slurs at his courage," wrote Red Fisher in the *Montreal Star*, "because while he is not alone in these departments, he takes a backseat to nobody in this or any other league."[23]

Days after Plante first donned the mask, the Montreal *Gazette* asked Toe Blake if Plante's early success had changed his own feelings regarding the mask.

"In a way, yes," Blake conceded. "When he was wearing it in pre-season training he wasn't sharp and my feeling then was that the mask was to blame. But perhaps it was Jacques himself and not the mask. Anyway, he played very well on our three-game road trip, and appeared to recover his old form . . . and the mask didn't seem to handicap him." Blake hastened to add that Plante "can wear the mask as long as he likes, if it doesn't interfere with his goaltending."[24]

Despite Blake's hope that the mask would just fade away, Plante continued to wear it, and followed the win over the Rangers by backstopping the Canadiens to a 10-game winning streak as part of a larger 18-game unbeaten streak. Surrendering only 13 goals in his first 11 games with the mask, Plante made a strong case against its opponents, including Blake.

But his coach's acquiescence came with one condition, remembers Bernie Geoffrion: "Toe made it clear that if Jacques started losing with the mask it would end up in the Forum dumpster."[25]

But even with Plante's and the team's success, the critics still howled their disapproval. When pressed by his detractors about the need for a mask, Plante always humbly replied that wearing the mask was nothing less than essential. He maintained throughout his life that wearing the mask was a necessity, born of his desire to continually change the way his position was played.

Ironically, during Plante's debut with the mask at Maple Leaf Gardens on November 21, 1959, the game had to be halted when the goalie for the Leafs, Johnny Bower, was struck in the mouth with a deflected shot by the Canadiens' Donnie Marshall. After receiving three stitches to close the wound, and short one of his teeth, Bower resumed his duties bare-faced.

After losing the game to the Canadiens 4–1, some in the media pressed Bower on why he wasn't wearing a mask like Plante's. Bower was a hockey veteran who had served a 12-year apprenticeship in the American Hockey League before winning the starting goaltender's job for the Maple Leafs. Quietly, Bower, like Plante, had been wearing a mask in practice with the Leafs, but unlike Plante he had no intention of wearing it in a game.

Bower claimed that for him the mask had "gotten in the way" of stopping the puck. "I'm also sure that if I had to wear a mask in a game I'd be lost. It's a great thing for other goaltenders – but not for me."[26] It would be another decade before Johnny Bower finally donned a mask, and then only in the last 17 games of a career that saw him play in more than 1,300 contests.

With only six professional goaltending jobs available in the NHL, many of the men in the nets were understandably reluctant to put on a mask. For most of them it came down to a choice between safety and performance, and because of the tenuous nature of the job, many, like Bower, knew that if their goals-against rose, their job security would decrease in relation.

This predicament was not lost on Plante. "It was fortunate that I was playing for the Canadiens," he recalled many years later. "They were a winning team. If I had been with a losing team, some bad goals would have been scored and everybody would have said it was because I started wearing a mask."[27]

In retrospect, it had to be Jacques Plante who took the first step towards wearing a mask. Rare was the player who challenged authority; even rarer was the player who didn't fear the wrath of NHL management.

Branded by his critics a rebel, and in some extreme cases a coward, Plante grew accustomed to hearing the scorn from fellow players, opposition coaches, and especially from the fans throughout the league. None of this, however, fazed him. "When I take it off, I'll also take off my skates," an exasperated Plante told his many critics. "In other words I'm wearing it from now until I retire."[28] Plante was fearless in the face of authority, especially when he felt he was in the right – and when he was aware of his value to the team. Because of his recent success, he had no fears about losing his starting position with the Canadiens.

Despite the criticism and negativity aimed at Plante, it didn't take long for others to follow his lead. The undeniable logic of protecting the goaltender from injury started to gain a foothold within the hockey world. Of course, this was boosted by Plante's performance – having surrendered only nine goals in the first eight games that he had worn the mask, he had continued the winning ways of the Canadiens.

Most surprising was the endorsement by Frank Selke, the Canadiens general manager, who did a stunning about-face in the *Hockey News* a month after Plante first donned the mask, exclaiming, "Every goalie should wear a protective mask."[29]

Five weeks after Plante began wearing his mask, Don Simmons, a goaltender with the Boston Bruins, donned one, in a game at Madison Square Garden against the Rangers, and proceeded to record a shutout.

Almost overnight, youth hockey associations in both Toronto and Halifax made masks mandatory for all goaltenders. Muzz Patrick, the general manager of the Rangers, one of Plante's most vocal critics a month earlier, now abruptly switched course and made all of his minor league goalies begin wearing facial protection.

Yet the one person whose opinion truly mattered the most still hadn't made a final decision. Blake had made it abundantly clear both to Plante and to the media that his acquiescence on the mask issue was dependant upon Plante's and the team's play. On December 2, Plante lost his first game in the mask: 1–0 to the Toronto Maple Leafs, snapping the Canadiens' 18-game unbeaten streak. This loss signalled a downturn in the team's fortunes, as they immediately lost six games in a row.

The Blake vs. Plante silent feud over the mask became a war of words fought in the newspapers. A headline in the January 2, 1960, issue of the *Hockey News* screamed, "Now It Can Be Told: Toe Would like Plante to Junk His Mask." "It seems the Habs coach has some misgivings as to whether the fibre-glass mask is actually what it's cooked up to be," wrote Charlie Halpin. "Toe hasn't directly told Plante to unmask, but the inference is there if there is any repetition of 'loose' goaltending that accompanied the Canadiens 6–5 loss to the Rangers [on December 20], then the mask has got to go. Blake, who is a conventional hockey man, expressed opposition to Plante's face mask but permitted him to wear the mask. For Blake, there was a question of how necessary the mask really is."[30]

The controversy over the mask temporarily subsided when the Canadiens went on a four-game winning streak right after Christmas, and followed it up by embarking on an eight-game undefeated streak to close out the month of January.

Typically of the headline-grabbing Plante, though, just as one controversy died down, another one flared up. As the Canadiens regained their winning ways, Plante publicly credited two things for his ability to bounce out of the slump: his mask and his newfound fondness for pep pills, which heightened his focus. Before a game on Boxing Day against the Black Hawks, Plante ingested half a pep tablet, and the Habs went on to win 9–2. The following night against the Red Wings he took another half pill, and the Canadiens won 3–1. Three nights later, with controversy raging in Toronto over his use of the pills, Plante passed on the drugs, and, according to Red Fisher of the *Montreal Star*, "contributed his most spectacular effort in weeks, a game that broke the hearts of the Leafs who did everything to Canadiens except put the puck in the net enough times."[31] The Canadiens skated to a 3–2 victory at Maple Leaf Gardens.

This latest controversy slowly faded away as Canadiens general manager Frank Selke made it clear that he would not tolerate any player using stimulants. "No player I manage will use any sort of drug for that purpose, victory is never that important," asserted Selke.[32] And with that edict, the pep pills disappeared from Plante's locker for good.

But for Plante, ever restless, the search for a better mask continued. In January 1960, Burchmore presented him with a new mask. Instead of the solid piece of fibreglass that made up the old mask, this one consisted of 540 fibreglass bars. A key improvement was the mask's lighter weight – only 10.3 ounces.

Plante's mask was firmly entrenched as part of his equipment, and the team clinched first place on March 3 with a 5–1 win over the Leafs at the Montreal Forum. "I am the best goalie in the league and with the mask I am even better," claimed Plante. "I can now laugh at getting hit in the face."[33]

But as the season progressed, whispers began to circulate about Plante's performance in the Montreal net since he put on the mask. "What has happened to the seemingly invincible Jacques Plante?" asked Charlie Halpin in the *Hockey News*. "The question has been on the lips of every hockey fan around the NHL circuit this past week, but no one has come forward with a solution. Plante's already steady decline in the Vezina Trophy race during the second half of the NHL schedule has been alarming. Plante himself is concerned. The Canadiens too, are worried. It is no secret that Plante has not been quite as efficient in the second half of the year as he was in the first thirty-five games, when Jacques had a 2.28 goals against average against Glenn Hall's 2.87 at the midway mark of the season. Today, Plante has skyrocketed to a 2.54 goals against as opposed to 2.55 for Hall."[34]

The situation came to a head on March 6, when the Canadiens and Plante lost 4–2 to Hall and the Black Hawks at the Chicago Stadium. Three days later, the *Toronto Star* headlined the slump in a banner headline on the sports page. "Jacques Plante's great and noble experiment has apparently ended in failure," wrote Jim Proudfoot.

> "We decided he'd better go without it in the playoffs," coach Toe Blake reported from Detroit yesterday, "so Jake agreed to try a few games beforehand without the protection."
>
> "We figure we've been getting one or two bad goals scored against us every game," Blake continued. "You just can't afford to give up these soft ones. And Jacques admits he hasn't been as sharp as he should be. So we'll see how things work out without the mask."
>
> Cold statistics suggest that Plante with the mask isn't quite as efficient as a nude-faced Plante. His net minding average has gone up half a goal per game this season over his lifetime NHL record. Blake was always skeptical. And now evidently Plante himself has begun to wonder – despite what exhaustive vision tests indicated.[35]

On the same page, in a little space at the bottom with considerably less fanfare, was the article "Plante Still Likes Mask." "I play just the same with or without it and I have just as much guts whether I wear it or not," he was quoted as saying, "but I'd like to wear it again."[36]

Plante, always candid with the media, explained what wearing the mask meant for him and his game. "When I stop pucks business is good," he said. "When I don't business is bad. The mask doesn't help me to stop pucks but when I don't have to worry about getting my face shattered, I can concentrate on stopping them."[37]

"During a game you don't have time to worry," Plante stressed. "But when you go home you lie awake thinking of that shot that just missed your face. You know if one hits your eye your career is finished. Once I put on the mask I didn't worry, not on the day of a game or afterwards either."[38]

What received considerably less attention in the paper was the result of the next game. Plante took to the nets at the Detroit Olympia against the Red Wings, bare-faced for the first time in 50 games, and lost 3–0.

With the playoffs a few weeks away, Blake needed to resolve the situation once and for all. Like all successful coaches, he was acutely aware that a goaltender's mental state was just as important as his physical skills. Plante had forcefully, both publicly and privately, and for quite some time, made his preference known.

At the conclusion of the Detroit game, Blake made the decision to allow Plante to wear the mask. Confronting Plante in the dressing room, Blake told him that he had a chance to win a fifth straight Vezina Trophy that year, and that if the mask would help him, he could do what he wanted. "The decision belongs to him, I won't force him to discard it," Blake informed the media in what was essentially a concession speech. "Anyway, I figure the percentage is in favour of him wearing it the rest of the season. The mask was a great thing with everybody when he went those eighteen straight games without a loss. Plante was wearing the mask then, and he'll be the same guy with it in the playoffs."[39]

"Coach Toe Blake is certain Plante will be alright for the playoffs," the *Hockey News* reported. "'I don't think Plante is feeling too good, he really doesn't look well, doesn't seem to have his usual pep,' said Blake, 'but what can you do about these things but rest.' As for the mask, Blake insists he will allow Plante to make up his own mind whether to wear it in the playoffs."[40]

With the playoffs mere weeks away, Blake wanted this distraction to go away, and since Plante was unwilling to discard the mask, he was left with no alternative. He had overcome his own preconceptions, and showed the ultimate confidence in Jacques Plante.

But with that confidence came pressure. Anything less than a fifth consecutive Stanley Cup would be a failure, for Blake, for Plante, for the Canadiens, and for the future of the mask.

"I'll be wearing it in the playoffs, don't worry about that," a satisfied Plante told the media. "Oh, I know I got it on, and it's hot. But since I don't find any difference playing with or without it, I may as well wear it and avoid facial injuries."[41]

Jacques Plante would never again step onto the ice without a mask.

15

THE PINNACLE

THERE HASN'T BEEN MUCH that's taken place in the world of hockey over the past half-century, both on or off the ice, that has escaped the keen attention of Red Fisher. The longest-serving beat writer in the NHL, he has written on the comings and goings of the Montreal Canadiens for the last 50 years.

Now, Red Fisher is able to look back at a career like no other. He considers himself lucky to have covered the Canadiens when they ruled the hockey world, like none before and none since. In his first 25 years on the beat, he was able to write the story of 17 Stanley Cup champions, and the story of the men who won has been at the core of Fisher's writing. And in his long and illustrious career, no player has fascinated him more than Jacques Plante.

"I started covering the Canadiens in the mid-fifties and you had to be aware of Mr. Plante from minute one," says Fisher today. "A great player, so confident in his own game, he was his own man. Along with being outspoken, he also had the brightest mind in hockey. I remember being on a weekly panel on the radio with Jacques Plante in the fifties. We had a panel comprised of Jacques Plante, Frank Selke Jr., Danny Gallivan, and myself. I thought it was a pretty darn good panel. Plante week in and week out was the guy who did the most talking on that show, and probably made the most sense. If he had something to say he said it, and it was always interesting."[1]

And rarely was Jacques Plante more interesting and more prominent than in the spring of 1960.

The 1959–60 season had been the most tumultuous season of Plante's career. He had introduced the mask to widespread scorn and derision, with some of the harshest criticisms coming from his fellow goalies and his own coach. His name was now known in most households, mentioned in the media along with Rocket Richard and Gordie Howe as the game's star players.

As the season drew to a close, Plante once again was in the spotlight. With five games left in the season and the Canadiens having clinched first place, coach Toe Blake decided that a weary Plante would sit out three of the games, with the reliable Charlie Hodge taking his place.

Throughout the league, the move generated simmering criticism. If Plante didn't play, he couldn't give up any more goals, thus helping to ensure another Vezina Trophy. Many came out and accused Plante of trying to back his way into a fifth consecutive Vezina win.

Two nights later, in his last game before his exile, Plante faced off with his closest competitor for the trophy, Chicago's Glenn Hall. Hall entered the game only one goal behind Plante in the race for the Vezina. After 60 minutes he found himself six behind the "tired" Canadiens netminder, as Plante turned back every shot from the Hawks in a 5–0 shutout.

After the game Plante didn't board the train for Boston with the team, instead retreating to the quiet comforts of home. The next night, with Charlie Hodge in goal, the Canadiens blew a 2–0 lead to the Bruins, who emerged with a 3–2 upset win.

Four nights later, the Canadiens were at home for a contest with the Toronto Maple Leafs, and contrary to what had been decided the week before, Plante was back in the nets. The lure of winning an unprecedented fifth consecutive Vezina Trophy had proved irresistible.

Perhaps he should have stuck to the original plan, for the Leafs handed the Canadiens their first home defeat in their last 19 outings, by pasting them 6–2. The six goals surrendered by Plante dropped him into a tie with Glenn Hall in the race for the Vezina, both men having allowed 175 goals throughout the season.

Their battle for the coveted Vezina hardware came down to the final games of the season, as Plante prepared to face the Rangers, and Hall took on the Bruins. The Rangers sought to ruin Plante's chances and did manage to put a third goal past him at the midway point of the third period. With the two games being played almost simultaneously, Plante stood alone in his net eagerly waiting for any word about Hall's progress in Boston.

Soon afterwards the updated score came in: 4–4. Plante knew that if he could keep the Rangers off the score sheet for the final 10 minutes, the Vezina would once again be his. True enough, with his defence throwing a checking blanket around him, the Rangers were unable to put another goal past him. And then, just as his game was ending, the announcement came in: Black Hawks 5, Bruins 5. As the final buzzer sounded that night in Madison Square Garden, Plante fell to his knees on the ice in celebration.

"In the dressing room he was crying unashamedly," wrote Red Fisher. "Some of the people with sterner backbones may have regarded Plante's emotional outburst with sly smirks, but nobody felt the tension as much as Plante did in this rink last night. The important thing, though, is that he didn't back into the Vezina. He won it because he had the least goals scored on him for the season, the only time a National Hockey League goalie has won five Vezinas in a row. Nobody, not even his severest critics, can take that away from him."[2]

And he did it all while wearing a mask.

Jacques Plante had the grand total of four days to savour his accomplishment. On the fourth day, the playoffs would begin as the Canadiens began the push for an unprecedented fifth consecutive Stanley Cup. In a rematch of the memorable semifinal from the year before, the Canadiens would once again face off against the Chicago Black Hawks, with one of the more intriguing subplots being the duel between the two men who had vied for the Vezina.

Both goaltenders were a study in contrasts, according to the *Montreal Star*. "Montreal's worried, jumpy, accident prone Jacques Plante . . . and Glenn Hall, the calm young iron man of hockey who disdains Plante's innovations such as face-masks and the wandering style and who hasn't missed a single game since he made the NHL in the 1955–56 season."[3]

But for a moment it looked like the hyped goaltenders' duel might not even take place. The day before the opening game of the series, Plante was hit on the Adam's apple by a puck. After spending the night in the hospital, a sore-throated Plante was pronounced fit to play.

"Neither team won any prizes for their display last night," wrote a disappointed Red Fisher in the aftermath of the first game, a 4–3 win for the Canadiens.[4] But if the first game of the series turned out to be a disappointing bore, the second game, two nights later, was anything but.

With the Canadiens nursing a 3–2 lead with a little over a minute and a half remaining in the game, the puck found its way onto the blade of the team's steadiest stick.

"I wanted our team to keep possession and I saw Tom Johnson and the 'Rocket' along the side," Doug Harvey told the assembled reporters after the game. "So I tried to drive the puck hard against the boards. I guess maybe the puck flipped a little and I got my stick caught. So instead of a hard pass, all I got off was a blooper. Billy Hay picked it up and you know the rest."[5]

The rest included Billy Hay, the league's rookie of the year, breaking in on Plante, unobstructed, and then placing a deke that ended with the puck tucked in between Plante's outstretched pads before it reached the back of the net.

The tying goal by Chicago was monumental, and it left the Canadiens shaken. Thanks to Harvey's rare gaffe, the two teams finished regulation tied. As the players shuffled off the ice, the spectre of overtime hung over a suddenly silent Montreal Forum.

"I've never seen Harvey as dejected as he was during the rest leading up to the start of the overtime," Toe Blake said. "Frankly, I was a little worried he'd go all to pieces in the overtime."[6] As some of his teammates, including fellow defenceman Bob Turner, tried to console him, Harvey kept muttering to himself that he owed his teammates a goal.

The Forum patrons sat nervously in their seats as the overtime commenced. After eight minutes of play, Bobby Hull, almost always an unstoppable force when headed towards the opposing goal, single-handedly rushed into the Montreal zone with the puck cradled on his stick. His charge ended with him crashing into the net, leaving three Canadiens as well as Jacques Plante sprawled on the ice.

The loose puck found its way onto the stick of Billy Hay, the man who had tied the game only minutes before. This time he saw an empty net yawning in front of him. Taking his time, Hay shot the puck towards the upper corner, seemingly a sure goal.

But Hay's slight hesitation had given a fallen Plante enough time to desperately stab at the oncoming puck with his goal stick. Amazingly, the puck struck the outstretched stick and deflected over the net.

Henri Richard gobbled up the puck and headed up ice towards the Chicago goal. He quickly passed it forward to Dickie Moore, who spotted an onrushing Doug Harvey. Moore left the puck for Harvey, as he and Richard headed towards Glenn Hall and the Chicago net.

From just inside the blue line, Harvey shot the puck towards the net. It never made it that far and luckily bounced right back onto his stick. Given a second chance, Harvey's aim was true, and his 40-foot shot somehow travelled through a maze of legs, and before a screened Hall could react, the puck was resting behind him in the back of the net.

The crowd exploded, his teammates poured off the ice, and in the space of a half-hour Doug Harvey had gone from the goat to the hero, as the Canadiens took a 2–0 series lead over the demoralized and stunned Black Hawks.

When the series headed to Chicago, the Canadiens should have been a comfortable lot. However, Toe Blake was far from content; he was, in fact, on edge. Memories of what had happened a year ago were still fresh. Then, like now, saw the Canadiens up 2–0. The year before, the Black Hawks took both games in Chicago to even the series. Blake was eager to avoid a repeat.

The third game dawned as 20,000 made their way to the sold-out Chicago Stadium. Once again, the Canadiens would find themselves playing in the sport's harshest and most rowdy venue.

As expected, the Black Hawks came fastest out of the gate, out-shooting the Canadiens 12–10 in a scoreless first period. According to the *Montreal Star*, "it was Plante who finally emerged from an undistinguished series thus far to play the kind of hockey of which he's capable. He produced three key saves – one off Eric Nesterenko, another off Elmer Vasko, who streaked in on him from nowhere, and another less dangerous one from Ron Murphy."[7]

Midway through the second period, Montreal's Billy Hicke broke the scoreless deadlock. Minutes later Jean-Guy Talbot made the score 2–0, and then a defensive curtain enveloped the desperate Black Hawks, who managed only four third-period shots at Plante.

The Canadiens' 4–0 victory was devastating in its effectiveness, and disheartening to the sellout home crowd. The final period was a long affair as the fans frequently interrupted the game by throwing fire-crackers, cans, paper, and other debris onto the ice.

"Plante saved us in the first period," an impressed Blake told the *Montreal Star*, "and he did it by playing like the Plante of old. He looked as if he wanted to eat the puck. He was moving surely, and he was quick. I don't know what made him return to form overnight, so to speak, and I don't care. All that worries me is whether or not he can keep it up."[8]

Blake needn't have worried for the next game. After another score-less first period, the Canadiens broke through for two quick goals in the second period, before hanging on in the face of a frantic Chicago onslaught in the third period.

"That's when Plante produced his finest hockey," wrote Red Fisher in the *Montreal Star*. "He was quick and agile . . . all this while he was harried and bothered by a crowd unhappy by the progress of events. They threw everything in the book from the stands: eggs, firecrackers, paper cups, rubber balls, and even a ladies shoe. The last object, Plante noted quickly, wasn't the right size for Mrs. Plante, so he hurled the shoe back in the stands."[9]

Out of time and patience, the Black Hawks took to running down the Canadiens' masked wanderer. "The first time it happened Plante suffered a one-stitch cut on the top of his head," reported Red Fisher, "but no further damage was done other than to hold up the contest for ten minutes or so."[10]

As the final buzzer sounded the Canadiens gathered around their goalie, whose play the last two games had spoken louder than any words. He had faced down the Black Hawks twice, shutting them out both times and banishing them to the sidelines.

The Canadiens now prepared for the Stanley Cup finals. It was their record tenth consecutive visit to the finals as they sought an unprecedented fifth straight Stanley Cup championship. It would be Jacques Plante's eighth straight appearance in the finals, a record that has yet to see another goalie come within three years of equalling.

As was the case the year before, the Canadiens matched up in the finals against the Toronto Maple Leafs.

Despite an extended layoff, the Canadiens wasted little time in putting the underdog Leafs on the defensive. The opening game of the finals saw the Canadiens jump out to a quick 3–0 lead against the over- whelmed Leafs. It wasn't until five minutes into the second period that Plante finally allowed a puck to reach the back of his net, snapping his playoff shutout streak at 150 minutes and 3 seconds. Another Leafs tally near the end of the second period added a glimmer of excitement to what had been a hopelessly dull game, but a goal by Henri Richard, who had already recorded three assists on the game, a minute and a half into the third, ended the scoring as the Canadiens prevailed 4–2.

The second game, played two nights later, followed a similar script, with the Canadiens jumping to an early lead 90 seconds in on a goal scored by Dickie Moore. Assisting were Henri Richard, for his fifth point of the series, and the Rocket. Jean Béliveau made it 2–0 mere minutes later, before the Leafs responded with a goal near the end of the first period to make it 2–1.

For the final two periods the Canadiens nursed their one-goal lead as an impenetrable Plante shut the door the rest of the way. Sitting in the crowd, carefully watching the game, was his old adversary Terry Sawchuk. After choosing Plante as the game's first star, Sawchuk commented to the media that "Plante was the difference."[11]

As the series switched to Maple Leaf Gardens for the pivotal third game, it appeared that Plante, as he had in the series before, was starting to take control of the finals as well. The game left little doubt to the series' outcome, as the Canadiens skated off with a convincing 5–2 win.

"Playing those Canadiens is like sitting on a horse with a noose around your neck," declared Boston Bruins coach Milt Schmidt. "The minute the horse gets hungry and moves for a bite of grass you've had it. Make one mistake against the Habs and you're dead."[12]

With the Canadiens now in control and the series' conclusion no longer in doubt, attention shifted to the Rocket, who had scored the final goal of the night. In adding to his own all-time record, the Rocket had scored the eighty-second playoff goal of his illustrious career. When cornered after the game and asked why he had kept the puck, a sly Rocket replied, "Just in case."[13]

As the Leafs faced elimination, they were left to ponder what had gone wrong against the dominant Canadiens. They found the main reason for their predicament standing in front of the Montreal net. "There's no doubt about it," Punch Imlach confessed to reporters. "Plante is murdering us. He's making the key saves." Added legendary Leaf and assistant coach King Clancy, "He's the best."[14]

For Plante, who had struggled through a second half of the season where the discussion focused on his mask and his rising goals-against, it was the sweetest of vindications. As for why his play had suddenly returned to the level of past years, Plante had no explanation.

"I was scared going in to the Chicago series," he revealed to the media. "I knew I wasn't playing well and that the Black Hawks were climbing all the time. But since the third game of the Chicago series, it all came back. I started making the right moves. I don't know what I'm doing differently. All I know is that I'm not being beaten by easy shots and it makes me feel good all over."[15]

"This is such an easy team to play for," Jacques continued, "and it is also such a tough team to play goal for, eh? When the team wins,

THE PINNACLE

people say Plante has a cinch, with defense guys like Harvey and Johnson in front of him. I've got to make saves, too, you know. Ah, but it's nice to have shooters like Jean and Dickie and Pocket Rocket and all the others on your side."[16]

Any thoughts that the Canadiens might let up were easily doused in a fourth game that was a display of utter hockey domination, the likes of which arguably have never been seen since. Jean Béliveau and Doug Harvey scored the opening two goals less than 30 seconds apart in the first period, with Henri Richard adding a third in the middle period, before Béliveau climaxed the scoring in the third period. The Canadiens' 4–0 Cup-clinching win was yet another shutout for Plante, his third of the playoffs.

As the final buzzer sounded, Plante took the mask off his face and held it high in the air for all to see. He had proved all the detractors and doubters wrong. Not only had he won another Vezina Trophy while wearing a mask, he had now captured a Stanley Cup with one of the most stellar goaltending performances of all time, all the while wearing a mask.

The Stanley Cup was wheeled to centre ice at Maple Leaf Gardens, and NHL president Clarence Campbell made his presentation, during which Maurice Richard made his way over and hugged the Cup. Soon Jacques Plante skated over, and there stood the Rocket and Jake the Snake. After the Rocket spoke to the remnants of that evening's crowd, he and Plante locked arms, and with the Cup between them posed for the assembled photographers.

The Canadiens' supremacy that spring was complete. They had captured their fifth consecutive Stanley Cup in the minimum eight games. They had scored the first goal in each of the eight games. They had never trailed on the scoreboard in any of the eight games. Henri Richard and Bernie Geoffrion led all playoff scorers with 12 points each, while Plante was at his stingiest, allowing only 11 pucks to cross his goal line in the eight playoff games.

In the days that followed, the accolades usually reserved for the greatest of all champions poured in when describing the Canadiens.

Even Conn Smythe, a man who rarely gave out any compliments when discussing the opposition, was forced to admit that his beloved Leafs "had lost to the greatest team of all time."[7] Such a sentiment no doubt warmed the heart of Smythe's long-time rival, Frank Selke.

As the Canadiens gathered for their team photograph the next day accompanied by the Stanley Cup, Jacques Plante stood at the pinnacle of his sport. He had claimed an unprecedented five straight Vezina trophies and six Stanley Cups all by the age of 31. As the years have gone by, the magnitude of his achievement and his contribution to that greatest of all teams has not diminished, especially in the eyes of his former teammates.

"When it came to the team that won five straight Stanley Cups, we had so much talent we never worried," remembered Hall of Fame defenceman Tom Johnson. "We never thought we'd lose. There was a real confidence factor on that team, plus we got the great goaltending from Plante. You knew if you got a goal, and if you ever got two goals, forget about it, you had a win with Jacques Plante in goal. We never even thought of losing."[18]

"Jacques Plante is my guy when you ask about a key player on that team," asserted defenceman Bob Turner to Habs historian Dick Irvin Jr. "As far as I'm concerned he's the best goalie of all-time. People talk about Sawchuk or Dryden or Fuhr and I just laugh. I don't care. Plante was the best."[19]

But perhaps the supreme testament to Plante's role and importance on that greatest of all teams came in a conversation a few years later, between two men who had seen it all first-hand. "I once asked Toe Blake who was the best goalie he ever saw," remembers Red Fisher today. "He told me that in the five years that the Canadiens won the Stanley Cup, Jacques Plante was the greatest goaltender he ever saw. For Toe to say that is really something. You have to have known Toe Blake. He threw around compliments like anchors. I was more than a little surprised, so I said to Toe that I didn't think you liked the son of a bitch, and Toe said to me that he was the best, what do you want me to tell you." And Red himself? "In my view he was the biggest reason the Canadiens won the Cup for five consecutive years. The 1959–60 team was the best ever and that was because of Jacques Plante."[20]

Fisher has also said that Plante "made goaltending an art rather than a profession. He set an entirely new standard of a way to play goal. He was a little more reliable all the time and he did more for the game of hockey than all the other goaltenders put together. He always ended up being a winner. Like him or not he was a winner."[21]

16

ONE STEP BACK

AS THE CANADIENS GATHERED for training camp in the fall of 1960, there was every expectation that this team would encounter little resistance on their way to a sixth consecutive Stanley Cup. Increasingly, many columnists, fans, and even executives urged NHL president Clarence Campbell to take measures to help bring an end to the Canadiens' run of success, claiming that their supremacy resulted in a lack of competitiveness and was bringing more harm to the game than good.

Campbell's intervention turned out to be unnecessary, as the passage of time began to undermine the Canadiens' dominance.

There was one major topic of discussion as training camp got under way: the career status of one Maurice "Rocket" Richard. On the morning of September 15, Richard scrimmaged with the team. The opposing goaltender was Plante. That morning, he put four pucks past a stunned Plante and added three assists. It was vintage Rocket. He then made his way up to Frank Selke's office and promptly retired. A press conference was held that very afternoon at the Queen Elizabeth Hotel.

"The fact is I didn't really give any serious consideration to retiring until my last season in the league," the Rocket remembered later. "That's when my weight started to bother me and I knew I was slowing down. When I arrived at the 1960 training camp I surprised myself. I played very well and was scoring goals, but also I was feeling it. I was obviously forcing myself and I seemed to be trying too hard. Back in the bench I'd get dizzy spells. And I started to fear getting hurt. Right in the middle of training camp I made up my mind that I had had it. The dizziness, the pushing, and the fact that it was so hard to lose weight convinced me that I'd be better off retiring."[1]

"If the Rocket was too old and didn't have 'it' anymore, what did that make me, huh?" said Plante, the victim of the Rocket's final four goals.[2]

In a closed vote, the Rocket's former teammates overwhelmingly voted Doug Harvey the Canadiens' next captain.

On the day of his retirement, the Rocket held or co-held 18 NHL regular-season records and 14 Stanley Cup playoff scoring records. But it would be his immense presence that the Canadiens would miss more than anything.

The Rocket's retirement was the only major departure from the team, and many still predicted a sixth straight Stanley Cup.

The team's first game of the season indicated that they were picking up right where they had left off the year before. The Boomer opened the scoring 66 seconds in, Henri Richard added two goals, and Jacques Plante didn't allow one to pass the goal line in a 5–0 whitewashing of the Toronto Maple Leafs.

However, unknown to his teammates or coach, Plante had begun feeling the effects of an earlier knee injury. He was unable to pinpoint when the pain began, only that it was there in spades. He hoped it would go away like many pains often do, but it didn't. That was when he noticed that he'd been subconsciously changing his way of play in an effort to relieve the pain. He was starting to make the first move against the opposing shooter, with often disastrous results.

As the Canadiens and Plante slumped in the early going, winning only six of their first 12 games, whispers again started that the mask was the problem. It was Toe Blake, the mask's biggest critic a year before, who now came to Plante's defence.

"I'm not gonna tell him to take off his mask for this reason: if he should ever get hurt, I'd be the guy they'd be blaming for the rest of my life," Blake told the media. "Plante knows how I feel about it. If he wants to take it off, it's up to him. I think he could play better without it, but I won't insist that he removes it."[3]

Unfortunately, the Habs' problems continued. The situation came to a head after the Canadiens narrowly avoided embarrassment at home on November 10. Plante allowed seven goals to beat him. Luckily, Jack

McCartan, a rookie goalie for the Rangers, allowed nine goals. "In a word, Plante is on the hot seat," wrote the *Montreal Star*, "and the Canadiens front office men are worried about the situation. The five times Vezina Trophy winner has allowed 56 goals in 16 games, and he shows no signs of improving."[4]

Plante's superiority in the playoffs a mere six months before now seemed like a lifetime ago. The seven goals allowed was a high in Plante's career and led to an emergency meeting of the Montreal brass. The following day, Frank Selke revealed to Red Fisher that he was in support of temporarily shelving Plante in favour of his perennial backup, Charlie Hodge, but that it was Toe Blake who had fought for and won the day for Plante.[5]

"I don't care what anybody says, Plante's still the best goalie in the league," a defiant Toe Blake announced to the *Hockey News*. "Sure, I admit he hasn't been as sharp as he was during the first half of last year or in the playoffs last spring, but neither has anyone else on my team, or at least most of them."[6]

Plante, keeping his sore knee a secret, responded to Blake's public vote of confidence with back-to-back weekend victories over Detroit and New York, temporarily silencing his critics. The team's next game was the following Saturday in Toronto, and the torrent of criticism was renewed in the face of a 6–3 loss at the Maple Leaf Gardens. The next night Plante battled Glenn Hall and the Black Hawks to a 1–1 draw at the Chicago Stadium before bowing to Terry Sawchuk and the Red Wings 3–1 four nights later in Detroit.

For the first time in memory the Canadiens were mired in a long-term slump. In hockey, when a team is struggling it is usually the goaltender who receives the majority of the blame, and in the case of Plante's higher goals-against average, it was becoming harder to defend him. He was ranked fourth amongst all goalies at this early stage of the season, having given up 18 more goals than the league leader, Toronto's Johnny Bower, and 15 more than his main rival, Chicago's Glenn Hall.

Frustration was mounting in all corners. Plante finally came forward with his sore knee and had it X-rayed, but doctors were unable to find anything amiss. This led some in the Canadiens organization to question whether there was indeed anything physically wrong with the underachieving Plante.

The irony was that Plante, who had suffered numerous severe and painful injuries and had played on when men of lesser fortitude would have stayed on the sidelines, was now being widely doubted when he complained about the pain in his knee.

Plante faced a difficult decision. He knew something was wrong with his knee, despite the X-ray results. He could play through the pain, he could rest and hope that the pain would subside, or he could undergo major invasive surgery that would threaten his chances of playing that season. This was the era before mini scopes that would have allowed surgeons to investigate before operating – it was either major surgery or none at all.

In the face of constant pressure from Selke and the team's vice-president, Ken Reardon, Blake finally gave in and started Charlie Hodge at the Forum against the visiting Chicago Black Hawks on November 26. Hodge was no stranger to the Montreal Canadiens. After all, he had been attending training camps for almost as long as the man who stood in the way of his professional advancement. While Plante had unprecedented success as the Montreal starter, Hodge had toiled in anonymity in various cities and leagues waiting for the phone to ring.

The call did come a few times through the years. Hodge played 14 games for the Canadiens in 1954–55, 12 games in 1957–58, two games in 1958–59, and a single game in 1959–60. Waiting for his chance, he had played for eight different teams in the past decade, in locales such as Rochester, Cincinnati, Seattle, Ottawa-Hull, and Plante's hometown of Shawinigan.

Now the door of opportunity had slightly opened. Hodge was determined to burst through. That weekend he defeated Glenn Hall and the Black Hawks 4–2, before shuttling off to Boston the next night and shutting out the Bruins 3–0. With Hodge manning the nets, the Canadiens were finally able to shake out of their early-season slumber and won the first eight games of his tenure.

Even though Plante was relegated to a spectator's role, he travelled with the Canadiens, practised diligently each day, and generously offered Hodge advice on how to deal with the circuit's more dangerous shooters. He did all of this without public complaint, and suffered his fate with grace and silence, as Hodge kept winning. Blake debated reinserting Plante, but the Canadiens brass, wishing to stay with the winning hand, were understandably reluctant to make the switch.

"I can't see any sense in making a change," Toe Blake told the *Toronto Star*. "Maybe it would be different if Plante could tell me his injured knee is 100 per cent right. He can't tell me that, so we'll go with Hodge."[7]

In an effort to relieve the ever-present pain in his knee, Plante began taking treatments from club physiotherapist Bill Head, who gave him a series of exercises designed to ease the throbbing in his leg. But the regimen brought little relief. "If you had seen Plante practice yesterday you wouldn't bet too much money that he'll be back for a long time," said Toe Blake. "He made a face every time he went after a puck. He seemed to be in pain with every move."[8]

As the calendar turned from 1960 to 1961, Hodge and the Canadiens continued to win at a torrid pace. After weeks of therapy, Plante was healthier, yet he continued to watch from the sidelines. This was out of character for him, and Canadiens beat writer Red Fisher sought to explain the mystery.

It is necessary to explore the character of the man to understand, in some small way, why he has been satisfied to sit on the sidelines all this time. He doesn't have to prove his ability. His record is proof enough of his talent. However, in many ways, the goalie is a strange man. He's a loner. He's supremely confident in his own talent, and as the games go by, he must find it increasingly difficult to believe that the Canadiens can win without him.

Thus, he's been leaving it to the Canadiens front office to take the initiative in his case. For a long time, he's been waiting for people like coach Toe Blake to ask him to return to his regular job, and this, Blake has found impossible to do, Hodge has been too good.

Any other player would have approached his employers a long time ago and asked to be returned to his position. Plante, though, isn't like any other player. His entire career has been one of nonconformity, and the system has worked for him. He has learned, though, that his employers can be just as stubborn as he is. It is their feeling that if Plante wants his job back, he has to ask for it – and then win it back.[9]

A few days into the new year, Jacques Plante finally swallowed his immense pride. Before one of the team's practices he approached Toe Blake and pronounced himself ready to play. Both Blake and Plante were proud and stubborn men, and their complex relationship was based more on professional respect than on any feelings of personal closeness. It had now been five weeks since Hodge had assumed the goaltending duties, and during that time Blake and Plante had not had a single discussion with each other about Plante's status.

"I talked it over with Plante and I told him the situation," Blake informed the press. "I can't take Hodge out of there, not with the way he's been playing. It would be unfair. Plante agreed completely. He realized that Hodge has been playing winning hockey for us. He accepts the idea of sitting on the sidelines. I was pleased with the way Plante took it."[10]

It had been a humbling season for Plante. He was the most accomplished goalie in the world, but for the first time in many years, there were now questions about his importance to the Canadiens. Jacques Plante was a driven man; he thrived when faced with a challenge and motivated himself in the face of doubt. Now he had to prove himself all over again. Such is the life of a goaltender: you're only as good as your last game. Jacques Plante emerged from his sabbatical a re-energized and reinvigorated man, despite the continuing pain in his knee.

But Plante had been on the sidelines for so long that the Canadiens were concerned about his readiness for action. Frank Selke summoned an eager Plante to his office. It was a meeting Plante never forgot.

"Jacques, you just aren't going to make it this way," a blunt Selke began. "I have to think of the end of the season and the possibility of having to replace Hodge for any reason. Your prospects of being ready are doubtful. I want to send you down in the hope that you will recover your sharpness."

"Down where?" asked Plante.

"To the Montreal Royals."

Plante was honest enough to know that his game needed improvement. Yet going to the Royals felt like a big step back. But these thoughts were soon overwhelmed by a familiar sensation – the excitement of a challenge.

"When do you want me to report?"[11]

It had been a little under nine years since Plante had suited up for the Montreal Royals. Now a team playing in the Eastern Professional Hockey League, they were anchored at the bottom of the standings. That the team was in last place mattered little to Plante. Unburdened of the pressure of chasing first place or trying to win a championship, he was free to focus on fine-tuning his own game.

There had not been a bigger story in hockey circles that season. Plante's quick and sudden transformation from Vezina Trophy–winning goalie to minor leaguer attracted widespread attention.

"Today one cannot spend five minutes in Montreal without hearing, in French or English, an explanation for this bizarre turnabout," wrote Jack Olsen in a *Sports Illustrated* profile on Plante entitled "Hero's Humiliation in Montreal."

Plante cooled off, they will tell you. Plante is hurt. Plante is being taught a lesson in humility. Plante asked to be sent down. Plante was thrown out kicking and screaming. Plante will be back next week. Plante will never be back.

Says a brooding, chastened Plante himself: "I have to face the fact, I may not play again for the Canadiens this year." The French-language newspaper *Le Dimanche-Matin* congratulated the banished goaltender for having "beaucoup de guts" about the demotion.[12]

Plante's "demotion" helped serve another purpose for Selke and the Canadiens organization. Attendance for the Royals' home games held at the Montreal Forum was averaging a mere 2,000 spectators. Plante, in his first game back, backstopped the last-place Royals to an upset of the first place Hull-Ottawa Canadiens in front of 5,198 fans. It was the lowly Royals' tenth game that season against the league-leading Hull team. Thanks to Plante they had their first win.

Playing in the rinks of the EPHL, Plante was a major gate attraction. Fans in these traditionally minor league cities now had an opportunity to glimpse a living, breathing hockey legend that many had seen only on television. In Kingston, 6,090 paid for the privilege to see Plante live. In Sault Ste. Marie, the second-biggest crowd of the year (3,357) came out to see him in helping the Royals to a 5–3 win.

According to the president of the EPHL, Plante upped crowds around the circuit by at least one-third.[13]

As his stay in the minors came close to the two-week mark, Plante began to openly wonder if returning to the Canadiens was a pipe dream and if his career might be coming to an end. "When you are sidelined like this, all kinds of thoughts go through the head," he confided to *Sports Illustrated*. "What am I going to do? What could happen? Charlie Hodge and I have been good friends since 1954. How can they take him out the way he's playing? And my knee is still bad. I have a lead boot at home. I strap it on and lift the leg for ten minutes every hour, all day long, hold it up there for 45 seconds. It hurts, but I want that job back. Maybe this year it is already too late. . . . I knew it had to happen sometime. Remember I am 32 years old. Charlie, he is just 26. I knew I would slip sometime, but, sonofagun, it is a little early, isn't it?"[14]

As Plante despaired about his future, events with the Canadiens began to take an unexpected turn in his favour. Since Plante's departure, the team with Hodge in net had emerged victorious only once in their last seven games, with Hodge surrendering 28 goals. The Canadiens' slump culminated on the weekend of February 4 and 5, when they dropped a 4–1 home decision only to follow it up with one of their worst performances in recent history, in a 7–2 whitewash by the Detroit Red Wings. The two losses knocked the Canadiens from their first-place perch and plunged them downward in the standings.

Charlie Hodge had just completed his thirtieth consecutive start in the Canadiens net. He had acquitted himself well, better than most expected, winning 18 games, losing only eight, tying four, and pitching four shutouts. But his time was up. Frank Selke convened an emergency meeting on February 6. The meeting included Plante and Blake, as well as the team's physiotherapist, Bill Head.

"We want to get back into first place," Selke told them straight off. "I think we need Jacques' experience and fighting spirit." Blake, who had always been Plante's biggest booster, remained skeptical as he stared at Jacques' bandaged knee.

"Tell me honestly, Jacques, how do you feel?" Blake asked bluntly.

Without hesitation, Plante replied, "About seventy-five per cent of my top form."

It was not the answer Blake wanted to hear and it did little to assuage his concerns. He took aside Bill Head, who soon came back and confronted Plante.

"They want to hear you say you're 100 per cent," Head told him. "As you know, in your job self-confidence means a lot."

Plante was annoyed. "And I want them to say to me. 'We know you are hurt, can play only seventy-five per cent, but we'll go with that.' What's more," he said, his voice rising in anger, "I feel that a seventy-five per cent Plante is as good as any goalkeeper in the National Hockey League."

Head smiled. "That answer ought to please them."[15]

In this trying season, Plante's confidence understandably may have wavered, but it had never disappeared, and his answer was exactly what a skeptical Blake wanted and needed to hear. And just like that, Jacques Plante found himself back where he always wanted to be.

Three nights later, on February 9, Plante skated out and made his return to the Canadiens lineup in a game at Boston Garden against the Bruins. He was aided by a brace on his troubled knee that his teammate Ralph Backstrom had provided.

In his first game, a refreshed and renewed Plante turned aside 20 Boston shots as the Canadiens pummelled the Bruins and their backstop Bruce Gamble with 48 shots in an easy 5–1 Montreal win.

Six nights later, the Canadiens travelled to Toronto for a showdown with the first-place Maple Leafs. For Plante, it was an opportunity to show the hockey world that rumours of his decline were grossly exaggerated.

"Maple Leafs got a message loud and clear last night," wrote the *Toronto Star*'s Red Burnett after a convincing 3–1 Canadiens win. "The message is that Jacques Plante is back in Vezina trophy form. And when Jacques is in that mood Montreal is next to unbeatable."[16]

The Jacques Plante who emerged from his sabbatical was a far different goaler than the one who had struggled the previous fall. In the 21 games that he played at the start of the season, he allowed 69 goals for a 3.50 goals-against average. After his return for the season's final 19 games, Plante allowed only 43 goals, for a 2.26 goals-against average.

The resurgence of Plante, along with Boom Boom Geoffrion's record-tying 50-goal season, helped push the Canadiens to the brink of first place. A win in the season's final game in Detroit would clinch first place. Jacques Plante, with a tumultuous year behind him, stepped confidently into the spotlight.

In a game in which the Canadiens outshot the Red Wings 39–20, only Jean Béliveau pierced the armour of Terry Sawchuk, who appeared to turn back the clock a decade by being the sole reason for such a close score. But on this night Plante was nothing less than perfect, and an empty-net goal with only one second on the clock by Claude Provost sealed the 2–0 victory and the Canadiens' fifth straight regular-season league title.

Jacques Plante had endured a year of humiliation and had even considered leaving the game that had been his life. But he had emerged from a career crisis to again take his place as the pre-eminent goalie in the game.

With the baggage of the season now behind him, Plante and the Canadiens could bask in a first-place finish that was their hardest and most satisfying yet. All that was left for them to accomplish was an unprecedented sixth consecutive Stanley Cup championship.

17

THE END OF THE LINE

AS THE CANADIENS BEGAN preparing for the playoffs and the possibility of a sixth consecutive Stanley Cup, they found themselves readying for a familiar foe. In the first round, for the third consecutive year they would face off with the Chicago Black Hawks, who had finished in third place, 17 points behind Montreal.

Having been swept by the Canadiens in the previous year's playoffs, and bowing out in five games the year before that, the Black Hawks had responded by building a bigger, more physical squad to augment their skilled players like Bobby Hull and Stan Mikita.

The first game seemed to bear out the media's prediction that the Canadiens would eliminate the Black Hawks for a third straight year. Chicago used its physical advantage to pound and outplay the Canadiens for the first two periods. However, after 40 minutes the game was tied at two, and the Black Hawks were overwhelmed by a four-goal barrage by the Canadiens in the third period. However, in the course of winning the first game 6–2 they had paid a heavy price.

"We didn't know it at the time but the most telling blow of all was dealt by Jack Evans against Jean Béliveau," recalled Bernie Geoffrion. "Jean was checked into the boards behind the net by the Chicago defenseman and struck his head on the glass as he was falling to the ice. The next day Béliveau still was complaining of a headache and would not be the same for the remaining games. If one check could turn a series, that was it."[1]

In addition to a suddenly impaired Béliveau, forward Billy Hicke was sent to the hospital with a slight concussion, and forward Donnie Marshall suffered a knee injury. Although the medical team recommended that he sit out at least the next few games, he chose to play, yet his effectiveness was unquestionably compromised.

For the first 40 minutes, the second game appeared to be following a script similar to the first. The two teams were tied at the conclusion of the second period. They exchanged goals in the third period, then Eddie Litzenberger, a former Canadien, beat Plante with less than three minutes to play, and the Black Hawks evened the series with a surprising 4–3 victory.

The series shifted to Chicago for game three. "This was not a game for the faint-hearted," Bernie Geoffrion later wrote. "Chicago Stadium was like a volcano waiting to erupt even before the opening face-off and it stayed that way throughout as bodies crunched bodies."[2]

In a career spanning more than 50 years, Red Fisher has been witness to over 4,000 hockey games, from regular-season tilts to playoffs, Canada Cups, World Championships, and the Olympics. When asked which is the greatest game he has ever seen, his answer is always the same: the third game of the 1961 semifinal series between the Canadiens and the Black Hawks.

"What occurred that night in Chicago was, arguably, the greatest performances by two goaltenders in NHL history," wrote Fisher. "From the start, the game belonged to Jacques Plante and Glenn Hall. Breakaways, long shots, slapshots, close-in shots – they saw them all and stopped them all for the entire first period and most of the second. Then, with less than two minutes remaining in the period, a gritty, hard-nosed left-winger named Murray Balfour, who had been 'sold' to the Black Hawks by the Canadiens in June of 1959, scored the game's first goal. The crowd erupted."

With 40 seconds left in the game, Toe Blake pulled Plante from the net in an attempt to tie the game. After a stoppage in play there was a critical faceoff in the Chicago end of the rink. Taking the draw would be Henri Richard, who decided to gamble. Instead of drawing the puck back like he would on almost every faceoff, he slapped at the dropped puck. The puck was in the back of the net before an unsuspecting Glenn Hall could react, and the game was tied.

The overtime was the height of excitement. Both teams exchanged numerous scoring chances as both goalies successfully defended their nets through the first overtime period and then a second overtime period.

"As the clock neared the twelve-minute mark of the third overtime, referee Dalton McArthur whistled down the Canadiens' Dickie Moore with a minor penalty," remembered Fisher. "Borderline stuff, particularly considering the time, the game's tempo, and the game's importance. Put it this way: there had been occasions earlier in the game when far more obvious penalties could have been called – against either team. Twenty-eight seconds later, at 12:12, Murray Balfour put the puck behind Jacques Plante from a scramble in front of the net. It was all over – except for the bedlam which followed."

The crowd went delirious in celebration. Making his way through the sea of debris that now littered the ice, an enraged Toe Blake made a beeline towards the scorer's bench, through the attempts of his players to restrain him. "McArthur still had his back to Blake when the Canadiens coach flung a punch which struck the referee on the shoulder and deflected onto his jaw," reported Fisher. "It was only then that McArthur turned, his eyes widening in surprise at the sight of Blake. That was also the moment when several Canadiens players wrapped their arms around their coach and led him from the ice."[3]

The repercussions from this chaos were sudden and severe. Toe's outburst would not go unpunished for long, and while he avoided a suspension, he was fined a then-record $2,000 by NHL president Clarence Campbell. For a man whose yearly salary was $18,000, it was a substantial amount. His punishment was not the only one. The following summer the NHL quietly relieved Dalton McArthur of his refereeing duties.

The loss of the game and Blake's record fine helped obscure a serious injury sustained by Geoffrion earlier in the game. Suffering from torn ligaments in his left knee, he had his leg secured in a cast, rendering him unavailable for the upcoming games in the series.

"We blew it against Chicago," Dickie Moore laments today. "I felt so bad at the end of game three because I took the penalty. It was a stupid penalty and the referee shouldn't have even called a penalty because the guy took a dive. I did put my stick on him, but not enough to pull him down. After the goal was scored, I slowly left the penalty box and felt horrible. I saw Toe coming across the ice, and I thought he was coming after me, but it turns out he was going after the referee." Moore laughs. "I was so thankful. I felt that I had cost the team the last game. And Toe, because of what happened with the referee, had taken all of the attention off me and the team and placed it all on himself. That was Toe Blake. I felt that I owed him and the team."[4]

Having scored only one goal in six periods against Glenn Hall two nights earlier, the Canadiens came out in game four and overwhelmed the Chicago goalie by bombarding him with 26 shots in the first period and 60 in total, for a 5–2 victory that evened the series. Leading the way was a spirited Moore, who paced the team with two goals.

In a series Rocket Richard called "the dirtiest I had ever seen," the physical play of the Black Hawks had been the main theme so far, and the Canadiens, despite having a generous rest in between games four and five, were a wounded group.

"The Black Hawks were kicking the stuffing out of us," wrote Bernie Geoffrion. "Their tough defense had practically nullified our offense. To give you an idea how much our attack was affected, our leading scorer for the series wasn't Béliveau, Moore, Henri Richard, or me, it was little Phil Goyette. Worse than that was the fact that we didn't have an antidote for their roughhousing."[5]

The list of the walking wounded now included Jacques Plante, who, despite playing with a brace since his return, was now suffering increased pain in his knee. Undoubtedly, the pressure of playing so many games in a row on an injured leg worsened the injury. Before games five and six, in the privacy of the dressing room, Jacques Plante was given a needle to anaesthetize his throbbing knee.

For the next two games, a weakened Jacques Plante knew he needed to be nothing short of great. He wasn't. Unfortunately for him and the Canadiens, Glenn Hall was perfect. Not one of Montreal's 32 shots beat Hall, as Chicago took control of the series with a 3–0 win in game five at the Forum.

"That was the worst we ever played in a play-off game since I've been here," complained Toe Blake. "But I still have confidence we'll pull it out of the fire. Our team always plays its best under the pressure."[6]

The desperate Canadiens, now facing elimination, boarded the train for Chicago for game six.

"Our predicament was clear," recalled Geoffrion. "We were a game away from having our Cup streak ended. My predicament was complicated. Dr. Larry Hampson had put my leg in a cast until April 7. But our do-or-die game in Chicago was April 4."[7]

On the train ride, Doug Harvey, the team's captain, ambled over and sat beside the injured Geoffrion. "Boom, we really need you tomorrow night," he said.

"Doug," replied Geoffrion, "I want to help but I've got this cast on my leg. What am I gonna do about that?"

"Why don't we cut it off, see how you feel without it?" suggested Harvey. "If you think it's okay, try working the power play."[8]

In the first five games of the series, the Canadiens had enjoyed a manpower advantage 22 times. They had scored the grand total of two goals. There was no doubt that the sudden disappearance of the Canadiens' vaunted power play was one of the series' enduring mysteries and a source of consternation for the increasingly frustrated Blake.

"I can't understand what's happened to our power play," Blake complained to the media. "I've told them over and over again that they've got to shoot the puck. But it happens all the time. They hold on to it, or they make that extra fancy pass, and the next thing we see is the puck going into our own end."[9]

With all that in mind, a hesitant Geoffrion acceded. "Doug got a knife from the train kitchen and the two of us sneaked into the ladies' washroom," Geoffrion remembered. "With my leg up on a chair I watched my captain saw away at the heavy plaster cast. He cut it lengthwise and the way the train was bouncing around it was a miracle I wasn't cut. It seemed to take hours to complete the job. I breathed a sigh of relief when he was done but soon had second thoughts. Pain shot up my leg when I stood up. I began to consider the repercussions of what we had done. I had plenty of time to think it all over because the leg hurt so much that I hardly slept a minute on the train that night."

The next morning the entire team saw the results of Harvey's handiwork. To say they were shocked would be an understatement. Toe Blake and Frank Selke were less than thrilled with the amateur medical procedure, but Geoffrion begged the two men to allow him to play, and after much deliberation and an injection to freeze the injured leg, Geoffrion skated out for game six.

"I wasn't trying to be a hero by biting the bullet and all that but I did have a sense of loyalty to the Habs and if they ever needed a boost this was it. After all how many times do you get to go for six straight Stanley Cups?"

Blake decided to use Geoffrion solely on the power play, and an opportunity presented itself midway through the first period. The opposition knew of Geoffrion's weakness, and as soon as he touched the puck he was met by a charging Bobby Hull.

"Sure enough Hull connected," Geoffrion wrote. "In fact he connected so hard that I crashed backward onto the bad knee. I knew then that they were determined to get me out of the game. I hobbled back to the bench and begged for one more chance but when it came on another power play they just knocked me right off my gimpy leg once more and that was really it. I was finished."[10] A dejected Geoffrion spent the rest of the game sitting on the bench.

The Canadiens fired 27 shots at the sturdy Hall, who once again presented an impenetrable figure, which the injured Plante was unable to match in the 3–0 defeat that ended the series and the season. It was a depressed and damaged group of players who solemnly made the long train ride back from Chicago.

"What a difference a year makes," commented Charlie Halpin in the *Montreal Star*. "This could very well have been the reaction of the vanquished Canadiens who arrived home today to the almost hushed cheers of a few banner-waving fans at Central Station."[11]

The greatest team the game had ever known had been dethroned, and an era of unmatched stability was about to become a time of change for the Canadiens.

The postmortem on the Canadiens' season began right away as many sought to explain their failure to win a sixth straight Stanley Cup.

"They were a powerhouse," recalled Frank Selke Jr. "But when the Rocket retired in 1960, he not only took his talent and skills away with him, he took his heart, too. I think maybe that had more to do with the team not being able to win the next year, win a sixth straight, than anything else. It wasn't the same team without his fire."[12]

With the benefit of hindsight it is easy to see that the Black Hawks' victory over the Canadiens was merely the first step in a change of direction in the way the game was coached and played. Chicago had imposed its physical will on the skilled Canadiens. The fact that an average player like Jack Evans could render the great Jean Béliveau impotent for the whole series spoke volumes. Now a team of superior talent could be brought down to the opponent's level of play through some mere roughhousing and intimidation. Thus began an era in which brawn took over from skill as the deciding factor in many a playoff series.

As was usually the case, the astute Frank Selke had seen the writing on the wall.

"Canadiens are going to be a lot tougher next season," Selke promised on the train ride home. "We have been playing nice, clean hockey a little too long. The Black Hawks deliberately racked up five of our best players and not one of the Canadiens put a hand on them in retaliation. I'm tired of hearing fans calling our players 'yellow-bellies.' This is going to change."[3]

Selke also vowed that Jacques Plante would be his goalie the following year. "But Jacques has got to take things more seriously," Selke warned. "He wasn't up to par through the early part of the schedule although he played his position better than most of the other players in the latter part."[4]

With the season over, Jacques Plante wrestled with the weight of a critical decision. The pain in his knee was once again intense, resulting in many a sleepless night. His choices boiled down to two options: retirement or an operation.

Despite his inconclusive X-rays, Plante knew there was something amiss with his knee. Furthermore, he knew that there was no way he could play another season with the Canadiens in this condition. He did not take the decision lightly.

"I thought it might be the end of my career," Plante recalled a year later. "A friend of mine who played goal in the minors had the same operation and he had to quit playing."[5]

Plante decided to go under the knife. His career hung in the balance.

THE HART

JACQUES PLANTE WOKE UP from his surgery disoriented. He couldn't remember later if he saw a nurse or a doctor, but he had to ask the question that had been bothering him and selling reams of newspapers for the season past: "Did they find anything wrong in the knee?"

"You had a torn cartilage, but it will be all right now."

He soon fell back asleep, comforted by his feelings of vindication. He had been right all along.

When he awoke later, he heard his wife, Jacqueline, at the end of the room, talking to his doctor.

"There's no reason why, with a summer of carefully directed exercise, Jacques won't be ready for September," the doctor told Jacqueline, unaware that her husband was now listening.

Jacques took a long, deep breath before cutting in on the conversation. "As soon as you let me out of here, I'll start exercising."

In the days after the surgery, Jacques was unable to do much of anything other than lie in his hospital bed. He found himself alone with his thoughts, many of which focused on the disappointment of the season before.

"It's astonishing what comes out when a man sits alone and gets honest with himself, just thinking," Plante reflected later. "I realized that I had started the last season over-impressed by the knowledge that

I had set a record no goaler would likely repeat in the stepped-up era of hockey, namely five straight Vezina Trophies. That egotistical satisfaction undoubtedly did me as much harm as the bad knee. . . . Subconsciously, I now realized, no desire was firing me to go after another Vezina. Whereas, during those five seasons, I had been fighting for every goal every night, I was making the knee an excuse not to go after every hard puck when we were leading by several goals. If they got another goal, or even two, so what as long as we won? I also realized that I had been letting up on the easy shots – stopping them, sure, but not with the extreme care that has to become a habit if you want to be a topflight NHL goaler. Then I began pitying myself because nobody would believe I was really hurt."[1]

Rare was the player who spent his summer working on an exercise routine. After all, that's what training camp was for. Much of training camp was spent skating laps, and after a few weeks it was believed that the players would be in game shape.

"I remember the first time I stepped into the Montreal Forum in 1969," remembers Réjean Houle today. "There was the dressing room, and a little side room for the training staff, along with the coaches' office. But what stuck out to me is how there wasn't any room dedicated to weights and/or exercise equipment."[2]

Off-season training was one of the few things that Plante previously shared with his fellow teammates. In his now decade-long professional career, he had never taken time out of his summer vacation to work on his fitness level. He had never engaged in a routine. Starting in the summer of 1961, he never again did without.

Following a regimen set out by the team's physiotherapist, Bill Head, Plante began rehabilitating his surgically repaired knee. It was a long, gradual, and often tedious process. After walking around gently and slowly bending the repaired knee, Plante was instructed to resume strapping a 16-pound weight to his foot. Whenever he would sit down to watch television or read a book, he would attach the weight to his foot and lift it at prescribed intervals.

As he built up strength in his leg, Plante was able to progress to longer and more hurried walks that grew to include up-and-down stair climbing. He started using a treadmill to speed up his walking, and soon advanced to jogging. He also played tennis, and it wasn't long before he was spending three hours a day on the local tennis courts.

When he wasn't hitting the tennis ball, he could usually be found on the golf course. For the past few summers, he and many of his teammates were employed by Molson Breweries, the Canadiens' new owners. Their job entailed playing in charity golf tournaments and attending celebrity banquets, and that was where Plante was able to interact with the public on a more personal level. He was pleased to discover that most of the people he met were very encouraging and supportive.

His recovery also allowed him to attend various hockey schools in the summer. A valued instructor across Canada and in Worcester, Massachusetts, he discovered that he loved imparting his wisdom to the next generation of goaltenders, who hung on his every word.

Jacques Plante emerged from his summer revitalized and determined to regain his former form. He felt that he had something to prove to those who had doubted him – and most of all to himself.

As Labour Day approached and training camp beckoned, Plante went to the Montreal Forum office of Frank Selke to discuss his contract for the upcoming season. A confident Plante showed off his improved knee, jumping around Selke's office. Selke remained firmly rooted to his chair.

"Jacques, I don't know what we are going to do with you next season."

Plante's elation quickly drained away as a cold silence gripped the room. Selke confessed that he was concerned about the rising number of goals against the Canadiens. He was not the type to overlook any detail, and in this case he was correct: over the last six years, Plante's goals-against had indeed steadily risen (1.86, 2.02, 2.11, 2.16, 2.54, and 2.80 the season before).

Many players would have been silenced when confronted with such numbers. Then again, not many players possessed a mind as quick as Jacques Plante's.

He quickly shot back: "So has the average of every other goaler in the league. If I was the only one I'd be worried."

Selke laughed and found himself agreeing with his goalie. Goals had been on the rise throughout the league the past few years as the slapshot started to become favoured among the players.

After a couple more visits to hammer out the details, Plante accepted a pay decrease of $1,000, leaving him with a base salary of $15,000 for the upcoming season. But the wise Selke dangled a carrot in front of Plante. If he won the Vezina Trophy in the next season, Selke would refund him his $1,000 and the team would pay him a bonus of $2,000 in addition to the $1,000 bonus paid out by the league.[3]

Selke knew his goaltender well. By flashing a potential financial reward in front of his frugal netminder, he was fuelling the man's intensity. In addition, the careful Selke was hedging his bet.

With the Canadiens beginning their training camp in Victoria, British Columbia, in the middle of September, the organization had decided to split their annual camp between the professional and amateur parts of the team. A week before the Canadiens began their professional training camp, the organization's minor league prospects gathered in Hull, Quebec. One veteran stood out among this group of youngsters. Imagine the surprise of the local reporters when they found Jacques Plante guarding one of the amateur nets. He was the only member of the Canadiens to attend the camp.

"I suppose I did work a little harder," he admitted later to the *Hockey News*. "But I've always tried to play as hard as I could and trained just as hard. After all if you can't do your job, somebody else will take your place no matter what business you are in. And if Canadiens didn't have a goalie, they'd get one. That's the way it goes in pro hockey."[4]

Plante didn't just merely show up at the rookie camp; instead he used it as a testing ground for his rebuilt knee. His knee passed the test, and his performance was so strong that Frank Selke crowed as the hockey experts predicted that the Canadiens would fall to fourth, fifth, or sixth place in the season to come. "Plante will make the difference," proclaimed Selke, who professed to have no worries about the season to follow. "Jacques is starting out with a different attitude than last year and his morale is marvelous. Don't be surprised if he has the best season of his hockey career."[5]

Few in the media gave much credence to Selke's prediction.

Upon his arrival in the Canadiens training camp a week later, Jacques Plante knew that the first question would be who would replace the team's former captain, Doug Harvey.

In the wake of the team's defeat the season before, Selke had promised that there would be changes to the Canadiens. That summer he made good on his vow when he shipped Harvey to the New York Rangers in exchange for the rugged defenceman Lou Fontinato.

The trading of Doug Harvey still elicits a wide range of debate. Seeing as he had just won his sixth Norris Trophy as the league's best defenceman, his trade made little sense to many observers. Perhaps the reason lay in Harvey's personality, which had him constantly at odds with the team's management. Whatever the reasons, having decided that Harvey had no future in the team's front office, the Canadiens management, tired of his antics and aware of his increasing age, shipped him out to the Rangers while he still had some value. (Doug Harvey would reluctantly become the new player-coach of the perennially struggling Rangers and become the highest-paid player in the game.)

Up to this point in Plante's career, the one criticism that had continually dogged him was that his success had more to do with the players in front of him than with his own skill. The critics said (incorrectly) that he faced on average a lower number of shots on goal than other goalies. And the one player who was always singled out above all of Plante's teammates was Doug Harvey. Without the presence of Harvey, there were those who wondered how effective Plante would be.

On the first day of training camp, Red Fisher posed the question that the entire hockey world wanted to ask. "How much is the team going to miss Doug?"

"I figured that would be the first question I'd be asked in training camp," Jacques replied with a grin before adding, "Listen to this: Doug Harvey is the greatest defenseman in the National Hockey League. All of us, and especially me, owe him a lot. He helped me win five Vezinas in a row. But now I'm going to show you how good Jacques Plante is, I'm going to win the Vezina without him."

"Do you really think you can?" Fisher asked.

"Watch me," replied Plante.[6]

On the eve of the season opener, the Canadiens gathered to select their team captain. In a vote held among the players, Jean Béliveau and Bernie Geoffrion tied for the honour, with Béliveau winning the tiebreaker.

Béliveau found himself in a cast to begin the season. He was joined on the sidelines by Dickie Moore. Yet despite these injuries and the absence of Harvey, the much-predicted collapse of the Canadiens never happened. The team unexpectedly thrived, and in the season's first eight games went undefeated, winning seven and tying one.

The Canadiens were now a team in transition. Bobby Rousseau, a native Montrealer, would take home that season's Calder Trophy as the league's best rookie, while second-year forward Gilles Tremblay blossomed with a 32-goal season, making him one of two Habs players to top the 30-goal mark. Sophomore J.C. Tremblay helped pick up the slack in the defensive end.

Surprisingly, the other Canadien to score 30 was not Geoffrion, Béliveau, or Moore but instead the previously unheralded defensive forward Claude Provost, who led the team with 33 goals. Now in his seventh year with the team, Provost took advantage of the offensive opportunity provided.

Yet the bulk of the credit for the Canadiens' strong start to the season went to Plante, who had been written off only months before by many of the same fickle critics.

Starting on November 18, the Canadiens embarked on a 13-game unbeaten streak that vaulted them into first place. "I don't want to take anything away from the other players," said Toe Blake. "But, let's face it. Without Plante, we wouldn't be as high in the standings as we are."[7]

For the first time in his career, Plante was being universally lauded for his play – without reservation.

"Maybe I'm just lucky," Plante told the *Hockey News*. "But I guess the operation on my knee had a lot to do with it. That cartilage trouble may have been bothering me for two or three years and I didn't notice it. My timing was off last year and I couldn't move as quickly as I wanted to."[8] Plante said he didn't think he was playing that much better. "Maybe it's just that people are noticing me more. I'm getting more shots to handle this season. That could be the reason. It's tough on a goalie when he has to go long stretches with just two or three stops. You get cold out there and lose your edge. When I get 10 or 15 shots a period, I've found I stay warm and play much better."[9]

When the season's first-half first all-stars were announced in the middle of January, the league-leading Canadiens were represented by only one player: Jacques Plante.

He was further disproving those critics who accused him of frailty by playing through some minor injuries. Early in the season in Toronto he suffered an asthma attack but played the next night in Boston. An ankle injury in early February had the Canadiens ready the standby goaltender, but Plante still played. At the end of the month a woozy Plante was lifted from a game after a goalmouth collision with Ken Schinkel of the Rangers. After a short break he returned to the game, despite a sore back and aching ribs.

"I'd seen him play four or five times that year," remembered noted hockey writer Jack Falla, "and I was thinking, I've never seen Plante play better than this. I've never seen anyone have a year like Jacques Plante had that year."[10]

For the first and only time in his career, he played the entire schedule of 70 games. And despite the much-publicized absence of Doug Harvey, the Canadiens allowed only 166 goals, 22 fewer than the previous year when Harvey had been on the team. Along with a modest goals-against average of 2.37 that led the league, the Habs finished in first place for the fifth consecutive year with 98 points.

After a one-year sabbatical Plante recaptured the Vezina Trophy, his sixth, tying the record of his hero, Bill Durnan.

The Canadiens' reward for finishing in first place was a fourth straight playoff showdown with the Chicago Black Hawks, who had finished 23 points behind them in the standings. Fully expecting a bruising battle, the Canadiens entered the series already down one of their superstars, as Henri Richard was forced to watch from the sidelines with a broken arm.

Much to the surprise of most observers, game one between the two rivals was a relatively tame affair that saw the Canadiens walk away with a 2–1 win.

The second game was more exciting. The Canadiens were trailing 3–1 with only 10 minutes to play. The close score was testament to the spectacular play of Plante, who was, in the words of the *Toronto Star*, "the whole show."[11] Inspired by their goalie, the Canadiens exploded for three late goals, in a come-from-behind 4–3 win that put the Habs up 2–0 in the series as the train pulled out for Chicago.

"The worst injury occurred during the third game of the 1961–62 play-offs," Jean Béliveau wrote later. "I was in the corner, scuffling for the puck with my former teammate Dollard St. Laurent, when suddenly the lights went out. While Dollard and I were scrambling, the other Chicago defenseman, big Jack Evans" – the same man who had left him with a concussion in last year's playoffs – "left his post in front of the net and charged me into the boards, catching me in the head with his stick, then driving my head into the glass. Even though I dressed for the remaining games, I was finished for the play-offs."[12]

Sadly for the Canadiens, Béliveau wasn't the only casualty in the 4–1 defeat. Ralph Backstrom separated his shoulder. This meant that the team's top three centres were all injured to various degrees. Furthermore, Bernie Geoffrion twisted his knee and was ineffective for the remainder of the series.

With Richard out, and Béliveau, Geoffrion, and Backstrom not playing at full strength, the Canadiens faced a daunting task. The young stars who had carried the team in the regular season failed to come through in the playoffs, and Montreal was unable to win another game. They bowed out for a second straight year to the Black Hawks in six games.

It was another disappointing ending to what had seemed a promising spring. Once again, the Black Hawks had neutralized the Canadiens' talent advantage and asserted their physical superiority.

As the dispirited Canadiens flew home, the players began their off-season. Jacques Plante was set to begin the longest road trip of his life. Representing Molson Breweries, he embarked on a 10,000-mile trip that would see him attend 21 banquets from Vancouver to Winnipeg. It would turn into one of the most memorable experiences of his rich life.

At the age of 33, Jacques Plante was taking stock of his life. He was at the highest point of his professional career. Now he was able to take the time to reflect on how far he'd come. Over the years, he had grown accustomed to a certain level of fame. He was unable to go anywhere in the province of Quebec without being noticed, and in the league's other five cities he was one of hockey's most recognizable faces. On this extended trip, however, he would realize the true extent of his popularity, giving him a new perspective on what he had accomplished in his professional career.

Always a man in search of a new discovery, and one who enjoyed his own counsel, Plante took advantage of the time to venture out and explore places he had only read about. This solitary trip also gave him a chance to temporarily enjoy a modicum of relaxation far from home. To that end, he decided to stop reading newspapers as he began his trek.

In Winnipeg, Jacques was the guest of honour at the annual Sportsmen's Dinner sponsored by the St. Boniface Optimists.

"Since Tuesday night, I have been besieged by sundry friends and acquaintances who keep asking what I think about Jacques Plante now," wrote Jack Matheson in the *Winnipeg Tribune*. "I tell him I think Jacques is quite a guy. He has intelligence, poise and an incredible ability to communicate. I also tell people that I am surprised, because Plante has always struck me as being something of a showboat who indulges in tantrums every time he finds a puck behind him in the net. Most remarkable was his comment to me that he had to learn to play goal all over again after having the cartilage operation."

After the last date of the tour, in Calgary, Plante hopped into his car to head to Seattle and take in the World's Fair. Soon he found himself a ways beyond Fort Macleod and noticed that his gas gauge was running low. Realizing he hadn't filled the tank since Calgary, he decided to stop at the first gas station he saw.

He came across a cluster of six houses, what he took to be a small village, with one of them possessing a gas pump in the front yard. Jacques pulled in and honked his horn. An older man, clad in overalls, ambled out towards the car and greeted Plante with a brief "Good day." After turning on the pump, the man slowly began to wipe the dirty windshield. Once he finished he turned his gaze towards Plante.

"Tell me, son," the elderly gentleman asked, "do you happen to be that goalkeeper fellow from Montreal – Jack Plant?"

Jacques was taken aback for a few seconds. "That's close enough," he responded. "I am Jacques Plante of the Canadiens, and how do you do?"

So thrilled was the old man that he hurriedly brought the famous goaltender into his humble abode to meet his wife. Despite the urge to keep travelling, Jacques enjoyed a cup of coffee with the elderly couple and answered all of their mostly hockey-related questions.

"I was completely overwhelmed," he wrote later, "being recognized in that remote southern Alberta village 2,300 miles from Shawinigan Falls where I had played hockey as an unknown kid. Never before had it struck me how much the game means to all Canada; what enjoyment it brings to people far beyond the rinks in lonely little places. I promised myself when driving away that because of what the game was doing for so many and had done for me, I would never knock it."

After being one of nearly 10 million attendees at the World's Fair in Seattle, he made his way down the American west coast for the first time, stopping in San Francisco and Los Angeles before travelling east towards Las Vegas.

In avoiding the newspapers, he had missed a significant news item. It took an unwitting blackjack dealer to break the news. Plante had been sitting at the casino for an hour, and with only twelve fewer dollars to show for it, when his table saw a change in dealers. Looking around the half-moon table, the new dealer gazed at the players while shuffling the cards.

"Hey, aren't you Jacques Plante?" asked the dealer.

"Yes, I am," replied a surprised Plante.

"Congratulations," offered the joyful dealer. "You sure deserved it."

Plante was puzzled. The dealer couldn't be talking about the Vezina Trophy; after all, that had been decided over a month before. It dawned on him that he must be talking about the all-star selections, which would have been announced a few days before.

"Thank you," replied Plante. "It's always a big thrill to be named an all-star."

The dealer shook his head. "All-star? I mean the top award, the Hart Trophy. You won it – didn't you know?"

Plante sat back in his chair in shock. The Hart Trophy is the ultimate prize, given to the league's most valuable player.

Plante quickly excused himself from the table and phoned home. Jacqueline happily told him how they were being bombarded with congratulatory telegrams. There was one that she read to him personally.

"Dear Jacques if you win any more honors I shall have to move out and make room for you because there seems to be nothing left to win unless it is the Stanley Cup just for you. Congratulations and best wishes once again from everyone here – Signed Frank J. Selke."[3]

The achievement humbled Plante. He had become only the fourth goalie to be awarded the Hart Trophy in its then 39-year history. It would be another 35 years before another goalie, Dominik Hasek, would take home the same award.

19

TOE

AS JACQUES PLANTE BASKED in the glow of a summer of redemption and adoration, his coach, Toe Blake, spent the same few months stewing over what had happened the previous spring, with an increased focus on the upcoming fall. Defeat did not rest lightly on Toe Blake's shoulders.

"He was rough, gruff, intimidating, wise, compassionate, unforgiving, scheming, and hard working – all of it dedicated to winning," Red Fisher wrote later. "Winning wasn't merely a worthwhile target for Toe Blake. It was everything."[1]

No aspect of the team or its performance on the ice escaped Blake's devout attention. If things weren't going to his liking, he believed that he could bring about change through the sheer force of his will. He embodied the old-time hockey coach like no other, seemingly having stepped out of a time and a generation that no longer existed.

"Back then the coaches didn't have the services of tapes, and they ran everything behind the bench," Jean Béliveau remembers today. "They sometimes employed assistants. Toe Blake, on the other hand, controlled everything, coaching the team with no assistants, handling all of the traveling details, handing out the train tickets to the players as well as our meal money and sometimes making the train arrangements for the opposing teams."[2]

Blake stood behind the bench alone, where he made all the decisions alone. Many of his former players today remark on the sharpness of his mind and on his innate ability to recall situations from even weeks before and then apply them at the most critical of moments.

"Toe was the ultimate coach," recalled John Ferguson. "He had a memory like an elephant and he treated players like men. He had a great feeling for the game and could mastermind behind the bench in a way nobody has ever been able to."[3]

Blake ensured that his players always travelled first class and stayed in the best hotels. Furthermore, Blake forbade them to carry their own luggage or suitcases in hotels. "When you play for the Montreal Canadiens," Blake implored his charges, "you go first class."[4]

As a former player himself, Blake treated his own players with the utmost respect. Nobody had a better understanding of a player's sense of pride. He never singled out an individual for criticism in front of the fans or the media. Blake's noted tough love was always delivered in private.

"Blake's players respected him, yet feared him," Red Fisher wrote later. "He was supremely loyal to them, and they to him. He had an uncanny talent of knowing when to raise and lower the volume. He produced winners, because he had no time to waste on losers."[5]

Yet some people were starting to question just how much of a winner Toe Blake really was. It had been over two years since a Stanley Cup parade had graced the streets of Montreal, and for many that was simply too long. Despite all that he had accomplished with the Canadiens over the past seven seasons, as he entered his eighth, Blake was inclined not to look at the five Stanley Cups he had won but to instead focus on the frustration of the last two seasons.

By October 1962, Toe Blake was even starting to hear the first whispers of doubt about his coaching expertise. These whispers were coming not from the Canadiens, who unhesitatingly re-signed him to his standard one-year contract, but instead from some of the team's supporters as well as a few in the media. Fingers were being pointed at him for the failures of the last two springs. The blame they placed on Toe, however, was no more intense than the blame the Canadiens coach put on himself.

Undoubtedly, the pressure had been ratcheted up on Blake this year. Unlike the season before, when many had predicted the Canadiens would finish fourth at best, this fall the experts were near unanimous in their belief that the Canadiens would repeat their first-place regular-season finish of the year before.

Blake had made no substantial changes to the team after its loss to the Black Hawks the past spring, and many pointed to the Canadiens' renewed health as a source of optimism. In addition, the continued excellence of Jacques Plante was considered a key factor in their predicted success.

The year before had been a serene one for Plante and the Canadiens, free of dissent, free of injuries, and free of conflict. It didn't take long, however, for the storm clouds to start brewing in the 1962–63 season. And the troubles began with a flare-up of Plante's asthma.

On the eve of the Canadiens' opener in Boston, Plante complained of feeling ill. But after a shot of adrenaline, he skated out for the opening game.

"I'll never go into the game in that condition again," Plante vowed after surrendering five goals in a 5–0 Bruins rout. It was a vow echoed by his coach. "It's the last time I'll put him in the nets when he's feeling that way," promised Blake.[6]

The hope for a strong season was shattered after a single game. Plante's illness would carry over to the Habs' first weekend set of games, where a young, untested Ernie Wakely filled in for him in a 6–3 win over the Rangers. The next evening in Detroit, Cesare Maniago was flown in from Spokane, Washington, to fill in for Plante, but still the Habs fell 3–1 to the Red Wings.

"Plante will have to win his job back," announced Frank Selke. Clearly agitated, Selke once again seemed to place the blame on Plante's mental state and not his asthma. "I can't understand why a man is all right on a Friday, as Plante was, and then turns up sick on a Saturday. He's got to show me that he deserves to be in the nets for this club. He's got to show me that his attitude is right."[7]

As Plante continued to miss games because of his asthmatic condition, one of his old rivals assumed the goaltending spotlight. Terry Sawchuk was gaining early-season accolades for his stunning play as the Red Wings went unbeaten in their first 10 games. What's more, he was playing with a mask. "I feel much more confident with the mask," Sawchuk said. "There isn't so much to worry about when the headhunters start shooting."[8]

After three years of being the man with the mask, Plante finally had company. Others, such as Don Simmons, had experimented with the mask before discarding it, but Sawchuk, along with Plante, the biggest goaltending name in the sport, was now wearing it full time. It was a turning point in the evolution of the mask. Plante had generally been viewed as an oddball for wearing a mask, but Sawchuk's adoption of it now gave it some legitimacy, a fact not lost on a bitter Plante.

"It wasn't until Sawchuk put on the mask that the Canadiens really accepted it," he told sportswriter Jim Hunt a few years later. "He was one of the game's superstars and if he wore one it had to be all right."[9]

Finally, after missing 10 games, Plante made his return to the Canadiens net. And once again it would be against the unbeaten Detroit Red Wings and their suddenly revitalized, masked goaltender, Terry Sawchuk.

Plante didn't disappoint, giving a masterful performance that saw him turn aside 42 Detroit shots, including nine off the stick of Gordie Howe, while his teammates were able to manage only 26 at Sawchuk. Still, the Canadiens skated off with a 4–1 victory that snapped the Red Wings' unbeaten streak.

The news was not all good. Plante aggravated a groin injury in the game. The result was that Cesare Maniago would serve as Plante's standby for the next couple of games. It would turn into a season-long role for the journeyman goaltender, and a source of aggravation for the Canadiens.

"I would have to sit in the stands behind Mr. Selke at the far end of the Forum," Maniago remembers today. "I wasn't allowed to go into the dressing room between periods. Ken Reardon told me to stay in my seat in between periods and if I need you I'll come and get you. Sure enough, several times he would come out from the walkway, he would look in my direction, and he would give me the finger, 'Okay, come on.' It was tough on me, from a preparation standpoint. Believe me, my heart was up in my throat. You anticipate it, but until it really happens you're not really prepared."[10]

Plante was only able to last through the first period of the game following his Detroit triumph, as Maniago got the call and took to the Montreal nets in a 3–1 defeat against Chicago, before leading the Habs to a win in Boston the next night.

Plante returned to action three nights later, in a 4–2 loss to the Leafs, before engaging in a classic contest with his old rival Glenn Hall in a 1–1 tie in Chicago against the Black Hawks.

It had become apparent the year before that the Canadiens were not the powerhouse they had once recently been. But to stay among the league's top teams they depended on one player more than any other. "We all know who put us in first place and kept us there last year," said teammate Tom Johnson, hoping that Plante would stay healthy. "We all know who has to keep us there this year."[11]

Unfortunately, health was the one thing that Plante was unable to maintain as the schedule trudged through February. A hip injury sidelined him at the start of the month, which was then followed by a groin injury. "It would be foolish to use me unless I'm perfectly all right," said Plante, "and traveling with the club hasn't helped. If I had stayed home, I could have been treated. As things stand now, the injury hasn't improved."[12]

The Canadiens continued to struggle with Plante on the sidelines and were unable to put together a winning streak of any consequence. After a 6–3 loss against the Rangers on February 6, with Maniago in the net, three nights later in Toronto Plante was pressed into action.

Blake's patience with Plante was starting to wear noticeably thin. The team was floundering without Plante. Yet Blake found himself in an impossible situation: he couldn't rely on Plante when he needed him more than ever. Plante's endless stretch of injuries were worrisome in their frequency and distressing in their variety.

"Plante has been complaining about a hip and a groin injury, which most people associated with the front office and the club's medical department have been inclined to shrug off," reported Red Fisher. "It is their view that injuries are something of an obsession with the goaltender, an escape hatch, so to speak, for what has amounted to several unhappy experiences in the nets in recent games."[13]

Plante claimed to be suffering from a pelvic disorder that caused a tremendous surge in pain in his right leg. However, he starred in a weekend of ties, firstly a 3–3 draw in Toronto, followed by a 5–5 tie with Boston the next evening, all the while claiming to still be injured. "It hurts all the time and my leg goes numb," Plante told the reporters after Saturday's game. "I can't feel a thing now."[14] And yet the next night he played.

No wonder nobody around the team was listening to Plante's complaints. In the space of one year he had gone from the league's best player to a pariah on his very own team. Even though Plante considered himself unfit for duty, Blake still wanted him to play. As a consequence, their relationship collapsed completely.

In retrospect their professional relationship had suffered its first break a few years earlier over the mask issue, which had been followed by a downturn in Plante's play and later Plante's knee injury. Plante may have eventually triumphed with the Stanley Cup, but it was clear that their bond had been irreparably broken. Although the previous year had been a harmonious one, culminating in Plante's Hart Trophy, it was now clear that the rift between the two was too wide.

Without consulting his coach, Plante decided to begin skipping the team's pre-game skate. Of course, this new attempt at innovation wasn't lost on Blake.

"I knew what was in Jacques' mind. He has an idea that the spare goalie should work the pre-game warmup. Then the regular goalie goes in and plays the game. But what good is that? He starts the game cold. First thing you know, he has to do the splits to stop a shot – and he pulls a muscle. I'm not in favour of a goalie wearing himself out in the warmup. But at least he has to take the stiffness out of his muscles." Ordered by Blake to resume taking the pre-game warm-up, a bitter Plante could only grouse that the warm-up "is the worst part of our business."[15]

Despite all the problems off the ice and Plante's inconsistencies on it, the Canadiens found themselves in familiar territory: eight points behind the league-leading Black Hawks with three games in hand. Plante had assumed the lead in the chase for yet another Vezina.

But another first place finish was not to be. The Canadiens finished the season in third place, a mere three points behind the Toronto Maple Leafs, snapping the Habs' streak of five consecutive league titles. Plante also came up short in the race for a record seventh Vezina Trophy by a measly five goals.

For the first time in four years the Canadiens' first-round opponents wouldn't be the Chicago Black Hawks. Instead, they would be facing the first-place Stanley Cup defending champion Maple Leafs. For the first time in many years, the Canadiens were beginning the playoffs as decided underdogs.

"Toronto should handle Canadiens because this team can skate with the Montreal athletes, and since they're physically tougher, the outcome – barring serious injuries to key personnel – isn't difficult to visualize," wrote Red Fisher on the eve of the series.[16] A desperate Blake told the media that the Leafs would win in a sweep unless the Habs found that seemingly elusive spark.

Plante was a standout for the Canadiens in the opening game, although according to Red Fisher, it was a "faint light in an otherwise dark picture" as Montreal went down to a 3–1 opening-game defeat "in a dreary, dispirited, mediocre effort."[17]

After the game it was revealed that Plante had played though he'd professed another asthma attack in the moments leading up to the game. "The goaltender's uncertainty distressed Coach Blake, who feels that things like these disturb the rest of the players," wrote Fisher. "Hence, he along with other members of the Canadiens executive – decided that a call for Charlie Hodge was in order." And it was Hodge in the Canadiens' net the next game. Blake gave Plante permission to sit out the team's practice on the day between games. When asked why, he responded that "some of the players needed a rest . . . Plante needed one too, I guess."[18] To those around him, Blake appeared like a man near the end of his rope.

On March 27, watching yet another practice that seemed like every other practice, the assembled reporters were looking for an angle to liven up what was shaping up to be a dull series. Jacques Plante provided them with that angle and more.

Plante was asked by a reporter to explain the reasons behind the Canadiens' fall from grace. In a moment of poor judgment and misplaced honesty, he replied: "We haven't got a leader. We used to have guys like Butch Bouchard, Bert Olmstead, Doug Harvey, guys who would tell you if you weren't going well. We don't have anyone like that now. We need a guy to give you the occasional whack on the seat."[19]

The reporters ran with the story, creating another unnecessary distraction for a team struggling to prolong their season. Many interpreted Plante's words as a direct shot at the Canadiens' captain, Jean Béliveau.

Amid the media frenzy ignited by Plante's remarks, the Canadiens fell 3–2 to the Leafs in the second game.

The black cloud that had followed the Canadiens only grew bigger on their return to Montreal, as the Leafs took a commanding series lead with a 2–0 shutout in front of a disgruntled sellout crowd at the Montreal Forum. Two nights later, the desperate Canadiens peppered Johnny Bower with 40 shots and staved off elimination with a 3–1 win.

Plante had been singled out for praise in the Canadiens' victory. Two nights later in Toronto, however, there would be no repeat performance. "The Canadiens have finished their dreariest season in recent memory the way they started it; no scoring, no goaltending," wrote Red Fisher in the wake of the Leafs' series-winning 5–0 thrashing of the overmatched Habs.[20] It was a distressing end to the season.

In the immediate aftermath of the debacle, Toe Blake debated whether to come back for the following season. Bitter and disillusioned, he began to question his ability to coach and wondered whether he was still able to get through to his players. "When I think of the chances we've had this year, when I think of the number of big games we've blown it makes me sick. With this team, we shouldn't be where we are. We have enough good players but I can't get anything out of them anymore. I tell them something, and they look at me as if I'm crazy. What is it? Will somebody please tell me what's happened?"[21]

It was a disillusioned, disappointed, and disenchanted group that peeled off their sweat-soaked uniforms that warm spring night in the bowels of Maple Leaf Gardens. Jacques Plante was taking off his Canadiens sweater not only for the last time that season but forever.

20

THE BETRAYAL

HUGH TOWNSEND WAS LIVING a uniquely Canadian dream.

For as long as he could remember, Hugh's life had revolved around the sporting scene in Pictou County, Nova Scotia, and more particularly, its largest town, New Glasgow. New Glasgow is located on the north shore of the province, about 165 kilometres northeast of Halifax.

As the bureau chief for Pictou County at the Halifax *Chronicle-Herald*, then the biggest daily in the Maritimes, Hugh was able not only to maintain strong ties with his home community but also to become a voice of its people.

Hugh wore a variety of other hats connecting him to the greater sporting world. In addition to writing for the *Chronicle-Herald*, he was the Maritime correspondent for the *Hockey News*, covering all aspects of the Maritime hockey scene. Possessing a keen eye for local hockey talent also helped him in his other job as the regional scout for the Toronto Maple Leafs.

His connections also led to some highly publicized visits in Pictou County as spring turned to summer in 1963. In his role as scout, in May Hugh had been able to procure a promotional visit from Maple Leafs superstar Frank Mahovlich, fresh off a second consecutive Stanley Cup. There were few names bigger in the hockey world at that time than the man known as "the Big M." The visit had been a smashing success, with only a note of dissent as Stellarton, the town situated next to New Glasgow, expressed mild disappointment that Mahovlich wasn't able to visit them as well because of his tight schedule.

In an effort to placate the Stellartonians, Hugh quickly arranged for Kent Douglas, another member of the Stanley Cup champions who had also won the Calder Trophy as rookie of the year, to come and visit them two weeks later.

A week or so later, the Trenton Legion approached Hugh about bringing in another Maple Leaf to visit the area. After plans to bring Carl Brewer fell through, the Legion asked Hugh if a player from another team could make the promotional visit.

And that's how Jacques Plante came to visit Pictou County on the first weekend of June 1963. To say that the first Saturday of June was a hectic one for the visiting Plante would be an understatement. Townsend picked him up at the Halifax airport mid-morning and drove him an hour and a half to begin his day in Stellarton, at the local Sobey's grocery store, sponsors of his visit, who had him draw a ticket for a $50 food order. Then he quickly made his way to Trenton, where he attended a youth track and field meet and handed out the winning medals.

Through the years, one of the constants on the Stellarton sporting scene had been a woman by the name of Mildred Dorrington. Mildred attended all types of events, photographing the participants and teams, all for the benefit of her bedridden husband, Aubrey, a noted sporting fan. In an act of kindness and generosity, Hugh arranged for the famed Plante to pay a surprise visit to their home, which became a treasured family memory.

In the early evening Plante was the guest of honour at a local golf club, and was then paraded through the streets of New Glasgow in Townsend's convertible. The parade eventually wound its way to the New Glasgow Stadium as day turned to dusk. There, Plante was a guest at a fundraising event being held by the New Glasgow Rangers of the Maritime Senior Hockey League. Speaking briefly to the hundreds present, he enjoyed a rapturous reception.

Soon it was time for Plante to be driven back to the airport. It had been a whirlwind 10 hours for him. Like Mahovlich and Douglas before him, Plante went home with a beautiful painting of a Pictou County scene done by a prominent local artist – and a carton full of Nova Scotia lobsters.

Being an enterprising reporter, Townsend had questioned Plante on their trips from and to the airport about the status of the Canadiens, who'd been bounced from the playoffs for a third consecutive season. Rumours of an impending shuffle swirled around the Canadiens. The only things that anybody knew for certain were Toe Blake's return and that there would be some changes on the roster.

"Montreal Canadien goaltender Jacques Plante said here Saturday that he does not expect a major shakeup in the Canadiens roster 'as Montreal writers are saying will take place,'" wrote Townsend in that Monday's *Chronicle-Herald*. "Taking a break from a busy schedule on his Pictou County visit, Plante said he does not expect any big names on the club to be traded. He said that Bernie 'Boom Boom' Geoffrion 'definitely will be back with us next season. There isn't a team in the league that would give us in return what Bernie is worth to us.'"[1]

On the day after his Nova Scotia sojourn, Plante had an appointment with Frank Selke at the Forum. Selke asked Plante if he could represent the team at a league meeting taking place two days hence regarding the players' pension fund. Plante readily accepted. Along with captain Jean Béliveau and Bernie Geoffrion, Plante was now one of the Canadiens who enjoyed the longest tenure with the club. At age 34, he was looking forward to taking more of a mentoring role with the team.

Two days later, on the morning of the meeting, he found himself roaming the golf course with teammate Jean Gauthier by his side. Gauthier was a nervous wreck that Tuesday morning. A rookie the year before, he loved being a Montreal Canadien, but feared that a late-season dip in his play could cost him his spot.

"I'm afraid I'm going to be traded," he confided to his team's goaltender in the clubhouse locker room. "You're going to the meeting today. Maybe if you said a word to the management . . ."[2]

Jacques, looking to reassure his younger teammate, promised to help in any way he could.

Plante was driving to the meeting in downtown Montreal, enjoying the vocal strains of Egyptian-Italian songstress Dalida, when a news bulletin came on. "We interrupt the program to bring you a sports bulletin. One of the most spectacular trades in National Hockey League history has just been announced by the Montreal Canadiens. A seven-player trade with the New York Rangers revolving around their 10-season goaling star, Jacques Plante."

A shocked Plante immediately pulled over to the curb as he turned the radio up. "Plante goes to New York together with Don Marshall and Phil Goyette in exchange for goalie Gump Worsley, Dave Balon, Léon Rochefort, and Len Ronson, a minor leaguer . . ."

The voice trailed off as unadulterated shock consumed Plante. He sat motionless, unable to move. Later on, he couldn't remember how long he had sat in that car.

Since he had first learned to skate, Plante had dreamed of being a Montreal Canadien. Now, with a lifetime spent as a goalie, he still wanted nothing but to be a Montreal Canadien. He had never wanted to play elsewhere for anybody else. They had discovered him, nurtured him, moulded him, and guided him into the professional he was today. And now they had discarded him, traded him away like a piece of meat, after all he had brought them.

Phil Goyette, part of the trade, tells what it feels like to be traded. "It's always a shock, especially when you're with an organization for so many years like I was and like he was. I was from Montreal – I was established here, had a home, children, and school and so on."[3]

It was a different world back then. Despite establishing himself as the game's pre-eminent goaltender, Plante had acquired no more professional rights than he had the moment he signed his first contract with the Canadiens. A decade of starring for the team had brought him no say in the course of his career.

Nobody had considered what this meant to him personally. His family, his business interests, his property interests were all firmly established in Quebec. Now, without any question or consideration, he was expected to uproot himself to what was not only a new city but an English-speaking city, in a new country.

At that moment, sitting in his car, he had an immediate decision to make: should he still attend the pension meeting? Finally, he yanked the car into gear. He would still go to the meeting, but not as a Montreal Canadien. For the first time, he would appear as a New York Ranger.

Jacques Plante was not the only one shocked by the trade. Many in the media had a hard time swallowing the deal, as did some in the hockey world. Punch Imlach, the coach and general manager of the Stanley Cup champion Toronto Maple Leafs, spoke for many when he commented, "I still rate Plante the finest goalie in hockey, certainly far superior to Gump Worsley."[4]

Even Frank Selke, the Canadiens managing director, fanned the flames when he was quoted a few days after the trade as saying that "Worsley never saw the day he could play like Plante when Jacques was at his best." However, Selke revealed the reasoning behind what was viewed by many as a most puzzling transaction. "We got rid of Plante because we couldn't depend on him anymore. Toe Blake couldn't have taken much more without punching him on the nose. He's the best goalie I've ever had and close to the best I've ever seen. But that doesn't say he can run the hockey club."[5]

"Jacques Plante is an extrovert who can't put his personal interests aside for the benefit of the team," continued Selke. "In the circumstances, no matter how brilliant a goaltender he may be, it was better that he left."[6]

A day later in his column in the *Montreal Star*, Red Fisher recalled a brief discussion between himself, Blake, and Canadiens executive Sam Pollock that took place shortly after Montreal had been eliminated from the playoffs.

> The three of us stood in the lobby of a downtown hotel, each a little fearful of saying the first word. After all, what do you say to a coach after his employees have been embarrassed in front of an entire country?
>
> Finally Blake spoke. "I've had it, I'm through."
>
> Pollock shook his head sadly: "It's natural to feel that way after losing 5–0."
>
> "Lookit," hissed Blake, "how would you like it, Sammy, to have a goalie who doesn't know when he's gonna play. How would you like to go from city to city and never be sure you'll have a goalie on the ice? As far as I'm concerned, I can't take it anymore."[7]

"Plante was the scapegoat for the Canadiens fall to third place," wrote Fisher in the days following the trade. "The front office wanted to make an example of a big player to wake up the rest."[8]

The Canadiens brass believed that they had acted in the best interests of the organization. To them, Plante had become more trouble than he was worth. That the team wasn't winning Stanley Cups any more, and an unstated worry that Plante was starting to physically break down, influenced the decision.

Yet it was the strain of the relationship between Toe Blake and Plante that was the true spur for the trade.

"Blake thought he was a hypochondriac and that he dreamed up things," journalist Frank Orr remembers today. "Blake was a very macho man, a man of his time, and expected all of his players to be the same. He would get mad when guys got hurt and he thought they were loitering when they didn't come back. He would rail on about Plante. The Canadiens back then wouldn't tolerate injuries. It was a pretty cruel system. If you got hurt a second time you were gone. When you slipped a little, that was it."[9]

"Jacques' trade wasn't much of a surprise, because of his character," Dickie Moore says. "He was bigger than the team, and nobody's ever bigger than the team. Ultimately, it's a team game."[10]

"It might have been a surprise when he was traded but nobody complained," reflects Henri Richard.[11]

"I wasn't surprised when he was traded," says Cesare Maniago. "When you are as highly regarded as Montreal was during that time and you don't win the Stanley Cup, then there's going to be the odd change made. In that season, we had a strong team, but Toronto beat us out. There was such a strong following in Montreal. If you lost one game that was tough enough, but if you lost two in a row, then don't even show your face around town because the people would be asking you all kinds of questions."[12]

"They treated me like a traitor when all I'd done was give them my life and the best I had," Plante confided to Frank Orr years after the deal.

"He solely blamed Blake for the deal," says Orr today, "yet he refused to say an unkind word about Toe. You could tell that he really respected him. His story was a classic French-Canadian story, and then, as Plante put it, they shit on him and all because Blake wouldn't indulge him."[13]

What took place that warm June day in Montreal would never leave Plante. He would go on to star for other teams, but on that day he had his heart broken by his first and truest love.

21

ALONE ON BROADWAY

AS MANY SETTLED IN to watch news of the trade on television, they were confronted on their screens by a grim-faced Jacques Plante outside the downtown hotel that housed that day's pension meeting. "The Rangers are on their way up," Plante boldly pronounced with the stinging news of the trade still achingly fresh, "and the Canadiens are on their way down."[1]

The gauntlet had been thrown down, and so began a summer in which a bitter Plante waged a one-man war of words in the media, all of it aimed directly at his former employer, the Montreal Canadiens. The result was that he quickly became ostracized from the only team he had ever known, and the fans who had always supported him began to desert him in droves.

It was quite a different story in New York. In a city that offered the country's finest entertainment district and largest and most competitive sporting scene, the hockey team seemed to always come out second best. New York in 1963 could boast of the dynastic Yankees and the woeful Mets in baseball, the championship Giants and the nascent Jets in football, as well as the Knicks in basketball. There were also numerous boxing and wrestling cards held every week at the Garden, horse racing out at Aqueduct, tennis at Forest Hills, and golf at Shinnecock. As a result the Rangers had to constantly battle for newspaper space.

It was usually a losing battle, until that summer of 1963, when a noted French-Canadian goaltender entered the local sporting scene.

Hoping to capitalize on the excitement building throughout the city, the Rangers rushed Plante down to New York to sign a contract instead of waiting until the traditional September signing period.

"General manager Muzz Patrick greeted him at Madison Square and they sat behind closed doors," wrote Andy O'Brien later. "They talked for quite a while; Plante reported his eyesight and reflexes were good, he had no weight problem, his golf handicap was down to six."

As Plante and Patrick got acquainted, waiting outside the closed doors was an impatient throng of New York media, eager for the introduction of the newest Ranger star. Inside the room, Patrick quietly slid the contract across the table for Plante's approval. Plante scanned the contract for the salary, and his eyes bugged out at the sight of the figure: $24,000 per year. It was far more than he was making in Montreal and equal to, if not more than, what anybody else in the league was making. Jacques didn't hesitate to reach for the pen.

"It is the first time in Ranger history," Patrick announced to the assembled media minutes later, "that the Rangers ever signed a player this early in the summer, but in Jacques' case we figured we should be different. After all, he's the best goalie in the business and he deserves the best."

As soon as a member of the media ventured a question about Plante's history of asthma, the newest Ranger took over. "I've still got it, always will," Plante admitted, "but I don't think I will have the same trouble here. In Montreal the winters are much more severe; besides I think a lot of my trouble was caused by the unnecessary pressure under which I had to play there."

The *New York Times* asked him about the pressure of playing in Montreal. "I'm glad to leave Montreal for New York because things have changed up there. The fans and the management have gotten so used to winning they put the pressure on you. You don't mind the pressure when you have the players to handle it. At one time last year I was thinking of quitting but Jacqueline wouldn't let me. 'You can't quit,' she told me, 'the boys need you.'"

The *New York News* asked him to expand on his earlier comment about the Canadiens being on the downswing and the Rangers on the upswing. Plante gladly obliged. "Canadiens have only four good scorers left: Boom Boom Geoffrion, Jean Béliveau, Henri Richard and Gilles Tremblay. The Boomer doesn't shoot as hard as he used to. Béliveau has been sick. Henri loses too many scoring chances trying to pull the goalies and Tremblay always shoots off the wrong foot."[2]

He said the Canadiens had weakened themselves in goal by replacing him with Worsley. He railed that the Habs were on an excessive "youth kick" and that many of Montreal's newest recruits were at best unproven and at worst not up to the task.

And when the reporters asked what the trade meant in the standings, a confident Plante replied: "This means that the Rangers make the playoffs and Montreal finishes fifth."[3]

It was a tirade built out of spite and loaded with malice. It isn't clear whether Plante was convinced of his own words or whether this was merely the bluster of a disheartened man.

For Emile Francis, then the Rangers' assistant general manager, Plante's tirade was unforgettable. "I'll never forget that first press conference," says Francis today. "He started talking about the Montreal Canadiens. I'm sitting there saying to myself, would you keep quiet, what are you doing? The Canadiens never forgot that. It was like committing suicide."[4]

The New York newsmen couldn't write down Plante's harsh critique fast enough. His words were a reporter's dream and a boon for newspaper sales. In Montreal, his increasingly estranged teammates took in every word, every description of their abilities and lack thereof, and circled October 12 on their calendar, the date when they would face the Rangers and their alienated former goaltender.

Behind the scenes, however, there were more important considerations at work. It was decided by Plante and his wife that he would go alone to New York, leaving his wife and two sons behind in Quebec. For the first time he would be separated from his wife and family. In time, it would prove to be a tremendous strain for all.

As training camp approached in New York, the Rangers went out of their way to accommodate their newest acquisition, adopting what the newspapers called a "Be Kind to Plante" movement. Reporters asked general manager Muzz Patrick how the Rangers would deal with Plante's infamous asthma attacks that always seemed to plague him in Toronto, and most specifically at the Royal York Hotel. Patrick informed the newsmen that Plante wouldn't have to go near the Royal York, and would be excused from any pre-game meeting or meal that would be held there. "If he wishes," Patrick added, "we'll book a flight that lands at Toronto International Airport two hours before face-off time. In that way he'll arrive at Maple Leaf Gardens full of vim and oxygen."[5] Plante's new coach, Red Sullivan, took the special treatment even further, announcing that Plante was exempt from practising with the team if he felt tired.

"He just about drove our trainer and equipment guy crazy in New York," remembers Emile Francis. "He had 42 pieces of equipment. He just kept coming up with all this stuff. I think you could have hit him with a bullet and not hurt him. He had pieces of equipment for inside his knee and outside his knee. You name it, he had a piece of equipment for it."[6]

Jacques was in heaven. The high salary, the perks, the special concessions – he viewed them all as his due after a decade in professional hockey. "I would have liked to finish my career in Montreal," Plante admitted to Red Fisher, "but if I had to change, I'm glad it's New York. I couldn't be happier with my contract. I like the team and we're on the way up."[7]

Plante's new team shared his enthusiasm. "In all my years as a member of the Rangers, I've never seen anything to match the spirit on this year's club," proclaimed Muzz Patrick. "The reason? Plante. He's working hard. He's yelling at the forwards and the defensemen. He's doing everything we expected of him."[8]

Plante's tenure with his new team officially began on October 9, 1963, in Chicago against the Black Hawks. It was an inauspicious debut. Plante was peppered with 43 shots, and the game was held up for 20 minutes in the third period so that he could receive seven stitches to close up a wound to the top of his head. In what would become an all too familiar pattern, Plante would allow only three goals, yet the Rangers would score only one in the 3–1 setback.

Of course, this was merely a prelude to the much-anticipated game two nights later in Montreal, where Plante would square off against his old teammates, many of whom had been relishing for months the opportunity to face their old goalie.

"Let them come," Plante proclaimed from the front of the sports pages the day of the game. "I've been waiting for them too and I feel I'm in the best shape in some years right now. I look at their lineup, and too many of the big names are missing. As for our team we've got good spirit. . . . We have enough talent to handle the Canadiens."[9]

If there had been one player who had taken the most offence to Plante's public lambasting of the Canadiens and their players, it was Boom Boom Geoffrion, a man who according to Plante had lost some power off his famed slapshot.

"It happens to all of us sooner or later," Plante reiterated on the eve of the game, fanning the flames, "but I expect him to try his hardest against us. He'll probably shoot harder than he has in some time, but I'll be waiting for him."[10]

The Canadiens rewarded Plante for his bravado with a barrage of 59 shots in a 6–2 drubbing by the Canadiens.

"The fifty-nine shot output was a new high for the club at least in recent memory," wrote Red Fisher. "Along the way Plante had to be spectacular to keep the count from mounting into the double figures in a game that saw the Habs score twice in the first, once in the second period, and then put the game beyond reach with a three-goal outburst in the final period."[11]

"We were delighted to beat him," Jean Béliveau told the *Hockey News*, "especially after some of the statements he made last summer."[12]

Of all the shots that blitzed the besieged Plante, none were harder than the one that came off the stick of the Boomer.

"The first time we met I got hold of the puck close to the crease and put everything I had behind the shot," Geoffrion remembered. "Plante still hasn't seen the puck. It went like a bullet right between his legs and into the net. But I wasn't through with him. As soon as the red light went on I skated up to the crease and gave him a little dig: 'Hey Jacques, if my shot is so weak how come you can't see it anymore?'"[13]

As Jacques slowly peeled off his sweat-soaked uniform in the unfamiliar confines of the visitors dressing room at the Forum, many newsmen pressed in to see what they had thought would be a humbled goalie. Instead they were confronted by a still defiant man, beaten but unbowed.

"In ten years with the Canadiens, I never saw them better," he admitted. "Henri Richard told the boys at the All-Star game that they had to beat me tonight or they'd be all sent to Siberia. They won't be that good again."[14]

That same night he said, "I am not saying any more about Montreal. All I did was get them mad at me."[15] It had been a painful lesson.

In his first two games as a Ranger, Plante had been blitzed with 102 shots and allowed nine goals. Yet the results on the road did nothing to dampen the enthusiasm that greeted him on his home debut with the Blueshirts on the night of October 16, 1963. It was the largest opening-night crowd to attend Madison Square Garden in 16 long years. Although there was overwhelming support for Plante, there were still a few lingering doubts. Hanging from the rafters was a large banner that read, "Bring Back the Gump." But by the time the second period came to an end, the banner had vanished. Plante exceeded all the hopes of the Rangers fans with a 34-save shutout over the Red Wings.

As the final buzzer sounded, his new teammates rushed out on the ice to surround an overcome Plante, who ripped off his mask and jumped for joy at the fifty-seventh shutout of his illustrious career and first victory as a Ranger. Plante was named the game's first star, and the photographers begged him to repeat his victory leap. Plante happily complied as the crowd granted him an unprecedented standing ovation.

"Veteran hockey observers couldn't recall the last time the Garden rattled with applause for an athlete as it did the night Plante skated from the ice after shutting out the Detroit Red Wings 3–0," reported the *Hockey News* on its front page. "It was the greatest ovation ever given a hockey player."[16]

"I had to play well tonight," Plante told a crowded room of reporters after the game, "if only to make those guys in the balcony take down the sign."[17]

Plante's first win as a Ranger may have been the high point of his two-year stay in New York. Struggling with inconsistency, the Rangers split their first eight games, then lost seven straight, went undefeated in the next four, before going winless in their next nine to fall out of the playoff chase.

As New York floundered in the standings, the bloom soon fell off the rose for Plante and the Rangers. Plante's early euphoria was replaced with the hard reality of a lonely life in an unfamiliar town. Perhaps expectations were too high for Plante. While still a great goaltender, he was apparently not the saviour the team had believed him to be.

And it didn't help when his asthma flared up at the end of October.

"One afternoon in Montreal I went for a short walk," Plante recalled. "We were staying in the Mount Royal Hotel. I got as far as the corner of Peel and St. Catherine Streets – barely 100 yards away – when I was seized by an attack. It was so bad that I couldn't make it back to my hotel room for my spray and had to go into the drugstore at the corner for help."[18]

And as the losses mounted, so did the schism between Plante and the Rangers, and in particular their head coach, Red Sullivan.

One night on a road trip, Plante was woken by the sound of his phone ringing. He found his coach on the other end of the line executing a curfew call.

"I was really mad," Plante said later. "I told him 'I have been in bed since nine o'clock and had just fallen asleep. Now I might be awake until three or four in the morning.' I told him never to do any phone checking on me again. He didn't."[19]

Plante later admitted that he never could talk with his hard-nosed coach, especially when his left knee began to bother him. (His cartilage operation a couple of years before had been on his right knee.)

He also was coming to the realization that what he had left behind in Montreal could never be replicated in New York. "I had gone from a winner to a loser. You'd have to get a doctor of psychology to explain it but once a team gets that loser feeling, it takes a lot of inspirational work by management and an on-ice leader or two to shake them out of it. With the Canadiens, winning was a built-in complex and still is."[20]

"It was difficult playing for the Rangers at the time," remembers a sombre Andy Bathgate today. "We were just a fill-in for Madison Square Garden – we were not the number one priority. Plus, the ownership was changing all the time."[21]

"The management wasn't dedicated to winning," says long-time Ranger Earl Ingarfield Sr. "They cared more about making money. I don't think they appreciated the players very much."[22]

Plante found out first-hand about the intentions of the Rangers ownership when he suggested that the team was defending the wrong end of the ice for two periods of every game at home. Because of the unique configuration of Madison Square Garden, the home team found their bench away from the net for the first and third periods, unlike in all the other rinks in the league. Plante believed – and justifiably so – that it made more sense for New York to defend the net closest to its bench for two periods so that the goalie could get to the bench quicker on a delayed penalty. After all, this was the way it was in the other five NHL ranks.

But the Rangers never acquiesced to Plante's logic, because season-ticket holders had always picked their seats based on two periods of action. Rather than adjusting the seat holders, the Rangers maintained the status quo, which Plante felt was a detriment to the team.

Plante accepted the Rangers' decision grudgingly, but made it clear that because of the distance, he couldn't be expected to come sprinting off the ice whenever a delayed penalty was whistled.

"In Montreal and Toronto the rink was their own," recalls Dick Duff. "If you were a player and you were injured and you needed to do a little skating on your own you would be given time at the Gardens or the Forum to work out alone on the ice. In New York, you didn't have that luxury. You had to practise in a little tiny ice surface a few floors up that had aluminum boards. We were spoiled in Montreal and Toronto, where as opposed to New York hockey was given a higher priority."[23]

Such was the heavy schedule of events at Madison Square Garden that the team was sometimes forced to practise out in Long Island. "In the 12 years that I played for the Rangers I never once practised on the Madison Square Garden ice," remembers Bathgate. "Every game you went out there was a new experience. It was the worst ice in the league at the time."[24]

As he settled in as a Ranger, Plante's reputation as a loner grew. He had decided to live out in Long Island with some of his teammates but tended to keep to himself. He didn't partake in the New York nightlife and remained distant from many of his new teammates.

"All the Montreal fellows lived in New Jersey," recalls Bathgate. "That was one of the problems in New York: we were all so spread out. You don't have that closeness that other teams do. It would be too expensive to live in the city, so everybody was spread out. I don't think Plante enjoyed it in New York. His wife stayed behind in Montreal and his heart wasn't in it."[25]

As the year wore on, Plante found himself buckling under the strain of an increased workload every night. Night after night he faced more shots than he ever had in his career. Undoubtedly, the fact that the Rangers were fading from the playoff race while his former team in Montreal was romping to a first-place finish exacerbated the strain.

"He played a lot better in Montreal than he did in New York," remembers Ranger teammate Harry Howell, "but we didn't have the same team as the Canadiens. Instead of getting 20 shots a night in Montreal he was getting 40 in New York. It had to be quite a shock to him."[26]

In his first year with the Rangers, Plante faced an average of 38 shots against him every game, the league's most, and a full 10 shots more a game than he had faced as a Canadien the year before. Averaged over the whole season, it was an increase of 700 shots over the 1963–64 season.

In a season marked by disappointment and dashed expectations for the Rangers, there were isolated moments, however, where Plante still demonstrated his greatness.

No team had tormented Plante more that year than the Canadiens, who had beaten the Rangers in nine of their 11 confrontations and outscored them by a cumulative total of 51 to 27. Heading into a weekend home-and-home series beginning in Montreal on March 7 and culminating in New York on March 8, Plante was still searching for his first win in Montreal as a Ranger after five unsuccessful tries.

The Canadiens and Rangers were two squads travelling in opposite directions. Much to the chagrin of Plante's earlier predictions, Montreal was fighting for first place, while the Rangers were staring on the outside of the playoff race yet again.

Such was the deteriorating status of Plante's relationship with his coach that when Plante told Red Sullivan on the morning of the game that he was suffering from a 102-degree fever, he was brusquely told, "I don't care if it's 105, you're playing."[27]

That night Plante stopped 38 of the 40 shots fired in his direction, as he led the Rangers to their first win of the year in Montreal, 3–2. Plante's opposition in the net, Charlie Hodge, faced only 19 shots, in what should have been a Habs rout. The next night in New York, Plante stopped all 33 Montreal shots as he and Hodge duelled to a scoreless tie.

"Jacques Plante is not only the National League's most colourful goalkeeper but now he has to be ranked as its most courageous as well," announced the *Hockey News* on its front page, pronouncing Plante "one of the few bright lights in a dismal Ranger hockey season."[28]

It was a sweet moment of vindication for Plante, albeit a fleeting one. The Canadiens went on to finish in first place; Charlie Hodge, long Plante's understudy, won the Vezina Trophy. And for the first time in his illustrious career, Jacques Plante found himself a spectator when the playoffs opened, watching the playoffs from the Forum press box.

As the playoffs progressed, the TV producers scoured the arena for guest analysts. In years past it had become common for superstar players on the sidelines to step into the studio and offer their analysis of the game.

In the playoffs of 1964, Jacques Plante didn't need to be asked twice for his opinion, and typical of Plante, even when he wasn't playing, he found a way to gain the spotlight.

Soon, Plante was in the unusual position of being praised not in the sports pages but instead in the entertainment section, as TV reporters applauded his every utterance.

"Jacques Plante should be on every hockey playoff intermission," raved Frank Moritsugu in the *Toronto Star*. "Last night he turned up for the second time in this round, and gave the between-period break a refreshing lift. The New York Ranger goalie is not only an articulate and thoughtful commentator, but he has more on-screen charisma and ease than the TV regulars surrounding him. Plante saved the two inter-missions, which badly needed him, not having much videotape recaps to unspool. And after the game his explicit reasoning for his three star choices was the best example of conscientious consideration for the fan I have yet heard from a chooser. Ranger loyalists will froth at the thought, but it's my hope that New York doesn't make the playoffs next year either. Then we mistreated viewers could have Plante as a TV commentator as soon as the season ends."[29]

"Two minutes with Plante and he would point out three things in the game that the casual observer wouldn't have noticed," remembers Frank Orr. "You go to Jacques for two minutes and you'd have your story."[30]

Jacques Plante returned to Quebec that summer after his first year in New York a tired and disillusioned man. In contrast to the off-season before, the summer of 1964 was a quiet one for him. The fickle media had moved on to the next story. Jacques Plante in New York was simply not the newsmaker he had been the year before.

For his wife, Jacqueline, who cherished her privacy, it was a welcome relief, but for Plante, a man who yearned to be in the spotlight, the absence of cameras and newsmen was a little disheartening.

But it wasn't long before he found himself back in the news when he signed up for the new four-team lacrosse league financed by some Quebec sportsmen. Plante starred for the Montreal Nationals, in a uniform strikingly similar to the Canadiens jersey he had once worn so proudly.

Playing lacrosse that summer, Plante rediscovered his love of competition, but when he rejoined the Rangers that fall, his renewed love was sorely tested. Some in the media questioned why he would go back to the Rangers at all. He was the most decorated goaltender in league history, and at 35 surely there was nothing left to prove. Many speculated that the money must have been too good to pass up. But for Plante, the motivation was a feeling of unfinished business.

"It wasn't the money, believe me," Plante said, "but because of something it may be hard for you to understand. I have always been win-crazy. . . . So, with that mentality, I just couldn't go out on a dismal note. I wasn't a starry-eyed rookie anymore. I knew the harsh side of pro hockey only too well. But I loved the game, loved its endless challenge and high excitement. One more big season – just one more, pray God, and I could say farewell to the Rangers and the New York fans with a feeling of all debts squared."[31]

For those watching in the pre-season, it quickly became apparent that something was wrong. Plante claimed for all to hear that his left knee was in constant pain, but in a replay of what had happened in Montreal years before, his complaints went unheeded. The Rangers decided to send him down to Baltimore of the American Hockey League to "work himself into shape" on the eve of the season's beginning.[32] The truth was that New York's newly installed general manager, Emile Francis, had seen enough.

Francis, put in charge with the directive to rebuild the Rangers, had come to the conclusion that the future of the team did not include Jacques Plante. It had only been a year since Plante had joined the Rangers to much fanfare, and so Francis kept his cards close to his vest. Despite his own doubts about Plante, Francis realized that he was still an asset, one that at the end of the season he would be able to cash in.

"I sent him down to Baltimore to give somebody else an opportunity," Francis recalls today. "I wanted to see what I had. . . . I could see in building that team up that the goaltending wasn't going to be good enough. Plante wasn't the type of a goalkeeper that you'd want to build a team around. Plante had been on a winning team and he sure as hell didn't want to be on a losing team. He was a loner, he didn't mingle with the players. He was never going to be the type of goalkeeper that the players were going to work their ass off for. As a former goaltender I could pick that up right away."[33]

Plante accepted his demotion, although according to various media reporters he didn't do it quietly. Upon his arrival in Baltimore, there were reports that he called the Rangers "a cheap organization" and said he would never play for Red Sullivan again.[34]

Such was the extent of the firestorm that erupted that Plante was taken back to New York and dragged in front of the media, where he publicly denied the quotes attributed to him. For Emile Francis, it served to confirm his earlier decision. After this latest act of contrition, Plante was sent back to Baltimore, where he donned the jersey of the Baltimore Clippers, all the while believing that he would soon be called back to the Rangers.

Baltimore in the mid-sixties was unquestionably a football town, where the Colts, led by Johnny Unitas, were firmly established as a civic institution. Hockey was more of a curiosity, and in Plante the team now had a spectacle for the public to come out and see.

"Having Jacques Plante in the lineup is like taking unfair advantage," wrote John Steadman in the *Baltimore Sun*. "The other team ought to be gifted with a courtesy goal to keep from getting discouraged. The Baltimore Clippers have Plante guarding their net and he really has no professional business being in the American League. He's much too good."[35]

On October 10, Plante made his debut as a Clipper in front of a crowd of 4,704 at the Baltimore Civic Center in a 3–3 tie. It had been a decade since he last suited up in the AHL, as a Buffalo Bison, and had played his last game against the Cleveland Barons. Now, after a decade distinguished by his goaltending excellence and innovation, he played his first game back against the same Cleveland Barons.

Plante soon discovered that the American Hockey League of 1964 was made up primarily of former NHL players as well as young prospects on the way up. Just one level before the NHL, the quality of competition was extremely high. On October 20 he squared off against the Rochester Americans, led by a young up-and-coming goalie named Gerry Cheevers. Five and a half years later, Cheevers and Plante would face each other in game one of the Stanley Cup finals.

"He was one of the best goalies to ever play the game," Cheevers recalls today. "He played his angles so well, but above all, when I think of him, I think of a winner, and ultimately that's what it's all about."[36]

Four nights later, Plante faced off against another future Hall of Fame goaltender, Ed Giacomin. However, this was merely the prelude to Plante's return to his home province for a showdown with the Quebec Aces.

This game was easily Plante's most noteworthy as a Clipper and attracted a tremendous amount of media attention as well as a season's record crowd of 11,852. The Aces came into the game undefeated. Many of the faces on the Quebec roster were familiar to Plante. Coached by his former teammate Boom Boom Geoffrion, who was in his first year as a coach, and anchored on defence by his former partner in defensive dominance, Doug Harvey, the Aces also featured Plante's oldest goaltending adversary, Gump Worsley, in the nets.

Since the Plante–Worsley trade a year and a half earlier, Gump had found himself struggling to stay in the Canadiens' plans. Outshone by Charlie Hodge, Worsley, like Plante, was stuck toiling in the AHL. Now the Gumper and Plante crossed paths once again.

The record crowd that night didn't go home disappointed, as Plante rose to the occasion. "Plante gave a superb exhibition of goaltending, but lost a 3–2 overtime decision," wrote the *Baltimore Sun* the next day. "After being beaten at 1:25 of the first period, he booted out every conceivable type of shot up to the very final second of regulation time, when Léon Rochefort scored on a rebound to tie the score at 2–2 and send the game into overtime. Then with 44 seconds remaining in overtime, Ed Hoekstra scored the winning goal, to ruin a fine display by Plante. . . . It was one of the most exciting games played here in years, with Ace's sensational finish setting the fans into a state bordering on delirium."[37]

Plante was revitalized in Baltimore. He rediscovered his love of the game, and away from the withering spotlight of the New York Rangers and the NHL, he began to shine.

However, the Rangers soon came calling, and in this case it was an emergency request for him to come to Toronto to face the Leafs on November 7 for one game only. Marcel Paille, his replacement as the Rangers goalie, had suffered a twisted ankle, and Plante was suddenly thrust into the New York goal before a national television audience on *Hockey Night in Canada*. And with his usual flourish and impeccable timing, he proceeded to shut out the Leafs 1–0. "First star – Jacques Plante!" the public address system blared.

"I brought him up from Baltimore – you should have seen the exhibition he put on in Toronto," Emile Francis remembers today. "He really didn't want to go back down to the minor leagues."[38]

"Did it practically on one leg," Plante later told the Toronto reporters. "My right knee is so bad it needs surgery. I'm trying to convince the doctor. I had the left knee done a few years ago."[39]

Plante's single-game elevation to the Rangers roster was quickly extended into a 32-game stay, during which he shared goaltending duties with Paille.

Despite his best efforts, though, the Rangers were once again on the outside looking in, and the Rangers decided to send Plante back to the AHL. This time he went down to Baltimore without complaint and actually seemed to appreciate the demotion. "The Rangers have been good to me and this doesn't affect the salary in my contract. Besides I like Baltimore and want to see the Clippers win the championship."[40] He happily rejoined the Clippers at the beginning of March, despite increasing pain in his knee.

Plante quickly made his mark in Baltimore, proceeding to win his first five games as the Clippers readied for the Calder Cup playoffs and a best-of-five series against Hershey.

"He had a bad knee in the playoffs against the Hershey Bears, and would get a needle before each game in the side of the knee," remembers teammate Bryan Hextall. "I could hardly watch as it was a big needle."[41]

Plante may have been playing in pain, but his performance didn't betray any signs of discomfort. "The Masked Marvel turned back 31 shots during the long evening, with many of his saves near spectacular," raved the *Baltimore Sun* the day after the Clippers' overtime win in the series' opening game. "His wandering out of the net also served to upset the Bears who had intentions of bearing down on the Baltimore goal, only to be confronted by some unorthodox tactics on Plante's part, tactics which proved beneficial in the long run."[42]

Plante was even better in the series' second game. "The master was at work last night at the Civic Center," wrote Albert Fisher of the *Baltimore Sun*. "Master, Masked Marvel, Jake the Snake, call him what you will, but goalie Jacques Plante put on one of the greatest exhibitions of goaltending ever seen in the Civic Center and the Clippers, with 9,621 fans looking on, whitewashed the Hershey Bears, 2 to 0, to take a 2–0 edge in the Eastern Division quarter-finals of the Calder Cup playoffs. Plante turned back 26 shots and again confounded the Bears with his incessant wanderings. He protected the shutout in the final 15 seconds, going behind the goal to rag the puck before finally passing out to a team-mate in the last five seconds."[43]

Far away from the NHL, Jacques Plante was once again proving the doubters wrong with his stellar play. Throughout his career he had showcased his ability to elevate his game when the most was on the line. Now in Baltimore, he was weaving his special brand of magic again.

And while Hershey would go on to win the next three games and eventually the series, Plante had proven that he was still a big-league goaltender. Now, as teams in the NHL began adopting a two-goalie system, which he had been advocating for years, Plante saw an opportunity to extend his distinguished career.

By sharing the load with another goaltender, Plante would be able to play a reduced schedule that would in turn reduce the wear and tear associated with playing every game, night after night.

With the end of his season in Baltimore, he made plans to have surgery on his injured right knee as well as a sore right hand, painful from years of catching the puck. He even predicted in the *Toronto Star* that these two surgeries, in addition to the two-goalie system, would allow him to play goal for another decade.

Plante's future with the Rangers was further cemented on May 17, when the Blueshirts traded Marcel Paille along with three other players to Providence of the AHL in exchange for Eddie Giacomin. It was assumed that Giacomin would share the goaltending duties for the next season with the resurgent Plante.

All that changed, however, upon Plante's return to his home in Laval-des-Rapides.

22

RETIREMENT
AND REBIRTH

JACQUES PLANTE WAS UNPREPARED for what he saw when he walked through the front door of his house that spring day. When he pulled into the driveway, he had been entertaining thoughts of playing another decade of professional hockey, but as soon as he saw his wife, dreams of playing the next season, much less the next ten, quickly left his mind.

Jacqueline looked gaunt and sickly. All the while that he had starred in New York and Baltimore, she had hidden her gradual physical deterioration from him. Now there was no hiding the obvious, and he rushed her to the doctor. Her weight had dropped from 125 to 98 pounds, and her blood pressure had dropped from 120 to a dangerous 85. After treating Jacqueline, the doctor quickly took aside Jacques and informed him that his ill wife was on the verge of a serious mental breakdown.

Plante pondered his own role in his wife's decline. She had stopped going to his games in 1959, incapable of dealing with that small group of rowdies who continually hurled verbal abuse at her husband. But it was a different type of fear that rendered her unable to even watch him play on television. She lived in dread of his being seriously injured or being discarded by the game he loved, all the while allowing him the space and time away from his family that he needed to be a better professional.

"We professional athletes regard injuries as an occupational hazard," Plante reflected later. "But the wives can't take it that casually. When their husbands land in hospitals in faraway cities they can't shrug it off as a tough break. Also, I was in a lot of stormy situations and she had to handle her own uneasiness as well as our boys' questions – often nasty things said about their father in school."[1]

"Yes it is true, I hid any illness from Jacques when he phoned me," Jacqueline confided to Andy O'Brien years later, "because he knew me so well. I knew he was what you call a 'loner' and did a lot of thinking in hotel rooms where worrying over small things makes them big things. A touch of flu being suffered by one of the players could become threatened pneumonia – just by thinking. So I was always cheerful, no matter how we felt or what we read or heard on the air. I knew that any bad news would be carried by him into the next game and I didn't want him ever to blame, even secretly, the loss of a game on some worry transmitted from home. I knew hockey was something very much a part of him. He even avoided business entanglements because he said they were distracting and demanding. He wanted to keep his mind free for his business of playing goal in the National Hockey League."[2]

At the age of 36 Jacques Plante felt it was time to change his priorities. Financially, the family was well off, owning their own house as well as rental properties and the beauty salon. Furthermore, he had a full-time job waiting for him at Molson Breweries, as supervisor of sales promotion. He was healthy and in full possession of his faculties. Now seemed the perfect time to leave the game behind and focus on his family; he felt pangs of guilt for neglecting them in pursuit of his hockey career.

"I will be 37 next winter," he confided to his wife. "I have had a lot of good times in hockey but a lot of bad times as well. And we saw how injuries caught up with the Rocket and so many others."[3]

Two weeks later, the surprised Rangers made the official announcement at the annual NHL meetings. Only two years before, Plante had been the centre of attention as one of the main figures in the biggest of all trades. Now, suddenly, it was all over.

"Hockey has been wonderful to me," Plante told the assembled media. "You get top money, travel first class and become an idol and hero to the fans. It was a wonderful experience."[4]

Many expressed shock at Plante's announcement and some even questioned whether the retirement would stick. "Despite his disclosure that he was through, many hockey men believe when they put the dollars on the line at contract time and the pucks start to fly in the fall, Jake will be back at his old stand whether it be with Rangers or Baltimore," opined the *Hockey News*.[5]

Plante's oldest adversary, Gump Worsley, echoed those sentiments, predicting that the retirement would be temporary: "Wait until the greenbacks start flashing."[6]

But Plante dismissed the suggestion. "I have never been as well paid or any happier than I have been with New York. I won't make near the money in my new job but I'll be with my family and that is the most important thing right now."[7] Plante stressed that a life in hockey was great. "I enjoyed it, but it takes you away from your family for most of the year."[8] He told the *Montreal Star*, "It's especially difficult for me to leave hockey now that the two-goalie system has been introduced. The only difference between a good minor leaguer and a good National Hockey League goalie is the pressure. I've always felt that if a goalie could get the benefit of a rest from time to time, he'd be better off. But this is the end."[9]

"Plante rates with the greatest goalkeepers of all time," admitted his old rival Jack Adams, the former Detroit Red Wings general manager. "I'm sorry to see him go. Not only was he colorful but he revolutionized the business of goaltending."[10]

Standing in the corner watching the drama unfold was the Rangers' general manager, Emile Francis, who had duelled Plante in goal more than a decade before in the American Hockey League. "I feel that Jacques could have played another couple of years," Francis said. "I'm sorry to see him go."[11]

Francis's feelings were not entirely altruistic. What he didn't share with the assembled media that day was his belief that Plante could have played for another couple of years *on some other team* and that his sorrow in seeing him go was that Plante had beaten him to the punch, so to speak.

"I was surprised when he retired," says Francis today. "I was completely caught off guard by it. At the end of the year I knew that was it. I acquired Cesare Maniago from the Montreal Canadiens and I got Eddie Giacomin from Providence of the American Hockey League to be the starter. So Plante was gone. My next move was going to be the trading of Jacques Plante. I just hadn't gotten around to it yet." Francis adds, "He may have known something was up as well. He knew that being sent down was kind of a sign that his career with the New York Rangers may have been coming to an end."[12]

The next phase of Jacques Plante's life began the next morning with a long phone call. Jacqueline noticed that afterwards he seemed preoccupied. He quickly sipped on a coffee, then left for his first day of work with Molson Breweries.

The phone call had been from the Quebec Aces of the American Hockey League. Coached by his former Canadiens teammate Boom Boom Geoffrion, the team offered Plante a five-year contract at $25,000 per season with a provision that he would only have to play the games, and not practise with the team.

That night he informed his wife of the extraordinary offer.

"Are you thinking of accepting?" a hesitant Jacqueline asked.

"No, it's out of the question," Jacques reassured her. "I thought I should take up the matter with Lou Gemus" – Plante's immediate boss at Molson's. "He told me there was no way I could carry on as supervisor of sales promotion if I tried to play organized hockey at the same time. It's a full-time career job he said, and I agreed."

"So it is settled?" asked a doubtful Jacqueline.

"Yes, it is settled, but –" Jacques hesitated before breaking into a wide grin, "isn't it good to know that in the city where I was once so pleased with junior hockey pay, somebody thinks your has-been husband is worth a $125,000 contract?"[3]

Plante's job with Molson involved numerous appearances at golf tournaments and on the banquet circuit, where he was constantly reminded of his popularity. He took the time to work at hockey schools as well as finding the time to engage in another summer of lacrosse. Most important, he was able to spend more time with his two sons, Michel and Richard, aged 14 and 10.

"For me to have him at home, that was more a relationship of friendship because I was getting older," Michel remembered years later. "I felt good having him at home. He could coach me if I was playing baseball during the summertime. It was good to see him back. As a father he gave us a good basic discipline. He was a loner even when he was at home, there was nobody around him. He read, painted, made home movies, creating a whole different scene at home apart from hockey."[4]

Plante also took his first steps into the business of mask making. Over the past few years he had been sporting a pretzel mask and hoping to manufacture mass-produced pretzel masks modelled on his own.

"The masks tended to fit badly, were uncomfortable, and difficult to see out of," commented Jim Hynes and Gary Smith in their history of the goalie mask, *Saving Face*. "Made with too much resin, they would also chip in cold arenas. The masks were strong enough, but in their attempt to produce a one-size-fits-all mask, the manufacturers managed to make a 'one size fits none.'"[15]

Over the next decade Plante would strive to expand on the initial business model, seeking opportunities to mass-market fibreglass masks to the general public.

He also was not above using his hockey fame for other business opportunities. "We worked together as spokespersons for a car dealership in the sixties, Park Avenue Chevrolet," laughs Dickie Moore today. "We were both supplied with a free car, we had to pay for the gas, and we made appearances for the dealership. Jacques would make a point of driving to the dealership, which was a ways for him, to get the free car wash. That way he'd save the dollar from doing it where he lived."[16]

As the summer turned to fall, there was some surprise in media circles when Plante, true to his word, stayed away from participating in professional hockey. But that's not to say that he kept his skates sitting on the shelf.

He was invited to play goal for the Quebec NHL Old Timers League alongside many of his former teammates. He was asked to pay $3.50 every practice night to contribute to the ice rental and to chip in for a few beers, which he gladly did. The Old Timers played charity contests throughout Quebec and in other provinces.

Playing for fun, alongside old teammates like the Rocket and Dickie Moore, brought back memories of the reasons he had begun playing the game. Any ill will that had built up from his departure from the Canadiens was quickly forgiven and forgotten. Performing in front of sellout crowds, Plante basked in the glow of the fans' adoration and the camaraderie of his former teammates.

He also started regularly going to the Montreal Forum, filing a weekly column for the Sunday paper *Dernière Heure*. Each Saturday night he trudged up to the Forum press box, high above the ice surface, lugging a typewriter at his side. Along with the other newsmen he tapped out his thoughts as his former team played below him. Still he was dogged by questions about a possible return to the nets.

"I'll tell you one thing," Plante told the *Hockey News* one night in the press gallery, amid the sound of clattering typewriters, "they'll never see me back in the game again. I'm through, finis, as we say. No more hockey for Jacques." Of his nascent writing career he explained, "I only cover Saturday games. I don't travel. One of my chief reasons for quitting hockey was to be able to spend some time at home with my family. That's the situation now, and I'm happy about it. My wife is also happy. The whole family is happy."[17]

He was also asked to provide colour commentary for televised hockey games, by both the CBC French network and CFCF, Montreal's independent English station.

"When he retired and he was an analyst on TV and radio, and in both languages, he was the best analyst I'd ever heard," Red Fisher says today. "He had the game down pat in his mind and made it very easy for his listeners to understand him. I've heard many great analysts over the years, Scotty Bowman was one, but Plante was the best."[18]

Plante was apparently content in retirement, carving out a whole new life that didn't include facing oncoming pucks. That is, until the Russians came to town.

On December 15, 1965, the highly touted touring Russian national team came to town to play the amateur Montreal Junior Canadiens at the Forum.

The utter domination of Russian hockey was slowly beginning to take hold in international hockey as the sixties progressed. Canada, long considered the world's premier hockey nation, had for years been able to send amateur teams overseas to claim championship after championship over European opposition. That began to change in the fifties. Canada had last captured an Olympic gold in 1952, and the Trail Smoke Eaters had been the last Canadian amateur team to capture a World Championship four years prior. It had been three years since a Canadian team, the Windsor Bulldogs, had beaten a Russian team on Canadian soil.

Canada's constant inability to beat the Russians at hockey was taking its toll on the national psyche. Fans had witnessed the superiority of the Russians first-hand the year before, when the Montreal Junior Canadiens, bolstered by six established professionals on loan from the Quebec Aces, including Gump Worsley and Doug Harvey, lost 3–2 to the touring Russian team. The Russians concluded their 1964 exhibition tour undefeated.

A year later, the Junior Canadiens prepared for the rematch. Once again, the team was allowed to reinforce their roster with six professionals not playing in the NHL. Having lost the year before, there was a pessimism among both the fans and the media about the chances of the Junior Canadiens against the mighty Russian bear.

Scotty Bowman, the team's head coach, placed a call to David Molson, the Montreal Canadiens president, asking for permission to speak to the New York Rangers, who still held the playing rights to the player that Bowman desired the most. The Rangers gave their permission for Bowman to pursue his first choice for the Junior Canadiens goal for the game against the Russians.

Jacques Plante initially declined Bowman's offer. "His retirement decision had been firm and final," Andy O'Brien wrote later. "It was obvious, too, that he was in the position of having nothing, really, to gain and everything to lose. True, he had resumed play with the Quebec Old Timers but that had been only a few games in a relaxed, no body-checking, no slap-shooting atmosphere with any game proceeds going to charity. Obviously, the required sharpness for a major test of skill was not there, nor would there be time to get back into reasonable shape."[19]

But it seems that Plante's deeply ingrained love for the spotlight, the temptation to be seen as the conquering hero, and the inherent challenge of facing the mighty Russians were impossible for him to ignore. He called Bowman back and accepted the offer.

"We brought him in for two reasons," Bowman says today. "We wanted to hype the crowd for the Russian game and we were looking for experience."[20]

Canadiens president David Molson agreed: "We know the Russians and their capabilities and it is unfair to expect a young, junior goaltender to try and hold them, Plante is certainly a well tried and proven NHL calibre player and should prove a great asset for this game."[21]

Almost overnight, the Forum sold out. The chance to see the returning Jacques Plante against the unbeatable Russians enticed the sporting public.

"Plante appears to have his work cut out for him against the Russians," opined the *Hockey News*. "The touring Soviets teed off on Canada's unbeaten National hockey team trouncing them 4–0 and 8–6 in the first two games of their North American tour. The Russians are an imposing crew on the ice. They don't shoot as hard as National Leaguers, which could be some consolation to Plante, but they aim the puck well and this could give Plante trouble."[22]

With only one week before the game, Plante threw himself into practising with the Junior Canadiens as well as with members of his former team the Montreal Canadiens. He also took the time to illustrate on the blackboard for his young defencemen how he wanted them to play and what positions he wanted them to take in certain situations, many of which he then went out and demonstrated on the ice.

"He's a real perfectionist and is as serious about this game as he was for NHL play," commented Scotty Bowman in the days leading up to the game. "Jacques has the names and numbers of all the juniors and has been watching their habits closely in workouts so he will know just who does what. He has been getting in all the ice time possible and is looking sharp."[23]

The night before the game, the Russians faced off against a team of Ontario Junior All-Stars before a sellout crowd at Maple Leaf Gardens. Bolstered by the presence of Canada's junior hockey sensation, Bobby Orr, the Ontario team fought a close game but lost 4–3 to the Russians.

After their victory, the Russian team immediately departed for Montreal for their showdown the next night with the Junior Canadiens. "None of us there from the communications media had seen a game that so focused the spotlight on one goaler," journalist Andy O'Brien wrote later. "True, the Junior Canadiens were reinforced by five players from the Houston Apollos" – the Canadiens' team in the Central Professional Hockey League – "but everybody seemed aware from the start that – as Scotty Bowman had sensed – the key figure would be Plante."[24]

Throughout his career, Jacques Plante had shown the ability to rise to the occasion when the spotlight shone the brightest, to perform at his best when the pressure was the harshest. But that was before he had left the game behind eight months earlier.

"I went in with the damndest case of the jitters I had ever known because I just didn't know what to expect," Plante confessed. "I had never seen the Russians play even on television. I had a crash program of practices for the last six days, but even that didn't ease the jitters. In Stanley Cup games I had been playing for a team and a city but tonight, it seemed, I carried all of Canada with me and I dreaded letting my nation down."[25]

Before a crowd that was perched on the edge of its collective seat, Plante emerged from the catacombs of the Montreal Forum, wearing the familiar jersey of the Montreal Canadiens with the unmistakable number 1 on his back.

The first period only heightened the tension in the arena as both teams skated to a scoreless standoff. Halfway through the second period, the Russians struck first, breaking the ice with a power-play goal by Vladimir Brezhnev at 9:04. In the middle stanza the Russians continued to hold the advantage while Plante's counterpart in the Russian net, Victor Zinger, held the Canadian shooters at bay, and the period ended with the Russians ahead 1–0.

The third period would prove to be a rollercoaster of emotions. A few minutes into the third period, the Junior Habs appeared to tie the game, only to have the goal immediately waved off by referee Frank Daigneault, who had whistled the play dead mere seconds before.

A disapproving crowd barely got settled before the home squad equalled the score. With Zinger's view of the puck obstructed by one of his teammates, Larry Pleau converted Norm Ferguson's perfect set-up to tie the game at one with a little over 12 minutes remaining on the clock.

The tension reached a fever pitch as the clock ticked towards the game's conclusion and both teams struggled to score that elusive winning goal.

"Plante was never better," the *Montreal Star* commented. "He didn't miss a trick as he gave the visitors a display of the 'old pro' in action. Jacques made the big saves. He delayed the game to adjust his padding, made several long sorties from his goal crease, and humbly skated around with bowed head as the fans cheered him after dramatically turning back the determined third-period stand by the Russians. Jacques stopped the Russians on five breakaways with Alexander Almetov and Victor Polupanov each turned back twice and Veniamin Alexandrov once."[26]

The conclusion to this anxious drama came with only 20 seconds remaining on the clock. André Boudrias checked a Russian defence-man inside his own blue line, jarring the puck loose and onto the stick of Bill Inglis, who quickly laid the puck on the blade of Norm Dennis, who backhanded it into the back of the Russian net. The final score was 2–1.

In its long, glorious history, the Montreal Forum has rarely heard a roar as deafening as the one that now filled the arena. "Plante got a breath-taking ovation from the fans and after the final siren sounded, his teammates carried him shoulder high in a sincere expression of their appreciation for his superb efforts," wrote the *Montreal Star*.[27]

After the game, before the assembled reporters, the Russian coach, Arkady Chernyshev, was full of praise for Plante's performance. "It was he who held us from winning and I consider him the best player we have faced on this trip."[28]

The dean of Russian hockey, Anatoly Tarasov, also paid tribute. "You want me to talk about Jacques Plante? We only knew him by name.

Tonight, not only did we meet him, we felt his presence. I'd like to ask you to thank him – to say thank you to Jacques Plante on behalf of all of us. I am speechless when I see him play. I hope I can say that the Russian team deserved to meet such a goaltender. It was a great honour for us to play against him."[29]

Back in the familiar confines of the Canadiens dressing room, the *Montreal Star* reported, "Plante was visibly shaken by the standing ovation he had received moments before and basked in the accustomed role of being the centre of attention."[30]

One of the reporters suggested that Plante could – or should – seek his reinstatement as an amateur, join the Canadian National hockey team, and head to Europe as an avenger for a wounded nation. With Plante, it was argued, Canada could regain its lost prestige on the international hockey scene.

"Hold on now," Plante replied, raising both of his hands. "This is it; this is the end of the line. I worked long and hard to become Jacques Plante, the goaltender. To me, that meant going to bed at eight or nine every night and naps in the afternoon so I was always fresh. It meant working at being in shape. It meant concentrating and worrying. I retired to get away from all these things and I'm not prepared to start all over . . . and I wouldn't be able to settle for anything less. I am Jacques Plante and people expect things of me. If I come back, even as an amateur, I still have to approach the game the way I always did and I don't want to. No this is it. The end."

David Molson, the president of the Montreal Canadiens, made his way towards the exhausted Plante. He had a simple request: could he get a picture with the man of the hour? Plante stood up and put back on his Canadiens jersey.

"It's a wonderful sweater," he remarked. "It's a pleasure to have it on again."[31]

The next morning he returned to work for Molson Breweries.

23

BACK IN THE SADDLE

AFTER THE EUPHORIC HIGH of the single-game performance against the Russian National team, Jacques Plante quickly and quietly slipped back into the tranquility of retirement. It was at this time that the NHL went through a major transformation.

At the same time that Plante was playing for the Baltimore Clippers, the NHL began expanding, doubling in size by adding another six teams, chosen from among 14 applicants. The new franchises were Pittsburgh, Philadelphia, Minnesota, Los Angeles, and St. Louis, in addition to a team operating out of the Oakland–San Francisco area known forevermore as the California Golden Seals. Each of the expansion six were set to begin play in the fall of 1967.

With the league doubling in size, so did the number of jobs available to aspiring hockey players. For many who had longed to play in the NHL, their moment of opportunity had arrived. The new teams would be made up of discards from the original six, career journeymen, and older players who brought name recognition to new franchises desperately in need of credibility.

No position in hockey was more changed by the expansion than goaltending. In the years immediately preceding the expansion, the original six franchises had slowly begun to adopt a two-goaltender system, which had long been advocated by its foremost proponent,

217

Jacques Plante. With the travel schedule becoming more arduous, the days of one-goaltender teams were no more. During the 1964–65 season, coincidentally Plante's last year in the league, Roger Crozier of the Detroit Red Wings became the last goaler to play his team's entire schedule.

The proof of the value in the two-goalie system could be seen in the last year before the expansion, when the Chicago Black Hawks, with Denis Dejordy and Glenn Hall splitting duties in the nets, gave up the least goals in the league, while the combo of Terry Sawchuk and Johnny Bower backstopped the Toronto Maple Leafs to a Stanley Cup championship.

With expansion, many of the old guard found themselves fronting new teams, clad in unfamiliar uniforms; Terry Sawchuk was now a Los Angeles King and Glenn Hall a St. Louis Blue. Their replacements among the established teams represented a changing of the guard, as the young goalies Gerry Cheevers, Rogatien Vachon, Eddie Johnston, and Bernie Parent began their careers in the NHL.

However, goalie was not the only position that was opening up. Each of the six new teams began their search for head coaches willing to guide the new teams through their formative years – plus add some name recognition. In addition to possessing sound hockey minds, many of the new coaches were former players.

Nowhere was this more apparent than with the Golden Seals, who hired Bert Olmstead as their first coach. Olmstead, a former star with both the Canadiens and the Maple Leafs, had long desired an opportunity to step behind the bench of an NHL team. After a year's apprenticeship in the Western Hockey League as the coach of the Vancouver Canucks, Olmstead was given his chance in the new and unlikely hockey environment of the Oakland–San Francisco region.

Olmstead realized that he didn't possess enough knowledge about one particular aspect of his team. Reaching for his phone, he dialed the number of the one person he knew who could solve his problem, the one person who knew more about goaltending than anyone else.

In the more than two long years since Jacques Plante had left the game behind, he had continued with his job at Molson Breweries, all the while tending goal for the Quebec Old Timers. He had moved further and further away from the public spotlight as he coached his sons' sports teams and pursued his burgeoning broadcasting career.

In the spring of 1967, Montreal's CFCF began airing a series of junior games from the Montreal Forum on Saturday afternoons.

Spotlighting the Montreal Junior Canadiens of the Ontario Hockey Association, the games featured many future NHL stars such as Brad Park, Garry Unger, Pierre Bouchard, and Walt Tkachuk. The lead broadcaster on the games and the sports director for CFCF was Dick Irvin Jr. The son of Plante's first coach with the Canadiens, it was Irvin who hired the retired Plante to be his partner in the broadcast booth. It was not a move wholly endorsed by the upper brass at CFCF.

"I hired Jacques as the colour man, which bothered my boss at CFCF, Bud Hayward," Irvin later wrote.

Bud wasn't sure Jacques' English would be good enough, not realizing Plante was perfectly bilingual. We had a meeting shortly before our first telecast. I had warned Jacques about Bud's fears over his English pronunciations. Jacques didn't say a word at the meeting. Then Bud gave us a pep talk about the kind of show he wanted and how important it was for junior hockey to receive exposure of this kind for the first time in the Montreal market.

"You okay, Jacques?" asked Bud when the meeting was coming to an end. "Think you can handle it?"

With a straight face, Plante replied, "Don't worry you. I try to do best I are."

The colour drained from Bud's face for a few seconds, until we started to laugh and let him in on the joke.[1]

"He was a very good analyst, a very smart man," Irvin recalls. "Those were tough times for junior hockey in Montreal. I remember shifting all the people over to the other side of the arena so when the camera focused on the ice and the crowd above them it would create the illusion of a much larger crowd."[2]

Plante quickly discovered that he was well suited to broadcasting. Always comfortable in front of a camera, he was able to convey his thoughts to his audience with equal amounts of precision and intelligence.

In early September, a few months after he started broadcasting, Plante received the call from Olmstead, offering him the job of goal-tending consultant. Plante immediately accepted, and hurried to the Seals training camp in Port Huron, Michigan.

Plante had always professed an interest in coaching. As his teammates could testify, he never hesitated to offer his advice and guidance to them, even if it wasn't always well received. In retirement, in an effort to keep his reflexes sharp and his body in shape, Jacques had taken to practising with the Montreal Junior Canadiens.

No sooner had Plante arrived at training camp than rumours started circulating throughout the league that his coaching had quickly taken on a more active role. Weighing in at a lean 174 pounds, a full 12 pounds lighter than when he had starred in Montreal, he was in stellar physical condition. Clad in full equipment, he found himself increasingly taking to the nets to demonstrate his coaching points. Being around the game again, with an NHL team, proved to be an irresistible lure to Plante.

"I read in the newspaper that Plante was there to help the young goalies, but he never talked to me and I was the only young goalie in camp," remembers prospect Gary Smith, who speculates, "He must have been trying out for a contract."[3]

The rumours of a comeback only intensified when Plante returned in an exhibition game on September 21, 1967. Before a sparse crowd of 1,176 at the McMorran Arena, Plante skated out in the unfamiliar uniform of the Seals. That night's opposition was another one of the expansion teams, the Los Angeles Kings. In their goal stood the legendary Terry Sawchuk.

This latest confrontation between the two long-term adversaries would be a brief affair, as Sawchuk played only the first period and Plante departed halfway through the second.

"I feel like I've never left," a confident Plante told the *Hockey News*. "My reflexes haven't changed a bit and my eyesight is as good as ever. I proved to myself that I could still play in the NHL. The two goals scored were well played by the other team. But I wasn't weak and I think to myself that if I had played those shots another way, I might have stopped them."[4]

With Charlie Hodge, the Seals' first pick in the expansion draft, staging a contract holdout from training camp, many speculated that the Seals were clearing the way to bring Plante out of retirement. But speaking to the press after the game, Coach Olmstead sought to downplay the notion of a Plante comeback, stating that his appearance was nothing more than a chance for Plante to see how he felt in the nets, and that there was no intention on the Seals' part to sign him to a player's contract.[5]

The very next morning, Plante abruptly departed the Seals training camp and returned home to Quebec.

Seals president Frank Selke Jr. (son of Plante's former boss with the Canadiens) offered the following explanation for Plante's sudden exit: "He was very perceptive. He evaluated the team and its chances and decided he didn't want to be a part of it. I think the final straw was getting bombarded in an exhibition game. He knew before anyone that the team wasn't very good. He packed up and left."[6]

Yet the records of the game show that Plante had not in fact been "bombarded" as Selke remembered. In his period and a half of play, he had faced only 10 shots, a far cry from the number he'd taken only a few years before as a New York Ranger.

In truth, Plante's NHL rights were still held by the Rangers. Before travelling down to Port Huron to be the Seals' goaltending consultant, he had to receive permission from the Rangers. However, once he stepped out onto the ice to play, it was a different matter entirely.

By letting Plante play that evening in Port Huron, the Seals violated NHL rules. Plante's playing rights were still held by the Rangers, and they were not about to give them up to the Seals without compensation. As an expansion team, however, the Seals had precious little to offer one of the established "original six" clubs. With the two sides unable to come to any agreement, Jacques Plante was prohibited from playing for the Seals or coaching long-term and was still bound to the Rangers. Hence, Plante bolted from the training camp.

"I want to play but I can't because of my family," a coy Plante informed the *Hockey News* after his departure. "The Seals wanted me to come here to help coach; that's why I came. There were others who did want me back as a player, though."[7]

Plante celebrated his thirty-ninth birthday in January 1968 and continued to play for the Quebec Old Timers and work for Molson Breweries. He also continued to mull over a return to the bright lights of the NHL. By the time the annual NHL meetings were approaching in June, he had decided.

Jacqueline had noticed her husband's increasing restlessness after three years away from the game. Nights that were once filled with oncoming pucks and the adulation of the crowd had been replaced by long stretches of boredom. Jacqueline could sense her husband's excitement over a possible return to the game, and she came to the realization that that's what he would do.

"I am perfectly well now, Jacques," she informed him on the eve of the NHL meetings. "If you would like to go back to hockey, go if you really want to."[8]

Because they still held his rights, he first approached the Rangers about a potential comeback. However, under the rules of the draft, the Rangers were allowed to protect only two goalies, and a 39-year-old Plante was on the outside looking in as the team protected starter Eddie Giacomin and backup Gilles Villemure. Realizing that he would be left unprotected, Plante turned his focus to the teams at the top of the draft order, beginning with the holders of the first selection, the St. Louis Blues.

Just a few months earlier, the Blues had become the first expansion team to make the finals. Led by Plante's greatest rival, Glenn Hall, in the nets and made up of many of his former teammates with the Canadiens, including Dickie Moore, Doug Harvey, and Jean-Guy Talbot, the Blues gallantly marched to the Stanley Cup finals before being swept aside by the new, more powerful Canadiens.

Luckily for Plante, the Blues were looking for a goaltender to share the load with the great Hall in the upcoming season. As well, they were coached and managed by Scotty Bowman. It had been two and a half years since Plante had dazzled the Russians in a virtuoso performance as a one-time add-on for the Montreal Junior Canadiens, coached by the same Scotty Bowman. That game had given both men a special appreciation of each other's talents. Plante had been showered with praise for that night's performance and had gone out of his way to praise Bowman too.

In 1965, Plante had been the perfect choice to face the unbeatable Russians. Now, as Bowman huddled with Blues officials, there was no doubt in his mind that Plante was the perfect fit for his team.

"He made an appearance at the Queen Elizabeth Hotel and he announced that he was going to come out of retirement," Bowman remembers today. "I thought he was perfect for what we were looking for and that we should take him with the first pick. Lynn Patrick, the Blues vice-president and former general manager, however, thought that we should wait and try and pick him later, but I was adamant. When it came to that first pick I told Lynn, 'I don't want to leave this guy.'"[9]

On June 12 the draft commenced, with the St. Louis Blues selecting Jacques Plante with the first overall pick.

Three years after announcing his retirement, Jacques stood in the same spot and announced his return to the game for the 1968–69 season. No goaltender had ever returned from a three-year absence successfully, much less one entering his fourth decade. Many of those gathered to hear him that day doubted that he could match his rich list of past accomplishments.

Then again, Jacques Plante had carved out an unparalleled career by defying convention.

24

THE PRIDE AND
THE MONEY

IN THE FACE OF the reporters' endless stream of questions that warm June weekend in Montreal, Plante was withholding a critical piece of information, not only from the media but from his new team as well.

"The biggest concern came a couple of weeks after we drafted him when he called me to say that he thought he needed some surgery on his knee," Blues coach Scotty Bowman remembers today.[1] Only to Bowman did Plante reveal that his left knee had been giving him problems since his final days in Baltimore. He also admitted that after three years away from the game his knee felt much better, but he wondered if it would be up to the strain of a season in the NHL.

Bowman set up an appointment with noted Montreal orthopaedic surgeon Dr. Edward C. Percy. Percy had quickly made a name for himself as the pre-eminent expert in the field after performing several successful surgeries on members of both the Montreal Canadiens and football's Montreal Alouettes.

Bowman pleaded with Plante to keep the surgery as quiet as possible. "Don't let the news media know about it. They'll be accusing me in St. Louis of hiring a goal-keeper with two bum legs."[2]

Normally, a signing of such a prominent player as Plante would occasion a press conference in St. Louis. But it was announced that, due to "previous commitments," Plante would be unavailable to visit St. Louis until the middle of July, a month later. It was a convenient ruse dreamed up by Bowman, who, along with Plante, hid the truth from a prying media.

The surgery took place July 1, Canada Day – to further distract the media. As Plante had long thought, there was torn cartilage in his knee. Percy was able to remove it and pronounced the surgery an unqualified success.

Three days later, Jacques was able to walk with the assistance of a cane. Within two weeks, the doctor determined that Plante had recovered his full range of motion. Plante immediately placed a call down to St. Louis and notified an anxious Bowman. Not only was he now walking without a limp but he was ready for the upcoming season. Bowman set the much-delayed press conference for July 15, and no one was any the wiser about Plante's secret surgery.

Upon Plante's arrival in St. Louis, Bowman put him to the test to make sure that the knee was sound. The two men took in an afternoon St. Louis Cardinals baseball game at Busch Memorial Stadium. "The temperature was nudging 115 degrees," Plante remembered later, "and I sat in a box seat sweltering while Bowman worked on a schedule for exhibition hockey games to be played by the Blues. He watched me as I walked up and down the stairs and to the car lot. He was happy and I felt real good about everything."[3]

After the game, the two men went to the Blues offices and worked out the details of a three-year contract that paid Plante $26,000 a season, with $12,000 of that being deferred until 1972, four years later. Plante's financial stability allowed him to defer parts of his salary, a move extremely rare among NHL players at the time. He then sat down in front of a bemused Bowman and performed an even rarer task for most NHLers. It was a weekend, and there was no secretary in, and so Plante typed up the contract himself.

Jacques Plante was now officially back in the National Hockey League.

A few days later he appeared before the St. Louis media. Upon first glance the only evidence of his advancing age were the white hairs that had started populating his long sideburns.

"Flawlessly dressed, slender, nervous, six feet tall, with black hair and a serious elongated face, he impressed all more as a successful, middle-aged businessman than the veteran of over a dozen rugged NHL campaigns," noted Montreal newsman Andy O'Brien. "Could this maskless one really be the fabulous figure who had won the Hart Trophy as the most valuable player on a team as talent-loaded as the Canadiens of '62?"

Almost immediately the media attempted to play up a potential rift with the Blues' goaltending incumbent, Glenn Hall, asking Plante if his salary exceeded Hall's. Plante, a savvy veteran of media skirmishes, easily evaded the meddlesome queries and instead answered, "I would never have thought of coming out of retirement – even for the most generous contract I have ever signed – if it weren't for the two-goaler deal. When the other goaler is one of the stature of Glenn Hall, how could I refuse Scotty Bowman?"

He was asked if he had spoken with Hall. "Yes and he seems as happy as I about the deal," Plante said. "Certainly we've both been around long enough to realize that neither of us could handle the full 76-game schedule. What's more, Scotty has assured us that we won't be competing against one another. Instead of one goaler staying in the nets as long as he's hot and healthy, we will be alternating."

"All of hockey will be watching as Bowman tries his great experiment," wrote a St. Louis newsman in the next day's paper, "which is the equivalent of trying to platoon Willie Mays and Mickey Mantle."[4]

As had been the case a few years before in New York, the Blues saw an increase in season's ticket sales right after Plante's unveiling.

In the three years since he'd left the game, hockey had undergone many changes. The keen-eyed Plante had noted one particular transformation on the ice. Plante had always been a master of playing the angles. Now, with the game increasingly being played out on the perimeter as ever more players used the powerful slapshot, he found his style more suited for the game than it had ever been before.

"Before I quit there were maybe one or two players on a team that had the kind of hard shot that made it necessary for a goaltender to play the angles very close," Plante told the *Hockey News*. "I could bear down on these fellows by coming out and cutting down the shooting angle. Now there are seven or eight players on every team who can score on you from the blueline, so you gotta come out and block the angles. If you know you gotta player coming at you that can't break an egg with his shot then you can stay in the net and you know you have plenty of time to move and make your play. You stay put because you know he's going to make some fancy play."[5]

The St. Louis Blues were the most successful of all the expansion franchises in the late sixties. Their team was a collection of former stars, rejects, has-beens, and never-weres, marshalled together under the coaching genius of Scotty Bowman and united by a work ethic unequalled in the NHL. For Plante, playing with the Blues would also bring some sense of familiarity, as two of his defencemen with the powerhouse Canadiens of the 1950s were now reunited with him in St. Louis: Doug Harvey and Jean-Guy Talbot.

The Blues also possessed the most generous owners in the league in the Salomon family. No owner ever loved his players more than Sid Salomon Jr. and his son Sid III, each of whom had secured their riches through the insurance business.

"There's a different atmosphere in St. Louis," said Phil Goyette, a teammate of Plante's in Montreal, New York, and now with the Blues. "You want to work harder. Naturally, the ownership has something to do with it. The Salomons mix with the players more than most owners. They give you the impression that you're part of the organization. There's something special about playing for the Blues."[6]

Every move that the Salomon family made was designed to increase their players' comfort and productivity. When they heard that several of the players made their home at a local hotel, the Salomons renovated a nearby clubhouse so the players could have somewhere to congregate if they wanted to watch TV, play pool or Ping-Pong, or just talk.

"I mentioned one day that I used table tennis to improve my timing," Plante told the *Toronto Star*. "That's all that was said. Next thing I know, there's a table in the rink. We also have a billiard table, television, sauna bath. It's almost like belonging to a private club."[7]

With the Salomons' guiding hand, the Blues quickly became the NHL's model expansion franchise.

A large part of their on-ice success could be attributed to the man Plante would share goaltending duties with. Among all his opponents, Glenn Hall stood out as Plante's main rival. They had clashed five times in the playoffs in their careers. Each time they faced off it was an epic showdown between two goaltenders who shared an unequalled proficiency for stopping the puck but approached it in two very different yet effective ways. Now paired, each still played the position in his individual way, but together formed the league's most formidable goaltending duo.

"I had no difficulty playing with Plante, I really didn't," Hall later told Dick Irvin for his study of goaltenders, *In the Crease*. "We weren't going to teach each other anything new. He was different but he was a dedicated hockey player. So often your skilled players are not dedicated, but Plante was. Plante liked to do different things, experiment, fool around with ideas."[8]

"Nobody would have ever thought that the two of us would be on the same team," Plante said at the time. "For all those years Glenn was the guy that I was fighting for the Vezina trophy and for the All-Star selections. Now I'm his biggest booster. And I was glad to hear that he wanted me with him on the team. Over all the years that Glenn and I were on opposing teams we never talked on any occasion for more than a few minutes together; we were strangers. Now Glenn and I sometimes talk over the game while we're on the plane. Sometimes we mention the old days, but mostly we just talk about the next game or the last game."[9]

Coach Scotty Bowman wisely left his two legendary goalies to their own devices. "Plante helped a lot in regard to goalie instruction," says Bowman today. "He liked to set up plays in practice. He wanted me to structure practices around game situations, like two-on-ones, etc. He was a very technical type of goalie. He and Glenn Hall played two different styles, so we had to practice, two different ways, depending on who was playing."[10]

"With Glenn Hall you had to play and practise a certain way and with Jacques you had to play and practise another way," confirms defenceman Al Arbour. "They were both so different. Glenn was a butterfly goalie and Jacques an angle goalie. For example, on two-on-ones, Glenn would take the pass, and Jacques would take the shooter."[11]

Before the season began, Bowman, Hall, and Plante sat down and went over the schedule, figuring out who would play whom. "Plante wanted to start by playing the home games against the West [Division] teams, because they would have less powerful shooters," explains Bowman today. "Glenn and him would split the West road games and Glenn could have the East teams in St. Louis and whoever else you're trying to break in can have the East games on the road because they would be the toughest games for us to win. He always had everything figured out."[12]

Right before the season was slated to begin, Bowman announced that when the Blues had back-to-back games scheduled on the weekend, either Hall or Plante would work on Saturday night and then stay behind in St. Louis on Sunday while a third-string goalie made the trip to back up the goalie who hadn't played the night before.

Realizing that his treasured goalie was alone in St. Louis on a Sunday, Sid Salomon III would invite Plante to come fishing with him, giving his aged goalie a restful day on the water. Soon Plante went out of his way to spend even more time with the Salomons – on their dime.

"They tell a lot of stories about Plante being cheap," recalls rookie goaltender Gary Edwards, who bunked at Plante's apartment. "I know that after the home games he would always show up at the apartment long after I got home. When a game was over Jacques always said he had to see the owners, the Salomons, about something, and he would go to the private club in the arena. They would invite him to stay and eat with them, so Jacques would sit with the owners and have a steak dinner, on the house, while the rest of the guys were out somewhere paying for theirs."[13]

A team of veterans, Plante's Blues teammates not only tolerated his eccentricities but on some occasions had fun with them. In earlier years Plante may have taken offence, but now a new, more mature Plante took it all in stride.

"He was pretty cheap with a penny, very, very frugal," recalls teammate Frank St. Marseille. "One year when we did a Christmas exchange we decided to have a little fun with him. A few of us chipped in some money and we bought him a pair of sunglasses and a tin cup. I remember we all got a laugh out of that one, including Jacques."[14]

The Blues began their second season in Chicago on October 11, 1968, with Hall in the nets, and were edged by the powerful Black Hawks 4–3. Back in St. Louis the next night before a capacity crowd, the Blues had their home opener against the Los Angeles Kings. Jacques Plante skated out for his first NHL game in three and a half years. He shut out the Kings 6–0, for the sixty-fourth shutout of his illustrious career.

In St. Louis he made some subtle adjustments to his rigid routine, many of which reflected a mellowing of the man, something even Plante readily admitted. "People just don't understand," Plante wrote later. "From noon on before a game, I had trained myself to concentrate on the players I would be facing that night, running and rerunning mental films on how they'd look coming in and what they would most likely do – shoot high, shoot low, fake then backhand, or try to deke me out of the way and just push the puck in. I wanted to be left alone until the game was over. But, beginning in St. Louis, I was less tense before games; I even stopped and signed and chatted with kids some nights like a kindly old man."[15]

A few years earlier, in both New York and Baltimore, he had allowed himself to wallow in the loneliness inherent in being so far away from his family. However, in St. Louis he was able to effectively channel his energy, all the while satisfying his insatiable curiosity. He began composing long daily letters, some as long as four pages, to Jacqueline. Having always enjoyed writing, he found that detailing the events of his days was extremely therapeutic. He also became more interested in cooking, especially Italian cuisine.

Plante even took one of St. Louis's goaltending prospects under his wing. His name was Gary Edwards, the Blues' first selection, sixth overall in the 1968 NHL entry draft. "When I was in St. Louis I bunked in with Plante in his apartment," Edwards later told broadcaster Dick Irvin. "He was very analytical about goaltending and he would go over a lot of things with me. He kept notes on how he had done against every team, the goals against him and who scored them, and charts on everything."[16]

That January 17, Plante celebrated his fortieth birthday. The very next night he found himself manning the Blues nets against one of his former teams, the New York Rangers.

"Jacqueline had phoned, of course, but I thought nobody in St. Louis knew about it and I sure wasn't yelling the news," Plante remembered later. "Then I skated out onto the arena ice to play against the Rangers and, suddenly, organist Mary Kramer gave a long blare and began playing, 'Happy Birthday to You.' The crowd stood up and sang, adding the word, 'Jacques.' Would you believe it, I stood and bowed my head to hide the tears."[17]

He said later that he tried his hardest to reward the St. Louis fans with a shutout, but his former team refused to cooperate as the two teams skated to a 2–2 tie.

Plante had always been seen by his critics as a bit of a showboat, whereas his supporters hailed him as a showman. Now he would take his act to even bigger heights. Touched by the response of the fans in St. Louis, he designed a routine to show his appreciation. After every home victory, and if he played well, Plante, after receiving the congratulations of his teammates, would slowly make his way to the exit. But just as he neared the exit, he would throw his arms in the air, a V for victory salutation. The fans in St. Louis loved it.

At the halfway point of the season, the tandem of Hall and Plante had given up the fewest goals in the league, with each man pitching five shutouts apiece. For the first time, the all-star game would see the East All-Stars face off against their Western counterparts. Both men, at the ages of 37 and 40 respectively, were named to the Western roster, becoming the oldest goaltending tandem to put on the all-star sweaters.

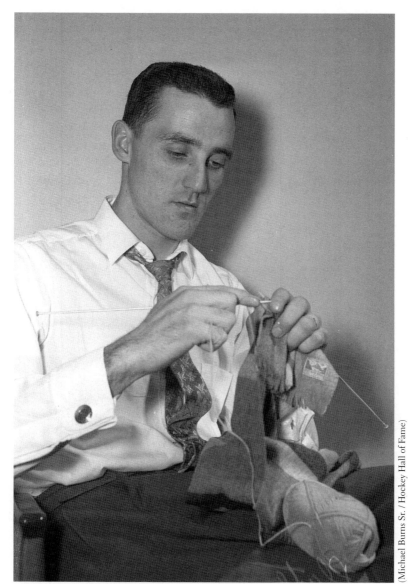

Plante was a proficient knitter, making his own toques, socks, and undergarments. And while his teammates rolled their eyes in disbelief, the media couldn't get enough.

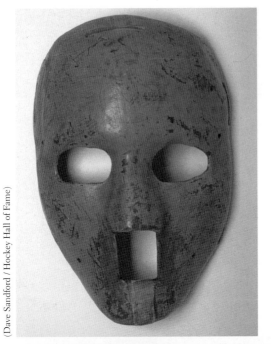

The first mask that Plante wore in an NHL game (currently on display at the Hockey Hall of Fame). After two months he switched to what is commonly referred to as the "pretzel mask."

Led by Plante (here thwarting Ron Stewart), the Canadiens won their fifth consecutive Stanley Cup defeating the Leafs in the 1960 final. Along the way he silenced many of his critics, going undefeated in the playoffs while allowing only 11 goals in 8 games.

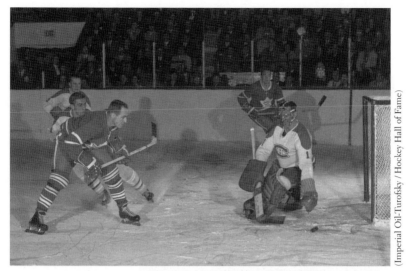

After an off-year in 1961, Plante (here stopping Red Kelly) came back with a vengeance in 1962, winning the Hart Trophy as the league's most valuable player. It would be 35 years before another goalie claimed the Hart Trophy.

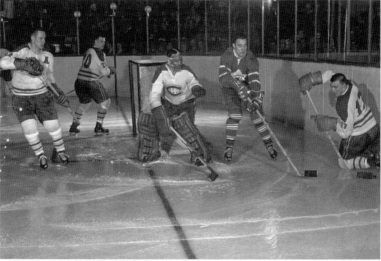

The Canadiens lost to the defending champion Maple Leafs in the opening round of the 1963 playoffs, bringing to an end Plante's glorious tenure with the team. (L to R: Tom Johnson, Phil Goyette, Plante, Frank Mahovlich, and Jean-Guy Talbot).

Plante's trade to the New York Rangers was the talk of the hockey world in the summer of 1963.

Plante's time in New York was a disappointment to both him and the Rangers. After only two years with the team, he retired from the game. Here, he makes the save on the legendary Gordie Howe.

(Frank Prazak / Hockey Hall of Fame)

After three years away from the NHL, Plante made his comeback with the St. Louis Blues in 1968.

Plante joined the Toronto Maple Leafs in the fall of 1970. At the age of 42, he was named to the second all-star team and set a still unmatched record with a .942 save percentage.

In 1972, Plante published the first instructional manual devoted exclusively to goaltending.

Plante's professional career finally came to an end with the
Edmonton Oilers of the WHA in the fall of 1975. He was 46 years old.

In the spring of 1984, the previously unknown Steve Penney led the Cinderella Canadiens to within two games of the Stanley Cup finals. Much of the credit for his success went to the team's goaltending coach—Jacques Plante.

In honour of the 50th all-star game in 2000, Canada Post issued a set of stamps honouring six greats of the game. The chosen goaltender was Jacques Plante.

On paper it seemed like a horrible mismatch. But for Plante the significance of the moment went beyond the game. That year the all-star game was to be held at the Montreal Forum, making it a special homecoming for Plante.

"He had a terrific all-star game," remembered Scotty Bowman of the 3–3 tie. "He, Glenn Hall, and Bernie Parent played and the shots were something like 50–12 against them. Plante hurt his knee in that game and he made a slow recovery. He came back with about four games left in the season. He was gonna play half the game for the first three that were left and then maybe the full game in the last game of the season. His goals-against average was below two a game."[18]

Plante was set to play the final game of the year in Los Angeles. However, he begged off, claiming that he had a twinge in his knee. Bowman and his teammates believed that the knee was merely an excuse, as Plante knew that if he sat out his goals-against average would end the season below two. With Plante unable – or unwilling – to play, Glenn Hall stepped into the breach and played the Blues' final game of the 1968–69 season, a 2–1 victory.

"He was always conscious of his goals-against average. That was the number that meant the most to him," Bowman recalls. "People called it selfish, but for me a goalie who wants to keep his goals-against down is an asset and not a detriment. He was a very studious guy."[19]

The Blues finished in first place in the West Division that year by nine and a half games. Together Hall and Plante allowed only 157 goals that year, the fewest in the league, to capture the Vezina Trophy together. For Hall it was the third time that his name would be etched on the trophy. For Jacques Plante it was the seventh, breaking the standard set by Bill Durnan, his idol. To this day, Plante retains the record.

"I keep telling myself that all this can't be happening," Plante told the *Hockey News*. "It really is hard to believe, isn't it? I mean it when I say I never played this well before."[20]

"I wasn't as personally excited over the comeback angle as I was in beating the six-win Vezina record held by the Canadiens immortal Bill Durnan," Plante admitted. "But I just couldn't explain about standing on my sisters' bureau as a kid, listening spellbound to the radio upstairs and pretending I was stopping shots with Durnan . . . How many people in St. Louis would have heard of Bill Durnan? And how could they possibly visualize how great he was? I couldn't rave about that either because the NHL record book now said I was greater and that would make me sound immodest."[21]

In the days following his seventh Vezina win, Jacques Plante basked in the praises and the accolades from the media and the fans, but in the St. Louis Blues dressing room one would be hard pressed to find a player less popular among his teammates. By sitting out, Plante had ensured that his goals-against average finished at 1.96, but he had paid a price for it.

"The players were upset with Plante, so they put all kinds of white tape around his luggage and painted a big red cross on it," recalls Bowman.

Somebody wrote on the tape, "Win #76 for Jacques." He came down to the room about two minutes before the game was over and he was upset the players felt that way.

That was on a Saturday. We went home the next day to start the playoffs on Wednesday. On Monday Plante came in and told me he wouldn't be able to play. By that time I had had it with him, I guess, so we went out of town to a hotel and I told him to stay in St. Louis. The day of the game we're getting off the bus at the Arena just as Jacques was pulling into the parking lot. Camille Henry, and I give him a lot of credit for this, came to me and said, "I know how you feel. But he's not coming back, Scotty, unless we make a fuss over him, make him feel wanted. I know everybody's cheesed off with him, but I'm telling you I know what he's like. He'll coast right through the playoffs unless we appeal to his pride."

I thought that was a pretty good idea, so I talked to Plante and asked him how he felt. He had received a special treatment that day for his knee at the clinic run by the football clinics. I tried to sympathize with him and that seemed to pep him up. He told me that he thought he could dress as a back-up that night but he still didn't think he could play.

Officially, Plante was listed as the backup to Glenn Hall as the Blues opened their first-round playoff series against the Philadelphia Flyers. Plante chose to watch the game from the Blues dressing room. In the second period, with the Blues ahead 1–0, a lunging Hall pulled his hamstring making a save and had to leave the game.

"So we had to go to Plante," remembers Bowman. "I didn't know it, but he was in the dressing room with hardly any equipment on. So he had to put his pads and everything on and it took ten or fifteen minutes.

Then he made his big entrance in the St. Louis Arena. He always had the crowd on his side and they went for it as if he was Napoleon coming in. And he played, well, you can check the records, but he played just great. We beat Philadelphia four straight, and then we played Los Angeles and beat them four straight. We won eight straight games and they were eight of the greatest games I've ever seen a goalie play."[22]

In the Blues' eight-game march to the Stanley Cup finals, Plante had only allowed an astonishing eight goals to get past him. It was a performance worthy of the greatest goaltenders ever, much less a 40-year-old man coming off a three-year retirement.

"Most goalies need work in order to stay sharp," Bowman says today. "Plante's concentration was so intense, however. He was always in the game, always mentally sharp, always in the game, even when he wasn't in the middle of the action."[23]

In the finals he was matched up with his old team, the Montreal Canadiens. However, in the six and a half years since he had been traded, much had changed. Both Frank Selke and Toe Blake had retired. The Montreal Forum, site of many of Plante's greatest triumphs, had been completely renovated. Gump Worsley, the goalie who had gone in the opposite direction in their blockbuster trade, could only watch from the comfort of the bench, as he had been usurped by the young Rogatien Vachon in the Montreal nets.

Yet the more things change, the more they stay the same. The Canadiens, winners of three of the past four Stanley Cups, were heavy favourites to make it four out of five. The team was still captained by the incomparable Jean Béliveau, whose two assistants, Henri Richard and Claude Provost, were the only other remnants from the greatest team hockey had ever known, sharing with Plante in an unequalled five consecutive championships.

In a rare Sunday-afternoon game televised throughout North America, the Canadiens scored two early goals in the first game, taking the steam out of Plante's return to his old haunt. The Blues answered near the end of the first period but were unable to get the tying goal. Plante, pulled from the game for an extra attacker, watched helplessly from the bench as Montreal iced the opening game with an empty-net goal.

Bowman reverted back to Glenn Hall for the second game, in which the Canadiens once again triumphed with another 3–1 victory. With the series heading back to St. Louis, a desperate Bowman went back to Plante, but the 4–0 defeat once again showed that the talent difference between the two teams was a disparate one. Simply put, the Blues, having scored only two goals in the first three games, were putting their goaltenders in an impossible situation.

Hall returned to the Blues nets for the fourth game as the team hoped to avoid a Stanley Cup sweep. Jacques Plante could only watch from the bench as the Canadiens overcame a 1–0 deficit to win another Stanley Cup with a 2–1 win.

One can't help but wonder what went through Plante's mind that afternoon. He had achieved one of his goals in his return to the game that year: a record-breaking seventh Vezina Trophy. Yet his other goal, a Stanley Cup, had eluded his grasp. It had been his first appearance in the finals in nine long years. To sit there and watch his former teammate Jean Béliveau celebrate another Stanley Cup must have only added to the hurt.

"Even though it was a sweep, if it hadn't have been for our goaltending it wouldn't have been close," says Frank St. Marseille today. "We overachieved because of our work ethic. The established teams were much more powerful than we were. We were overmatched."[24]

For his second season in St. Louis, Plante unveiled a new mask. During his first season with the team he had continued to wear the pretzel mask that he had been sporting for most of the past decade. Now he arrived in camp with something entirely different. The mask was a solid white that gleamed under the lights of the arena. It had been developed in collaboration with David Britt, a Montrealer and a former goaltender.

Britt worked in the airplane industry and preferred to do most of his business in various airport terminals throughout North America. He was familiar with the next generation of resins and cloths and put this knowledge to use in developing the latest models in the continuing evolution of the goalie mask.

The two men would meet up in airports and sketch out mask designs, then send them out to mask makers. Since Plante was busy tending goal with the Blues, it was left to Britt to sell the masks to the league's other goaltenders, quite often in an airport departures terminal. It was Britt who would take the face moulds of the goalies who agreed to wear the mask, later delivering the finished product to the goalie when his team came to play at the Montreal Forum.

Plante was once again dipping his toe into the mask-making business. By the end of the season, the sturdiness of his newest design would be put to the ultimate test.

The Blues coasted that season, decimating their expansion brethren and finishing an astounding 22 points ahead of the runner-up Pittsburgh Penguins in the West Division standings. In addition, Hall and Plante were nine goals short of repeating as winners of the Vezina Trophy.

Without question, the highlight of the season for Plante was his appearance in the all-star game held on January 20, 1970, in the friendly confines of the St. Louis Arena and in front of its raucous fans. As they did the year before, the league utilized an East–West match-up. Plante was joined in the West lineup by six of his Blues teammates, and the reception afforded them was as loud as any hockey fan could remember.

"Plante's spectacular performance in this year's All-Star game was a tremendous individual effort that could serve as a model for goalies," opined the *Hockey News*. "He twisted, squirmed, kicked the puck, stopped it with his elbow, dropped to the ice, bounced up again, darted from side to side – all with the lightning speed of a rookie phenom. Plante was playing with a pulled hamstring muscle but he stopped twenty shots in the final period for an All-Star game record and shut out the big guns of the Eastern Division while playing half the game."[25]

"You know I play for pride and the money," a smiling Plante told the newsmen.[26]

Plante found his second season in St. Louis a little more trying. He appeared in five fewer games, posting a respectable 2.19 goals-against average and adding five shutouts to his career total. His goaltending partner, Glenn Hall, wavered about playing again and appeared in only 18 games, resulting in a 2.91 goals-against and a single shutout.

Into the breach stepped career journeyman Ernie Wakely, whose decade-long career had been marked with two career starts as a Montreal Canadien. Playing 30 games, only two games fewer than Plante, Wakely posted a lower goals-against average than his more esteemed teammates, along with four shutouts.

Entering the playoffs, Bowman took the highly unusual step of alternating all three of his goalies as the Blues attempted to advance to the Stanley Cup finals for a third consecutive year.

In the first round of the playoffs, the Blues were matched up against the Minnesota North Stars. The opening game saw a renewal of goaltending's oldest rivalry as the league's two most experienced netminders once again stood at opposing ends of the rink.

"The first game at St. Louis was a battle of old men – me against Jacques Plante," Gump Worsley remembered. "Plante had celebrated his forty-first birthday in January, I was one month shy. Our defense was having trouble clearing the puck that night and I had to handle 41 shots. We only got 21 shots at Plante and the Blues won 6–2."[27]

Still using their unique three-goalie rotation, the Blues went on to eliminate the North Stars in six games before advancing to take on the Penguins in the West Division finals.

With the series deadlocked at two games apiece, the crucial fifth game was set for the St. Louis Arena. Bowman was faced with a critical decision, which he announced on the eve of the game to the impatient press: "This will be the key game and I am starting Jacques Plante."

Pacing nervously behind the bench, Bowman needn't have worried. The greatest clutch goalie of all time added to his already remarkable résumé by shutting out the Penguins 5–0 before a raucous home crowd that shook the old, decrepit foundation of the St. Louis Arena.

The crowd was already hoarse when the public announcer informed the fans that this was the fourteenth playoff shutout of Plante's career, an NHL record. Plante, his arms raised in triumph, left the ice to a rapturous reception from the adoring throng. This euphoric celebration, unbeknownst to anyone, was Plante's goodbye to St. Louis and its magnificent fans.

Two nights later, in Pittsburgh, Bowman continued his rotation, with Glenn Hall thwarting the Penguins as the Blues closed out the series with a 4–3 win, advancing once again to the Stanley Cup finals.

The previous two years the Blues had been defeated by the Montreal Canadiens. The opposition in the 1970 finals would be the Boston Bruins. Led by Bobby Orr and Phil Esposito, the young and powerful Bruins were viewed as the sport's next dominant team and were overwhelming favourites to defeat the resilient Blues.

If the Blues had any hope, it rested on the shoulders of Jacques Plante, who entered the finals with a stunning 1.48 goals-against average. This was his tenth appearance in the finals, another record that still stands. It had been 17 years since his memorable playoff debut in the Chicago Stadium. He was now the oldest player on the ice by three years, and was 11 years older than his counterpart in the Boston nets, Gerry Cheevers.

He readied himself in the nets. Plante, as always, relished the challenge. In his mind he raced through the many times he had been underestimated or counted out by those supposedly in the know. He had shocked the world before. Now he set out to do it again.

Early in the second period his dream of another Stanley Cup championship rapidly crumbled to the ice. The play started out like so many before it as Boston's Fred Stanfield moved in from the point. As he lifted his stick, Plante fearlessly moved out to challenge him, cutting down the angle. Stanfield, his stick arched in the air, violently connected with the puck. As the slapshot steamed towards him, Plante was, as usual, in perfect position. Suddenly, Phil Esposito jerked his stick at the oncoming puck. The speeding puck glanced off Esposito's outstretched stick, leaving Plante absolutely no time to react.

The puck struck him right in the middle of the mask, knocking him out cold. The paramedics called for the stretcher and then wheeled out the unconscious Plante, right past the shattered remnants of what had once been his mask.

25

ONE MORE MOMENT
FOR THE MASTER

JACQUES PLANTE SOON FOUND himself laid up in the Jewish Hospital of St. Louis, where he was subjected to a battery of tests that quickly concluded he had suffered a serious concussion. His hockey season had come to an end, but after spending a few more days in the hospital, followed by a few weeks of rest and relaxation, he was fully recovered – a recovery he felt he owed entirely to his most famous innovation. "I'm convinced that the mask saved my life," Plante later told *Sports Illustrated*.[1]

As soon as he was able he phoned home to speak with his wife, Jacqueline. "She was relieved to hear from me," Plante later told Andy O'Brien. "Normally, Jacqueline doesn't watch television, but she knew I was playing that night and the kids were watching the game. They didn't tell her when I was hurt but late in the game while walking through the room she took a quick glance at the screen and asked: 'Where's your father?' The youngest boy [aged 15], trying to act nonchalant, replied: 'Oh, they carried him off on a stretcher in the second period.'"[2]

Red Fisher had been there in the days before the mask, through the four broken noses, the shattered cheekbones, the fractured jaw, all the stitches, the bruises, the cuts, and there when Plante first put on the mask over his battered face. Yet this injury was different.

Fisher saw Plante lying in bed, a red welt over his left eye. "Plante looked like a man who had run into a wall," Fisher observed. "He felt even worse because he's hurt and he's in pain and even though he would like it otherwise, he knows his time has run out in this city."

Plante told Fisher, "When I started playing with the mask, I always told myself that if necessary, I would put my face in front of a shot. I always felt it was another piece of equipment, just like a glove or a pad. But now . . . the pain every time I move my head . . . I don't think that way any more. I'll get out of the way even if a goal is being scored. Nothing is worth this. But ah, I suppose I am talking this way because I am hurt now. I am hurt and I don't feel like playing any more, but after a few days I'll be better and then I'll want to play again because I like to play. It won't be here, but whoever wants me can have me next year."[3]

Two months before the Stanley Cup finals, the Toronto Maple Leafs traded defenceman Tim Horton to the New York Rangers. The Blues had owed the Rangers a player to be named later. As part of the Horton trade, the as yet unchosen player the Blues owed to the Rangers was now transferred to the Leafs. Toronto made no secret of their desire to acquire Plante, who was unlikely to be one of the goalies protected by the Blues in the June draft.

Soon after Fisher excused himself from Plante's room, a cluster of reporters from Toronto found their way in. With the Leafs having just finished a last-place season, many of the city's sportswriters found themselves in St. Louis covering the Stanley Cup finals, and they took advantage of the opportunity to ask him about the Plante-to-Toronto rumours.

Plante had trouble wrapping his head around the thought of playing in Toronto. "It's not that I don't think highly of Toronto, but you fellows know only too well the trouble I've had there with my asthma. The last thing that can happen to me is Toronto."[4]

Beyond Plante's hospital room, the world once again witnessed the Blues being swept in the finals as the Boston Bruins skated off with the Stanley Cup. Plante was released from hospital in time to partake in the team's annual paid vacation in Miami Beach, with the plane and hotel on the Salomon family's tab. Lounging in the warm sun by the pool, he was able to enjoy a full prescription of rest and relaxation.

At the end of the vacation, Plante stood with his teammates at the hotel entrance, waiting for the bus to take them to the airport. A sombre Scotty Bowman pulled him aside.

"I'm sorry to do this," Bowman began, "but I didn't want to spoil your holiday. Before leaving St. Louis we sold you to Toronto. With the league expanding again next season to add Vancouver and Buffalo, it's vital that the Blues build their rosters with an eye on the future. As you know, we will be able to protect only two goalers in the June draft. After the season he's had, Wakely has to stay. And Hall is almost three years younger than you. I really wish it could be otherwise, Jacques, I am."

"Don't feel badly about a thing," Plante answered. "If I had been in your place, Scotty, I would have done the same. You and the Blues and St. Louis have been wonderful to me for the last two years."[5]

The two men shook hands and Plante made his way to the bus and an uncertain professional future. With his career at a crossroads, and at the age of 41, retirement seemed to be once again a logical option, but Plante quickly dismissed it, even though he knew his wife would most certainly object. "How could I think of quitting after playing what I honestly consider to have been my best two seasons in goal?" Plante said at the time.[6]

In that summer of 1970, Plante threw himself into his newest and largest venture yet: Fibrosport, a company dedicated to producing and selling goaltender masks. He had attempted to market masks before, but never on this large a scale.

Installing himself as president of Fibrosport, he purchased a building in Magog, Quebec, for its headquarters. The first task of his new company was to quickly produce a prototype of a mask stronger than the one that had shattered under the impact of Fred Stanfield's shot a few months back. Fibrosport would sell both custom-made masks and mass-produced masks designed to replicate Plante's own. Each mask was made of high-impact fibreglass and epoxy resin, and featured ridges meant to deflect pucks away instead of absorbing the full impact straight on. Plante soon began to aggressively market his latest mask, pronouncing it the finest ever made.

Plante used the platform of the NHL's annual June meetings to introduce his latest creation. It was a shining white mask that upon demonstration was able to withstand the impact of the hardest and fastest of shots.

"My latest design has been tested by an air cannon firing pucks at 135 miles per hour," Plante boasted to those assembled. "The results have been so spectacular that the engineering department at Sherbrooke University has endorsed my new mask." Beaming like a proud father, he pointed at the mask and proclaimed, "This is it, the ultimate in protection . . . gruesome but efficient."[7]

The mass-produced masks usually retailed for between $12 and $18 each, while the professional model, similar to Plante's own, retailed for $150. He found himself frequently fielding requests for technical guidance from many European countries, particularly Sweden, as well as throughout North America. Fibrosport proved to be a highly successful venture, starting with a staff of 12 and boasting sales worldwide, while producing upwards of 8,000 masks a year.

When not focused on Fibrosport, Plante spent his time on an increased physical training regimen. Each day he would spend 20 minutes on calisthenics, in addition to three 10-minute intervals on the exercise cycle. Any free time he could find usually saw him on the tennis court.

Plante wanted to continue playing but wasn't sure he wanted to do it in Toronto. And truth be told, Plante had not been the Leafs' first choice. Ironically, they had first set their sights on Gump Worsley, but they soon found it impossible to pry him away from Montreal, and, on the suggestion of the Leafs' legendary vice-president, King Clancy, went after Plante.[8]

In his first meeting with Jim Gregory, the Leafs' general manager, Plante's uneasiness quickly transformed into enthusiasm as Gregory outlined the potential terms of the contract: $75,000, with two-thirds of it being deferred until 1981. It was a long way from the 50 cents a game he'd earned with the factory team in Shawinigan Falls.

However, no amount of dollars could buy a cure for Plante's Achilles heel: his asthma. The Leafs had prepared by subletting for Plante an apartment in the city's north end, and far away from Lake Ontario, which he felt exacerbated his condition. Plante was even offered his choice of specialty pillows. Furthermore, the Leafs assured a skeptical Plante that the city of Toronto boasted the top asthma specialists in Canada.

The Leafs also told him that in the event that he suffered an attack, or even if he just didn't feel like playing on a particular night, he only had to say so. "We have four other goalers, including Bruce Gamble, reporting to training camp," Plante remembered Jim Gregory telling him, "but we need your experience to help them and the team in general. You have been in the league a long time, Jacques, and we also want you to sit down at lunch with the defensemen and explain just how they should work with a goaler in the NHL. We have a lot of young talent, but we need you to guide them along in your own sphere."[9]

It was this bare expression of need that most appealed to Plante. Sure, the money was exceptional, but by this point he was relatively well off, and the apartment was a considerate touch. Here were the Toronto Maple Leafs, second only in prestige to the Montreal Canadiens, begging him to join them.

"I was wanted and it felt good," Plante admitted later, "particularly since I had just come out of two good seasons and I honestly felt I had something to give, something fresh and not from yesteryear. And it also seemed to offer a most satisfying way to end my NHL career."[10]

Unlike the Blues, the Leafs were a team composed of veterans and raw youngsters. Over three years removed from a Stanley Cup championship, many of the members of that veteran club had long departed. Veterans who remained, like Dave Keon and Ron Ellis, were joined by a group of youngsters trying to find their way in the post-expansion NHL. When asked about the Leafs' young players, Plante joked, "The Leafs are on a youth kick – and for me, life begins at 41."[11]

The detailed contract called for Plante to stay in the organization at the conclusion of his career, either as a scout or as a goaltending instructor. The agreement also required Plante to make promotional appearances on the team's behalf.

It looked like Jacques Plante had found the final destination of his long, accomplished hockey journey. The irony was that it was with the Toronto Maple Leafs, a team that a quarter century before had put a claim on his professional services before dropping him from their junior negotiation list.

For Jacques Plante, playing hockey meant no distractions. If he was to be at his best, it required his full focus and attention. He put his son Michel, 19, in charge of all production operations at Fibrosport.

The usually confident Plante was surprised to be battling his nerves as he entered the team's training camp. But head coach John McLellan and his teammates made him feel at home right away. In McLellan, Plante found a coach who treated him more like an assistant coach than a player and gave him the freedom to make many of his own decisions.

In training camp, as management had hoped, Plante set about imparting his methods to a young and inexperienced crop of defencemen.

"The puck is a magnet for these kids," Plante explained to the *Hockey News* on the eve of the season. "I'll try to teach them that in our zone, the man with the puck is mine. I want them to take care of the other guys. It's a matter of split seconds and if I have to worry about a man in front of me or to the other side of me, I'll lose that split second. So that's the rule. The man with the puck is mine and I don't want them rushing at him."[12]

"At first, it was kind of daunting having him as a teammate," remembers defenceman Brad Selwood. "For the first month or two I found it tough to approach him. He was kind of intimidating. Once you did, however, he was very good, very approachable. His intensity stood out, he was all business. He was very focused in both practices and games. He used the practices to work on game situations. He was a true student of the game. In addition, he was also an outstanding communicator. In practice, he'd lay out situations so you knew what to do in the game. If you made a mistake, he let you know about it but not in a nasty way. I personally took it as constructive criticism. It was never to the point that it was your fault – he just hated to get scored on."[13]

Plante was more amiable and open with his teammates in Toronto than he had been before. Put it down to age or the passage of time, but he was definitely a more peaceful and calm man at this point of his life. His new teammates were the beneficiaries of his relaxed personality.

The changes in Plante, however, did not extend to his wallet, as he continued to live a very frugal lifestyle. He continued to beg off players-only meetings where he might be required to chip in for something. And while his demeanour was more relaxed, he was still intensely private.

Despite any mellowing, Plante was determined to keep himself near the top of the goaltending fraternity. He discarded his habit of occasionally smoking a cigar and put an end to the couple of beers he usually imbibed each day. As a result his weight dropped from 184 pounds at the beginning of training camp to 171 when the regular season began.

To the surprise of many observers, Plante made it through the Leafs' September training camp without an asthma attack. Free to concentrate on his game, he focused on both the physical and the mental demands that lay in the season ahead.

"It's the month that bothered me the most," he reflected later, "and to be free of it in Toronto was unbelievable. I have to conclude that the mental aspect is a dominant factor. Previously, when I came in with the Canadiens, I had to play. Now that pressure was removed; even when the season started I knew one week ahead when and against which team I would be playing. That way I could plan my game by thinking and rethinking the habits of the players who would be shooting at me. The stars who average about four shots a game were familiar but the others took some memory strain because many average only one or one and one-half shots per game. But all can score if you're careless."[14]

Much as he had in St. Louis with Glenn Hall, Plante consulted with his coach and Bruce Gamble, the backup goalie, about the playing schedule, trying to maximize the Leafs' chances for success. It was an arrangement that drew a fair share of criticism in hockey circles, as some felt that Plante was choosing his spots and avoiding many of the league's better teams in an effort to pad his own stats.

"Plante has a bad reputation for picking his spots," wrote Boston Bruins goalie Gerry Cheevers in his diary of the 1971 season, *Goaltender*, "but he's doing this for a purpose. He picks the games where the Leafs have a good chance to win – playing at home or against expansion teams. And he helps them win, you can't deny that."[15]

There was one team that year with which Plante didn't pick his spots. For the first time, he found a modicum of success against his old team from Montreal. He had always been nervous when facing his former club, but in 1970–71 he seemed to overcome this particular malady. Over the course of the season he defeated the Canadiens on three occasions.

Even at that point, almost eight years after he had been traded by Montreal, his fondness for the Canadiens was still apparent, as was the lingering hurt of the trade that sent him away. "He mentioned to us one time that the CH was stamped on his heart," remembers Brad Selwood. "'I'm a Montreal Canadien forever,' he liked to say."[16]

A month into the season, Leafs general manager Jim Gregory swung the first of two trades that would benefit Plante and the Leafs. Bob Baun was already a Toronto Maple Leaf legend before he began his second stint with the team on October 13, 1970. A winner of four Stanley Cups with the team in the sixties, he was most famous for scoring an overtime winning goal in game six of the 1964 finals and then playing the seventh game – on a broken leg. Now he returned to the Toronto fold and provided a stabilizing influence, both on and off the ice.

"It was a real treat playing with Jacques Plante," Baun wrote in his memoirs. "He was notorious as a loner and eccentric, but no one could fault his hockey knowledge."[17]

In the middle of January 1971, Plante celebrated his forty-second birthday. Yet many of those in the media chose not to report his advancing age. Instead they were filling up their copy space looking for adjectives to describe his outstanding play.

Even the venerable *Time* magazine, whose coverage of hockey was cursory at best, heaped praise on Plante. "Plante's playing has been, well, spectacular. In 26 games this season, he has shut out the opposing team three times and allowed an average of only 1.90 goals per game."[18]

As for the Leafs, finishers in last place the year before, they were now in fourth place, with the third-place Canadiens firmly in their sights. "Plante is the reason we're in fourth place now and why we're going to finish third," beamed King Clancy.[19]

"He is the greatest thing that ever happened to me," raved Leafs coach John McLellan. "Does he second-guess me? Hell no. In fact, I ask him. I say, if you notice anything, Jacques, you let me know. He could be a success at anything he tried. He's got a remarkable mind."[20]

As he continued to excel into his forties, Plante's position in hockey and its history seemed secure. Furthermore, many of his innovations, once ridiculed by many, were now accepted throughout the game.

When Plante first left the game, he and Terry Sawchuk were the only two starting goalies wearing a mask. A mere six years later, in a league comprising 14 teams with 28 professional goalies, there remained only one bare-faced puck stopper. It was the same man who had been the opposing goalie on that historic night a little over a decade earlier: Gump Worsley.

"I never got around to trying a mask and it's too late now," said Worsley at the time, before adding, "But it has helped a lot of guys, believe me."[21]

As well, the two-goalie system that he had long advocated was now being used by every team in the league.

Plante was now playing against a new generation of goalies who had grown up in the shadow of his greatness and openly spoke of him as their inspiration. And no player spoke more freely or candidly about his admiration for Jacques Plante than Bernie Parent. On January 31, 1971, the Leafs traded Bruce Gamble to the Philadelphia Flyers and acquired Parent. In time, he would become Jacques Plante's prized pupil.

Parent's admiration for Plante had started early in life. He used to spend hours sitting out on his front porch patiently waiting for a mere glimpse of the great Jacques Plante, whose married sister lived next door. As he got older he began to pattern his goaltending style after his idol's.

After a couple of seasons with the Boston Bruins, Parent was selected by the Philadelphia Flyers in the 1967 expansion draft and immediately established himself as one of the league's brightest young goaltenders. He starred in both the 1969 and 1970 all-star games, sharing the goaltending duties alongside Plante.

Despite his success, however, there still seemed to be something missing from his game, as fellow goaltender Gerry Cheevers noted in his 1971 book, *Goaltender*. "He's probably got more natural ability than any goaltender in the league. I don't know too much about his desire though. . . . He's not the most enthusiastic goaler I can think of."[22]

"During the early years in Philadelphia, my work habits were only fair and even though I played well for the Flyers, I never really understood my full potential," Parent admitted years later, confirming Cheevers' assessment.[23]

When first told of the trade by Flyers general manager Keith Allen, Parent was visibly upset. Having laid down roots in the area, he was not particularly eager to leave. That cloud of disappointment began to lift the moment that he stepped into the Leafs dressing room for the first time.

"Jacques Plante came over and grabbed my arm," Parent remembered. "Cripes, Plante was like a god to me. He was my idol. I had been watching him on TV since I was a kid. Now I was on the same team with him. It was then that I knew that even though I still felt the hurt over the Philadelphia trade, this trade was going to be the best thing that ever happened to me in hockey."[24]

It wasn't too long before many noticed Parent's transformation under Plante's tutelage as Bernie Parent began to fulfill his immense potential.

"There was no one in the world quite like Plante," Parent has said. "I learned more from him in two years with the Leafs than I did in all my other hockey days. He taught me a great deal about playing goal both on the ice and in my head off the ice. He taught me to be aggressive around the goal and take an active part in play instead of waiting for things to happen. He showed me how I kept putting myself off-balance by placing my weight on my left leg instead of on my stick side. He taught me how to steer shots off into the corner instead of letting them rebound in front of me. That old guy made a good goalie of me."[25]

One day at practice, Parent asked Plante how he was able to read the shooters so well. "I've studied them all and have a book on them," Plante quickly answered. Parent remembers: "The next day I started putting together a similar book. I found out that Plante had more than just a book on a bunch of shooters. He kept notes on every arena, how to play the boards in each one and how the lighting affected playing goal. Cripes, the old man – he knew everything."[26]

The Leafs would finish the regular season in fourth place as the Canadiens held firm to the third position in the final standings. Jacques had gone the whole year without a debilitating asthma attack. That didn't mean that he made it through the season injury free, though.

Near the end of the season the team had been on a road swing through California. They had a day in L.A. before a game against the Kings, and Jacques took in some sun rays at poolside. The next day, his face was so sunburned that he couldn't wear his mask. In stepped Bernie Parent, and a suffering Plante looked on from the bench. After the game he was sent to the hospital, before being sent back to Toronto for further tests. For official consumption the cause of his injury was altered.

"They say he has an infection from having his teeth cleaned by a dentist," Jim Gregory informed the unsuspecting media. "My face hurts like hell," added a pained and surely embarrassed Plante.[27]

With the season coming to a close, the magnitude of Plante's first season in Toronto was starting to come into focus. He had played in 40 games that season, with a record of 24 wins, 11 losses, and four ties, and added four shutouts. Without him in the net the Leafs had sputtered to a 13–22–4 record.

Even more impressive was his goals-against average of 1.88, which topped the league. For Plante, it was the eighth time he had achieved this remarkable feat, to this day an NHL record. The other two Leaf goalies that season, Gamble and Parent, combined for a goals-against average of 3.39. Plante finished in fifth place in the voting for the Hart Trophy, nine years after he had won the award with the Canadiens.

At the conclusion of the season, the professional hockey writers mailed in their ballots for the post-season all-star teams. Plante was named goaltender on the second team, finishing behind the Vezina Trophy winner for that season, Ed Giacomin of the New York Rangers.

At a time when many of his contemporaries were leaving the game, Plante continued to excel. Glenn Hall would retire for good that summer, Johnny Bower had taken his leave a year earlier, and Terry Sawchuk had passed away the summer before. Only Gump Worsley continued to put himself before the oncoming pucks. In an anonymous poll conducted by the *Toronto Star*, the league's coaches voted Plante the league's top netminder.[28]

"I know it's incredible, almost unbelievable, but I'm playing better now than when I was with the Montreal Canadiens," a high-spirited

Plante told writer Stan Fischler in 1971. "My reflexes are just as fast, and I have far greater knowledge."[29]

As the playoffs beckoned, many wondered if he had one last glory ride left in him.

In their first-round showdown against the second-place Rangers, Plante struggled and was unable to maintain the magic of his regular season. In the opening game of the series, held at Madison Square Garden, he "played poorly," according to the *Toronto Star*'s Red Burnett, in a 5–4 Leaf defeat. He was replaced in the second game by Bernie Parent, and the Leafs evened the series in a game interrupted for 20 minutes by two brawls in the third period.

During the first brawl, Parent had his mask thrown into the Madison Square Garden stands by the Rangers' Vic Hadfield. Without a backup and adamant that he wouldn't play without his mask, Parent stood at centre ice while Leafs vice-president King Clancy, aged 68, desperately scoured the crowd, hoping to find the lost mask.

"I saw Vic throw the mask in the crowd," remembers Rangers coach Emile Francis. "I can still see it coming down and this young guy grabbing it and going 100 miles an hour up the stairs and out the exits. I don't care if King had lived to be a hundred years old – he was never going to catch that guy."[30] To this day the whereabouts of Parent's Fibrosport mask are unknown.

So with four minutes and 42 seconds remaining, the man who had brought the mask to prominence came off the bench and finished the game, a 4–1 Leaf victory. As soon as the game was over, Plante rushed off the ice and placed an emergency order to Fibrosport for another mask, which made it to Toronto in time for Parent to play game three, a 3–1 Leafs victory. The Rangers, however, followed up their game-three defeat with back-to-back wins, putting the Leafs on the verge of elimination as the two teams returned to Maple Leaf Gardens for the sixth game.

With their offence at a standstill and their season in the balance, the desperate Leafs turned to Plante. "Admittedly, the ôdds against Les Leafs would be shortened by all reputable books if Jacques could also be expected to chip in a couple of goals," wrote Milt Dunnell in the *Toronto Star* the day of the game. "It isn't the goals which they've allowed, that are driving the Leafs towards seasonal unemployment: It's the one which they haven't scored themselves."[31]

That night against the Rangers, the anemic Leafs' offence could muster only a single goal against New York goaltender Ed Giacomin.

Plante had to be perfect, but for the only time that glorious season he was not up to the task.

"Maple Leafs coach John McLellan and his veteran goalkeeper, Jacques Plante, ran out of miracles last night," wrote Red Burnett the next day in the *Toronto Star*. "For the first time since the National Hockey League season opened Plante failed in his role as 'stopper' in a key game. But it took a thrilling overtime contest to shunt Plante and McLellan out of the Stanley Cup spotlight."[32]

Amid the disappointment and gloom of the Leafs dressing room in the wake of the 2–1 defeat, Plante attempted to put the season in some type of perspective. "This team has come a million miles since I first skated on the ice with them in training camp. I rate it as a tremendous year for a club in the first season of a rebuilding program. The players and management deserve a lot of credit and can be proud of their efforts."[33]

Plante failed to mention his own role in the Leafs' success that year. His contribution had been immense. Even though the defeat to the Rangers left a bitter taste, it couldn't erase the shine of a season for the ages.

At the age of 42, Jacques Plante had fashioned one of the greatest seasons of any goaltender in the history of the game.

It would take another 30 years to recognize exactly how transcendent a season it had been.

For that we can thank a gentleman named Edward Yuen from Regina, Saskatchewan, and authors Jeff Klein and Karl-Eric Reif, who published Mr. Yuen's findings in their 2001 book, *The Hockey Compendium*.

During Plante's time in the league, the primary statistic for measuring goaltenders was their goals-against average. Even Plante was obsessed with this statistic each season, to the point that he was accused of sitting out games in an effort to keep his personal goals-against under two in his first season in St. Louis.

However, as a means of measuring a goaltender's performance, the goals-against average is flawed. The statistic is calculated by dividing the number of goals a goalie allows by the number of minutes he plays, then multiplying that figure by 60. Essentially you're dividing his goals-allowed figure by the number of games he played to see how many goals he allows per game on average.

In a seven-game series, say goaltender A faces 50 shots in each game, allows only four goals each game, while making 46 saves in each game. His goals-against average is 4.00.

In that same seven-game series, goaltender B faces 20 shots in each game, allows only two goals each game, while making 18 saves in each game. His goals-against average is 2.50.

Goaltender B has the far better goals-against average, yet he has faced 30 fewer shots a game and made 28 fewer saves a game than goaltender A. With much less work to do, has goaltender B necessarily played better than goaltender A?

What does a goaltender do? He stops shots. Yet the goals-against average does not take that into account. In an effort to remedy this discrepancy, the statistic known as save percentage came into vogue, with the NHL officially keeping track of the numbers beginning in the 1982–83 season.

Save percentage answers a basic goaltending question. What percentage of shots does a goalie save? Let's go back to our earlier example.

Goaltender A saves 46 shots a game while allowing four goals on average. Therefore he stops 92 per cent of the shots he faces. His save percentage is .920.

Goaltender B saves 18 shots a game while allowing two goals on average. Therefore he stops 90 per cent of the shots he faces. His save percentage is .900.

Given the same number of shots, goaltender A would stop the puck more frequently.

With the NHL keeping track of the save percentage only since the 1982–83 season, Edward Yuen was curious to know the save percentages of some of the great goalies of the past. He researched the shot and save totals for every goalie in every NHL regular-season game from 1954–55 through 1966–67, in addition to a few selected years in the 1970s. By using the game reports found in the *Winnipeg Free Press*, *Le Devoir*, the *New York Times*, and the *Globe and Mail*, he was able to double-source his raw data. After all the information was compiled, he did the math.

What he discovered was that Jacques Plante had led the league in save percentage four times in his career with the Montreal Canadiens:

- In 1954–55, his first full season with the team, he posted a .929 save percentage.

- In 1955–56, the first year of the Canadiens' five-year Stanley Cup run and Plante's five-year Vezina run, he once again posted a .929 save percentage.
- In 1958–59, the fourth year of the Canadiens' five-year Stanley Cup run and Plante's five-year Vezina run, he posted a .925 save percentage.
- In 1961–62, the year he won both the Vezina and the Hart Trophy, he posted a .923 save percentage.[34]

Yuen also documented the 1970–71 season, Plante's first with the Toronto Maple Leafs and the season he led the league with a goals-against average of 1.88 and was named to the second all-star team.

What he found when he crunched the numbers from that season was startling. Over the course of the 1970–71 season, Jacques Plante had posted an astonishing save percentage of .942. The runner-up that year in save percentage was Ed Giacomin of the New York Rangers, whose save percentage was .921. The gap between him and Plante was the widest of any first- and second-place finisher in recorded save percentage history. The .942 save percentage was the highest of Plante's career, shattering his career high with the Canadiens of .929 achieved in the 1954–55 and 1955–56 seasons. In addition, and most astounding, the .942 save percentage recorded by Plante in 1970–71 is the highest ever in NHL history, surpassing the official NHL record held by Dominik Hasek, who posted a .937 save percentage in the 1998–99 season.

Jacques Plante, the most accomplished goalie in hockey history, the winner of seven Vezina trophies, one Hart Trophy, and six Stanley Cups, may have in fact had the greatest season of his career on a Toronto Maple Leaf team that finished fourth in its division and was eliminated in the first round of the playoffs. He didn't play on a powerhouse team and he didn't play behind a Hall of Fame defenceman, but statistically, his goaltending has gone unmatched since. And all of this was accomplished at the tender age of 42.

26

THE LIVING LEGEND

FIVE AND A HALF weeks after the Leafs were eliminated from the 1971 playoffs by the New York Rangers, Jacques Plante was back in the nets at Maple Leaf Gardens. But even though he was in full uniform, he wasn't playing another game of hockey. On May 24, 1971, he was acting as a goalie in the movie *Face-Off*.

The film, which would go on to become the first million-dollar-grossing film in Canadian cinematic history, was billed as the story of Billy Duke, the hottest prospect to hit the NHL since Bobby Orr. Sherri Lee Nelson is the singer in a rising rock group, and *Face-Off* is the dramatic and moving story of the growing love between these two young and exceptionally talented people. It is also the story of Billy's rookie year with the Toronto Maple Leafs, of the thousand and one pressures on the most publicized and highest-paid rookie in hockey history.

That day of filming at the Gardens was devoted to the hockey scenes, with 30 NHL players dressed in different uniforms simulating various game scenarios. Plante appeared only briefly in the movie, but sought to make his time on the screen as close to perfect as possible.

"Filming had been rolling along smoothly," wrote Brian Mockler in the *Toronto Star*.

NHL'ers in various sweaters had been letting Leafs defenceman Jim McKenny, the on-ice double for the film's star, Art Hindle, score on a dazzling series of three-on-ones, two-on-ones and solo dashes.

The trouble started when the script called for a scene of an opposition player scoring on the Leafs goal. The player in question was former Leafs bad boy Mike Walton, by then a Bruin. Three times Walton was sent in alone on Plante. And three times Plante refused to yield.

There was an anxious confrontation between the film's production staff and the Leafs netminder. Plante was visibly agitated, his mask bobbing up and down throughout the exchange. Suddenly the consultation ended. Then after a short delay came the familiar voice of Gardens PA announcer Paul Morris: "Monsieur Plante," he intoned, "wishes it to be known that he is consenting to allow the puck to enter the net."

Walton raced in alone on Plante again, a goal now assured. What did Plante do?

He did what he did flawlessly thousands of times during his career whether he was playing behind the all-stars who worked on the Canadiens blue line or the sad-sack Ranger defence.

He stopped Walton cold. The Gardens erupted, the few hundred fans making more noise than was heard at most games of that era. As for Plante himself, he skated about thirty feet from his crease, his narrow shoulders drawn together in a theatrical shrug as if to say he couldn't help himself.

There was another consultation, more exasperation and yet another breakaway. This time Monsieur Plante consented to allow the puck into the net. Walton got his goal and Plante had made his point.[1]

Among the fans in the crowd that day was a nine-year-old boy named Stephen Taylor. Thanks to the generosity of the *Toronto Star*, Stephen, who had cystic fibrosis, watched the day's filming with his father.

During a break in the filming, Gerry Cheevers skated over to Stephen's front-row seat and signed his prized autograph book. And then Plante, proving to be far more obliging with the awestruck young boy than he had just been with the film crew, took Stephen and the boy's grateful father into the Leafs dressing room. He allowed them to sit down and soak in the atmosphere. He let Stephen try on his famous mask and explained how it protected his face. As they were leaving, Plante promised Stephen a stick signed by the Leafs team. Indeed, a week later, the mailman showed up bearing a special package for young Stephen Taylor: a stick autographed by the Toronto Maple Leafs.

In the fall of 1971, Plante, now the oldest player in the league, returned for his second year with the Maple Leafs, with whom he signed for another year for the princely sum of $75,000. The contract was unlike many being signed by those in the NHL.

Plante received no signing bonus. In fact, much of the money was deferred, with the first payment of $10,000 due on January 1, 1972. The remainder would be paid in annual installments each January 1. The last payment, of $5,000, was made in 1979.

Plante's response to the constant questions about his retirement: "I will quit the day it becomes a chore."

With Fibrosport still a nascent enterprise, Plante found another reason to continue playing. In a feature article in the February 1972 issue of *Hockey Pictorial*, Plante said that his playing increased the company's sales. "My company is not big, it cannot yet afford expensive marketing programs," admitted Plante. "But since I'm playing and wearing the mask I sell and Bernie's wearing my mask and a few other goaltenders are as well, kids know the mask must be good. If I wasn't playing, what I'm saying now would be advertising and I would have to pay for it."[2]

There was no doubt that Plante was the most popular of all the Leafs. During the season he would receive upwards of 200 letters a day, the most of any player. The majority of these came from young, aspiring goaltenders who were searching for advice from the man widely considered the expert.

In order to expedite his responses, Plante carefully put together a list of 15 tips for young goalies. The tips were not listed in order of importance, as Plante believed they were all equally imperative in the development of young goaltenders.

1) You must be a good skater.
2) You must learn how to clear the puck with your stick.
3) You must keep your stick on the ice at all times while waiting for a shot.
4) You should use a stick that is correct for your height. If you are 6 ft tall or so, use a stick with a long wide part. You can use up

to 24 in. If you are small, use one with a shorter wide part. Never cut the handle of your stick. This often prevents you from reaching for a loose puck away from you.

5) Try to play standing up as much as possible. This helps on the high shots and the rebounds.
6) Block your angles well. Do not play with your back against the goal. Try to stand at the edge of your goal crease.
7) Do not move backward when the puck carrier comes towards you. In doing so, you give him more room to score and you are off balance.
8) Always keep your eyes on the puck.
9) Do not anticipate plays.
10) On a breakaway, do not rush toward your opponent. Wait for him at the edge of your goal crease.
11) You must learn how to use your two gloves and your skate on the stick side.
12) You must talk to your players and tell them what to do with the puck.
13) Never criticize a teammate if he makes a mistake. Your job is to correct mistakes.
14) Do not be afraid to ask your Coach for help. If you do not understand his explanation, make him repeat it. He prefers that, to seeing you repeat the same mistakes.
15) Watch the other goalies. You will learn a lot from them – I still do after thirty years.[3]

In addition to getting bags of mail, Jacques was increasingly in demand as guest lecturer or special guest at various social and sporting events. He often used these platforms to express his original thoughts and ideas.

He complained that minor league hockey was obsessed with winning, to the detriment of the fun of the game. For children under 10 he advocated an increased emphasis on the game as recreation as opposed to the current climate that preached competitiveness. He also strongly urged that the focus of youth hockey should be on the development of skills.[4]

On the ice, after such a promising season the year before, the Leafs stagnated. They certainly weren't helped by the controversy surrounding the team off the ice throughout the 1971–72 season. With his trial on income tax evasion slated to begin, Leafs co-owner Stafford Smythe unexpectedly passed away on October 13, from a bleeding ulcer. Ultimately, his partner Harold Ballard assumed majority ownership of the team. He was soon confronted with his own criminal trial on 28 counts of fraud involving $82,000, 21 counts of theft involving $123,000, and tax evasion. A few months after the conclusion of the season he would be found guilty on 47 counts of fraud and grand theft and sent to prison.

One can only wonder how much personal issues weighed heavily on Plante that season. In 1972, his 23-year marriage to Jacqueline came to an end. The divorce was not made public, and nary a mention of it cropped up in the papers.

He still posted a winning record, but his 16–13–5 record was not as good as it had been the year before. Furthermore his goals-against average, which had led the league with a 1.88 the year before, soared to 2.63.

Somehow, the Leafs once again managed to grab the fourth and final playoff spot in the East Division, only four points ahead of fifth-place Detroit. Matched up in the first round against the Boston Bruins, the Leafs were no match for the eventual Stanley Cup champions, who brushed Toronto aside in five games. In Plante's only game of the series he was bombarded; he failed to stop the puck five times.

That showing certainly didn't diminish his greatness in the eyes of others. Around the world, Plante "was acknowledged as the master by other goalies, who frequently sought his advice when they were having problems. Most netminders admitted that they studied his technique closely," wrote Frank Orr in his book *Great Goalies of Pro Hockey*.[5]

Proof of his global stature as the game's unquestioned goalie guru came with an invitation in the spring of 1972 from the Swedish Hockey Federation, asking Jacques to come and give tutorials to some of the country's goaltenders. And so the last weekend of July found Jacques Plante in Lexsand, Sweden, about 250 kilometres from Stockholm, sharing his wisdom with the country's eight best goaltenders, in addition to 20 coaches from the Swedish National League.

Plante extended his lessons far beyond the technique of stopping the puck. His primary objective was to have his students analyze the game more critically, and to become knowledgeable about various strategies. As he had his whole career, Plante stressed that they should make use of their intelligence and imagination.

News of Plante's sojourn in Sweden was eclipsed by the birth of a rival professional hockey league, christened the World Hockey Association. In an effort to make an immediate impact, they began signing stars away from the established NHL. Bobby Hull, J.C. Tremblay, and Gerry Cheevers were just some of the big names who signed big-money contracts with the new league.

Almost overnight, the economics of the sport began to change. Leafs owner Harold Ballard, staring at prison time, spent his summer refusing to match the staggering salaries doled out by the upstart league, a few of which approached the million-dollar mark. The Leafs were more vulnerable than most teams to the overtures of the WHA. Heading into the 1972–73 season, the team had only three players under contract: Plante, Bob Baun, and forward Rick Kehoe. With Ballard unwilling to budge on issues of salary, the promise of a young hockey team quickly unravelled as many of the Leafs joined the new league.

Among them was Bernie Parent, who was joined in the WHA by Rick Ley, Jim Harrison, Brad Selwood, and Guy Trottier. The next year they would be followed by Paul Henderson and Mike Pelyk.

A new era in hockey was dawning, and as could be expected, Jacques Plante was at the forefront. That September was witness to the greatest hockey series ever when Team Canada, made up of the NHL's best players, faced off with the best from the Soviet Union. It was a match-up that the public had been craving for years, a chance for the Canadian professionals to put an end to the international success enjoyed by the Russians.

Having played the Russians seven years before, Plante was one of the few in Canadian hockey who knew anything about the Soviet game. That, combined with his broadcasting experience, helped contribute to his placement in the booth as the colour commentator on the French telecasts of the eight-game series.

Minutes before the series' opening game, an unexpected visitor entered the Soviet dressing room. For Vladislav Tretiak, the young Soviet goaltender, the stranger's appearance was still a source of disbelief years later.

"It was Jacques Plante, the famous 'pucktamer,' the best Canadian goaltender of all time," Tretiak recalled in his memoirs. "Plante came in to our room with an interpreter and amazed us by sitting with me and explaining in detail how I should play against the likes of Mahovlich, Esposito, Cournoyer, and Henderson. To help me visualize it, Plante showed me everything on a blackboard. Then he said goodbye and left. I am still puzzled by what motivated him to do that. He probably felt sorry for me, the little guy, in whom Esposito was going to shoot holes. I don't know, but I will always be very grateful to Jacques Plante, whose suggestions helped me so much."[6] (This was not the first time Plante had met Tretiak. The two men had spent time together the day before, when Plante presented Tretiak with a Fibrosport mask straight from his manufacturing plant. With the help of an interpreter, the two men sat with each other and discussed the finer points of playing goal.)

Many have since questioned Plante's motives in advising Tretiak that evening. Plante does appear to have taken pity on Tretiak, as he publicly shared in the opinion that Team Canada would prevail in the series, and like most he predicted that the Russians would be unable to score a single victory. But watching that opening game from the broadcast booth, Plante saw the folly of his prediction. The Soviets skated off with a 7–3 opening-game triumph.

Ed Johnston of the Boston Bruins, and now the third goaltender for Team Canada, claimed that Plante's influence on Tretiak's style was easily detectable. "You can see Jacques' scientific approach in the way Tretiak plays. He doesn't go down on the angles. And he turns with the play when an attacker cuts in front of the net, just the way Jacques does."[7]

Asked by the media to comment on his unofficial student's play, Plante maintained, "I didn't really teach him that much, just a little about playing the angles and positioning himself in the net. Tretiak has to learn to use his stick a little more and how to control the puck with it in the goal area."[8]

Moving to Moscow for the final four games, the series was not decided until Plante's Toronto teammate Paul Henderson scored the winning goal with 34 seconds remaining in the eighth game.

Hockey had been forever changed. Suddenly, Canada realized it was not alone at the top. Soon the NHL would be populated by players from European countries as international hockey gained a whole new level of respect in the hockey world.

No player was more prominent in that greater hockey world than Jacques Plante, who in the fall of 1972 published his long-awaited instructional manual on playing goal. Published simultaneously in English as Goaltending and in French as Devant le Filet, the book was the first to deal exclusively with the position of goaltender. It touched on all aspects of the position, with the aid of drawings and photographs. "Goaltending is such a highly specialized job that players in that position need special exercises and coaching that doesn't apply to any other position," wrote Plante. "I hope this book will help both them and especially their coaches."[9]

Plante needn't have worried. *Goaltending* quickly ascended to its well-deserved status as the definitive book on the position. For the next few decades it was the bible of goalies everywhere, at all levels and in all leagues.

Between his broadcasting duties, publishing his book, and the continued operations at Fibrosport, Jacques Plante was an extremely busy man. But he still showed up at the Leafs training camp in September. Looking around, he saw 14 players who hadn't been there in his first season with the team, a mere two years before.

The team's prospects for the 1972–73 season weren't helped when in the fifth game of the season Bobby Baun suffered a career-ending neck injury. This was a huge blow not just to the Leafs but to Plante, both personally and professionally. Not only had he lost his best defenceman but he also had lost a man he had grown close to off the ice.

As well, Plante no longer had the benefit of Bernie Parent as his goaltending partner. His goals-against average ballooned to 3.04 as he posted a losing record of 8–14–6 in 32 games that season. Plante's average looked better when compared to those of the other two goalies who manned the Leafs nets that year. Gord McRae and Ron Low posted goals-against of 3.77 and 3.89 respectively.

The promise of only two seasons before seemed a distant memory as the Leafs plummeted to the league's fourth-worst record. On many nights Plante was alone in the Toronto goal, scrambling to hold off the opposition.

On March 2, 1973, Plante found his professional salvation when the Leafs traded him along with a third-round draft choice to the defending Stanley Cup champion Boston Bruins in exchange for a first-round pick and future considerations.

Plante had been given a golden opportunity to try once more to win another Stanley Cup. The Bruins, winner of two of the past three Stanley Cups, were still smarting over the loss of Gerry Cheevers to the rival WHA. With superstars like Bobby Orr and Phil Esposito dotting their star-studded lineup, Bruins general manager Harry Sinden hoped that Plante would help shore up their goaltending.

Sinden, the head coach for Team Canada in the previous fall's Summit Series with Russia, was considered one of the game's brightest minds. He had long professed his admiration for Plante.

The trade was announced on Saturday night, and Plante was pressed into immediate action, appearing in Boston on Sunday afternoon in front of a national television audience. Playing the Chicago Black Hawks, Plante once again rose to the occasion, making 27 saves in recording the eighty-first shutout of his career. Even more impressive was that Plante had blanked Chicago without the services of Bobby Orr in the Boston lineup.

"I was nervous before the game," said Plante, "more nervous even than when I was a rookie. A rookie doesn't think about this kind of a game. But here I am, 44-years-old and the team wanted me. I didn't think I'd get another chance at a playoff game."[10]

Playing eight games for the Bruins to finish the season, Plante caused a sensation by winning seven, including a shutout against the New York Rangers, Boston's first-round opponent in the playoffs.

"We just wouldn't have wrapped second place without him," Sinden told the *Toronto Star*. "We've lost one game in 12 since he got here; evidence enough of what he's done. His average is 2.00 goals per game and it's been a long time since any goalie on this club had a mark that low."[11] Countering questions about Plante being a rent-a-player, Sinden informed the media, "We're counting on Jacques to play for us again next season."[12]

Amid the enthusiasm, however, some voices of dissent could still he heard. Punch Imlach, now the general manager of the Buffalo Sabres, predicted, "Boston will go down the drain in a hurry with trades like that. Plante's finished. He'll give you a good game now and then, but he makes mistakes in judgment. He's too old."[13]

Unfortunately, the dissent began to infect the Bruins' own dressing room. In retrospect, it is easy to see how ill matched Plante was with the Bruins. Boston was the defending Stanley Cup champion. A group of players in their mid to late twenties, they had grown up together and were an extremely close team. When Plante arrived in town, he began instructing the players, particularly his defencemen, on how he wanted them to play. That may have worked with a veteran squad in St. Louis or with a young, unproven club in Toronto. But when you try to instruct Bobby Orr, winner of the previous five Norris trophies and on his way to a sixth, how to play his position, you're going to cause friction. And when you clashed with Bobby Orr in Boston in the early seventies, you were a man alone. "If you think there was confusion in the room before," an anonymous Bruin told the *Sporting News*, "you should have seen it after Plante arrived."[14]

Nevertheless, the Bruins, holders of the league's second best record, were widely seen as the favourites in their first-round series against the New York Rangers, the same team they had defeated in the Stanley Cup finals the year before.

The first game, at the Boston Garden, was an unmitigated disaster for both the Bruins and Plante. "The Rangers checked the Bruins to a standstill, threw a barrage from long range and short at a very shaky Plante and routed the Bruins 6–2," reported Mark Mulvoy in *Sports Illustrated*. "Orr spent much of the night futilely seeking new avenues out of the Boston zone, and when he did get the puck to a teammate one of the Rangers quickly took it away. The Phil Esposito–Wayne Cashman–Ken Hodge line, which led the NHL in scoring, did not get a shot against Ranger Goalie Eddie Giacomin until the game was nearly over. For Plante, every Ranger shot was an adventure. Three of New York's six goals were scored on blasts from at least 40 feet away."[15]

Despite the urging of the Boston players, Coach Bep Guidolin chose to stick with Plante in the second game. To those who watched the spectacle, Plante appeared an old and tired man. He tried all the tricks he had gathered in his long career, in an effort to slow the game down. But the Rangers won, 4–2.

Jacques Plante had played the last game of his illustrious NHL career.

Down 2–0 in games, and with Phil Esposito out of the series after undergoing a knee surgery, it was only a matter of time. As Plante watched from the bench, the desperate Bruins managed to scrape out a win in game three, but lost the next two and were eliminated.

27

A MAN CONFLICTED

PACING BEHIND THE BENCH of the Quebec Nordiques, a stoic Jacques Plante was once again alone. The thought of being a coach had crossed his mind many times during his playing years, as had the notion of returning to the province of Quebec in some sort of hockey capacity. Now, at the age of 45, he had realized both of these desires as the coach and general manager of the Nordiques of the World Hockey Association for the 1973–74 season. Furthermore he was being paid a salary far better than any he'd seen as a player.

As the two teams skated in front of him, he was not a content man, though. His thoughts drifted back to the previous April, when he decided to take the Nordiques up on their tremendous offer. Despite the compensation, a 10-year contract with a salary rumoured to be a million dollars, he had still had difficulty making up his mind.

The Nordiques had approached Plante in February 1973, when he was still a Toronto Maple Leaf, but Plante hedged on making a decision before, in early April, expressing his desire to stay with the Bruins for another year.

"I changed my mind about retiring since I came to Boston," he explained. "I like the setup. And it changes a goalie's attitude quite a lot when he finds himself playing behind a strong defense again. Suddenly, it seems like an easier job. You don't get so tired anymore. We've got everything worked out for next season already – how much money I'm to be paid and what my working arrangements are going to be."[1]

And then, on May 3, in a startling about-face, Plante publicly spurned the Bruins and signed the contract to become the Nordiques' head coach and general manager.

At the press conference announcing his hiring, he said that despite taking over both the coaching and managerial duties of the Nordiques, he still wanted to play in goal. With a year still remaining on his Bruins contract, he would be unable to tend the nets for Quebec in the upcoming season, "but next year I'll definitely play. I feel like I've got five years left in me."[2]

In Boston, a stunned Harry Sinden held his own press conference. It was clear to all those in attendance that it was not a happy occasion, especially considering that earlier in the week Sinden had told the media that Plante would be wearing a Bruins uniform in the upcoming season. "I talked with Jacques Friday" – five days earlier – "and he told me: 'Give me a good deal and I'll stay.' We gave it to him and we were counting upon him to play about 30 games for us next year. Then I began hearing reports and called him Tuesday. He told me not to worry, our deal still stood. Now I get this news. He probably had the contract with the other team when he talked to me. If that's true, I never want to speak to him again."[3] Plante, knowingly or not, had publicly embarrassed Harry Sinden. He would soon learn of the consequences.

As he settled in to his new job in management, Plante sought to make a splash. The Nordiques had failed to make the playoffs the season before, and in an effort to sell more tickets and improve the team, he hit upon an ingenious idea: he would make his former teammate Jean Béliveau a member of the Quebec Nordiques.

Béliveau had retired from the NHL only two seasons before in fitting fashion, hoisting the Stanley Cup aloft for the tenth time as he skated off the ice at Chicago Stadium in his last game as a professional. In retirement, he moved into the Canadiens front offices as the team's vice-president. During his junior days in Quebec he had been the biggest star the city had ever seen. A return to Quebec, now, at the rink he once filled to capacity would be a tremendous publicity and marketing coup for the two-year-old Nordiques. So Plante and Paul Racine, the club's principal backer, offered Béliveau a four-year deal for one million dollars.

"Whatever you put on the table, I won't go back on the ice," Béliveau told them. "Ten million, twenty million, it doesn't matter. I'm forty, going on forty-one. I can't play the quality of hockey I like any more. If I could, and if I wanted to play again, I'd play with the Canadiens. It wouldn't be fair to you, the fans, or me . . . I just can't do it anymore, and I'm the first guy to recognize it."[4]

Having failed at his first attempt to land a marquee player, Plante took aim at a second, albeit lesser target. Réjean Houle had been the first overall selection by the Montreal Canadiens in the 1969 entry draft. A prolific scorer in junior, with the Canadiens he had assumed a checking role that had brought him a modicum of success, as he was now the proud holder of two Stanley Cup rings. In the hot summer months of 1973, he found himself in the middle of a contractual tug-of-war between the Canadiens and the Nordiques. Ultimately, he jumped the Canadiens ship and joined Quebec for what was rumoured to be a three-year, $100,000-per-season deal.

Plante next turned his attention to Serge Bernier, then starring with the Los Angeles Kings. A star with the Quebec Aces when in junior and a first-round draft pick of the Philadelphia Flyers, Bernier was coming off a 22-goal season. Plante had correctly predicted that the return of Bernier would help create some excitement at the ticket office. Picking up Bernier was undoubtedly Plante's finest move as an executive, as Bernier would score 37 goals and 49 assists, resulting in 86 points that season, and become one of the WHA's top offensive players.

With Houle and Bernier under contract, Plante was able to turn to another matter that had been on his mind over that summer. On August 8, he pulled out a sheet of Nordiques stationery and began typing a letter to Harry Sinden, the general manager of the Boston Bruins, and the man he had left a few months earlier.

Dear Harry:
I should have met you, talked with you or at least wrote to you much earlier than to-day to let you know that even if I decided to come to Quebec City, I will never forget the few weeks I spent in Boston.
   I felt wanted from the start and this made me want to play for you and the Bruins. When I accepted to go to Boston, I was sure we could win the cup and all the time I was there, I conditioned myself to my utmost (physically and mentally) to be at my best.
   I had confidence till the very end, but we didn't make it. I wish I could have done better against New York, but I didn't have it. One thing for sure, is that you got from me everything I had left.

I must thank you for the good words you had for me when we met in your office after the season was over. They made me feel very good . . . so good, that even if I was drained then, I could have gone back and played all those games all over again. I did many times in the following weeks and still think about them now and then.

When at the end, you told me that I did what you got me for, I felt warm and, on the way home. I started to dream about the coming year . . . that will not be. I am very sorry about this (not as much as you, you might say), and this was the most difficult decision I had to make in my life. But, as I explained earlier, I had no choice . . .

I had to tell you all this but something else too, and I wonder what can be your policy here. I would like to find out how I can have my equipment back. All of it was given to me by Emile Francis when I left New York. I brought it back to St. Louis, to Toronto and then to Boston. Naturally, some of it was replaced over those five years . . . and if you want me to pay something, I will gladly pay you back . . . but I need it badly as I want to play with the "Oldtimers" and keep in shape at the same time.

There is <u>NO</u> chance for me to come back to active playing. The more I think about it, the more I cannot see myself back in "Pro Hockey" facing the hard shots and having to stand all the pressure. So, would you please ask your trainer and put it aside and give it to the Whalers for me. We play them during training camp. Lefty Reed of the Hockey Hall of Fame also wants my last mask to put in his building with the other ones I used (He has 5 already).

Before closing, may I ask you what happened to my share of the money for the second place finish, the playoffs and my expense money to go to Boston from Toronto ($100.00 plus) and to come back home in Magog. Please ask your accountant.

We had agreed that my meals at the Sonesta would be paid by the Bruins, since I had to stay at the Hotel. I am enclosing a Memo from my contract with Toronto about the room. I understand that from the amount there can be a few expenses to take out.

Please do not take this letter the wrong way. I wish this situation would never have happened but since it has to be, let's make the best out of it and not hold grudges. Who knows, maybe some day we will need each other again.

I am sorry, I took so much of your time but I had to let you know how I felt about you, the Bruins, Boston and playing there . . . and about to leaving.

Again, many thanks for everything and if you need me, please call me. (Even if we are in two different leagues, this is always hockey).

Until I hear from you, I remain.

Sincerely,

Jacques Planté[5]

The letter elicited no response from Harry Sinden. Plante waited, and phoned, and all he would find was the sound of silence. After three months, and increasingly desperate, he sent out another letter, dated December 6, 1973, this time to Weston W. Adams Jr., the Bruins president. This letter, too, received no response.

Plante couldn't comprehend the position of the Bruins and the depth of their feelings of betrayal. In their trade with the Leafs, they had paid a high price for Plante, a first-round pick, as well as goalie Eddie Johnston. And while Plante helped the Bruins finish in second place, his playoff performance had been undeniably poor. With the Bruins' goaltending in a state of flux, Sinden had been counting on Plante to play at least 30 games the next year. After all, he was under contract to play the 1973–74 season with the Bruins. By jumping to the Nordiques, Plante had violated the terms of his signed contract, after giving his word that he would come back. This had to be especially embarrassing for Sinden, who had publicly talked of Plante's imminent return.

As a last resort, on March 21, 1974, after seven months without an answer from either Sinden or Adams, Plante wrote a letter to NHL president Clarence Campbell. He summed up his list of grievances with the Bruins and went so far as to claim that he had "found it necessary" to leave the Bruins for the Nordiques, and that Sinden "was very satisfied with me and the way I played and that even if I left for the W.H.A., the deal was worth it since according to him, Ken Broderick was as good as the departed Eddie Johnston."[6] Once again, it appeared that Plante felt his difficulties with the Bruins lay in his playoff performance and not in his decision to walk out on the last year of his contract.

Campbell responded to Plante four days later, informing him that his letter had been forwarded to Sinden. Campbell received a response from Sinden a week later. That letter helped reveal the depth of the bitterness that the Bruins organization had for their former goaltender. After dealing with the various financial issues, Sinden wrote about Plante's still missing equipment: "I do not know what happened to the goalkeeper's equipment which Plante brought with him from Toronto and which we feel became the outright property of the Boston Bruins at that time. In any event, the equipment is no longer in inventory here in Boston. I suspect that players or personnel in the organization may have taken action to rid the Boston organization of any memories that may exist of Jacques Plante's short tenure here."[7]

The last line of Sinden's letter dripped with disdain. Campbell immediately forwarded the letter to Plante, and the dispute quickly degenerated into a squabble in which Plante continued to make accusations that Sinden denied.

On June 1, Plante responded to Sinden's statement through Campbell, now acting as more of an intermediary than an adjudicator, and the two men began a written battle.

Looking over the increasing pile of letters between Plante and Sinden, Campbell sat down to make his decision. In early August he decided that the Bruins did in fact owe Plante $859.99 in bonus money from the previous year's second-place finish, since the Leafs had no record of ever receiving the payment that Sinden had always maintained was sent. Plante also received his $2,500 share for finishing in the quarter-finals, minus the $500 fine for missing training camp, a fine that Campbell admitted to Sinden "was questionable."[8]

Plante and the Bruins had finally extricated themselves from one another, with neither being satisfied with their brief tenure together or with their messy and prolonged parting.

28

THE LION IN WINTER

THE ITCH TO PLAY again had come early in Plante's time as the Nordiques coach and general manager. When he had signed his contract in the summer of 1973, he made a point of mentioning to the media that he was going to come back and play goal the next year, after sitting out the first year because of his contract with the Bruins. A few weeks later he distanced himself from those comments.

In October, with the season barely under way, he confessed that he was going through a period of feeling ambivalent about the game. "Some days, I feel good and the thought comes to me: I can still stand it. There are times when I'm involved in the administration of the team and I'd just love to be getting ready to fly somewhere to play a game. Then, I ask myself: Why would I want this again? Over the last few years it was tough. I'd get the shakes during warmup and they would disappear for a period. It was no longer a sport for me."[1]

As an executive he was now working 16-hour days, but thoughts of returning to the nets were never far from his mind. As the months passed by, Jacques gradually grew more disenchanted with his new role. Like many great players who had gone before him and tried their hand in coaching, he soon realized the one inescapable fact that confronted him behind the bench: no matter how hard he pleaded or how many drills he ran, he couldn't give his players his own talent or skill. Some things cannot be taught.

As the games continued, he came to understand his limitations as a coach. Communication was not one of Plante's strong suits as a head coach. A loner by nature, he tended to be distant from many of his own players, and they became accustomed to stretches of prolonged silence behind the bench.

He was also not well versed on running the game from the bench. He could not emulate previous coaches like Toe Blake and Scotty Bowman, who were masters of matching lines and achieving strategic advantages over their opposition. "Plante tried to give us all the information he could give from his own experiences," says Réjean Houle. "But you couldn't compare him as a coach to Scotty Bowman. Plante knew a lot about the technique, but he was not a head coach type. He would have been much better suited to being a goalie coach."[2]

Both Blake and Bowman had coaching experience before becoming professional coaches and were able to grow into their position behind the bench. That season in Quebec, Jacques Plante enjoyed no such advantage.

Years before, when he was with the Canadiens, Toe Blake had totally entrusted Plante with the goaltending. Blake, himself a former forward, claimed ignorance, admitting to Plante that he was ill suited to offer any goaltending advice. Now Plante discovered that he was just as ill suited to offer any advice to his team's forwards. He was a renowned expert on hockey in the defensive end and could talk for hours about goaltending and defensive strategies, but once the puck crossed the red line into the offensive zone, he was a limited if not ineffective coach.

Plante's problems in Quebec were not restricted to the team. Always a favourite of the media, he alienated the local press almost immediately when he began writing a column in the newspaper *A-propos*. His own column bypassed the media, allowing him to speak directly to the fans, and lost him the support of the local newsmen, and when the team struggled he found the support of many influential reporters had evaporated.

The one bright spot in his life that year was far from the rink. Jacques had first met Caroline Raymonde Udrisart a decade earlier in New York City, when he was playing with the Rangers. Born in Switzerland, she worked at the Swiss Pavilion at Expo 67 in Montreal, and had proceeded to stay in Canada. Over the next couple of years she assumed

a larger place in Jacques' life, to the point where they were now insep-
arable. In time, she would become the second Mrs. Plante.

As the season dragged on to an inglorious end, with the Nordiques
missing the playoffs for a second consecutive season, there were whispers throughout the city about the wisdom of signing Jacques Plante
to a 10-year, million-dollar contract. Rumours quickly spread about
his commitment to the club, as stories of him polishing his skis in his
coach's office spread through town.[3] In March 1974, at a WHA
meeting in Chicago, a frustrated Plante made his bid for professional
independence.

A little over six months earlier, in a transaction that garnered virtually no press or public notice, the Edmonton Oilers had selected Plante
in the June 1973 WHA professional player draft. With Plante joining
the Nordiques the month before on the basis of a 10-year contract, the
Oilers' selection was viewed as nothing more than a lark. But that
changed in March of 1974.

At a league meeting, Plante informed Edmonton Oilers owner Wild
Bill Hunter that he wanted to come out of retirement and was in perfect
shape to play. Hunter was stunned when he realized Plante was serious.

After the meetings, Plante went about his business as the coach and
general manager of the Nordiques. However, as the season slowly
plodded towards its merciful conclusion, unhappiness about Plante fes-
tered in the Quebec ownership. The question soon became not
whether Jacques Plante would be back next year but instead whether
he would resign his post or if the team would be forced to fire him.

On Saturday, May 4, Plante would be making his presentation on
the season past at the Nordiques' annual shareholders meeting. Many
in the press braced for a confrontation between the proud Plante and
the angry shareholders. Two days before the conference, Paul Racine,
the Nordiques president and the man so instrumental in the team's
earlier negotiations with Béliveau, Houle, and Bernier, announced that
he would not be continuing in his current position. By the eve of the
meeting, rumours were running wild that Plante would be resigning
both of his positions as soon as he finished his speech.

Talking to the media in the days before the meeting, Plante said he
felt "that a coach should not automatically be held responsible for a
team's failures. He said he knew there were several people after his head
because the Nordiques had failed to make the playoffs."[4]

With cameras documenting his every move, Plante, with his chin
jutting slightly forward, walked into the meeting that Saturday a proud

man. It was widely known inside hockey circles that he was likely to be forced out by the Quebec brass by the end of the meeting. He presented his report and then stunned the shareholders by announcing his resignation from both positions.

"The news is stupefying at first glance," wrote *Le Soleil* the next day. "But if we look closer, we understand that Plante, a man who has always been affable and reasonable until the end had to admit the facts – the facts that were obvious to everyone who was following his progress with any attention. A superb goaltender and a refined game analyst, he wasn't able to transpose onto the ice what he could express so well in words. He didn't have what it takes to be a manager. He was certainly aware that the shareholders' case against him was getting more serious and more irrefutable every day."[5]

Many in the media were puzzled by Plante's decision to walk away from the final nine years of his Nordiques contract. Had the team fired him, he would have been owed the entire amount. By resigning, he received nothing. But a few days later the picture became a little clearer.

If the media were caught off guard by Plante's actions that Saturday in Quebec, then they were downright shocked four days later when he suddenly appeared in Edmonton to announce his latest comeback, with the WHA Oilers as their newest goaltender.

It was a stunning return to the nets. It soon became obvious to the public that the sudden resignation from the Nordiques and the almost simultaneous signing with Edmonton had been planned well in advance.

"Jacques trained religiously and watched his diet closely," remembered Oilers owner Bill Hunter. "And so for $150,000 a season, the great Jacques Plante pulled on an Oilers jersey. It was a thrill for me to sign one of the great men of hockey, and it was pretty good publicity too."[6]

Many questioned this latest comeback. Plante would turn 46 in January, and his critics wondered why a man with his financial house in order and in good health would go back into the nets. After all, what was left to accomplish? He had done everything in the sport – as a matter of fact he had done more than anybody who had ever put on a set of pads.

It may sound simplistic, but Jacques Plante wasn't playing hockey for money, even though his salary was the highest he had ever received in his professional career. And he wasn't playing the game for fame and glory – he had more of both than any other goalie.

No, he was playing the game once again because it remained a challenge to him, and because he lived for it. "I have nothing to prove,"

Plante said, "because I'm not going to get any better. At my age it is all down for me. I play because this is what I like to do best."[7]

In August it was announced that the returning Plante had been added to the extended roster of Team Canada as the WHA prepared to have its own version of the Summit Series. For the 45-year-old Plante, it was the first time that he had put on the jersey of his country. It was also a rare instance when he wasn't the oldest player. Gordie Howe, 10 months older, also skated for the team. Sadly, Plante would only be a spectator, as a valiant if not undermanned Team Canada lost to the powerful Soviet squad.

One of the major considerations behind the signing of Plante was the Oilers' desire to sell tickets to their new rink, the Northlands Coliseum, capacity 15,326. It was quite an improvement from the home rink they had used in their first two seasons, the Edmonton Gardens, capacity 5,200.

Sunday, November 10, marked the grand opening of the Coliseum, coinciding with Plante's debut as an Oiler. The opposition would be provided by the Cleveland Crusaders and their star goalie, Gerry Cheevers, two-time Stanley Cup winner with the Boston Bruins. This perfect confluence of events and legendary goalies resulted in the game's being sold out two days before the puck dropped. Workers were installing the last seats mere hours before the game began.

That Sunday evening, 15,326 people, the biggest crowd to watch a WHA game in the league's three-year history, watched Plante officially become the oldest professional goaltender in the history of hockey. He didn't disappoint: the Oilers won 4–1.

In the fall of 1974, Plante was once again the talk of the hockey world. In his first nine games with the Oilers he won eight. He was careful to point out to the media that his wins had been against the league's best teams. "You can't say I've been avoiding the tough teams like they were trying to say a couple of years back. I've played against Houston, Winnipeg, Toronto, New England and everybody."[8]

"Jacques was exceptionally popular with the fans," said Bill Hunter. "The phone would constantly ring asking if Jacques was playing tonight. He meant two to three thousand extra fans a night if not more."[9]

Much as he had been in Toronto, Plante was a steadying, calming influence on the Oilers' young defence corps, constantly communicating with them and directing traffic in his own end. If there was one criticism of Plante, it was that he rarely played away from Edmonton. Not only did he not play in many of the road games, he seldom bothered to attend them. He would stay behind in Edmonton, where he practised with the Edmonton Oil Kings, a junior team in the Western Hockey League.

"That is Bill Hunter's decision," Plante explained. "After he signed he said they'd try to play me at home mostly. What tires me most is the traveling part."[10]

Then disaster struck. On December 11, Plante was practising with the Oil Kings when he was bowled over by an oncoming player. Struck on the side of the head by the player's helmet, he was knocked out cold. Later, the doctors confirmed that he had suffered an injury to his ear drum that affected his equilibrium. "Right now the doctors say I can skate," Plante announced, "but don't think I should play because of the balance factor, if I was to pivot quickly or make a sudden shift. But they tell me it's nothing serious really."[11]

Unfortunately, the doctors were wrong. Many have argued, including Bill Hunter, that Jacques Plante was never the same goaltender after that. The statistical record supports this theory. Before the accident, Plante had won eight games and lost only one. After the accident, he won seven games, lost 13 and tied one.

On December 22, he attempted to play for the Oilers, but after 18 minutes dizziness and a sick stomach forced him to leave the game.

As the calendar turned into 1975, the Oilers had the best winning percentage in their division. However, as Plante's equilibrium problems and inconsistent play lingered, the team soon went into an unavoidable and seemingly inevitable descent down the standings.

With two games left in the season, the Oilers announced that Jacques Plante was done for the season thanks to a broken index finger. At the same time, however, Plante was quick to state that he would be returning to the Oiler nets the next season, while also announcing that the next season would definitely be his last. "I've had the dizzy spells all year," he admitted. "There was no use of me complaining about that after a while. So if I was scheduled to play, I played. I was much sharper earlier in the year, when I was healthy I was playing great."[12] The Oilers would finish the season in fifth place, and on the sidelines when the playoffs began.

After a summer spent in Switzerland with Raymonde, Jacques Plante, at the age of 46, arrived in the Edmonton Oilers training camp in mid-September. He soon found out that the team's newest goaltending acquisition, Dave Dryden, had been handed the starting position in the nets. This helped put him at odds with Clare Drake, the Oilers' new coach.

As camp began, Drake, eager to test the fitness of his players, set up a two-mile run. Plante, in front of all his teammates, informed the new coach that he couldn't take the course because of his asthma. Drake calmly informed his legendary goaltender that he would run the two miles the following Monday or else, and then turned his back to Plante. The coach had the backing of the team's owner, Bill Hunter, who stated publicly that if Plante couldn't meet the team's physical requirements, his contract would become null and void.

As Plante struggled to find his spot on the Oilers in the first week of October, he received a phone call from his oldest son, Michel. It was a phone call that no parent ever wants to get. Michel told him that his youngest son, Richard, had committed suicide. Michel recalled the awful moment years later: "He said to me, 'Let me call you back,' and he just hung up and called me back about 15 minutes later. So in that period of time he probably cried a lot. It really hurt him because he wasn't there at the time."[13]

Plante immediately left the Oilers training camp and returned home to Quebec.

Still grieving, Plante returned to the Oilers camp the next week. He was living a parent's worst nightmare, but compassion and empathy were in short supply that fall in Edmonton.

At camp he was confronted by a coach who didn't want him on the team, and the team's ownership was searching for ways to get out of his contract. Plante's fall of discontent was compounded by an inter-squad game in front of the public, in which he was roundly booed by the crowd for allowing seven goals.

A few nights later, on October 9, the Oilers played their final exhibition game of the pre-season against the Calgary Cowboys. With the regular season starting the next night against the Minnesota Fighting Saints, the Oilers attempted to cancel the game because of poor ticket sales, yet Calgary refused.

Clare Drake's decision to carry two goaltenders meant that Jacques Plante was the odd man out. He played the first two periods of the exhibition game that night, allowing three goals on 17 shots. That night's crowd of 1,620 had witnessed the final game of Jacques Plante's glorious hockey career.

A few days later, Plante was told there wasn't a space for him on the team's roster. He quietly returned home.

There was no press conference. There were no ceremonies to honour a man whose contributions to the game were immense. There was no farewell tour. It would be another week before the Oilers took the trouble to announce in a press release that Plante had retired from the game. Even that announcement was pushed out of the sports head-lines by Carlton Fisk's home run in game six of the World Series.

It was an inglorious exit for a man who had forever changed the game, a sad and silent ending to the greatest goaltending career the sport of hockey had ever known. On the day of the press release, there wasn't a goalie in professional hockey that wasn't sporting a mask. Jacques Plante the player may have left the game, but Jacques Plante's legacy would forever be an integral part of hockey's fabric.

29

THE MENTOR

IN 1974 AND 1975 no goalie was more dominant than Bernie Parent. He had led the Flyers to back-to-back Stanley Cups, while winning consecutive Vezina trophies and becoming the first player to win two Conn Smythe trophies in a row as the playoffs' most valuable player.

After recovering from a back injury the previous season, Parent returned as the Flyers starter for the 1976–77 season. And even though the team had the league's second-best record, Parent was unhappy with his play, as his 2.71 goals-against average was a significant increase from his Cup-winning seasons a few years before (in 1974 and 1975 he had posted league-leading averages of 1.89 and 2.03 respectively). In the playoffs he struggled mightily, losing all three games he played in, with an unsightly goals-against of 3.90, before being replaced by Wayne Stephenson in the Flyers nets.

Now 31, Parent, indisputedly the game's pre-eminent goalie a few years before, was now facing a crisis in his career. When the Flyers training camp convened, the once confident Parent was starting to doubt if he could ever regain his championship form of a few years before. He had spent much of the last two seasons looking for the answer to his problems and was even considering retirement. He had consulted a psychiatrist. The year before he had begun devouring self-improvement books, while swearing off cigars and alcohol. Yet he still struggled.

The Flyers were running out of options in an effort to help Parent recapture his form. During a meeting of the team's brass at the conclusion of their four-game sweep to the Bruins, it was the Flyers' captain, Bobby Clarke, who hit on the solution. "There's one guy who might be able to help," Clarke told the room. "Jacques Plante."

Any person who had spent any time with Bernie Parent was aware of the influence that Jacques Plante had had on his career. Parent felt that everything he had achieved in hockey – Stanley Cups, Vezina trophies, Conn Smythe trophies – was owed to Jacques Plante.

In hiring Plante, the Flyers were hoping for a stabilizing influence on Parent as well as a coach to specifically work with the goalies in the system. And who better fit that role than the most decorated goalie in hockey history and the man viewed as the leading expert on the position? And that's how Jacques Plante became the first goaltending coach ever employed in the NHL.

Plante spent his first two days at the Flyers training camp as an interested spectator. He took a seat in the stands and watched Parent intently. So heavy was his concentration that he didn't speak to Parent. After two days of study, Plante bluntly told Parent exactly what he was doing wrong, boiling it all down to three problems: Parent was sitting back on his heels, backing into his crease, and losing concentration.

"Twenty-five percent of goaltending is talent," Plante told Jay Greenberg, the Flyers beat writer from 1975 to 1989. "Twenty-five percent is positioning. The other 50 percent is concentration."[1]

Parent heeded Plante's advice and in the process rediscovered the Bernie Parent of old. "It's fun again," he remarked. "It's back. I was off almost the whole year [following the neck operation] and I forgot how to tend goal. How to stand, how to challenge the shooter. I had fallen into all kinds of bad habits. Jacques got me back into the right ones."[2]

The proof of Plante's wisdom and knowledge was in Parent's re-emergence during the 1977–78 season. He won 29 games, lost only six, and tied three. He finished the season with a league-best seven shutouts, and had a goals-against average of 2.22, second only to Ken Dryden of the Montreal Canadiens. Under Plante's tutelage, the team gave up the second-lowest number of goals in the league.

For the next five years Plante served as the goaltending coach for the Flyers. It was a job he enjoyed thoroughly. In addition to working with the Flyers goalies, he also coached the goalies within their organization, particularly with their minor league affiliate in Maine. In his first two seasons with the Mariners, playing in the American Hockey League, they won the Calder Cup. In his five-year tenure with the team, the Mariners finished in first place three times, in addition to a second- and third-place finish.

Thanks to Plante's coaching, goalies such as Rick St. Croix, Phil Myre, Pete Peeters, Bob Froese, and Pelle Lindbergh were able to advance to the NHL, with Peeters and Lindbergh both capturing the Vezina in the years after their apprenticeship with Plante.

"Plante is responsible for much of what success I've had," claimed Peeters in 1980. "Nobody knows more about goaltending and nobody is a better teacher. Here I was coming out of junior, a flopper, relying mostly on reflexes. . . . Plante gave me a lot of things to think about and I had a few ideas of my own and it took me time to sort everything out. Sometimes, facing a shot, I would try to remember all of what he told me and before I knew it the puck would be in the net. It took me time to develop the skills I needed."[3]

Plante was reinvigorated by his experience in Philadelphia. He had found his calling as a goaltending coach. He enjoyed interacting with the young goaltenders and being able to teach these aspiring youngsters the nuances of the position, imparting his voluminous knowledge to the next generation.

The Flyers occasionally sent him on scouting jaunts to rival cities like Boston, New York, and Pittsburgh. Plante would sit in the arenas and take studious notes about what he saw. He had spent a lifetime observing the game, and now the Flyers were smart enough to take advantage of his knowledge and experience.

But not every aspect of Plante's life was perfect.

At its peak, Fibrosport had been producing close to 10,000 masks a year. However, the company's fortunes began to head downward in February 1977, when Buffalo Sabres goalie Gerry Desjardins, wearing a fibreglass-style mask – not one sold through Fibrosport – was clipped in the eye by a puck, ending his career.

The Desjardins injury left the league's other goalies jittery. Tony Esposito put a protective metal lattice across the eyeholes in his Fibrosport mask. The Canadian Standards Association, in charge of certifying sports equipment through the country, banned fibreglass masks from minor hockey. For Fibrosport this decision had devastating consequences.

Two years later, in February 1979, Bernie Parent suffered a career-ending eye injury when an opponent's stick entered the right eye hole of his mask. After the injury to Parent, not only the most prominent goalie to wear the Fibrosport mask but one of its leading proponents, many goalies switched to the cage-and-helmet version used by most today.

After almost a decade of business, Plante's dream of a mask-making empire crashed and burned. Soon after the demise of Fibrosport, he packed up his remaining belongings, and he and his wife, Raymonde, began a new life together in Switzerland.

Sierre is a small town of 10,000 people, located in a part of Switzerland noted for its fertile winemaking. Called "the town of a thousand hills" by the Romans, Sierre has a landscape dotted with castles and vineyards. Sierre is famous for its hospitality as well as for having the most sunshine of any town in Switzerland.

Jacques Plante settled down to live his golden years amid the peace and tranquility of this small town. Alongside his beloved Raymonde, he felt free to indulge in his wide range of passions, like painting and tennis, in addition to skiing in the Alps.

Always a very private man, he revelled in the privacy and serenity that he enjoyed in his Swiss enclave.

"His health was better," remembers his son Michel. "He put his asthma pump down and never used it there."[4]

Plante also took an interest in the local hockey scene, helping coach many young goaltenders and running numerous hockey clinics. He renewed acquaintances with Jacques Lemaire, who moved to Sierre in the fall of 1979 after concluding his Hall of Fame career with the Montreal Canadiens. Lemaire had played on the Junior Canadiens team that Plante had famously backstopped to victory against the visiting Russians in 1965. Playing two seasons with the local Sierre team, Lemaire also acted as coach, learning the rudiments of the profession.

In the fall of 1983, two years after leaving Sierre, Lemaire rejoined the Canadiens as an assistant coach. The Canadiens were by then a team in transition. They had last won the Stanley Cup in 1979 and had since fallen victim to some spectacular playoff flameouts. Now, with their front office overhauled and Serge Savard, a former teammate of Lemaire's and another who had played with Plante against the Russians in 1965, in the general manager's chair, they immediately set out to find the man to help with their group of inexperienced goaltenders. They knew the perfect person for the job.

Twenty years after he had been traded away, Jacques Plante triumphantly returned to the Montreal Canadiens organization as their goaltending coach. To be back in the Canadiens fold meant a lot to Jacques, and he cherished his time in the organization. He had always considered himself to be foremost a Montreal Canadien. And even though he wasn't playing, the fact that the Canadiens needed him once again was a source of tremendous pride for him.

Much as he had done before in Philadelphia, he attended the team's training camp before making a few in-season visits, as well as a visit during the playoffs.

However, there was one change in his coaching style compared to his previous stint in Philadelphia.

"As a goaling instructor, Plante tells it as it should be – rather than showing how it's done," wrote Milt Dunnell in the *Toronto Star*. "He wears the armored skates on the ice but the other tools of ignorance have been abandoned." Not playing in net was a decision he had made while coaching in Philadelphia, Plante explained to Dunnell. "I used to stop some shots until one day Reggie Leach rifled one that broke my thumb. I told the trainer I never wanted to see the equipment again."[5]

"The most important thing for the goalies is to have somebody to talk with and somebody that speaks the same language," Plante told Montreal TV station CFCF. "The goalies need somebody that understands their problem and that can correct them. My job is to find out what's wrong, so they don't go into a slump, so that we know what's going on."[6]

Although many of the goalies on the Canadiens roster had read Jacques' book, *Goaltending*, this was their first experience working with a goaltending coach in person. Both in print and in person, Jacques made an impression, as Canadiens goalie Rick Wamsley attested. "Other guys in Port Dover were reading *Tom Sawyer* or *Treasure Island*. With me it was Jacques Plante's primer on how to play goal. I read it dozens of times. Fifteen years later, I can still recite pages out of that thing."[7]

"He's helped me tremendously with angles," Wamsley professed as training camp came to a close. "His big theory is to get hit by the puck. I've been concentrating on getting in a good position to get hit by the puck."[8]

With his reputation once again firmly intact, Plante was in constant demand among coaches and others involved in junior hockey, especially in Quebec. More often than not he was asked to provide his expert opinion on prospective goaltenders and advise what they might need to do to take their game to the next level.

In the fall of 1983, Roger Picard, the coach of the Granby Bisons, asked Plante to make a special visit to the junior team's training camp to check out his young goaltending prospect. Plante had no way of knowing that the young goaltender he was about to evaluate would one day challenge his unofficial title as "the greatest goalie who ever lived." The young goaltender's name was Patrick Roy.

"He wanted me to do things," remembers Roy, "that didn't make sense to me. I told him 'I have a lot of respect for you. You're one of the greatest goalies of all time, but I don't believe that what you're asking me to do is right.' That annoyed him, and after the practice, he told Mr. Picard that I would never make the National Hockey League."[9]

Roy was the definitive butterfly goalie, employing a style of goaltending in direct contrast to Plante's stand-up angular style. Plante advised Roy to ditch the butterfly, a piece of advice that the obstinate Roy quickly rejected. Plante took this as an affront. What Plante failed to see in the young man's stubbornness was a streak of independence similar to what he himself had possessed in his younger days.

Full of optimism, the Canadiens broke camp and then proceeded to have their worst regular season in over 30 years. Finishing with a losing record, the team snuck into the playoffs with a fourth-place finish in the Adams Division. With 17 games left in the season, Jacques Lemaire ascended to the head coaching job. Not many took notice. After all, the Canadiens were given no chance to defeat the Boston Bruins, a team that had finished 29 points ahead of them in the standings, in their first-round best-of-five playoff series.

Plante flew in from Switzerland and sat in on a critical meeting to settle the most important decision facing the Canadiens as the postseason loomed. In an effort to catch the heavily favoured Bruins off guard, and because Lemaire found his current goaltending duo unacceptable, the Canadiens decided to start the unknown, unheralded, and seemingly over his head Steve Penney in the Montreal goal. Penney had played in only four games that year. He lost all four, while allowing 19 goals, for an unsightly goals-against average of 4.75.

After a satisfying training camp spent under Plante's tutelage the previous fall, Penney had been sent down to the AHL, where he stuck with the team as the third-string goaltender. Over the course of the season, again under Plante's influence, Penney had played himself into the starting job.

As the Canadiens skated onto the ice at the Boston Garden, there stood Steve Penney in front of the Montreal net. What went under-reported at the time was that Penney, who had considered retiring before the season, had come under the influence of Jacques Plante.

What happened next was one of the most surprising playoff performances in league history.

In the opening game of the series, Penney allowed only one goal in a 2–1 Canadiens upset victory. The second game, once again held in Boston, saw Penney repeat his performance, this time in a 3–1 win. Back in Montreal, Penney and the Canadiens completed the unlikeliest of upsets, with a 5–0 whitewash that sent the stunned Bruins home.

In the next round the Canadiens faced off with their provincial rivals from Quebec, the Nordiques. The WHA had been absorbed into the NHL in the fall of 1979, and since then the rivalry between the two clubs had grown to be the bitterest in the entire league. They had first met in the playoffs two years before, with the Nordiques scoring an over-time goal in the deciding fifth game.

Now Penney, with Plante watching intently from the sidelines, led the Canadiens in a fight-filled series that stood out for the level of passion displayed, with Montreal emerging as the winner.

Amazingly, the Canadiens found themselves as part of the NHL's final four, where they were paired off against the New York Islanders, the league's four-time defending champions. The magic continued in the first game as Penney and the Canadiens shut out the stunned Islanders 3–0 and then followed it with a 4–2 victory in the second game.

And although the Canadiens' dream run would come to an end with the Islanders winning the next four games over a beat-up, battered, and overmatched Montreal team, nobody would soon forget that thrilling spring when the unknown Steve Penney took the city on an exhilarating journey.

Standing in the background stood Jacques Plante, the architect of Penney's success, the author of his improbable transformation, and the man who brought him back from the brink of retirement.

30

SWITZERLAND

AFTER HIS RETIREMENT, Jacques Plante basked in the accolades and honours that can only come with a legendary career.

Less than three years after he had left his playing career behind, Plante received the phone call informing him of his induction into the Hockey Hall of Fame. Two months later, on September 13, 1978, he and Raymonde were the guests of honour at the presentation dinner for the Hall of Fame. The dinner was held at the Royal York Hotel, ironically a venue that had throughout Plante's career been a source of anxiety, as he readily blamed the hotel for his asthma attacks.

Plante shared the stage with two fellow inductees. The first was Marcel Pronovost, who had grown up with him in Shawinigan Falls, and the second was Andy Bathgate, the man who had taken the shot that night in Madison Square Garden, leading to Plante's donning a mask for the first time in league play.

Jacques' induction speech was given by Frank Selke, the man who had signed him to his first contract and who had assembled a team that many still regard as the game's greatest. For Jacques, enshrinement in the Hockey Hall of Fame was a validation, an acceptance by a hockey establishment that had so often been at odds with him. Following Selke's speech on that emotional night, Plante said, "The awards I won were for one season's play or a month's work in the playoffs. To be named to the Hall of Fame, however, is to be recognized for what you did in your lifetime and that's the best reward of all."[1]

Three years later Plante was inducted into another honoured institution when he was named to the Canadian Sports Hall of Fame. And while Jacques took special pride in these honours, one above all brought him the most personal satisfaction.

On the night of January 12, 1985, at the Montreal Forum, the Canadiens, the greatest of all sports franchises and an institution recognized worldwide, honoured their all-time "dream team" in recognition of their seventy-fifth anniversary. In a vote decided through a fan ballot, the team would be made up of one coach, one left winger, one centre, one right winger, two defencemen, and one goalie. The players, chosen from more than 20,000 ballots, would be honoured in a ceremony before the Canadiens' game that evening against the Buffalo Sabres.

The coach, decided in a landslide, was the great Toe Blake. The defence tandem was made up of Doug Harvey and Larry Robinson, the only active player chosen. On the left wing was Dickie Moore, while on the right wing Maurice "Rocket" Richard took the honours. Centring the two was the incomparable Jean Béliveau. And rounding out the team in goal was Jacques Plante.

The vote for the goaltender may have been the toughest, as it was the one position that had the longest list of legendary players. Yet Plante triumphed by a nearly two-to-one margin over his nearest competitor, Ken Dryden, the man who had led the team to six Stanley Cups in the 1970s. Following Dryden in the balloting was Plante's idol Bill Durnan, then Georges Vézina, and finally George Hainsworth.

In front of a standing-room-only crowd that included Canada's prime minister, Brian Mulroney, each man was introduced one by one, starting with Toe Blake, who took his bow at centre ice.

And then in the corner of the rink stood the man who had back-stopped the team to six Stanley Cups, including an unmatched five in a row, listening as his accomplishments were read over the loudspeaker. Jacques Plante had left the team more than 20 years before under the bitterest of circumstances, feeling hurt and betrayed. Tonight, he was back in the uniform he had once worn so proudly and with such distinction. After such a long absence, he had finally returned home.

He skated out to thunderous applause and raised both his arms in the air in his trademark acknowledgement of his fans' adoration. He skated towards centre ice and shook hands with his old coach before skating to where he had always felt the most comfortable – in front of the Canadiens net.

And then one by one each of the legends was introduced and came down and took a shot at him, Harvey, Robinson, Moore, Béliveau, Richard, and the team's oldest alumnus, Aurel Joliat. After dropping the ceremonial puck, the all-timers made their way off the ice, while the inheritors to their thrones took over.

It would be the last time that Jacques Plante ever skated on the hallowed Forum ice.

The next night at a fundraising gala dinner celebrating the team, attended by Prime Minister Mulroney and Montreal mayor Jean Drapeau, $35,000 was raised for needy and disabled children. As each member of the "dream team" was introduced, a video montage played of his greatest moments. It was a night to reminisce, to bask in the glow of what they had accomplished, and a chance for old friends to talk about the good days.

What none of them could have known that wonderful night was that they were also saying goodbye to Jacques Plante.

A year later, in January 1986, the St. Louis Blues came calling for Plante's services as a goaltending consultant. Working with Greg Millen and Rick Wamsley, who had studied under him with the Canadiens a few years before, he signed a contract to immediately begin tutoring the Blues goalies and promised to follow it up with a visit on the eve of the playoffs.

"Our goaltending has been good but we want it to get better," admitted St. Louis head coach Jacques Demers. "And we're not talking about just any guy. We're talking about Jacques Plante, the best there ever was."[2]

"He's your basic walking encyclopedia of how to play goal," said a happy Wamsley. "Instead of going to Page 347 you just ask him the question."[3]

"I don't want a full-time job," Plante stressed. "I'm doing what I like best now, talking goaltending. This has been my life, talking with goaltenders and knowing they appreciate it. My reward is seeing a big smile on their faces when they see me around. I don't want any more."[4]

Plante had been on the ice only for a few practices before, during a lunch break one day, Jacques Demers noticed that he spent the time poking at his food, hardly eating anything at all. A concerned Demers shared his observations with the Blues' team physician, Dr. J.G.

Probstein, who examined Plante. Probstein discovered that Plante had dropped over 15 pounds in the previous two weeks.

Probstein, who had held the same position with the Blues during Plante's tenure there, decided to X-ray Plante's stomach, even though he hadn't complained of feeling any pain. As soon as he looked at the results, Probstein knew immediately that it was cancer. He apprised Raymonde Plante of the situation, and it was agreed that it would be best not to tell her husband until they had returned home to Switzerland.

Probstein later said that he had been amazed that Plante had been so active, considering the advanced stage of the cancer. "He landed here with a hell of a mess in his stomach and he's out teaching guys how to play hockey."[5]

Plante and his wife immediately left for Switzerland, where he was diagnosed with stomach cancer and admitted to a Geneva hospital. But little could be done for him, as the cancer was so far advanced.

As time grew short, it was finally released to the media that Jacques had cancer, something that he had fought to keep private.

On the night of February 26, Raymonde Plante stayed by her husband's side until 10 o'clock. For the past three weeks she had held a constant vigil at his bedside. After watching the late-night news on the television, she returned home for the evening. At 5:25 a.m., Jacques' aorta burst, and he expired due to the resulting hemorrhage. He was 57 years old.

Like the rest of the world, Jean Béliveau had heard the news of Jacques' passing, and like many he assumed that Plante's remains would be flown back to Canada for burial. The day after his death, Béliveau was told that his old teammate would be going to his final resting place in Switzerland – in about 36 hours.

François Seigneur, the Canadiens' vice-president of marketing, asked him to go. "We've found a ticket on Air Canada to Zurich via Paris and the plane leaves at seven-fifty tonight from Mirabel," Seigneur said. "You're the only one who can go, and the league is asking, too. They'd like to be represented there, if possible. It's your choice, but you're the last person in the current organization who knew him and his family well. Can you make it?"[6]

Béliveau didn't hesitate. He quickly gathered a few things together in an overnight bag and headed for the airport. For him it was one last trip to pay respect to his former teammate. The two of them had come such a long way since the first time they met on the junior rinks of Quebec as teenagers. Once, they had spent time on the train as young men talking with each other about life and their goals and aspirations. Each of them had succeeded in his own way. And now Jean Béliveau was going to say goodbye.

The next morning, in a small church packed to overflowing, Jacques Plante was laid to rest.

"At the church, Raymonde led me by the hand into the first row of family mourners and I sat beside her during the service," Béliveau wrote later in his memoirs. "Outside the church, I learned once again how small our modern world can sometimes be. Two teams of peewee hockey players, wearing their sweaters over shirts and ties, had formed an honour guard at the door. One of their coaches looked very familiar to me – and I was staggered to learn that the peewees came from Victoriaville, my hometown. They were scheduled to play an exhibition game in Sierre later that day, having just crossed the Alps from Chamonix, France. When the coach heard of Jacques' death, and learned when his funeral would take place, he booked his team on an earlier train, to ensure they could attend and pay their respects to a fellow Canadian and Quebecer. It was a beautiful gesture appreciated by everyone."[7]

As the casket made its way from the church, it passed beneath two rows of the peewees' sticks, held aloft. It was a moving moment that seemed so right.

That evening Béliveau and Raymonde went out and watched a hockey game between Sierre and Kloten from the Swiss National League.

The next morning Béliveau packed his belongings for the trip back, then paid Raymonde one last visit. It was there that she presented him with a very precious and heartfelt gift. Handing him the homemade bottle of wine, Raymonde explained that Jacques had hand-picked the grapes from a small vineyard nearby, recording and numbering all the bottles by hand.

Béliveau looked down at bottle number 187 – a last gift from his teammate and friend.

AFTERWORD

THE SUDDEN DEATH of Jacques Plante prompted an outpouring of tributes and remembrances from those who had known him best, mixed in with praise reserved only for those who ascended to the highest levels of achievement in their chosen profession. Throughout Quebec the provincial flag flew at half-mast as a tribute to one of the greatest sportsmen the province had produced.

"The hockey world has lost one of its greatest stars, a true innovator whose influences helped shape the modern art of goaltending," said John Ziegler, president of the NHL. "Jacques' love of the game, along with his many talents, accomplishments, and durability over 17 National Hockey League seasons will always be remembered."[1]

"It's a big loss for hockey," remarked his old coach Toe Blake. "I had him through those five Stanley Cups the Canadiens won. Everybody said what a great team we had, but we also had a guy who could stop the puck. Without him we probably wouldn't have won five in a row."

"He was an individual who portrayed his own style," remembered Dickie Moore. "He wasn't a student of the game, he was the professor and he did it while he played, as well. He changed the style of the game. He loved being part of the game."

"He taught me some things on the ice," recalled Steve Penney, "but when I look back on it, he taught me a lot more on how to handle this game off the ice. He showed me how to forget bad games."[2]

Red Fisher, who had watched more Jacques Plante games than anybody else, simply stated, "He was the greatest goaltender I ever saw."[3]

On March 11, almost two weeks after his death, a memorial service was held at the Church of the Immaculate Conception in Montreal. Organized by the Montreal Canadiens at the urging of Jean Béliveau, the service was attended by Jacques' first wife, Jacqueline, his son Michel, and many former teammates.

Six months after her husband's death, Raymonde Plante established the Jacques Plante Foundation to aid in the development of young prospective Swiss goaltenders. On August 29, 1986, she wrote a cheque to begin the foundation's work.

Since Jacques' death, Raymonde has dedicated her life to preserving his legacy, while at the same time transferring his ideals to the next generation of puck stoppers. For the next 19 years she ran the foundation, often hand-picking the selected goalies herself, using criteria her late husband had taught her. Since its inception the foundation has sponsored clinics for minor league goalies and provided equipment for those less fortunate.

On the twentieth anniversary of her husband's death, Raymonde, with the assistance of Classic Collections, put together the Jacques Plante auction. Made up of 53 items, consisting of masks, jerseys, and personal memorabilia, the proceeds were to go to the Jacques Plante Foundation. The auction was a smashing success, with the highlight being the purchase of a game-worn mask, thought to be the third that Plante ever wore, by the Canadian Museum of Civilization, for $19,000. It's hard to imagine the government ever again bidding on a goaltending mask because of its historical value.

Raymonde also established the Jacques Plante Trophy, awarded annually to the best goaltender in the Swiss National League as voted on by the captains and coaches of the circuit. A glance at some of the names on the trophy illustrates the influence Jacques and Raymonde have had through their tireless efforts on behalf of Swiss hockey. Past winners include Jonas Hiller and Cristobal Huet, two Swiss-born goalies who are now starting goaltenders in the NHL, among an ever-growing list of Swiss players now populating the NHL.

In 2006, two decades after Plante's death, in what may have been the greatest moment in Swiss hockey history, the country's national team defeated Team Canada 2–0 at the Turin Olympics. Days later, Raymonde Plante received a postcard in the mail, signed by the whole Swiss team.

Despite his passing, a string of honours continued to be bestowed on Jacques Plante, many of them of the highly exclusive variety.

He was the subject of a *Heritage Minute*, one of only two hockey players so honoured. *Heritage Minutes* are 60-second films that illustrate a key moment in Canadian history. Now a whole new generation of Canadians was able to experience the night Jacques Plante changed the game of hockey forever, brought to life on their TV and cinema screens.

The *Heritage Minute* brought about a heightened awareness of Jacques Plante's role not only in hockey history but in Canadian history as well. Today, Canadian students are taught about Jacques Plante as part of their Canadian history curriculum.

On September 23, 1994, Plante was inducted into the Quebec Pantheon of Sports Heroes.

The Jacques Plante Trophy is awarded to the goaltender in the Quebec Junior Hockey League with the lowest goals-against average. The Shawinigan Arena, where Plante was once denied entry because of his age, now carries his name above the door.

In 1998 the *Hockey News* celebrated its fiftieth anniversary by convening an esteemed panel of writers, journalists, broadcasters, coaches, general managers, referees, and former players to select the top 100 players in hockey history. Ranked as the thirteenth best player in the game's history, Plante trailed only his rival Terry Sawchuk for the top goaltending honour.

As the millennium approached, *Time*, in a series of special issues commemorating the twentieth century, chose the 10 most influential athletes of the century. The list contained the giants of sport: Babe Ruth, Muhammad Ali, Pele, Michael Jordan, Secretariat – and Jacques Plante. Not only was Plante the only hockey player featured on *Time*'s prestigious list, he was also the only Canadian. "Gordie Howe was great, Bobby Orr greater, Wayne Gretzky the greatest – yet none altered the course of hockey quite so much as the piece of molded fiberglass that Jacques Plante affixed to his head on November 1, 1959," wrote Daniel Okrent, spotlighting the chosen 10.[4]

Magazines weren't the only media celebrating the twentieth century as it came to a close. ESPN assembled a multimedia project highlighting the greatest athletes of the century. *SportsCentury*, their acclaimed biographical show, used interviews along with archival footage to tell the stories of those that had forever shaped sport. Jacques Plante was one of a few hockey players to be featured among a list of well over a hundred luminaries from the sports world. The one-hour episode dedicated to him was aired in 2000.

TSN, Canada's sports network, produced its own special on Plante, as did the History Channel, which devoted an hour to his story on an episode of *The Canadians: Biographies of a Nation*.

On February 5, 2000, Canada Post, in commemoration of the fiftieth NHL all-star game, selected six of the game's greatest legends to be honoured with their own stamp: Wayne Gretzky, Bobby Orr, Gordie Howe, Maurice Richard, Doug Harvey – and Jacques Plante.

Yet among all these posthumous honours and accolades, it is hard to imagine Jacques Plante finding one more important than the one he received on October 7, 1995, when his number 1 jersey was raised to the rafters of the Montreal Forum, forever retired in his honour. On that most emotional of nights, his son Michel, flanked by Gerry McNeil on his left and Gump Worsley on his right, accepted the ultimate honour, thrusting his father's jersey in the air as the banner carrying his name and number took their rightful place among the greatest to ever wear the red, white, and blue. Finally, Jacques Plante was back home, this time for good.

Yet the greatest tribute to Jacques Plante can't be found on a trophy, or through a television show, or even on a stamp. The greatest tribute to Jacques Plante takes place every time a game of hockey is played. Many of those practising his methods today never saw him play, and many still may not know who he was, but every time a goaltender puts on a mask, or plays the puck, or talks with his defencemen, he is the heir to the legacy of Jacques Plante, a man whose continued influence lingers over the game that he loved so much.

ACKNOWLEDGEMENTS

Writing a biography is similar to putting together a puzzle. You start with a quantity of different-sized and different-shaped pieces and a clean slate. Over time the pieces are slowly placed on the table as you try to find the ones that interlock with what you already have. Often, the pieces you thought would fit don't, while the ones that at first glance appear to be totally wrong later, after some trying it this way and that way, take on a perfect fit.

You spend what seems like an endless amount of time envisioning what the finished puzzle is going to look like as you assemble it one piece at a time. Then there are times when you think the final puzzle has eluded you or that you must have lost some of the pieces.

It is in those moments that you understand that even though it is your name on the book cover, a book is truly a collaborative effort that would be impossible without the help and encouragement of many people.

First and foremost, I would like to thank my agent, Arnold Gosewich, who not only took a chance on a first-time author but was also the guiding force in getting this book done.

I would also like to thank my publisher, McClelland & Stewart, and more specifically Doug Pepper and Eric Jensen for their unbridled enthusiasm for the book. In addition, I would like to thank my editor, Elizabeth Kribs, for bringing a fresh perspective and her keen insight to the manuscript, and my copy editor, Shaun Oakey, for steering the manuscript to completion.

In the course of my research I was able to spend a few days at the Hockey Hall of Fame's resource centre, where I was able to peruse their wide variety of archival materials. In particular, I would like to convey my gratitude to Miragh Addis for being extremely helpful and accommodating and to Craig Campbell for opening up the Hall's photo archives for use in the book.

A researcher's work is only as good as the libraries he or she frequents. The library at Queen's University houses a treasure trove of archived newspapers and was extremely crucial to my research. I would like to express my appreciation to Karen MacLeod of the New Glasgow Library as well as the Pictou County Roots Society, both based in New Glasgow, Nova Scotia. David Smith of the St. Clair County Library System, in Port Huron, Michigan, and Lisa Greenhouse of the Enoch Pratt Free Library, in Baltimore, Maryland, were both kind enough to forward me photocopies from their newspaper archives. I would also like to thank Nancy Fay of the National Archives of Canada for the use of some of the photographs.

I was extremely fortunate to be forwarded video footage of Jacques Plante from the archives of CTV Montreal, formerly CFCF. I would like to express my appreciation to Bob Turcotte and Bob Povacz for taking time out of their busy schedules.

Allan Stitt may possess the finest private collection of original hockey contracts and NHL correspondence in the world, and I was fortunate enough to spend a morning in his office going over his documents that featured Jacques Plante. The chapter on Plante's grievance with Harry Sinden and the Boston Bruins would have been impossible without his help.

I wish to extend my heartfelt thanks to my fellow members in the Society for International Hockey Research, many of whom have been extremely generous and forthcoming with their suggestions and advice. In particular, I would like to thank Kevin Shea, Paul Patskou, Lloyd Davis, and Len Kotylo.

I am wholly indebted to the following people for going out of their way to help me along the path: Red Fisher, Dave Stubbs, Robert Lefebvre, Joe Pelletier, David Shoalts, Howard Morenz, Matt Gauthier, Sebastien Tremblay, Philip Abbott, Glen Woodrow, and John Ovens.

On a personal note I would like to single out the following people for their unwavering support and enthusiasm during the course of writing this book: Michael and Jane Thompson, Lloyd and Fran Jones, Derek and Sandra Eagleson, Nate and Jennifer Jones, Matt and Delta Jones, Nick and Mandy McKinley, Brett Mills, James Jones, Tim Horgan, Michele Labossiere, Rob Davis, Denis Collier, James Baxter, and Terry Connors.

Most of all I would like to thank those who accepted my request to be interviewed for the book. Without them this book would not have been possible. I would like to thank each of these men who took the time to share their memories, allowing me a better understanding and appreciation of the life and times of Jacques Plante.

NOTES

PROLOGUE

1   Andy O'Brien and Jacques Plante, *The Jacques Plante Story*, p. 94.
2   O'Brien and Plante, *The Jacques Plante Story*, p. 94.
3   O'Brien and Plante, *The Jacques Plante Story*, p. 94.
4   "Tape Measure Gives Plante Last Laugh," *Toronto Star*, January 29, 1963, p. 9.

CHAPTER 1: THE SEEDS OF THE MAN

1   Ben Olan, "The Jacques Plante Story," *Hockey Illustrated*, November 1962, p. 32.
2   Andy O'Brien and Jacques Plante, *The Jacques Plante Story*, pp. 3, 26.
3   O'Brien and Plante, *The Jacques Plante Story*, p. 27.
4   O'Brien and Plante, *The Jacques Plante Story*, p. 27.
5   "Jacques Plante," *ESPN SportsCentury*, interview with Frank Orr, November 8, 2000.
6   Dickie Moore, interview by the author, November 14, 2008.
7   Frank Orr, interview by the author, January 9, 2009.
8   Marcel Pronovost, interview by the author, November 29, 2008.
9   O'Brien and Plante, *The Jacques Plante Story*, p. 27.
10 O'Brien and Plante, *The Jacques Plante Story*, p. 110.
11 Frank Orr, *Great Goalies of Pro Hockey*, p. 128.
12 O'Brien and Plante, *The Jacques Plante Story*, p. 28.
13 Mike Leonetti, *Canadiens Legends*, p. 6.
14 O'Brien and Plante, *The Jacques Plante Story*, pp. 3–4.
15 Raymond Plante, *Jacques Plante*, pp. 16–17.
16 O'Brien and Plante, *The Jacques Plante Story*, p. 29.
17 Chrys Goyens and Allan Turowetz, *Lions in Winter*, p. 160.

CHAPTER 2: THE ARCHITECT

1   Chrys Goyens and Allan Turowetz, *Lions in Winter*, pp. 106–7.
2   Goyens and Turowetz, *Lions in Winter*, p. 102.
3   Goyens and Turowetz, *Lions in Winter*, p. 109.
4   Goyens and Turowetz, *Lions in Winter*, p. 105.
5   Frank Selke with H. Gordon Green, *Behind the Cheering*, p. 134.
6   D'Arcy Jenish, *The Montreal Canadiens*, p. 120.
7   Goyens and Turowetz, *Lions in Winter*, p. 105.
8   Goyens and Turowetz, *Lions in Winter*, p. 108.
9   Jenish, *The Montreal Canadiens*, p. 118.
10 Goyens and Turowetz, *Lions in Winter*, p. 109.
11 Goyens and Turowetz, *Lions in Winter*, p. 111.

CHAPTER 3: NECESSITY IS THE MOTHER OF INVENTION

1   Frank J. Selke to Clarence Campbell, December 15, 1947. Allan Stitt collection.
2   Selke to Campbell, December 15, 1947.
3   Bernard Geoffrion and Stan Fischler, *Boom Boom*, p. 19.
4   Andy O'Brien and Jacques Plante, *The Jacques Plante Story*, p. 30.
5   "Quebec Citadels Win Over JAHA Royals," Montreal *Gazette*, November 7, 1947.
6   Conn Smythe to D. Pinard, December 12, 1947. Allan Stitt collection.
7   Selke to Campbell, December 15, 1947.
8   Dickie Moore, interview by the author, November 14, 2008.
9   O'Brien and Plante, *The Jacques Plante Story*, p. 32.
10 O'Brien and Plante, *The Jacques Plante Story*, p. 32.
11 Frank Orr, *Great Goalies of Pro Hockey*, p. 24.
12 Frank Orr and George Tracz, *The Dominators*, n.p.
13 Orr and Tracz, *The Dominators*.
14 Jean Béliveau, Chrys Goyens, and Allan Turowetz, *Jean Béliveau*, p. 41.
15 Lorne Worsley and Tim Moriarty, *They Call Me Gump*, pp. 11–12.
16 O'Brien and Plante, *The Jacques Plante Story*, p. 32.

CHAPTER 4: PATIENCE IS A VIRTUE

1   Andy O'Brien and Jacques Plante, *The Jacques Plante Story*, p. 33.
2   "Jacques Plante," *ESPN SportsCentury*, interview with Michel Plante, December 8, 2000.
3   O'Brien and Plante, *The Jacques Plante Story*, p. 33.
4   O'Brien and Plante, *The Jacques Plante Story*, p. 33.
5   Douglas Hunter, *A Breed Apart*, p. 85.
6   http://www.legendsofhockey.net/html/spot_oneononep196402.htm.
7   Elmer Lach, interview by the author, January 15, 2009.
8   "Plante Risked Wrist Operation in Effort to Gain Greatness," *Hockey News*, April 10, 1954, p. 3.
9   O'Brien and Plante, *The Jacques Plante Story*, p. 34.
10 Dick Irvin, *In the Crease*, p. 11.
11 "Plante Risked Wrist Operation," p. 3.
12 "Plante Risked Wrist Operation," p. 3.
13 O'Brien and Plante, *The Jacques Plante Story*, p. 34.

CHAPTER 5: A GRAND ENTRANCE

1   Andy O'Brien and Jacques Plante, *The Jacques Plante Story*, p. 35.
2   O'Brien and Plante, *The Jacques Plante Story*, p. 35.
3   "McNeil Out Indefinitely; Plante Takes Over," Montreal *Gazette*, October 31, 1952, p. 29.
4   Dick Irvin Jr., interview by the author, September 29, 2008.
5   O'Brien and Plante, *The Jacques Plante Story*, p. 37.
6   O'Brien and Plante, *The Jacques Plante Story*, p. 38.
7   Elmer Ferguson, Montreal *Herald*, November 1, 1952, quoted in O'Brien and Plante, *The Jacques Plante Story*, pp. 38–39.
8   Raymond Plante, *Jacques Plante*, p. 39.
9   O'Brien and Plante, *The Jacques Plante Story*, pp. 39–40.
10 O'Brien and Plante, *The Jacques Plante Story*, p. 40.
11 O'Brien and Plante, *The Jacques Plante Story*, p. 40.
12 Dink Carroll, "Richard Fails to Break Record as Habs Win," Montreal *Gazette*, November 3, 1952, p. 22.
13 O'Brien and Plante, *The Jacques Plante Story*, pp. 40, 41.
14 Baz O'Meara, *Montreal Star*, November 3, 1952, quoted in O'Brien and Plante, *The Jacques Plante Story*, p. 41.

CHAPTER 6: JAKE THE SNAKE

1   *TSN Profile*, interview with Ken Reardon, 2001.
2   Jack Horrigan, "'Jake the Snake' Plante Big Boon to Buffalo Bisons," *Hockey News*, February 7, 1953, p. 12.
3   Horrigan, "Jake the Snake," p. 12.
4   Larry Bortstein, *My Greatest Day in Hockey*, p. 126.
5   Andy O'Brien and Jacques Plante, *The Jacques Plante Story*, p. 45.
6   O'Brien and Plante, *The Jacques Plante Story*, p. 45.
7   O'Brien and Plante, *The Jacques Plante Story*, p. 46.
8   O'Brien and Plante, *The Jacques Plante Story*, p. 46.
9   O'Brien and Plante, *The Jacques Plante Story*, pp. 44–45.
10 O'Brien and Plante, *The Jacques Plante Story*, p. 46.
11 Bud Booth, "Playoff Madness Grips Chicago, Frenzied Fans Envision Stanley Cup," *Hockey News*, April 11, 1953, p. 2.
12 O'Brien and Plante, *The Jacques Plante Story*, p. 47.
13 Dick Irvin, *Now Back to You, Dick*, p. 59.
14 O'Brien and Plante, *The Jacques Plante Story*, p. 47.
15 O'Brien and Plante, *The Jacques Plante Story*, p. 47.
16 *Don Cherry's Grapevine*, interview with Danny Gallivan, 2001.
17 O'Brien and Plante, *The Jacques Plante Story*, p. 48.
18 Bortstein, *My Greatest Day*, pp. 126, 128.
19 Baz O'Meara, *Montreal Star*, April 5, 1953, quoted in O'Brien and Plante, *The Jacques Plante Story*, p. 48.
20 Dink Carroll, "Canadiens Rout Hawks 4–1 to Reach Stanley Cup Final," Montreal *Gazette*, April 8, 1953, p. 21.
21 Douglas Hunter, *A Breed Apart*, p. 119.
22 O'Brien and Plante, *The Jacques Plante Story*, p. 51.

CHAPTER 7: A SENSATION

1   Andy O'Brien and Jacques Plante, *The Jacques Plante Story*, p. 52.
2   O'Brien and Plante, *The Jacques Plante Story*, p. 52.
3   O'Brien and Plante, *The Jacques Plante Story*, pp. 52–53.
4   O'Brien and Plante, *The Jacques Plante Story*, p. 53.
5   Vince Lunny, "Plante Gains Big League Rating, Has Phenomenal 1.58 GA Average," *Hockey News*, April 10, 1954, p. 2.
6   D'Arcy Jenish, *The Montreal Canadiens*, p. 140.
7   Jack Horrigan, "When Plante Left Buffalo for Montreal He Expected to Be Back in a Few Days," *Hockey News*, April 17, 1954, p. 8.
8   Lunny, "Plante Gains Big League Rating," p. 2.
9   Lunny, "Plante Gains Big League Rating," p. 2.
10 Lunny, "Plante Gains Big League Rating," p. 2.
11 Pat Curran, "Bewildered Hero Says 'Thanks' as Pals Roar," Montreal *Gazette*, March 26, 1954, p. 23.
12 Dick Irvin, *The Habs*, p. 105.
13 Irvin, *The Habs*, p. 107.
14 Irvin, *The Habs*, p. 111.
15 Irvin, *The Habs*, pp. 108–9.
16 "Plante Uncertain Starter in Cup Series Opener in Detroit," Montreal *Gazette*, April 3, 1954, p. 23.
17 Dink Carroll, "Wings Strike Early, Jolt Habs 5–2, Lead Series," Montreal *Gazette*, April 9, 1954, p. 22.
18 Baz O'Meara, *Montreal Star*, April 11, 1954, quoted in Brian Kendall, *Shutout*, p. 107.
19 "Irvin Undecided About Goalie? The Gloomy Dean Is Only Kidding," *Toronto Star*, April 15, 1954, p. 20.
20 Irvin, *The Habs*, p. 111.
21 Pierre Proulx, *La Presse*, April 17, 1954, quoted in Jenish, *The Montreal Canadiens*, p. 141.
22 Dick Irvin, *My 26 Stanley Cups*, p. 63.

CHAPTER 8: THE ROCKET

1   Dickie Moore, interview by the author, November 14, 2008.
2   Douglas Hunter, *A Breed Apart*, p. 119.
3   Hunter, *A Breed Apart*, p. 119.
4   Pat Curran, "Habs Goalie Gerry McNeil Decides to Retire From Hockey," Montreal *Gazette*, September 27, 1954, p. 27.
5   Curran, "Habs Goalie Gerry McNeil," p. 27.
6   Vince Lunny, "History Repeats – McNeil Quits as Nerves Give Out!" *Hockey News*, October 9, 1954, p. 3.
7   Andy O'Brien and Jacques Plante, *The Jacques Plante Story*, p. 54.
8   O'Brien and Plante, *The Jacques Plante Story*, p. 54.
9   "Dial 'M' for Montreal Misfortune!!!," *Toronto Star*, September 28, 1954, p. 20.
10 "Plante, Defence Shine for High-Flying Habs," *Toronto Star*, November 1, 1954, p. 18.
11 Chrys Goyens and Allan Turowetz, *Lions in Winter*, p. 94.
12 Jean Béliveau, Chrys Goyens, and Allan Turowetz, *Jean Béliveau*, p. 94.
13 Dick Irvin, *The Habs*, p. 116.

14 Béliveau, Goyens, and Turowetz, *Jean Béliveau*, p. 100.

15 "Tears, Threats Flow Over Rocket," *Montreal Star*, March 17, 1955, p. 50.

16 Irvin, *The Habs*, p. 122.

17 O'Brien and Plante, *The Jacques Plante Story*, p. 58.

18 Marcel Pronovost, interview by the author, November 29, 2008.

19 Dick Irvin, *My 26 Stanley Cups*, p. 71.

20 http://archives.cbc.ca/sports/hockey.

21 Frank Selke with H. Gordon Green, *Behind the Cheering*, p. 142.

22 O'Brien and Plante, *The Jacques Plante Story*, p. 65.

23 Bernard Geoffrion and Stan Fischler, *Boom Boom*, p. 79.

24 Marcel Pronovost interview.

25 Selke and Green, *Behind the Cheering*, p. 144.

CHAPTER 9: THE DAWNING OF A NEW ERA

1 D'Arcy Jenish, *The Montreal Canadiens*, pp. 151–52.

2 Jenish, *The Montreal Canadiens*, p. 152.

3 Dickie Moore, interview by the author, November 14, 2008.

4 Andy O'Brien and Jacques Plante, *The Jacques Plante Story*, p. 68.

5 Eric Duhatschek, "Canadien Dream Team," *Hockey News*, December 17, 1999, p. 14.

6 O'Brien and Plante, *The Jacques Plante Story*, p. 68.

7 O'Brien and Plante, *The Jacques Plante Story*, p. 69.

8 Jenish, *The Montreal Canadiens*, p. 153.

9 Dickie Moore interview.

10 Dickie Moore interview.

11 Andy O'Brien, "Andy O'Brien Says . . .," *Montreal Star*, December 3, 1955, p. 55.

12 Duhatschek, "Canadien Dream Team," p. 15.

13 "All Eyes on the Ice," *Sports Illustrated*, January 23, 1956, p. 13.

14 Jacques Plante and Len Bramson, "Jacques Plante on Goaltending: It's an Unpredictable Business," *Hockey Pictorial*, February 1956, p. 33.

15 Plante and Bramson, "Jacques Plante on Goaltending," p. 33.

16 Baz O'Meara, "Habs See Early Rout of Rangers After Sweep," *Montreal Star*, March 26, 1956, p. 28.

17 Baz O'Meara, "'Rocket' Equals Assists Mark as Canucks Eliminate Blues," *Montreal Star*, March 28, 1956, p. 62.

18 Ken Campbell, *Habs Heroes*, p. 40.

19 Brian Kendall, *Shutout*, pp. 135–36.

20 Baz O'Meara, "Habs Trounce Wings, Eye Stanley Cup Sweep," *Montreal Star*, April 4, 1956, p. 63.

21 "Blake Praises Plante for Puck-Stopping Job," *Montreal Star*, April 9, 1956, p. 18.

22 Baz O'Meara, "The Passing Sport Show," *Montreal Star*, April 10, 1956, p. 28.

23 Baz O'Meara, "Habs Seen Heavy Favourites to End Wings' Cup Domination," *Montreal Star*, April 10, 1956, p. 28.

24 Baz O'Meara, "The Passing Sport Show," *Montreal Star*, April 11, 1956, p. 54.

25 Baz O'Meara, "Canadiens Clip Red Wings to Grab Stanley Cup," *Montreal Star*, April 11, 1956, p. 54.

26 Baz O'Meara, "The Passing Sport Show," *Montreal Star*, April 11, 1956, p. 54.

27 Duhatschek, "Canadien Dream Team," p. 15.

1   Bernard Geoffrion and Stan Fischler, *Boom Boom*, p. 100.

2   Red Fisher, *Hockey, Heroes, and Me*, p. 119.

3   William Brown, *Doug*, p. 154.

4   Brown, *Doug*, p. 154.

5   Brown, *Doug*, p. 154.

6   "Jacques Plante," *ESPN SportsCentury*, interview with Scotty Bowman, December 8, 2000.

7   Ben Olan, "The Jacques Plante Story," *Hockey Illustrated*, November 1962, p. 73.

8   "Habs Play, Think as Team – Blake," *Toronto Star*, October 12, 1956, p. 26.

9   D'Arcy Jenish, *The Montreal Canadiens*, p. 155.

10 O'Brien and Plante, *The Jacques Plante Story*, p. 74.

11 O'Brien and Plante, *The Jacques Plante Story*, p. 74.

12 O'Brien and Plante, *The Jacques Plante Story*, p. 74.

13 Vince Lunny, "Acrobatic Jacques Plante Has Unique Style," *Hockey News*, February 9, 1957, p. 3.

14 Baz O'Meara, "Four-goal Eruption by 'Rocket' Sinks Hub in Playoff Opener," *Montreal Star*, April 8, 1957, p. 32.

15 John Devaney and Burt Goldblatt, *The Stanley Cup*, p. 165.

16 "Canadiens Set Sights on Stanley Cup Clincher," *Montreal Star*, April 16, 1957, p. 52.

17 Milt Dunnell, "The Secret of Jake the Snake," *Toronto Star*, April 12, 1957, p. 20.

CHAPTER 11: THE TRUE TEST OF A CHAMPION

1   "Jacques Plante," *ESPN SportsCentury*, interview with Jack Falla, December 8, 2000.

2   Milt Dunnell, "Jacques Sleeps Well, Eats Often," *Toronto Star*, December 6, 1957, p. 28.

3   Red Fisher, "'Boom Boom' to Leave Hospital Within Two Weeks, Says Doctor," *Montreal Star*, January 29, 1958, p. 36.

4   "Moore Suffers Broken Wrist, Tries Cast Against Rangers," *Montreal Star*, February 21, 1958, p. 28.

5   Red Fisher, "Hodge Called to Replace Injured Jacques Plante," *Montreal Star*, March 14, 1958, p. 54.

6   "Plante Says He Didn't See Play Which Put Him on Injury List," *Montreal Star*, March 15, 1958, p. 55.

7   Fisher, "Hodge Called," p. 54.

8   Red Fisher, "Goyette, 'Rocket' Blast Playoff Lead for Habs," *Montreal Star*, March 26, 1958, p. 52.

9   Red Fisher, "Wings Cup Hopes Fade After Habs' Great Victory," *Montreal Star*, March 31, 1958, p. 16.

10 Fisher, "Wings Cup Hopes Fade," p. 16.

11 Red Fisher, "Playoff Pressure Performance Old 'Hat' to Fabulous Rocket," *Montreal Star*, April 2, 1958, p. 56.

12 Red Fisher, "Quick Move by Béliveau Aids Habs' First Cup Win," *Montreal Star*, April 9, 1958, p. 54.

13 Red Burnett, "It Makes Me Feel Young: Rocket," *Toronto Star*, April 18, 1958, p. 18.

14 Dick Irvin, *My 26 Stanley Cups*, p. 80.

15   Burnett, "It Makes Me Feel Young," p. 18.
16   "Plante Breaks Down, Cries," *Toronto Star*, April 21, 1958, p. 22.

CHAPTER 12: SOLITARY MAN

1   Henri Richard, interview by the author, December 2, 2008.
2   Phil Goyette, interview by the author, October 5, 2008.
3   Ben Olan, "The Jacques Plante Story," *Hockey Illustrated*, October 1962, p. 74.
4   Jean Béliveau, interview by the author, October 6, 2008.
5   Jean Béliveau, Chrys Goyens, and Allan Turowetz, *Jean Béliveau*, p. 135.
6   Dickie Moore, interview by the author, November 14, 2008.
7   Jacques Plante, *On Goaltending*, p. i.
8   Henri Richard interview.
9   Phil Goyette interview.
10 Bob Duff, *Without Fear*, p. 33.
11 "Smythe May Gamble on Veteran Rollins, Hawk Deal Pending," *Toronto Star*, June 3, 1958, p. 17.
12 "Report NHL May Keep Goalie in Net," *Toronto Star*, June 2, 1958, p. 22.
13 Jean Béliveau interview.
14 Kenneth Rudeen, "The Habs Have Put It On Ice," *Sports Illustrated*, February 17, 1958, p. 32.
15 Red Fisher, "Plante Rises to Heights," *Montreal Star*, October 27, 1958, p. 21.
16 Red Fisher, "'Long Walk' for Goalie," *Montreal Star*, November 3, 1958, p. 27.
17 Fisher, "'Long Walk,'" p. 27.
18 Jim Proudfoot, "Jacques' Jitters Woe for Toe," *Toronto Star*, November 12, 1958, p. 24.
19 "Canadiens Watch Last Season's Film to Get in 'Winning' Mood for Playoffs," *Montreal Star*, March 24, 1959, p. 32.
20 Chrys Goyens and Allan Turowetz, *Lions in Winter*, p. 118.
21 "Pilous Praises Effort by Skov," *Montreal Star*, March 30, 1959, p. 31.
22 Bernard Geoffrion and Stan Fischler, *Boom Boom*, p. 34.
23 Red Fisher, *Hockey, Heroes and Me*, p. 146.
24 Geoffrion and Fischler, *Boom Boom*, p. 135.
25 Dick Irvin, *The Habs*, p. 167.
26 Geoffrion and Fischler, *Boom Boom*, p. 136.
27 "Selke Hopes Rivalry Won't Cause Flareup," *Montreal Star*, April 9, 1959, p. 48.
28 Dick Irvin, *My 26 Stanley Cups*, p. 80.

CHAPTER 13: CHANGING THE FACE OF HOCKEY

1   Bernard Geoffrion and Stan Fischler, *Boom Boom*, p. 17.
2   Geoffrion and Fischler, *Boom Boom*, p. 72.
3   "Masked Marvel," *Time*, November 23, 1959.
4   Glen Liebman, *Hockey Shorts*, p. 147.
5   Kenneth Rudeen, "A Long, Cold Road to Fame," *Sports Illustrated*, January 12, 1959, p. 32.
6   Rudeen, "A Long, Cold Road," p. 32.
7   Andy Bathgate, interview by the author, September 16, 2008.
8   Red Fisher, "The Night Jacques Plante Made Goaltending History," www.NHL.com, November 1, 2007.

9   Andy Bathgate interview.

10 Fisher, "The Night Jacques Plante Made Goaltending History."

11 Red Fisher, *Hockey Heroes, and Me*, p. 165.

12 Andy O'Brien and Jacques Plante, *The Jacques Plante Story*, p. 14.

13 Bob Carter, "Plante Changed Goaltending," www.espn.com, 2007.

14 *Hockey News*, October 3, 1959, p. 8.

15 Fisher, *Hockey, Heroes, and Me*, p. 166.

16 *Hockey News*, October 10, 1959, pp. 6, 12.

17 Fisher, *Hockey, Heroes, and Me*, p. 166.

18 "Plante Plumps for Face Masks for All Goalies," *Hockey Pictorial*, October 1959, p. 29.

19 Charlie Halpin, "Jacques Plante Wants to Be the Man in the Mask," *Hockey Pictorial*, November 1959, p. 10.

20 O'Brien and Plante, *The Jacques Plante Story*, p. 15.

21 Dick Irvin, *In the Crease*, p. 12.

22 Roch Carrier, *Our Life with the Rocket*, p. 284.

23 Fisher, *Hockey, Heroes, and Me*, p. 165.

CHAPTER 14: SELLING THE MASK

1   Jean Béliveau, interview by the author, October 6, 2008.

2   Bernard Geoffrion and Stan Fischler, *Boom Boom*, p. 143.

3   "Monster," *Toronto Star*, October 3, 1959, p. 35.

4   Arthur Pincus, *The Official Illustrated NHL History*, p. 94.

5   Stan Fischler, "Masked Marvel Plante Will Be Missed," *Hockey News*, March 14, 1986, p. 6.

6   Geoffrion and Fischler, *Boom Boom*, p. 144.

7   Stan Fischler, "More Chatter Brings Big 'Never' from Little Gump," *Hockey News*, November 14, 1959, p. 5.

8   Fischler, "More Chatter," p. 5.

9   Red Fisher, *Hockey, Heroes, and Me*, p. 166.

10 Kevin Allen and Bob Duff, *Without Fear*, p. 31.

11 Andy O'Brien and Jacques Plante, *The Jacques Plante Story*, p. 16.

12 Bob Carter, "More Info on Jacques Plante," www.espn.com, March 21, 1951.

13 Milt Dunnell, "About Masks, Men and Underwear," *Toronto Star*, November 5, 1959, p. 12.

14 Fischler, "More Chatter," p. 5.

15 Red Fisher, "The Night Jacques Plante Made Goaltending History," www.NHL.com, November 1, 2007.

16 "Masked Marvel," *Time*, November 23, 1959.

17 Fischler, "More Chatter," p. 5.

18 Fred Addis, "The Year of the Mask: 1959–60," *SIHR Hockey Research Journal* 2005, p. 42.

19 Bob Duff, "Do Fewer Stitches Mean More Red Lights?" *Hockey News Special Edition: Greatest Masks of All Time*, 2008, p. 53.

20 Arturo F. Gonzalez Jr., "Hockey's Faceless Wonder," *Modern Man*, November 1960.

21 "Masked Marvel," *Time*, November 23, 1959.

22 O'Brien and Plante, *The Jacques Plante Story*, pp. 17–18.

23   Red Fisher, "Plante Hits New Heights," *Montreal Star*, November 2, 1959, p. 18.

24   "Jacques Plante to Wear Mask Against Rangers Tonight," Montreal *Gazette*, November 5, 1959, p. 20.

25   Geoffrion and Fischler, *Boom Boom*, p. 146.

26   *Hockey 1964: Official Sports Magazine*.

27   "A Lifesaver Plante Says of His Mask," *Toronto Star*, September 29, 1983.

28   Charlie Halpin, "'Pocket' Real Vet as Habs Clutch Clouter," *Hockey News*, December 5, 1959, p. 5.

29   Halpin, "'Pocket' Real Vet," p. 5.

30   Charlie Halpin, "Now it Can Be Told: Toe Would Like Plante to Junk His Mask," *Hockey News*, January 2, 1960, p. 2.

31   Red Fisher, "Plante Checks Hot Leafs as 'Pocket' Scores Brace," *Montreal Star*, December 31, 1959, p. 13.

32   Jim Proudfoot, "Victory Never Has Been That Important – Selke," *Toronto Star*, December 30, 1959, p. 13.

33   Hal Bock, *Save!* p. 39.

34   Charlie Halpin, "Plante on Hot Seat in Vezina Cup Race," *Hockey News*, March 19, 1960, p. 1.

35   Jim Proudfoot, "Plante Is Unmasked He Still Gets Beaten," *Toronto Star*, March 9, 1960, p. 10.

36   "Plante Still Likes Mask," *Toronto Star*, March 9, 1960, p. 10.

37   O'Brien and Plante, *The Jacques Plante Story*, p. 13.

38   Jim Hunt, *The Men in the Nets*, p. 26.

39   Halpin, "Plante on Hot Seat," p. 1.

40   Halpin, "Plante on Hot Seat," p. 1.

41   Halpin, "Plante on Hot Seat," p. 1.

CHAPTER 15: THE PINNACLE

1   Red Fisher, interview by the author, September 6, 2008.

2   Red Fisher, "McNeil Happy Plante Played," *Montreal Star*, March 21, 1960, p. 24.

3   "Goalers' Duels Shaping Up for Stanley Cup Playoffs," *Montreal Star*, March 22, 1960, p. 32.

4   Red Fisher, "Hull Rated Likely Starter as Hawks Seek 'Equalizer,'" *Montreal Star*, March 25, 1960, p. 53.

5   Red Fisher, "Habs' Harvey Sheds 'Goat' Horns as Overtime Goal Beats Hawks," *Montreal Star*, March 28, 1960, p. 27.

6   Fisher, "Habs' Harvey," p. 27.

7   Red Fisher, "Habs Win Away From Final as 'Kids' Scalp Chihawks," *Montreal Star*, March 30, 1960, p. 53.

8   Red Fisher, "Habs Hope Plante Retains Edge," *Montreal Star*, March 31, 1960, p. 62.

9   Red Fisher, "Sweep Chihawks in Four Games," *Montreal Star*, April 1, 1960, p. 26.

10   Fisher, "Sweep Chihawks," p. 26.

11   Red Burnett, "Big Difference Is Down the Middle," *Toronto Star*, April 11, 1960, p. 10.

12   Red Burnett, "Can Leafs Stop 4-game Sweep?" *Toronto Star*, April 13, 1960, p. 14.

12   Red Fisher, "Rocket Grabs Ice Souvenir 'Just in Case' – Habs Romp," *Montreal Star*, April 13, 1960, p. 64.

14   Red Fisher, "Says Goaler Key to Canucks' Success," *Montreal Star*, April 14, 1960, p. 60.

15   Fisher, "Says Goaler Key," p. 60.
16   Milt Dunnell, "Wondering with Monsieur Plante," *Toronto Star*, April 13, 1960, p. 14.
17   D'Arcy Jenish, *The Montreal Canadiens*, p. 162.
18   "Jacques Plante," *ESPN SportsCentury*, interview with Tom Johnson, December 8, 2000.
19   Dick Irvin, *The Habs*, p. 147.
20   Red Fisher interview.
21   "Jacques Plante," *The Canadians*, interview with Red Fisher, 2000.

CHAPTER 16: ONE STEP BACK
1   Maurice Richard and Stan Fischler, *The Flying Frenchmen*, pp. 289–90.
2   Andy O'Brien and Jacques Plante, *The Jacques Plante Story*, p. 81.
3   Red Fisher, "It's Up to Plante Says Canuck Coach Over Mask Problem," *Montreal Star*, November 3, 1960, p. 60.
4   "Canadiens Goalie Plante on 'Hot Seat,'" *Montreal Star*, November 12, 1960, p. 61.
5   Red Fisher, "Close Call for Plante," *Montreal Star*, November 14, 1960, p. 36.
6   Dick Bacon, "Blake Gives Jacques Vote of Confidence Despite GA Record," *Hockey News*, November 19, 1960, p. 7.
7   Milt Dunnell, "Arab Plante and Camel Hodge," *Toronto Star*, December 7, 1960, p. 18.
8   "Canuck Goalie Plante Still Bothered By Knee," *Montreal Star*, December 10, 1960, p. 54.
9   Red Fisher, "Plante Wants Job Back," *Montreal Star*, January 5, 1961, p. 61.
10   Red Fisher, "Plante Agrees Hodge Remain in Canucks' Nets," *Montreal Star*, January 7, 1961, p. 21.
11   O'Brien and Plante, *The Jacques Plante Story*, pp. 85–86.
12   Jack Olsen, "Hero's Humiliation in Montreal," *Sports Illustrated*, February 6, 1961.
13   Lloyd McGowan, "Plante's Antics Boost Crowds for Circuit," *Montreal Star*, February 6, 1961, p. 13.
14   Olsen, "Hero's Humiliation."
15   O'Brien and Plante, *The Jacques Plante Story*, p. 87.
16   Red Burnett, "When Plante's in Best Form Then Habs Are Unbeatable," *Toronto Star*, February 16, 1961, p. 16.

CHAPTER 17: THE END OF THE LINE
1   Bernard Geoffrion and Stan Fischler, *Boom Boom*, p. 163.
2   Geoffrion and Fischler, *Boom Boom*, p. 163.
3   Red Fisher, *Hockey, Heroes, and Me*, pp. 176–77, 178, 180.
4   Dickie Moore, interview by the author, November 14, 2008.
5   Geoffrion and Fischler, *Boom Boom*, p. 165.
6   Geoffrion and Fischler, *Boom Boom*, p. 165.
7   Geoffrion and Fischler, *Boom Boom*, p. 165.
8   Geoffrion and Fischler, *Boom Boom*, p. 165.
9   Red Fisher, "Habs' News All Bad as Black Hawks Up and 'Boomer' Down," *Montreal Star*, April 3, 1961, p. 26.
10   Geoffrion and Fischler, *Boom Boom*, p. 165.
11   Charlie Halpin, *Montreal Star*, April 5, 1961.

12 Dick Irvin, *The Habs*, p. 169.

13 Geoffrion and Fischler, *Boom Boom*, pp. 167–68.

14 "Selke Says Big 'Chop' Coming in Habs' Camp," *Montreal Star*, April 6, 1961, p. 39.

15 Ben Olan, "The Jacques Plante Story," *Hockey Illustrated*, November 1962, p. 73.

CHAPTER 18: THE HART

1 Andy O'Brien and Jacques Plante, *The Jacques Plante Story*, p. 88.

2 Réjean Houle, interview by the author, December 29, 2008.

3 O'Brien and Plante, *The Jacques Plante Story*, p. 90.

4 Pat Curran, "Where Would Canucks Be Without Plante?" *Hockey News*, March 10, 1962, p. 3.

5 Bernard Geoffrion and Stan Fischler, *Boom Boom*, p. 172.

6 Red Fisher, *Hockey, Heroes, and Me*, pp. 168–69.

7 "Plante Habs' Saver," *Toronto Star*, December 28, 1961, p. 18.

8 Curran, "Where Would Canucks Be," p. 3.

9 Leo Monahan, "Prize Goalie Plante Shoots for Three Awards," *Sporting News*, February 28, 1962, sect. 2, p. 5.

10 "Jacques Plante," *ESPN SportsCentury*, interview with Jack Falla, December 8, 2000.

11 Red Burnett, "Stanley Cup Pressure Nightmare for Goalies," *Toronto Star*, March 31, 1962.

12 Jean Béliveau, Chrys Goyens, and Allan Turowetz, *Jean Béliveau*, p. 124.

13 O'Brien and Plante, *The Jacques Plante Story*, p. 93.

CHAPTER 19: TOE

1 Red Fisher, *Hockey, Heroes, and Me*, p. 15.

2 Jean Béliveau, interview by the author, October 6, 2008.

3 Michael Ulmer, *Canadiens Captains*, p. 8.

4 Ulmer, *Canadiens Captains*, p. 17.

5 Fisher, *Hockey, Heroes and Me*, p. 18.

6 Red Fisher, "Frisky Bruins Belt Sick Goalie Plante as Perreault Stars," *Montreal Star*, October 12, 1962, p. 48.

7 Red Fisher, "A Warning for Plante," *Montreal Star*, October 15, 1962, p. 62.

8 Leo Monahan, "Masked Marvel Sawchuk – Master Netminder," *Sporting News*, November 24, 1962, sec. 2, p. 9.

9 Jim Hynes and Gary Smith, *Saving Face*, p. 58.

10 Cesare Maniago, interview by the author, December 12, 2008.

11 Red Fisher, "Plante Hits Peak Form," *Montreal Star*, December 6, 1962, p. 52.

12 Red Fisher, "Warns Habs to Topple Toronto," *Montreal Star*, February 3, 1963, p. 18.

13 Red Fisher, "Plante Stirs More Fuss," *Montreal Star*, February 12, 1963, p. 64.

14 Jim Proudfoot, "Plante's Health of Deep Concern to the Canadiens," *Toronto Star*, February 11, 1963, p. 10.

15 Milt Dunnell, "A Cashier and a Psychiatrist," *Toronto Star*, February 21, 1963, p. 10.

16 Red Fisher, "Habs Finally 'Underdogs,'" *Montreal Star*, March 26, 1963, p. 49.

17 Red Fisher, "Leafs Whip Canadiens in Cup Start," *Montreal Star*, March 27, 1963, p. 66.

18 Red Fisher, "Will Handle Goaling if Plante's Ailing," *Montreal Star*, March 28, 1963, p. 72.

19 "Plante Says Habs Haven't a Leader," *Montreal Star*, March 28, 1963, p. 72.

20 Red Fisher, "No Scoring, No Goaling Spell Habs Elimination," *Montreal Star*, April 5, 1963, p. 30.

21 Red Fisher, "Blake Needs Rest Period," *Montreal Star*, April 5, 1963, p. 30.

CHAPTER 20: THE BETRAYAL

1 Hugh Townsend, "Plante Doesn't Expect Major Shakeup of Habs," Halifax *Chronicle-Herald*, June 3, 1963.

2 Raymond Plante, *Jacques Plante*, p. 124.

3 Phil Goyette, interview by the author, October 5, 2008.

4 O'Brien and Plante, *The Jacques Plante Story*, p. 104.

5 O'Brien and Plante, *The Jacques Plante Story*, p. 104.

6 D'Arcy Jenish, *The Montreal Canadiens*, p. 170.

7 Red Fisher, "Big Trade Took Time," *Montreal Star*, June 5, 1963, p. 62.

8 O'Brien and Plante, *The Jacques Plante Story*, p. 103.

9 Frank Orr, interview by the author, January 9, 2009.

10 Dickie Moore, interview by the author, November 14, 2008.

11 Henri Richard, interview by the author, December 2, 2008.

12 Cesare Maniago, interview by the author, December 12, 2008.

13 Frank Orr interview.

CHAPTER 21: ALONE ON BROADWAY

1 Andy O'Brien and Jacques Plante, *The Jacques Plante Story*, p. 101.

2 O'Brien and Plante, *The Jacques Plante Story*, p. 102.

3 Leo Monahan, "Free-for-All Forecast in NHL Race," *Sporting News*, October 12, 1963, p. 15.

4 Emile Francis, interview by the author, April 18, 2009.

5 O'Brien and Plante, *The Jacques Plante Story*, p. 106.

6 Emile Francis interview.

7 Red Fisher, "Plante Waiting for 'Boom' to Explode with Hard Shot," *Montreal Star*, October 12, 1963, p. 61.

8 Red Fisher, "Plante Adds New Sparkle to Rangers," *Montreal Star*, October 11, 1963, p. 40.

9 Fisher, "Plante Waiting for 'Boom,'" p. 61.

10 Fisher, "Plante Waiting For 'Boom,'" p. 61.

11 Red Fisher, "'Boom Boom' Leads Habs Over Rangers, Suffers Locked Hip," *Montreal Star*, October 15, 1963, p. 33.

12 Stan Fischler, "Plante Not Talking Anymore – About Habs," *Hockey News*, November 16, 1963, p. 8.

13 Bernard Geoffrion and Stan Fischler, *Boom Boom*, p. 189.

14 O'Brien and Plante, *The Jacques Plante Story*, p. 107.

15 Fischler, "Plante Not Talking," p. 8.

16 Stan Fischler, "Masked Netminder Given Standing Ovation," *Hockey News*, October 26, 1963, p. 1.

17 Fischler, "Masked Netminder," p. 1.

18 O'Brien and Plante, *The Jacques Plante Story*, p. 109.

19 O'Brien and Plante, *The Jacques Plante Story*, p. 109.

20   O'Brien and Plante, *The Jacques Plante Story*, p. 108.

21   Andy Bathgate, interview by the author, September 16, 2008.

22   Earl Ingarfield Sr., interview by the author, February 25, 2009.

23   Dick Duff, interview by the author, February 11, 2009.

24   Andy Bathgate interview.

25   Andy Bathgate interview.

26   Harry Howell, interview by the author, September 7, 2008.

27   Red Fisher, "Blues Happy When Plante's Ailing," *Montreal Star*, March 9, 1964, p. 42.

28   "Plante Ordered to Play – Temp 102," *Hockey News*, March 14, 1964, p. 1.

29   Frank Moritsugu, "'Hamlet' to Be Repeated in Fall," *Toronto Star*, April 22, 1964, p. 36.

30   Frank Orr, interview by the author, January 9, 2009.

31   O'Brien and Plante, *The Jacques Plante Story*, pp. 113–14.

32   "Rangers Send Plante to Baltimore in AHL," *Montreal Star*, October 9, 1964, p. 43.

33   Emile Francis interview.

34   O'Brien and Plante, *The Jacques Plante Story*, p. 114.

35   John Steadman, *Baltimore Sun*, 1964, quoted in O'Brien and Plante, *The Jacques Plante Story*, p. 115.

36   Gerry Cheevers, interview by the author, September 20, 2008.

37   "Goal Comes with Only 44 Seconds Left," *Baltimore Sun*, October 26, 1964, p. 19.

38   Emile Francis interview.

39   Milt Dunnell, "The Atmosphere Is Unfriendly," *Toronto Star*, March 1, 1965, p. 13.

40   O'Brien and Plante, *The Jacques Plante Story*, p. 116.

41   Bryan Hextall to the author, December 2008.

42   Albert Fisher, "Final Goal by Schinkel in Overtime," *Baltimore Sun*, April 1, 1965, p. 31.

43   Albert Fisher, "Baltimore Takes 2–0 Series Lead," *Baltimore Sun*, April 3, 1965, p. 15.

CHAPTER 22: RETIREMENT AND REBIRTH

1   Andy O'Brien and Jacques Plante, *The Jacques Plante Story*, p. 117.

2   O'Brien and Plante, *The Jacques Plante Story*, p. 118.

3   O'Brien and Plante, *The Jacques Plante Story*, p. 118.

4   Red Burnett, "Plante Retirement May Benefit Maniago," *Toronto Star*, June 8, 1965, p. 12.

5   "Plante Retires, Decides He's Had Enough," *Hockey News*, July 1965, p. 7.

6   Hal Bock, *Save!*, p. 52.

7   O'Brien and Plante, *The Jacques Plante Story*, p. 119.

8   Burnett, "Plante Retirement," p. 12.

9   "Plante Keeps NHL Guessing With Retirement Disclosure," *Montreal Star*, June 8, 1965, p. 26.

10   Burnett, "Plante Retirement," p. 12.

11   "Plante Keeps NHL Guessing," p. 26.

12   Emile Francis, interview by the author, April 18, 2009.

13   O'Brien and Plante, *The Jacques Plante Story*, p. 120.

14   "Jacques Plante," *The Canadians*, interview with Michel Plante, 2000.

15   Jim Hynes and Gary Smith, *Saving Face*, p. 54.

16   Dickie Moore, interview by the author, November 14, 2008.

17   Gil Smith, "'No Comeback for Me' Says Plante," *Hockey News*, October 23, 1965, p. 11.

18   Red Fisher, interview by the author, September 6, 2008.

19   O'Brien and Plante, *The Jacques Plante Story*, p. 7.

20   Scotty Bowman, interview by the author, February 7, 2009.

21   "Plante in Lineup Against Russians," *Montreal Star*, December 9, 1965, p. 21.

22   Gil Smith, "Ex-NHL Goalie Jacques Plante Ready for Comeback against Russian Team," *Hockey News*, December 18, 1965, p. 8.

23   "Pro-bolstered Junior Habs Loom Big Test for Russians," *Montreal Star*, December 14, 1965, p. 24.

24   O'Brien and Plante, *The Jacques Plante Story*, p. 7.

25   O'Brien and Plante, *The Jacques Plante Story*, p. 8.

26   Charlie Boire, "Plante Puts on Dazzling Show as Junior Habs Stop Russians," *Montreal Star*, December 16, 1965, p. 61.

27   Boire, "Plante Puts on Dazzling Show," p. 61.

28   "Plante Best We've Met: Russ Coach," *Toronto Star*, December 16, 1965, p. 14.

29   Raymond Plante, *Jacques Plante*, p. 150.

30   George Hanson, "Goalie Not Tempted to Try Amateurs," *Montreal Star*, December 16, 165, p. 61.

31   Hanson, "Goalie Not Tempted," p. 61.

CHAPTER 23: BACK IN THE SADDLE

1   Dick Irvin Jr., *Now Back to You Dick*, pp. 225–26.

2   Dick Irvin, interview by the author, September 29, 2008.

3   Brad Kurtzberg, *Shorthanded*, p. 90.

4   Spence Conley, "Plante Impresses in Comeback But Sudden Exit Puzzles Seals," *Hockey News*, October 14, 1967, p. 2.

5   Joe Walker, "Seals Show Improvement, Play L.A. Kings to Tie," Port Huron *Times Herald*, September 22, 1967, sect. B, p. 1.

6   Kurtzberg, *Shorthanded*, p. 8.

7   Conley, "Plante Impresses," p. 2.

8   Andy O'Brien and Jacques Plante, *The Jacques Plante Story*, p. 125.

9   Scotty Bowman, interview by the author, February 9, 2009.

CHAPTER 24: THE PRIDE AND THE MONEY

1   Scotty Bowman, interview by the author, February 7, 2009.

2   Andy O'Brien and Jacques Plante, *The Jacques Plante Story*, p. 130.

3   O'Brien and Plante, *The Jacques Plante Story*, p. 130.

4   O'Brien and Plante, *The Jacques Plante Story*, pp. 131, 132.

5   Geoffrey Fisher, "Plante Confesses He Came Back Because He Missed It," *Hockey News*, November 2, 1968, p. 3.

6   Stan Fischler, *Saga of the St. Louis Blues*, p. 42.

7   Milt Dunnell, "Age Now an Asset in Goaling Trade," *Toronto Star*, December 20, 1968, p. 15.

8   Dick Irvin, *In the Crease*, p. 67.

9   Donald Berms, "Blues Zero Heroes – Glenn Hall – Jacques Plante," St. Louis Blues Program, January 30, 1969, pp. 50–51.

10   Scotty Bowman interview.

11   Al Arbour, interview by the author, March 22, 2009.

12   Scott Bowman interview.

13   Irvin, *In the Crease*, p. 124.

14   Frank St. Marseille, interview by the author, March 5, 2009.

15   O'Brien and Plante, *The Jacques Plante Story*, p. 135.

16   Irvin, *In the Crease*, p. 124.

17   O'Brien and Plante, *The Jacques Plante Story*, p. 134.

18   Scotty Bowman interview.

19   Scotty Bowman interview.

20   Jim Proudfoot, "Plante Admits This Season He Never Played Better in Goal," *Hockey News*, May 10, 1969, p. 13.

21   O'Brien and Plante, *The Jacques Plante Story*, p. 137.

22   Dick Irvin, *Behind the Bench*, p. 171.

23   Scotty Bowman interview.

24   Frank St. Marseille interview.

25   Victor Berns, "Plante Still 'Mr. Spectacular,' Not Slowing Down Despite Age 41," *Hockey News*, February 20, 1970, p. 2.

26   Red Burnett, "Bobby Hull with Keon, Ellis Ruel's Idea of a Great Line," *Toronto Star*, January 22, 1970, p. 20.

27   Gump Worsley and Tim Moriarty, *They Call Me Gump*, p. 105.

CHAPTER 25: ONE MORE MOMENT FOR THE MASTER

1   Leo Monahan, "Got Those St. Louis Blues," *Sports Illustrated*, May 18, 1970.

2   Andy O'Brien and Jacques Plante, *The Jacques Plante Story*, p. 140.

3   Red Fisher, "Red Fisher's Column," *Montreal Star*, May 5, 1970, p. 32.

4   O'Brien and Plante, *The Jacques Plante Story*, p. 141.

5   O'Brien and Plante, *The Jacques Plante Story*, p. 142.

6   O'Brien and Plante, *The Jacques Plante Story*, p. 142.

7   Red Burnett, "Plante's New Mask Grotesque But Great," *Toronto Star*, June 9, 1970, p. 17.

8   Bill Libby, "An Improbable Hero," *Hockey News*, April 23, 1971, p. 8.

9   O'Brien and Plante, *The Jacques Plante Story*, p. 146.

10   O'Brien and Plante, *The Jacques Plante Story*, p. 146.

11   Burnett, "Plante's New Mask," p. 17.

12   Jim Proudfoot, "Plante Seen Ready for New Challenge, Aims at 50 Games," *Hockey News*, October 16, 1970, p. 28.

13   Brad Selwood, interview by the author, March 12, 2009.

14   O'Brien and Plante, *The Jacques Plante Story*, p. 148.

15   Gerry Cheevers and Trent Frayne, *Goaltender*, p. 92.

16   Brad Selwood interview.

17   Bob Baun and Anne Logan, *Lowering the Boom*, p. 217.

18   O'Brien and Plante, *The Jacques Plante Story*, pp. 148–49.

19   O'Brien and Plante, *The Jacques Plante Story*, p. 149.

20   O'Brien and Plante, *The Jacques Plante Story*, p. 149.

21   Red Burnett, "Gump at Birth of Mask But He's Still a Holdout," *Toronto Star*, October 31, 1970, p. 40.

22 Cheevers and Frayne, *Goaltender*, p. 92.

23 Howard Berger, *Maple Leaf Moments*, p. 257.

24 Bernie Parent, Bill Fleischman, and Sonny Schwartz, *Bernie! Bernie! Bernie!* p. 98.

25 "One on One with Bernie Parent," www.legendsofhockey.net, November 7, 2005.

26 Parent, Fleischman, and Schwartz, *Bernie! Bernie! Bernie!* p. 115.

27 Red Burnett, "Plante Home for Treatment," *Toronto Star*, March 26, 1971, p. 12.

28 Jim Proudfoot, "Plante Still Finest Goalie in Pro Hockey NHL Coaches Opinion in Star Poll," *Toronto Star*, March 13, 1971, p. 49.

29 Stan Fischler, *Go Leafs, Go!* p. 25.

30 Emile Francis, interview by the author, April 18, 2009.

31 Milt Dunnell, "The Impossible Is Jacques' Job," *Toronto Star*, April 15, 1971, p. 14.

32 Red Burnett, "Jacques Plante Runs Out of Miracles," *Toronto Star*, April 16, 1971, p. 14.

33 Burnett, "Jacques Plante Runs Out of Miracles," p. 14.

34 Jeff Z. Klein and Karl-Eric Reif, *The Hockey Compendium*, pp. 100, 102.

CHAPTER 26: THE LIVING LEGEND

1 Brian Mockler, "The Great Plante Gave Pro Hockey a Whole New Look," *Toronto Star*, March 5, 1986, p. B2.

2 Dan Proudfoot, "What Will the Great Jacques Plante Do Next?" *Hockey Pictorial*, February 1972, p. 46.

3 O'Brien and Plante, *The Jacques Plante Story*, p. 183.

4 Raymond Plante, *Jacques Plante*, p. 169.

5 Frank Orr, *Great Goalies of Pro Hockey*, p. 28.

6 Vladislav Tretiak, *Tretiak*, p. 51.

7 Orr, *Great Goalies of Pro Hockey*, p. 147.

8 Orr, *Great Goalies of Pro Hockey*, p. 147.

9 Frank Orr, "Plante Passes on Tricks of Trade," *Toronto Star*, November 21, 1972, p. 26.

10 Leo Monahan, "Goalie Plante Bruins' Lifesaver at 44," *Toronto Star*, March 24, 1973, p. 13.

11 Frank Orr, "Plante Is Bruin Playoff Key at 44," *Toronto Star*, March 31, 1973, p. 47.

12 Leo Monahan, "Goalie Plante Bruins' Lifesaver," p. 13.

13 "But Imlach Claims Goaltender Is Through," *Montreal Star*, March 5, 1973, p. B-1.

14 Stan Fischler, "Speaking Out on Hockey," *Sporting News*, April 28, 1973, p. 41.

15 Mark Mulvoy, "War for the Inscrutable East," *Sports Illustrated*, April 16, 1973, p. 30.

CHAPTER 27: A MAN CONFLICTED

1 Jim Proudfoot, "Plante Turns Down Quebec Offer," *Toronto Star*, April 10, 1973, p. 32.

2 "Nordiques Sign Jacques Plante," *Toronto Star*, May 3, 1973, p. 17.

3 "Nordiques Sign Jacques Plante," *Toronto Star*, p. 17.

4 Jean Béliveau, Chrys Goyens, and Allan Turowetz, *Jean Béliveau*, p. 228.

5 Jacques Plante to Harry Sinden, August 8, 1973. Allan Stitt collection.

6 Jacques Plante to Clarence Campbell, March 21, 1974. Allan Stitt collection.

7 Harry Sinden to Clarence Campbell, April 4, 1974. Allan Stitt collection.

8 Clarence Campbell to Harry Sinden, August 2, 1974. Allan Stitt collection.

CHAPTER 28: THE LION IN WINTER

1   Jim Kernaghan, "Jacques Plante Yearns to Play," *Toronto Star*, October 4, 1973, p. C05.
2   Réjean Houle, interview by the author, December 29, 2008.
3   Ed Willes, *The Rebel League*, p. 163.
4   "Nordiques in Big Shakeup as President, Plante Quit," *Toronto Star*, May 3, 1974, p. C02.
5   Claude Larochelle, *Le Soleil*, May 5, 1974, as quoted in Raymond Plante, *Jacques Plante*, p. 182.
6   Bill Hunter with Bob Weber, *Wild Bill*, p. 233.
7   Wayne Overland, "Plante's Goal: Survival," *Edmonton Journal*, November 7, 1974.
8   Terry Jones, "Practising Plante Knocked Out," *Edmonton Journal*, December 13, 1974, p. 73.
9   "Jacques Plante," *The Canadians*, interview with Bill Hunter, 2000.
10 Jones, "Practising Plante," p. 73.
11 Jones, "Practising Plante," p. 73.
12 Terry Jones, "Plante Plans to Play, 'Definitely' His Last," *Edmonton Journal*, April 4, 1975, p. 69.
13 "Jacques Plante," *ESPN SportsCentury*, interview with Michel Plante, December 8, 2000.

CHAPTER 29: THE MENTOR

1   Jay Greenberg, "Flyer Goal in Good Hands: Bernie and Wayne," *Sporting News*, January 28, 1978, p. 29.
2   Greenberg, "Flyer Goal in Good Hands," p. 32.
3   Rex MacLeod, "Flyers' Goalie Too Young for Neuroses," *Toronto Star*, February 27, 1980, p. B03.
4   "Jacques Plante," *The Canadians*, interview with Michel Plante, 2000.
5   Milt Dunnell, "A Lifesaver Plante Says of His Mask," *Toronto Star*, September 29, 1983, p. F1.
6   *CFCF News*, interview with Jacques Plante, October 1983.
7   Jim Proudfoot, "Plante Student Passes Exams as NHL Goalie," *Toronto Star*, March 28, 1985, p. H1.
8   *CFCF News*, interview with Rick Wamsley, October 1983.
9   Michel Roy, *Patrick Roy*, p. 149.

CHAPTER 30: SWITZERLAND

1   Frank Orr, "Bloodshed a Common Bond for Hockey Hall of Famers," *Toronto Star*, September 14, 1978, p. B01.
2   "Jacques Plante, 57, Dies, Called 'Best Ever' Goalie," *Toronto Star*, February 28, 1986, p. B3.
3   Tom Wheatley, "Blues Hire Plante to Coach Goaltenders," *Hockey News*, January 31, 1986, p. 27.
4   "Jacques Plante, 57, Dies," p. B3.
5   "Jacques Plante, 57, Dies," p. B3.
6   Jean Béliveau, Chrys Goyens, and Allan Turowetz, *Jean Béliveau*, p. 288.
7   Béliveau, Goyens, and Turowetz, *Jean Béliveau*, p. 290.

AFTERWORD

1 "Jacques Plante, 57, Dies, Called 'Best Ever' Goalie," *Toronto Star*, February 28, 1986, p. B3.

2 "Jacques Plante: Hockey's Masked Legend," Montreal *Gazette*, February 28, 1986, p. D1.

3 Red Fisher, "Former Habs Goalie Jacques Plante Dead at 57," Montreal *Gazette*, February 28, 1985, p. 1.

4 Daniel Okrent, "The 10 Most Influential Athletes of the Century," *Time*, June 14, 1999.

BIBLIOGRAPHY

BOOKS

Allen, Kevin, and Bob Duff. *Without Fear: Hockey's 50 Greatest Goaltenders*. Triumph Books, 2002.

Barris, Ted, John Short, and George Hanson. *Positive Power: The Story of the Edmonton Oilers*. Executive Sport Publications, 1982.

Baun, Bob, and Anne Logan. *Lowering the Boom: The Bobby Baun Story*. Stoddart, 2002.

Béliveau, Jean, Chrys Goyens, and Allan Turowetz. *Jean Béliveau: My Life in Hockey*. McClelland & Stewart, 1994.

Berger, Howard. *Maple Leaf Moments: A Thirty-Year Retrospective*. Warwick Publishing, 1994.

Bock, Hal. *Save! Hockey's Brave Goalies*. Avon Books, 1974.

Bortstein, Larry. *My Greatest Day in Hockey*. Grosset & Dunlap, 1974.

Brown, William. *Doug: The Doug Harvey Story*. Véhicule Press, 2002.

Campbell, Ken. *Habs Heroes: The Definitive List of the 100 Greatest Canadiens Ever*. Transcontinental Books, 2008.

Carrier, Roch. *Our Life With the Rocket: The Maurice Richard Story*, Penguin Books, 2001.

Cheevers, Gerry, and Trent Frayne. *Goaltender*. Dodd Mead, 1971.

Cole, Stephen. *The Last Hurrah: A Celebration of Hockey's Greatest Season '66–'67*. Viking Books, 1995.

Coleman, Charles. *1947–1967*. Vol. 3 of *The Trail of the Stanley Cup*. National Hockey League, 1976.

Cox, Damien, and Gord Stellick. *'67: The Maple Leafs, Their Sensational Victory, and the End of an Empire*. John Wiley & Sons, 2006.

Cruise, David, and Allison Griffiths. *Net Worth*. Viking Canada, 1991.

Devaney, John, and Burt Goldblatt. *The Stanley Cup: A Complete Pictorial History*. Rand McNally, 1975.

Diamond, Dan, and Eric Zweig. *Hockey's Glory Days: The 1950s and '60s*. Andrews McMeel Publishing, 2003.

Duplacey, James. *Forever Rivals*. Random House Canada, 1996.

Dupuis, David Michael. *Sawchuk: The Troubles and Triumphs of the World's Greatest Goalie*. Stoddart, 1998.

Etter, Les. *Hockey's Masked Men*. Garrard Publishing, 1976.

Fischler, Stan. *Go Leafs, Go! The Toronto Hockey Story*. Illustrated by Dan Baliotti. Prentice Hall, 1972.

——. *The Greatest Players and Moments of the Philadelphia Flyers*. Sports Publishing, 1998.

——. *The Rivalry: Canadiens vs. Leafs*. McGraw-Hill Ryerson, 1991.

——. *Saga of the St. Louis Blues*. Prentice Hall, 1972.

Fisher, Red. *Hockey, Heroes, and Me*. McClelland & Stewart, 1994.

Geoffrion, Bernard, and Stan Fischler. *Boom Boom: The Life and Times of Bernard Geoffrion*. McGraw-Hill Ryerson, 1997.

Goyens, Chrys, and Frank Orr. *Maurice Richard: Reluctant Hero*. Team Power Publishing, 2001.

Goyens, Chrys, and Allan Turowetz. *Lions in Winter*. Prentice Hall Canada, 1986.

Goyens, Chrys, Allan Turowetz, and Jean-Luc Duguay. *The Montreal Forum: Forever Proud*. Les Editions Effix, 1996.

Greenberg, Jay. *Full Spectrum: The Complete History of the Philadelphia Flyers Hockey Club*. Triumph Books, 1996.

Hall, Glenn, and Tom Adrahtas. *The Man They Call Mr. Goalie*. Douglas & McIntyre, 2003.

Hockey Hall of Fame. *Honoured Canadiens*. HB Fenn, 2008.

Hockey News. *Sixty Moments That Changed the Game*. Hockey News, 2007.

Hockey News. *The Top 100 NHL Players of All Time*. Edited by Steve Dryden. McClelland & Stewart, 1998.

Hood, Hugh. *Strength Down Centre: The Jean Béliveau Story*. Prentice Hall Canada, 1970.

Hunt, Jim. *The Men in the Nets*. McGraw-Hill Ryerson, 1972.

Hunter, Bill, and Bob Weber. *Wild Bill: Bill Hunter's Legendary 65 Years in Canadian Sport*. Fitzhenry & Whiteside, 2002.

Hunter, Douglas. *A Breed Apart: An Illustrated History of Goaltending*. Viking Press, 1995.

——. *Champions: The Illustrated History of Hockey's Greatest Dynasties*. Triumph Books, 1997.

——. *Scotty Bowman: A Life in Hockey*. Viking Canada, 1998.

Irvin, Dick. *Behind the Bench: Coaches Talk About Life in the NHL*. McClelland & Stewart, 1994.

——. *The Habs: An Oral History of the Montreal Canadiens, 1940–1980*. McClelland & Stewart, 1991.

——. *In the Crease: Goaltenders Look at Life in the NHL*. McClelland & Stewart, 1995.

——. *My 26 Stanley Cups: Memories of a Hockey Life*. McClelland & Stewart, 2001.

——. *Now Back To You Dick: Two Lifetimes in Hockey*. McClelland & Stewart, 1988.

Jenish, D'Arcy. *The Montreal Canadiens: 100 Years of Glory*. Doubleday Canada, 2008.

Kendall, Brian. *Shutout: The Legend of Terry Sawchuk*. Penguin Books Canada, 1997.

Kent, Geoffrey W. *Here Come the Vees: An Illustrated History of the Nova Scotia Voyageurs*. Nimbus, 1997.

Klein, Jeff, and Karl-Eric Reif. *The Hockey Compendium: NHL Facts, Stats, and Stories*. McClelland & Stewart, 2001.

Kreiser, John, and Lou Friedman. *The New York Rangers: Broadway's Longest-Running Hit*. Sports Publishing LLC, 1996.

Kurtzberg, Brad. *Shorthanded: The Untold Story of the Seals, Hockey's Most Colorful Team*. AuthorHouse, 2006.

Leonetti, Mike. *Canadiens Legends: Montreal's Hockey Heroes*. Raincoast Books, 2004.

———. *Cold War: A Decade of Hockey's Greatest Rivalry, 1959–1969*. HarperCollins Canada, 2001.

———. *The Game We Knew: Hockey in the Fifties*. Raincoast Books, 1997.

———. *The Goalie Mask*. Raincoast Books, 2008.

———. *Hockey's Golden Era: Stars of the Original Six*. Firefly Books, 1998.

———. *Hockey in the Seventies: The Game We Knew*. Raincoast Books, 1999.

———. *Maple Leaf Legends: 75 Years of Toronto's Hockey Heroes*. Raincoast Books, 2002.

———. *Maple Leafs Top 100: Toronto's Greatest Players of All Time*. Raincoast Books, 2007.

Liebman, Glenn. *Hockey Shorts*. McGraw-Hill Ryerson, 1996.

McDonell, Chris. *The Game I'll Never Forget: 100 Hockey Stars' Stories*. Firefly Books, 2002.

McFarlane, Brian. *The Habs*. Brian McFarlane's Original Six. Stoddart, 1996.

Melançon, Benoît. *The Rocket: A Cultural History of Maurice Richard*. Translated by Fred A. Reed. Greystone Books, 2009.

Mouton, Claude. *The Montreal Canadiens: A Hockey Dynasty*. Van Nostrand Reinhold, 1980.

———. *The Montreal Canadiens: An Illustrated History of a Hockey Dynasty*. Key Porter Books, 1988.

Obodiac, Stan. *The Leafs: The First Fifty Years*. McClelland & Stewart, 1977.

O'Brien, Andy. *Fire-wagon Hockey: The Story of the Montreal Canadiens*. Follett Publishing, 1967. Reprinted as *Les Canadiens: The Story of the Montreal Canadiens*. Toronto: McGraw-Hill Ryerson, 1971.

———. *Rocket Richard*. Ryerson Press, 1961.

O'Brien, Andy, and Jacques Plante. *The Jacques Plante Story*. McGraw-Hill Ryerson, 1972.

Orr, Frank. *Great Goalies of Pro Hockey*. Random House, 1973.

Orr, Frank, and George Tracz. *The Dominators: The Remarkable Athletes Who Changed Their Sport Forever*. Warwick Publishing, 2004.

Parent, Bernie, Bill Fleischman, and Sonny Schwartz. *Bernie! Bernie! Bernie!* Prentice Hall, 1976.

Pincus, Arthur. *The Official Illustrated NHL History*. Triumph Books, 2001.

Plante, Jacques. *Goaltending*. Collier-Macmillan Canada, 1972.

Plante, Raymond. *Jacques Plante: Behind the Mask*. XYZ Publishing, 2001.

Richard, Maurice, and Stan Fischler. *The Flying Frenchmen: Hockey's Greatest Dynasty*. Hawthorn Books, 1971.

Robinson, Chris. *Stole This From a Hockey Card: A Philosophy of Hockey, Doug Harvey, Identity, and Booze*. Nightwood, 2005.

Roy, Michel. *Patrick Roy: Winning. Nothing Else*. Translated by Charles Phillips. John Wiley & Sons Canada, 2008.

Selke, Frank, and H. Gordon Green. *Behind the Cheering*. McClelland & Stewart, 1962.

Sports Illustrated. *The Canadiens Century: One Hundred Years*. Time Inc. Home Entertainment, 2009.

Tretiak, Vladislav. *Tretiak: The Legend*. Penguin Books, 1987.

Ulmer, Michael. *Canadiens Captains*. Macmillan Canada, 1996.

Wakefield, Dan. *New York in the Fifties*. Houghton Mifflin, 1992.

Warchocki, Tim. *Before the Blade: The History of Buffalo Bisons Hockey*. Rama Publishing, 1999.

Willes, Ed. *The Rebel League: The Short and Unruly Life of the World Hockey Association*. McClelland & Stewart, 2005.

Worsley, Lorne, and Tim Moriarty. *They Call Me Gump*. Dodd, Mead, 1975.

ARTICLES

Addis, Fred. "The Year of the Mask: 1959–60." *Society for International Hockey Research Journal* 2005.

"All Eyes on the Ice." *Sports Illustrated*, January 23, 1956.

Bacon, Dick. "Blake Gives Jacques Vote of Confidence Despite GA Record." *Hockey News*, November 19, 1960.

Berms, Donald. "Blues Zero Heroes – Glenn Hall – Jacques Plante." St. Louis Blues program, January 30, 1969.

Berns, Victor. "Plante Still 'Mr. Spectacular,' Not Slowing Down Despite Age 41." *Hockey News*, February 20, 1970.

Booth, Bud. "Playoff Madness Grips Chicago, Frenzied Fans Envision Stanley Cup." *Hockey News*, April 11, 1953.

Byward, Garth. "Jacques Plante's Strange Story." *Hockey Pictorial*, March 1959.

"Canadiens Call on Toe." *Hockey Pictorial*, October 1955.

Carroll, Dink. "Plante in Hab Cage at McNeil's Request." *Hockey News*, April 11, 1953.

Conley, Spence. "Plante Impresses in Comeback But Sudden Exit Puzzles Seals." *Hockey News*, October 14, 1967.

Curran, Pat. "Jacques' Attitude Key to Habs' High Altitude Prayers." *Hockey News*, October 21, 1961.

——. "Plante Says Lack of Leader Hurting Habs, Another Olmstead, Harvey Needed by Club." *Hockey News*, April 6, 1963.

——. "Uncertainty of Plante's Health Has Blake Pulling His Hair Out." *Hockey News*, November 17, 1962.

——. "Where Would Canucks Be Without Plante?" *Hockey News*, March 10, 1962.

"'Daring Dick' Irvin Gambles on Rookies." *Hockey News*, April 11, 1953.

Duff, Bob. "A Brief History of the Mask." *Hockey News Special Edition – Greatest Masks of All Time*, 2008.

——. "Do Fewer Stitches Mean More Red Lights?" *Hockey News Special Edition – Greatest Masks of All Time*, 2008.

Duhatschek, Eric. "Canadien Dream Team." *Hockey News*, December 17, 1999.

Dulmage, Paul. "Plante: The Man Behind the Mask." Maple Leaf Gardens program, October 31, 1970.

Ende, Steve. "A Straight Talk with Ernie Wakely." *Sport Review Hockey*, March 1972.

Falla, Jack. "A Brash Act 20 Years Ago Became a Tribute to the Late Jacques Plante." *Sports Illustrated*, November 17, 1986.

Fischler, Stan. "Andy's Blast Puts New Face on Plante." *Hockey News*, November 14, 1959.
———. "Blues Going Up, Habs Down – Plante." *Hockey News*, September 1963.
———. "Goalie 'Highly' Confident He'll Be Great in Garden, Says Rangers On Way Up." *Hockey News*, October 19, 1963.
———. "Jacques Plante Sounds Off." *Hockey Pictorial*, October 1963.
———. "Mask Chatter Brings Big 'Never' From Little Gump." *Hockey News*, November 14, 1959.
———. "Masked Marvel Plante Will Be Missed." *Hockey News*, March 14, 1986.
———. "Masked Netminder Given Standing Ovation." *Hockey News*, October 26, 1963.
———. "Plante Not Talking Anymore – About Habs." *Hockey News*, November 16, 1963.
———. "Plante, Sullivan Relationship Could Be An Explosive One." *Hockey News*, August 1963.
———. "Speaking Out on Hockey." *Sporting News*, April 28, 1973.
Fisher, Gregory. "Plante Confesses He Came Back Because He Missed It." *Hockey News*, November 2, 1968.
Fisher, Red. "Rating the Goalies." *Sport Review Hockey*, March 1972.
Fleischman, Bill. "Plante Dons Pads." *Hockey News*, October 7, 1977.
Frayne, Trent. "How Doug Harvey Loafed His Way to Fame." *Maclean's*, February 15, 1958.
Gates, Bob. "New Bruin Netminder Bernie Parent Admits Early Hockey Days Grim Ones." *Hockey News*, December 18, 1965.
Gonzalez, Arturo F., Jr. "Hockey's Faceless Wonder." *Modern Man*, November 1960.
Goren, Herb. "Les Canadiens Rated as Best Bet to Topple Red Wings – If Jacques Plante Makes Grade." *Sporting News*, November 3, 1954.
Greenberg, Jay. "Flyer Goal in Good Hands: Bernie and Wayne." *Sporting News*, January 28, 1978.
"Habs Picked as Team to Beat." *Hockey News*, October 20, 1962.
Hahn, Reno. "The Blues 'Young Tradition.'" St. Louis Blues program, January 30, 1969.
Halligan, John, and John Kreiser. "Game of My Life: New York Rangers." *Sports Publishing*, 2006.
Halpin, Charlie. "Jacques Plante Wants to Be the Man in the Mask." *Hockey Pictorial*, November 1959.
———. "Now It Can Be Told: Toe Would Like Plante to Junk His Mask." *Hockey News*, January 2, 1960.
———. "Plante on Hot Seat in Vezina Cup Race." *Hockey News*, March 19, 1960.
———. "Plante's Goal: To Be Seeded Game's Best." *Hockey News*, October 24, 1959.
———. "'Pocket' Real Vet as Habs Clutch Clouter." *Hockey News*, December 5, 1959.
Horrigan, Jack. "Amazing Jacques Plante Injects Zip into Eddolls' Lonely Bisons." *Hockey News*, January 17, 1953.
———. "'Jake the Snake' Plante Big Boon to Buffalo Bisons." *Hockey News*, February 7, 1953.
———. "When Plante Left Buffalo for Montreal He Expected to Be Back in a Few Days." *Hockey News*, April 17, 1954.
Kuenster, John. "Will Canadiens Sag or Soar? Critics Ask." *Sporting News*, March 1, 1961.
Libby, Bill. "An Improbable Hero." *Hockey News*, April 23, 1971.
Lunny, Vince. "Acrobatic Jacques Plante Has Unique Style." *Hockey News*, February 9, 1957.

——. "History Repeats – McNeil Quits as Nerves Give Out!" *Hockey News*, October 9, 1954.

——. "Plante Faces Full Schedule as Canadiens' Goal-keeper." *Hockey News*, October 9, 1954.

——. "Plante Gains Big League Rating, Has Phenomenal 1.58 GA Average." *Hockey News*, April 10, 1954.

——. "Strange Illness Forces Plante into Hospital." *Hockey News*, November 17, 1956.

——. "Wrist Operation Changed Plante's Hockey Outlook." *Hockey News*, February 4, 1956.

"Masked Marvel." *Time Magazine*, November 23, 1959.

McCarthy, Jack. "Bruins' Goal Again Problem as Plante Defects to WHA." *Hockey News*, May 18, 1973.

McKenzie, Ken. "Blake Lauds Plante For 'Hart' Win." *Hockey News*, June 1962.

MacLean, Norman. "Hall or Plante – Who'll Be No.1 For Blues?" *Sporting News*, November 9, 1968.

——. "Oui, Oui Say the Rangers." *Hockey Pictorial*, January–February 1965.

——. "Plante Coming Back as Player; Gendron New Nordiques Coach." *Hockey News*, June 1974.

——. "The St. Louis Blues: Hockey's Wonder Team." *Sporting News*, February 22, 1969.

Monahan, Leo. "Canadiens Skating Off with Another Crown." *Sporting News*, March 9, 1960.

——. "Confidence, Relaxation Called Keys to Canadiens Juggernaut." *Sporting News*, March 26, 1958.

——. "Free-for-All Forecast in NHL Race." *Sporting News*, October 12, 1963.

——. "Goalies Called Keys to NHL Playoff Portals." *Sporting News*, February 26, 1958.

——. "Got Those St. Louis Blues." *Sports Illustrated*, May 18, 1970.

——. "Hawks Top Threat to Aging Canadiens." *Sporting News*, November 1, 1961.

——. "Jitters in NHL – Rangers Bust Out of Dungeon." *Sporting News*, December 12, 1964.

——. "Masked Marvel Sawchuk – Master Netminder." *Sporting News*, November 24, 1962.

——. "Prize Goalie Plante Shoots for Three Awards." *Sporting News*, February 28, 1962.

——. "Trigger Temper, Fast Reactions, A Publicity Flair – That's Plante." *Sporting News*, May 10, 1969.

Mulvoy, Mark. "Those Uppity Blues." *Sports Illustrated*, November 25, 1968.

——. "War for the Inscrutable East." *Sports Illustrated*, April 16, 1973.

O'Brien, Andy. "Long Season for Jake the Snake." *Weekend Magazine*, March 21, 1964.

——. "Who Couldn't Coach Canadiens?" *Weekend Magazine*, November 7, 1959.

Okrent, Daniel. "The 10 Most Influential Athletes of the Century." *Time*, June 14, 1999.

Olan, Ben. "The Jacques Plante Story." *Hockey Illustrated*, November 1962.

Olsen, Jack. "Hero's Humiliation in Montreal." *Sports Illustrated*, February 6, 1961.

Orr, Frank. "Plante: Man of Vision and Strength." *Hockey News*, March 14, 1986.

Plante, Jacques. "Let's Change the Vezina System!" *Hockey Illustrated*, January 1965.

——. "Let's Give Goalies a Break." *Hockey Illustrated*, January 1964.

Plante, Jacques, and Len Bramson. "Jacques Plante on Goaltending: It's an Unpredictable Business." *Hockey Pictorial*, February 1956.

"Plante Accepts Nordiques' Offer to Coach in WHA." *Hockey News*, May 18, 1973.

"Plante Battling Asthma Again." *Hockey News*, October 20, 1962.

"Plante Becomes Playoff 'Spectator', Sees Game as Slower from Rinkside." *Hockey News*, April 18, 1964.

"Plante Finally Receives Recognition." *Hockey Pictorial*, Summer 1959.

"Plante Ordered to Play – Temp 102." *Hockey News*, March 14, 1964.

"Plante Plumps for Face Masks for All Goalies." *Hockey Pictorial*, October 1959.

"Plante Retires, Decides He's Had Enough." *Hockey News*, July 1965.

"Plante Risked Wrist Operation in Effort to Gain Greatness." *Hockey News*, April 10, 1954.

"Plante Strikes It Rich on Bonuses with 'Extras' in $9,000 Vicinity." *Hockey News*, June 1962.

"Plante Suffers Broken Tooth While Singing." *Hockey News*, August 1959.

Proudfoot, Dan. "Surprised Plante Admits He's Never Played Better." *Hockey News*, January 29, 1971.

———. "What Will the Great Jacques Plante Do Next?" *Hockey Pictorial*, February 1972.

Proudfoot, Jim. "Plante Admits This Season He Never Played Better in Goal." *Hockey News*, May 10, 1969.

———. "Plante Seen Ready for New Challenge, Aims at 50 Games." *Hockey News*, October 16, 1970.

Richard, Henri, and Ben Olan. "I Made It on My Own." *Hockey Illustrated*, January 1963.

Ronberg, Gary. "An Icy Love-In with the Red-Hot Blues." *Sports Illustrated*, April 7, 1969.

Rudeen, Kenneth. "A Long, Cold Road to Fame." *Sports Illustrated*, January 12, 1959.

———. "The Habs Have Put It on Ice." *Sports Illustrated*, February 17, 1958.

"Sizzlers Gunning for Punch Line's Playoff Marks." *Hockey News*, April 10, 1954.

Smith, Gil. "Big Trade For The Best Says Toe." *Hockey Pictorial*, October 1963.

———. "Ex-NHL Goalie Jacques Plante Ready for Comeback Against Russian Team." *Hockey News*, December 18, 1965.

———. "Get the Money, Says Plante." *Hockey Pictorial*, January 1962.

———. "'No Comeback for Me' Says Plante." *Hockey News*, October 23, 1965.

———. "Plante Retires, Decides He's Had Enough." *Hockey News*, October 23, 1965.

———. "Plante's Predicament." *Hockey Pictorial*, April 1961.

Taylor, George. "Plante Battling Back with Clippers After Fearing Knee Gone for Year." *Hockey News*, October 31, 1964.

Wheatley, Tom. "Blues Hire Plante to Coach Goaltenders." *Hockey News*, January 31, 1986.

Woody, Mel. "Sullivan Says Plante Still Rangers' Goalie If and When – Paille Comes Through in Pinch." *Hockey News*, October 24, 1964.

Zanger, Jack. "A Goalie's Life Is a Nervous One." *Sport Magazine*, February 1957.

Zweig, Eric. "Benedict's Mask." *Society for International Hockey Research Journal* 2005.

INDEX

320